First publish

City Trail Pu

thecitytrail@t

Text copyright © 2013 Blake Evans-Pritchard and Violetta Polese
Maps © 2013 City Trail Publishing Ltd.
(Map on the inside back cover reproduced with the kind permission of HTM)
Photographs © individual photographers

British Library Cataloguing in Publication Data
A catalogue record for this book is available from the British Library

ISBN 978-0-9559274-1-6

Cover photograph by Violetta Polese
('*The Herring Eater*' sculpture by Tom Otterness at Scheveningen's beach, with Scheveningen pier in the background)

Typesetting by City Trail Publishing Ltd.
Printing by AGE, Urbino, Italy

Audio files for this guidebook can be downloaded from www.thecitytrail.com
Audio Download Code: LXT18623PQ

"Nature is under control but not disturbed."

Queen Beatrix of the Netherlands

Contents

BEST OF THE NETHERLANDS

Maps

City Trail Guide
to

The Hague
and the best of the
Netherlands

The guidebook for travellers and expats

BLAKE EVANS-PRITCHARD
VIOLETTA POLESE

www.thecitytrail.com

City Trail Publishing Ltd.

Foreword

When Andrew Carnegie was born, in 1835, colonialism was still very much at its peak. Explorers were still heading off to discover new worlds, and conquer them where possible. Slavery was rampant throughout Africa and elsewhere, despite efforts by some well-meaning Europeans. War was an accepted way to maintain power and influence.

A few years before Carnegie died, in 1919, war came to Europe's own battlefields. So great was the bloodshed that this war came to be known as the war to end all wars. It wasn't and in 1939 the same thing happened, only with different weapons.

Carnegie was a successful industrialist and had a vision that many shared at the time: that of world peace. The Hague, widely recognised as the International City of Justice, embodies this vision.

The iconic symbol of The Hague is the fabulous Peace Palace. Carnegie gave $1.5 million to set it up, although it wasn't his idea. The idea reportedly came from discussions between Russian diplomat Friedrich Martens and his US counterpart Andrew White.

The idea was for the Peace Palace to house the Permanent Court of Arbitration, which had been set up in 1899 to resolve disputes between countries without resorting to war. The court lives on in the Palace to this day.

Other judicial institutions permeate throughout the fabric of The Hague. The International Criminal Tribunal for Yugoslavia was set up to try war crimes that took place in the Balkans in the 1990s. Former Liberian president Charles Taylor was tried and convicted for war crimes in the city, under the auspices of The Special Court for Sierra Leone. In 2002, a permanent war crimes court — the International Criminal Court — was set up to make sure that atrocities could never be allowed to happen in the world again.

International justice is not without its critics, but the idea of a world without war, injustice or suffering is a noble one indeed.

As we researched this book, we encountered the indefatigable Ben Ferenz, the last prosecutor at the Nuremberg trials, held after the second world war. He has dedicated his entire life to international justice and using it to prevent future wars.

"We went in fast, we went in whilst the ovens were still burning," he reminisced, when asked about the Nuremberg investigation. His eyes glazed over as he drifted back to some distant memory in the past. Then he came back with alarming alacrity: "This can never be allowed to happen again. It... really... can... never."

A noble sentiment and, for all the flaws of international justice, one that is interwoven into the make-up of the The Hague.

We dedicate this book to peace, justice and an end to suffering. Wherever that may be needed. And however it may come about.

Blake Evans-Pritchard

Violetta Polese

February 26, 2013

Our Guides

Violetta Polese has been independently exploring the world for the past 15 years. Her travels have taken her all across Europe and the United States of America — and as far afield as Vietnam, India, Japan and Peru. She has spent some years living in Belgium, France, Spain, Portugal, Vietnam and Sudan.

Violetta was born in Italy. She studied Translation and publishing at university before deciding to pursue a life of travel, writing and photography.

Violetta is passionate about other cultures and strongly believes in living as the locals do. Her honed language skills come in useful when blending in with local customs and practices. She currently lives in The Hague and she has spent the last few years visiting every corner of the Netherlands.

Violetta continues to write articles for publication all around the world — in French, Italian and English. She is currently codirector of City Trail Publishing.

Blake Evans-Pritchard is a professional journalist. He has been writing for a number of years about Africa. He also likes to think he knows something about economics, and regularly writes on this subject for a variety of British publications.

Like Violetta, Blake is passionate about travel and has spent many years roaming the world. Although his travels have taken him all over the place, the lure of Africa has been too strong — and he has always found himself drifting back to the continent.

Blake studied computer science at university. Then one day, whilst he was travelling between Byron Bay and Cairns in Australia, it suddenly dawned on him that he wanted to be a journalist and writer instead. He has never looked back.

He cofounded City Trail Publishing in 2008, which he still has a hand in running.

THE CITY TRAIL TEAM

Authors
Blake Evans-Pritchard, Violetta Polese

Researcher support
Elkie Jordans, Jan Kooy, Andreas Zellhuber, Ana Uzelac, Laurence Carrier-Desjardins, Ronald Mik

Proof-readers
John Evans-Pritchard, Sheila Evans-Pritchard, Marie Thompson, William Baldwin, Richard Goodwin, Rebecca McCoy, Colin Cartmell-Browne, Simon Jennings, Brian Beary

Photographers
Violetta Polese, Giorgio Benassi, Blake Evans-Pritchard, David Wilkinson, Laurent Virassamy, Giorgio Benassi

Sales representatives
Stuart Coster (United Kingdom), Carmine Rossi (Italy), Brian Beary (United States)

Wildlife consultation
Bram Klundert

Archaeological consultation
Nadine Lemmers, Casper Gils, John Kuipers (💻 www.johnkuipers.ca)

Dutch language
Chamara Mahabier, Blake Evans-Pritchard, Violetta Polese

Dutch language proof-reader
Elkie Jordans

Audio files
Chiamara Mahabier, Anuradha Lachman, Blake Evans-Pritchard

Additional support
Wendel Broere, Bianca Niţă, Laurent Virassamy, Antoine Lucas

Additional thanks to
Laurence Blairon, Gonny Tafuni, Jos van Tegelen, Liz Charnock, Daisy de Krom, Chris Yachouh, Ingrid Klavertjevier, Vivian Andyka, Diana Necea

HOW TO SUPPORT INDEPENDENT PUBLISHING

We do our best to make our guidebooks the most accurate, up-to-date and useful of any destination that we write about.

We spend innumerable hours researching, investigating and writing our guides. Every single member of our team has the dedication, passion and determination to bring you the very best in travel guidebooks.

However, the publishing industry is tough and things are not always easy for the smaller player. Giant retailers and distributors take a significant share of profits for selling our book. They can sometimes demand as much as a 60% cut, which makes it very difficult for us to earn any money when we sell through third-parties.

We want to continue to offer quality books — but we need your help!

Buying directly from us (⌨ www.thecitytrail.com) not only helps us maintain our commitment to quality. It could also save you a bit of money, since we often have offers and discounts on our website. Suggest to your friends to buy directly from us, too!

We make every effort to provide you with the best and most up-to-date guidebook possible. But, of course, things will always change. We'd be really grateful if you could let us know of anything that has changed, so we can include this in the regular updates that we provide to our readers.

You can send us an email at @ thecitytrail@thecitytrail.com. We will give credit to every correction or amendment that we include.

SYMBOLS USED IN THIS BOOK

In the text

☎	Telephone number	⏰	Opening times
🖥	Website address	💰	Price
@	Email address	🕂	How to get there
👍	Top tip	🍴	Type of restaurant
📷	See photo	🏠	Address
M	Free entry with Museumkaart		

On maps

🚌	Bus station	☕	Where to drink
📚	Bookshop	▼	What to do
⛪	Church or Christian Centre	◉	What to see
💡	Education and learning	🏛	Embassy or government building
🛏	Accommodation	✉	Post office
❶	Information	🍴	Where to eat
@	Internet point	🛒	Where to shop
↯	Market	🚂	Train station
☪	Mosque		

PUBLISHER'S FORWARD

Here at City Trail Guides, we know the value of being armed with the most-informative, accurate and reliable travel companion possible.

A growing number of people are choosing to experience new cultures not just on vacation but by choosing to live and work in a particular part of the world. Guidebooks as they were seen when they were invented now need something more.

That's why we have pioneered a unique set of guidebooks that are researched by people who have spent time actually living in, and not just visiting, the places that they are writing about. So that they have experienced first-hand everything they write about.

Our researchers have actually gone though the experiences that those moving to a new place may face: looking for a job, renting an apartment, buying a house and all the other cultural experiences that do not come from just a brief visit.

Our core philosophy is simple but effective. Through our guidebook series, we offer travellers the opportunity to move beyond a superficial appreciation of a country and really start to understand the customs and cultures that are to be found there.

All updates to our titles are made through extremely detailed on-the-ground research. We do not cut corners. We make sure that we re-visit every place that we have written about, to make sure that nothing has changed. We do not just rely on Internet or phone calls. We actually go to the places — even those places that are a really, really long way away.

Our guidebooks are focused on the main city where expats are likely to end up living. But we also believe it is important to provide information on those areas nearby, because this is where our readers may end up staying or living.

We go further afield, too — showcasing those parts of the country that we believe are really not to be missed, so you can plan sightseeing weekends or longer trips away.

Above all, our researchers have an enduring enthusiasm for the country that they have chosen to write about — and it is this enthusiasm that permeates throughout the pages of this guidebook.

The City Trail Team

Itineraries

THE BEST OF THE HAGUE

Whilst The Hague isn't terribly big, it is perhaps best appreciated by bicycle. This will also allow you to reach the main highlights in a single day. If you don't have a bike, you can rent one at one of main train stations of The Hague.

We'll start this tour from Centraal Station. Opposite the station, you'll find the **Haagse Bos** (p162), which is a lovely park to ride through. It is here that you'll find **Huis Ten Bosch Palace** (p153), the residential palace of the Netherlands' reigning monarch. A 10-minute cycle ride northwards, along the Koningskade, is the miniature world of **Madurodam** (p152). Make your way through **Scheveningen Bosjes** (p162) and **Westbroek-park** (p162) until you reach the magnificent **beach of Scheveningen**.

Cycle in the direction of the pier. Along the way you will find some fabulous **fairytale sculptures** by Tom Otterness (p154). It is well worth dismounting to have a closer look. Just opposite the pier you will find the **Kurhaus** (p154), a magnificently iconic hotel; you should definitely consider parking your bike and casually strolling inside to appreciate the elaborate — not to say ostentatious — interior.

Since you have paused your journey here, now might be a good time to take a morning coffee from one of the many **cafés** along the waterfront, particularly if the weather is fine. Before you end your Scheveningen jaunt, cycle a couple of kilometres into the dunes on Scheveningen's easternmost side, known as the **Oostduinen**.

Now we're heading back into town. Cycle along Scheveningseweg until you reach the **Peace Palace** (p152), which now houses the International Court of Justice and Permanent Court of Arbitration. From here, cycle along Zeestraat and on your way pop in to appreciate **one of the world's finest panorama's**, painted by Hendrik Willem Mesdag (p149).

Continuing along this street, you will see the **Noordeinde Palace** (p152) to your right. Shortly afterwards, turn left and you will come across Lange Voorhout. At the end of the avenue is one of the most famous museums in The Hague: the **Escher Museum** (p139).

Make your way from here to the **Binnenhof** (p148), where you can see the **Dutch Parliament**. If you want a tour of this, you will have to arrange one with ProDemos, which has offices nearby.

If you haven't stopped for lunch already, there are a couple of good options nearby: try **Spize** (p180) for Thai, **Very Italian Pizza** (p177) for Italian or **Warung Mini** (p181) for Surinamese.

Park your bike and spend the rest of the afternoon strolling through the city centre. You might like to do a spot of **shopping** (p128), **explore Chinatown** or visit the **Van Kleef distillery** (p146).

THE BEST OF THE NETHERLANDS

The Netherlands isn't a big country so it doesn't actually take too long to travel around the country, You can visit the most spectacular attractions in the country over several weekends, spread throughout the year, or in a three-to-four week *tour de force*.

Much of the following tour can be attempted outside of summer, but it won't be nearly as pleasant and you'll find it harder to follow some routes (for example, many of the ferries between the islands run a severely reduced service out of season).

Take a train up to **Amsterdam** (p251) and spend a day visiting the amazing museums up there, such as the **Van Gogh Museum** (p254) and the **Anne Frank House** (p254). A night out in Amsterdam is a memorable experience — make sure you take a casual stroll through the **red light district** (p251) as dusk is depending. Head north to **Zaanse Schans** (p226), where you can spend a pleasant afternoon before heading up to Den Helder to catch the ferry across to the Frisian island of **Texel** (p243). During the summer months, you can hop between the islands all the way to **Ameland** (p249) and then take a ferry to Holwerd on the mainland. Here you can join a **Wadlopen tour** (p257) to trek through the mudflats of the Wadden Sea.

Take a trip to Borger in Drenthe to visit the discover the history of the **ancient megalithic tombs** there (p238), before heading down to one of the finest examples of a medieval cities in the country: **Deventer** (p229). Follow this with a trip to the primate park in **Apenheul** (p235) and a visit to **the Loo Palace** (p235) just outside **Apeldoorn** (p235).

Head all the way down to fabulous Limburg and its capital **Maastricht** (p266), stopping at **Nijmegen** (p236) on the way. With its historical charm and excellent restaurants, Maastricht is a lovely place to spend a few days before contemplating your journey back.

Take a train to the wonderfully historic city of **Dordrecht** (p219), and from here you can explore **the Biesbosch** (p232), one of the finest natural reserves in the country.

On your way back to The Hague, stop at **Rotterdam** (p196) for a few hours or so to appreciate the town's eclectic architecture. Hop across to **Delft** (p207) in order to discover the distinctive blue-and-white pottery known as **Delftware** (p208). The Hague is a mere 20 minute train ride away. What better way of rounding your trip than seeing the top sights of the International City of Justice: **the Escher Museum** (p139), **the Panorama Mesdag** (p149), **the Peace Palace** (p152) and **Scheveningen beach** (p154)?

If you still have the energy and the season is right (late March to mid-May), you might think about popping up to the Keukenhof gardens (p218), near Leiden, to see the tulips there.

CITYWALK: THE HAGUE'S CENTRE

You'll find the colour map for this city walking tour on the inside front cover of this guidebook.

You can begin the tour from anywhere along the route, but this itinerary assumes that you start at the **New Town Hall** (p144). Taking a trip up to the 11th floor of the building will give you a great view over The Hague, and allow you to appreciate something of this city's architecture.

Back on ground level, turn right out of the building and continue on up Spui, which soon becomes Hofweg. A little way up the street, you will find **the Passage** (p148) on your left and **the Binnenhof** (p144) on your right. Explore the Passage if you want, before crossing through the inner courtyard of the Binnenhof. If you want to arrange a tour of the **Ridderzaal**, **ProDemos** (p158) can arrange this for you; they have offices just before you enter the Binnenhof.

After the Binnenhof, take a right past the **Historical Museum** (p143). You'll then turn right on to Tournooiveld, followed by a left shortly afterwards, which will bring you to the **Escher Museum** (p139). Continuing along Lange Voorhout, you'll pass a street leading down to **Denneweg** (115), a particularly picturesque part of the city. Explore if you want and then continue along Lange Voorhout.

Cross into Heulstraat and turn right at the end. This will take you past the **Noordeinde Palace** (p146) and round to the **Royal Stables** (p147), neither of which you can get into but they are nice to behold from the outside. Turn right off Hogewal on to Prinsesswal and then continue past the **Palace Gardens** (p147), which will be on your right; you *can* enter here.

A little further on, you'll find a sushi restaurant **Sumo** (p178) on your left, which is a possible stop for lunch.

Eventually, you'll reach the **Grote Kerk** (p145). This may be a good time to stop for a coffee break. Just to the right of the church, you will find a number of cafés including the **Cheesecake Company** (p182).

Take Schoolstraat, which will bring you to **Grote Markt** (p147), a lively spot for a drink. Turn right Prinsegracht and continue until you get to **Hofje van Nieuwkoop**, the most impressive *hofje* (p144) of the city.

Double back along Spijkermakerstraat, which will bring you to Bouwersgracht. Zigzag on to Hoge Zand. Once you reach Lange Beestenmarkt, you might like to venture a few hundred metres down this street until you reach the **Van Kleef distillery museum** (p140), a good place for an afternoon tipple.

Continue on the road that you were walking along until you reach Paviljoensgracht, then left on to Bierkade. At this point, you may feel like stopping for a drink at beer specialist **De Paas** (p182), overlooking the canal. Round off your tour with a stroll through **Chinatown** (p147).

The Essentials

WHEN TO GO

The Netherlands has a temperate climate, not dissimilar to that of England, which it shares the North Sea with.

Deciding when to go depends on what you want to get out of your visit to the country. Each season offers something different.

Most hotels, shops, and attractions remain open all year. However, in high season (from May to September), some sights may extend their opening times. Theme parks and zoos may be closed during the winter months.

Dutch winters can be bitterly cold, but the Dutch make the most of them. During prolonged cold spells, the canals freeze and thousands of Dutch take to the ice with their skates.

Some consider spring to be the best time of year for visiting the Netherlands, when the flowers are in bloom. The famous Dutch tulips usually start to come out in late March and last until early May.

From May to October, the Netherlands is bustling with activity. However, you will have more tourists.

Remember though, that, no matter what the season is, the Netherlands is one of the rainiest countries in Europe — so don't bank on sunshine for your entire stay.

LANGUAGE

Dutch is the official language of the Netherlands. Although the majority of people in the cities have a good command of English, in some of the more rural areas you may find it harder to communicate if you don't speak Dutch.

In the large towns and cities, practising Dutch can be an uphill struggle. Start speaking the language in any shop or café and the chances are that your fumbling attempts will be rewarded with a response in near-perfect English.

Unlike in other European countries, the Dutch don't expect foreigners to have mastered their language or even attempt to learn it. Telling people that you are learning the language will often be met by amusement or sometimes a quizzical look that says it all: "why?"

Nonetheless, the Dutch do appreciate it when foreigners make the effort to learn their language, so it is always worth giving it a go.

A small part of the country in the north-west speaks a distinct language called Frisian. Frisian, which is spoken by perhaps no more than a few hundred thousand people, only has official status in Friesland — it is not an official language in the rest of the Netherlands. Limburgish is an official language in Limburg, around Maastricht.

▶ See p272 for help learning Dutch.

TOURIST INFORMATION

It may be confusing when looking for a tourist office in the Netherlands. The Dutch have a unique name for it: 'VVV'. Many Dutch don't even know what this stands for, since it is always used in acronymic form. It actually stands for *vereniging voor vreemdelingenverkeer* ('association for tourism').

The Essentials

LOOK FOR THE "VVV" LOGO

When looking for it, just follow the 'VVV' logo (see box).

Almost every town in the Netherlands has a tourist or information office. This office is usually located in the centre of town, often in or near the town hall.

Dutch tourist offices are different to what you might expect in other EU countries. They often feel like shops, where you can purchase maps and souvenirs, rather than somewhere to go for free information. Although some tourist offices do provide free maps, usually of the city centre, many are only available if you pay. Tourist offices can be useful for finding and booking accommodation.

Tourist offices are not allowed to provide specific recommendations for restaurants. They can provide general details about where restaurants are, but they are not permitted to favour one restaurant over another.

The official tourist website (💻 www.holland.com) is a good source of free information. The website has been translated into the more common languages.

The tourist board also has a representation in the UK (☎ +44 20 7539 7958) and in the US (☎ +1 212 557 3500).

In The Hague, the tourist office can be found in the city hall (🏠 Spui 70; ☎ 070 353 5043).

You are also likely to encounter ANWB (💻 www.anwb.nl) shops whilst in the Netherlands. This is a private organisation that sells guidebooks and maps.

GETTING THERE AND AWAY

By air

The Netherlands is exceedingly well-connected to most of the world's destinations by air. In fact, the country is something of a transit hub for those travelling between Asia or Africa and America.

The country's main airport is **Schiphol** (💻 www.schiphol.nl), which is a brief 30 to 40 minute train ride from The Hague and 45 to 50 minutes to Rotterdam. There is also a fast-train between Schiphol to Rotterdam, taking just 26 minutes. This train is run by the high-speed train company Fyra, and costs €13.50 each way.

Schiphol is the fourth busiest airport in the world and most airlines depart from or transit here.

Rotterdam and The Hague share an airport that connects with 40 other cities around Europe also has its own airport (💻 www.

TAKE CARE!

You can buy a train ticket at one of the airport's many ticket machines. However, if you choose to purchase a ticket in English (as many foreigners do), the default ticket option that will be selected will be for a full-fare first class ticket. Unless you do want to travel first class, you will need to manually change the category of ticket that you are buying.

rotterdamthehagueairport.nl), now known as 'Rotterdam The Hague Airport'. See p196 for information about how to get to and from the airport.

The low-cost airlines Ryanair, Transavia and Wizzair fly to Eindhoven in the east of the country. There are two trains an hour between The Hague and Eindhoven (journey time 1hr40). Regular buses shuttle between the airport and Eindhoven's train station (20 minutes).

By water

The Dutch city of Rotterdam is Europe's largest port. Many passenger and cargo services operate out of this port, and the occasional cruise ship often weighs anchor there.

Other main passenger ports in the country include the Hook of Holland, IJmuiden and Amsterdam.

Ostend and Zeebrugge, in neighbouring Belgium, are also convenient ports to use for people coming to the Netherlands.

If coming from the UK, you might consider sailing to Calais in northern France. It takes about three hours to drive from Calais to The Hague, depending on traffic. There are no direct bus or train links: you will have to change at Paris. The following section provides further details about overland travel from abroad.

By land

The Netherlands shares a land border with Germany and Belgium.

Rail connections between these countries are generally good. The Dutch Rail website (🖥 www.ns.nl) lists the times of trains to some destinations outside the country, but it is only possible to see the price and make a reservation for national journeys.

Consult the German railway website (🖥 www.db.de) for more international rail travel options. The Belgian rail website (🖥 www.belgianrail.be) lists connections between Belgium and the Netherlands.

For details of high-speed international connections, visit 🖥 www.nshispeed.nl.

At the end for 2012, the high-speed train service Fyra was introduced between the Netherlands and Belgium. However, it was beset

MAIN SHIPPING LINES BETWEEN THE UK AND NETHERLANDS / BELGIUM / FRANCE

UK port	Destination	Duration	Company
Harwich	Hook of Holland	6hr15	Stena Line
Hull	Rotterdam / Zeebrugge	14hr	P&O Ferries
Newcastle	Amsterdam (IJmuiden)	15hr	DFDS Seaways
Rosyth	Zeebrugge	17hr30	Superfast Ferries
Ramsgate	Ostend	4hr	Transeuropa Ferries
Dover	Ostend	2hr05	Hoverspeed Ltd.
Dover	Calais	1hr10	Sea France / P&O

by problems from the beginning and has been suspended until further notice.

Fyra was supposed to replace the regular international intercity train. This service has now been reintroduced, but travellers will have to change two or three times.

Tickets for some international destinations can be purchased at automated ticket tellers in the station. However, for many you must go to the station ticket office, where you will face a €3.50 surcharge.

Thalys (🖳 www.thalys.com), the international high-speed rail operator, runs regular services from Amsterdam and Rotterdam direct to Belgium (Antwerp and Brussels) and France (Lille and Paris). Reservation is obligatory.

If coming from the UK, you might consider taking the Eurostar (🖳 www.eurostar.com), the high-speed train link that runs through the Channel Tunnel between England and France. The train doesn't run as far as the Netherlands, but changing at Brussels allows you to take the Thalys to The Hague. You can purchase combined tickets for such a trip on the Eurostar website.

If you regularly travel abroad by train, you might want to get a yearly discount card that entitles you to 20% off international rail travel (p96).

Road travel between countries is also relatively easy. Whilst passports aren't generally checked at the border, random controls are sometimes carried out, with vehicles being stopped and searched for illegal immigrants or drugs.

If you plan to travel by road to Germany during the winter months, you must have winter tyres — even if the conditions seem perfect. Failure to comply with this could result in a hefty fine.

One of the cheapest ways of getting to the Netherlands, particularly for last-minute travel, is by bus. Eurolines (🖳 www.eurolines.com) runs regular services to The Hague. Long-distance bus travel in Europe demands a certain amount of patience. Be prepared to be stopped by the border control police, especially at night.

TRAVELLING AROUND

Within cities

One of the great delights of the Netherlands is how easy it is to get around without a car.

For many Dutch, the bike is the preferred means of transport. The terrain is generally flat and streets are well-laid out for this.

Most main Dutch train stations now have a facility for hiring bicycles. Ordinarily, this will cost €15 a day, but you can get a significant reduction by subscribing to the *OV-fiets* service (🖳 www.ov-fiets.nl). A yearly subscription costs €11, but you must already have some contract with Dutch Rail — whether that be a discount card or a season ticket for a particular journey. Note that the activation of the *OV-fiets* subscription is not immediate.

The *OV-fiets* card allows you to rent bikes for just €3.10 a day. The bikes available at train stations are typically Dutch, with back-peddle brakes and no gears. For those not used to this style of bicycle, riding one can take a little getting used to.

If you don't want to cycle, you can always take the tram or bus.

The easiest way of paying on trams and buses is to use the *OV-chipkaart*, which is periodically topped up with credit. The amount that you are credited for each journey depends on how far you travel. Rates are set by regional

---

DON'T FORGET TO CHECK OUT!

On both trams and buses, don't forget to check out with your *OV-chipkaart*! If you don't, you will be charged a fixed penalty (€4 for buses and trams and €20 for trains). It is very easy to forget to check out, since most passengers will put the card away once they have checked in. Best to keep the card to hand. On buses and trams, you are expected to check in while you are entering. At railway stations, there is no *OV-chipkaart* reader in the train so you must check in beforehand.

---

transport companies, but are usually at least €0.80 per kilometre. The *OV-chipkaart* can be topped up in the station, using the ticket machines or at the ticket desks.

The system has now largely replaced the old *strippenkaart* system (p92). On most buses and trams, you can still buy a paper ticket from the driver, although this is significantly more expensive.

The website 🖳 www.journeyplanner.9292.nl helps you plan your journey by public transport.

If you are going to drive, a word of caution: unlike many European cities, Dutch towns really do favour the bicycle. If you are turning into a street, check and double-check that there is no cyclist coming because, in most cases, they have the right of way.

Taxis are available in the major cities (p297). Watch out for deceitful taxi drivers who refuse to use the taxi meter and try to overcharge foreigners.

The national rail system offers a shared taxi service at certain stations — usually the smaller towns where commercial taxis are not

available. This service is not available in the major cities such as The Hague or Amsterdam. To find out which stations qualify, you will need to speak to Dutch Rail staff.

To use a *treintaxi*, you should call at least half an hour before, using the premium rate number 0900 873 4682.

The cost is extremely reasonable: €4.70 per person anywhere within a designated parameter.

Around the country

The Netherlands' **rail network** is probably the most convenient way of getting around, if you don't want to use your own car.

Although the rail system has a reputation for efficiency, the Dutch regularly complain about persistent disruptions to the rail network, particularly during cold weather or sporting events. Part of this is because there is little spare capacity in the rail network, so that any minor hiccup on the line is likely to have knock-on effects elsewhere.

A day-trip ticket, which allows you to travel to as many destinations as you want in a single day, costs €58. With a discount card, it costs €28. Sometimes, though, you can get the ticket even cheaper — look for deals that are regularly offered by Albert Heijn supermarket, Blokker, Jumbo and Kruidvat. It is often possible to get a day of unlimited travel for as little as €14. You can also sometimes find offers on 🖳 www.treinreiziger.nl.

Cross-country travel by **bus** generally takes longer than the equivalent journey by train. Buses also tend to be less direct and may require more changes. They are more useful for short hops between towns or to get to some of the Netherlands' more out-of-the-way places.

There are four main bus companies in the Netherlands: Connexxion (💻 www.connexxion.nl), Arriva (💻 www.arriva.nl), Veolia (💻 www.veolia-transport.nl) and Qbuzz (💻 www.qbuzz.nl).

Tickets can be purchased on board most buses, although this is generally more expensive than using your *OV-chipkaart*. Some companies also have their own promotional deals. For example, Connexxion offers a €10 ticket that allows a day of unlimited travel on its bus network. Such tickets can usually be purchased at the tourist office.

Trams connect nearby towns — such as Delft, Wassenaar, Rijswijk — to The Hague. Simply use your *OV-chipkaart* or buy a ticket as you board the tram.

If **driving**, note that traffic can be fairly heavy in the country, especially around major cities.

There is only one toll road, through the Westerscheldetunnel in Zeeland, which goes under the Westerschelde estuary. The tunnel is 6.6 km in length and costs €4.90 per car. The tunnel is a good way of avoiding the horrendous Antwerp road if you are travelling down to Belgium, whilst at the same time taking in the magnificent Zeeland Deltaworks (p269).

▶ See p88 for more information.

MONEY

The Netherlands has had the euro ever since it first entered circulation in January 2002. The former currency — the guilder — is no longer legal tender.

The most common ways of paying for goods and services in the Netherlands are cash and debit cards. Credit cards are not widely used, except for some large purchases or for online payments.

Small purchases are sometimes made using a type of smartcard called a *chipknip* or *chippas*, which has to be topped up with money from a bank account.

The most popular credit cards are Visa and Mastercard. Cirrus and Maestro are the most widely accepted banking cards.

Travellers' cheques can be converted to euros at a bank or exchange bureau. However, it is not usually possible to use them to pay in restaurants and shops.

Money can be changed at banks, post offices or exchange bureaux, which can be found at airports, major railway stations and in areas where tourists are likely to be.

Household bills are most commonly paid by bank transfer or direct debit. Most Dutch banks now offer online banking facilities, which makes paying bills even easier.

Note that, when writing sums of money, the Dutch reverse the English convention of using commas and decimal points. For example, €1.500 means one and a half thousand euros, whilst €1,50 means one euro and 50 cents.

The Dutch do not use one and two cent coins and shops will refuse to accept them. This also means that shops will round prices up or down to the nearest five cents. The one exception to this is the post office, where smaller-denomination coins can still be used.

EXCHANGE RATE	
£1	€1.16
us$1	€0.75
CA$1	€0.74
AU$1	€0.77
NZ$1	€0.63

THE COST OF LIVING

At first glance, the Netherlands seems to be a fairly expensive place in which to live. This is particularly true in Amsterdam, The Hague and Rotterdam, where the vast number of expats end up.

It is true that, since the introduction of the euro in 2002, prices have been steadily climbing upwards.

However, for some things, such as groceries, the Netherlands is actually cheaper than other West European countries. Recent statistics from the EU's statistical bureau show that, in terms of food and drink (excluding alcohol), prices were 2% below the European average. Other West European countries — including Belgium, Germany and Denmark — were far higher.

Prices will be higher if you regularly purchase specific products from your home country, which are available in specialist stores dotted around the main cities (p131 for the stores found in The Hague).

What really pushes the cost of living up is the price of rent, electricity and gas. In the main cities, budget for at least €300-400 for a single room. A one-bedroom apartment will cost at least €750. Prices in the smaller towns, or in the countryside, are likely to be lower.

Eating at good-quality restaurants can also be pricey, although it is possible to get some good deals on the Internet (p109).

Due to a high level of tax, petrol is also fiendishly expensive, second in Europe only to Norway, according to research from the British Automobile Association (AA). The average price at the pump for unleaded petrol is €1.63. If you're driving through any neighbouring countries, it is best to fill up on fuel before you get to the Netherlands.

▶ See p129 for the cost of basic produce

MAIL AND COMMUNICATION

The postal service

The Dutch postal service is operated by TNT Post and is generally fast and efficient. Post offices (🖵 www.postkantoor.nl) are typically open between 8.30am and 5pm, Monday to Friday, although some large branches may also be open on Saturday mornings.

Stamps are generally only sold at post offices and shops that offer TNT services. They are mostly sold in sets of five or 10, although some outlets will make an exception to this.

Post boxes are everywhere in the country. They are usually orange, though you may still get some of the older-style red post boxes, particularly in rural areas. There are usually two slots into which you can put your mail — one for postcodes in the immediate locality and the other for all other mail — so check carefully.

For urgent deliveries, consider using one of the main shipping companies that operate in the country: DHL (☎ 0800 0552; 🖵 www.dhl.com), TNT (☎ 0800 1234; 🖵 www.tnt.com) or UPS (☎ 0800 099 1300; 🖵 www.ups.com).

Internet

Getting an Internet connection at home is a fairly straight-forward process.

Inexpensive **broadband** access is now available throughout the country. The cheapest package is around €17 (for a 256 kbps connection), whilst faster packages are around €30. Connection fees tend to be around €70, but you can often find deals where the connection fee is waived.

The website 🖵 www.internetten. nl (only in Dutch) has a good price comparison of packages that are currently available. When ordering your Internet package, remember to check whether there is a limit on the amount of data you can download each month or an unlimited download allowance (look for the words '*geen datalimiet*').

It usually takes at least a week to set up an Internet connection, but it can be quicker if you select a self-installation option..

Public **Internet cafés** are not always easy to find in the Netherlands. As you might expect, Amsterdam has an abundance of them; but elsewhere you can spend quite a bit of time searching for one. The best place to look is usually around the central station.

Wi-fi spots, on the other hand, are prevalent throughout the Netherlands — many cafés and restaurants are now wired up for you to surf.

Libraries and tourist offices sometimes provide free Internet access, although at busy periods your time on the computer may be limited.

Internet coffee shops, where you can smoke cannabis as you surf, are popular in Amsterdam. Some can also be found outside of the capital.

▶ See p40 for more information about getting connected

▶ See p40 for a list of Internet cafés in The Hague

Phone

The country code for the Netherlands is +31. The area code consists of two or three digits, depending on the size of the area. Mobile phone numbers start with 06. Free service numbers start with 0800. Numbers starting with '09' cost more than

the standard rate: 0900 denotes informational lines, 0906 adult lines and 0909 general entertainment.

If you want to search for a number in the Netherlands, the official Yellow and White Pages can be found at 🖵 en.detelefoongids.nl.

Getting a **land connection** shouldn't be a problem, though you will need to provide a valid ID, BSN social security number and bank card. You may also need to pay a deposit, particularly if you are not an EU citizen.

The phone system is still owned by KPN (☎ 0800 0402; 🖵 www. kpn.nl), the previously state-run company. However, since privatisation, a number of other companies have also been given the right to operate telephone services over the KPN infrastructure. However, this does not mean that you need to have a landline subscription with KPN before you can have a phone in your house.

The largest providers include Ziggo (🖵 www.ziggo.nl), UPC (🖵 www. upc.nl), Tele2 (🖵 www.tele2.nl), Primus and Budget Phone (🖵 www. budgetphone.nl).

These companies offer very competitive rates, and sometimes include package deals that combine **Internet and television** with a telephone connection.

When getting connecting you have two options — either to go for the cheaper one-line option or the more expensive ISDN line, which may be more suitable if you're running a business.

Public telephone boxes have all but disappeared in the Netherlands. You can still find a few though, mainly at the larger stations and near tourist attractions. A very few of these accept coins, but for most you will have to buy a telephone card. These are available at tourist offices, post offices and smalls shops. But be warned: telephone boxes are provided by different companies, and therefore accept different phone cards. KPN is the biggest provider of them.

If you want to go for a **mobile phone** instead, there are a wide range of companies available, each offering slightly different options: KPN (💻 www.kpn.nl), Vodafone (💻 www.vodafone.nl), Telfort (💻 www.telfort.nl), T-Mobile (💻 www.t-mobile.nl), Lebara (💻 www.lebara-mobile.nl), LycaMobile (💻 www.lycamobile.nl), Simyo (💻 www.simyo.nl).

You have the option of whether to subscribe to a service (usually for at least a year) or to use pay-as-you-go top-up cards. A subscription will offer you cheaper calls, but you will be committed to paying a fixed amount. Symio allows subscriptions on a month-by-month basis.

Both Lebara and LycaMobile offer very cost effective pay-as-you-go deals, particularly for calling abroad.

▶ See p40 for more information about postal, Internet and phone services in the country.

PRESS

For such a small country, the Netherlands has a surprisingly vibrant and diverse media scene.

There are nearly a dozen nationwide daily **newspapers**, although a few of these only have fairly small circulations. Historically, these papers were linked to so-called 'pillars', which were set up by institutions according to political or religious ideology (p71). Such pillarisation has largely faded away, but in some cases hints of a paper's former ideology can still be spotted.

The country's most widely-read newspaper is De Telegraaf, considered a conservative liberal tabloid in terms of content (although, like other Dutch newspapers, it is printed in broadsheet format).

Also popular are the right-wing papers Algemeen Dagblad and the slightly more liberal NRC Handelsblad. The left-leaning De Volkskrant is widely read, too. Trouw, originally founded as an underground resistance newspaper during the second world war, is a protestant centre-left paper with a strong focus on religion.

Metro, Spits and De Pers are popular free newspapers, given away during weekdays on the underground or at popular transport hubs.

There is also a wide range of regional newspapers, published according to city or locality.

All newspapers are privately owned.

English and American newspapers are widely available in the main cities at higher prices.

Television and **radio** consist of a combination of public-broadcasting organisations and commercial operations.

There are three public television stations — Nederland 1, Nederland 2 and Nederland 3 — and five public radio networks — Radio 1, Radio 2, 3FM, Radio 4 and Radio 5).

Nederland 1 is orientated towards news, sport and family programming. Nederland 2 is for culture, arts, politics and religion. Nederland 3 concentrates on youth and progressive programming.

Radio 1 is a news and sports channel. Radio 2 and 3FM play chart and album music. Radio 4 plays classical, jazz and world music. Radio 5 offers easy-listening programming.

There are also a variety of commercial channels. The Netherlands has had commercial broadcasting since 1989 — before then, it was not permitted.

Radio Netherlands World (⌨ www.rnw.nl) is an English-language radio station, which broadcasts news from the Netherlands around the world. Around Amsterdam, you can pick up BBC World Service broadcasts on 648 (AM) or 198 (long wave). Cutbacks at the BBC means that the FM service is no longer available.

Cable networks offer a wide range of Dutch and foreign TV channels and radio stations.

Dutch TV and radio listings can be found at ⌨ gids.omroep.nl (only in Dutch).

ELECTRICITY, GAS AND WATER

Electricity in the Netherlands is 220 volts.

Most plug sockets in the country are the two-pin continental variety, with side grounding contacts. This is the same type as those used in neighbouring Germany and Belgium, but not the same as in the UK and the US.

The Dutch energy market was deregulated in 2004, and so you can find many utility suppliers offering very competitive rates. It pays to shop around. Green tariff options are also becoming increasingly popular in the country.

The main gas and electricity suppliers include Essent Groene Stroom (⌨ www.essent.nl), Nuon (⌨ www.nuon.nl) and Oxxio (⌨ www.oxxio.nl).

Water is generally of high quality and safe for drinking.

▶ See p35 for information about utilities

VISAS AND PERMITS

The Netherlands is a member of the Schengen border control system. This means that, if you are entering from another Schengen country, you will not usually have to show your passport (although spot checks can take place, so make sure you carry it with you).

Citizens of countries that belong to the EU or European Economic Area (EEA) do not require a visa to enter the country and can stay for an unlimited amount of time, although after 90 days they are required to register with the authorities. Those living in the Netherlands because of work are also required to register.

Visitors from the United States, Australia, Canada and New Zealand are visa-exempt for stays of up to 90 days. Visas are required for South Africans.

Nationals of Australia, whilst not needing a visa, may be required to show their return ticket, proof of sufficient funds and health insurance for the duration of their stay.

The website of the Ministry of Foreign Affairs (⌨ www.minbuza.nl) has the latest details about visa requirements.

If you find that you do need to apply for a visa, the Dutch embassy in your home country can help you with the process.

Under the Schengen system, visa applications from certain nationalities will require approval from the other Schengen partners. This process usually takes at least eight working days. The Ministry of Foreign Affairs has latest details.

All travellers visiting the Netherlands must have a passport that is valid for at least 90 days after expected departure date.

EU nationals have the automatic right to work in the country. Other nationalities may have to apply for a working visa — consult your local Dutch embassy for current rules.

Under Dutch law, all nationalities should carry valid photo ID at all times, although spot checks are rarely carried out.

If you have lived in the Netherlands for five years or more, you will be eligible for Dutch residence. The cost of this is currently €30.

▶ See p24 for more information about visas and permits.

HEALTH

The Netherlands has a good level of health care, which is an intriguing blend of social welfare coverage and private provision.

Unlike in the UK, the Dutch government is not in control of the day-to-day management of health services. This responsibility rests, instead, with private health care companies.

If you are living in the Netherlands for more than 90 days, or you are paying income tax in the country, then you are required to purchase health insurance from a Dutch insurance company.

Every health care insurance company must offer you a basic package, covering basic check-ups, hospitalisation where necessary, prenatal care and certain prescription medicine. This basic package does not generally provide for dental treatment. You can either take out additional insurance for this, or just pay the necessary amount at the dentist as and when.

When offering this basic package, insurance companies are not allowed to discriminate against people on the grounds of health or age. Although the government sets the basic price level for the package, it is up to individual companies to determine additional fees for providing such cover, so it pays to shop around.

As a rule-of-thumb, expect to pay around €100 a month for basic health care coverage.

To compare health insurance deals, visit 🖵 www.kiesbeter.nl/zorgverzekeringen.

Some insurance companies allow you to seek treatment at any health clinic, whilst others specify a list of approved places where you can go under the terms of your health cover.

Children under the age of 18 years are entitled to free health care.

People staying for less than three months in the Netherlands are not required to purchase health insurance.

You will be charged health insurance from the moment you move to the Netherlands, not from the moment you register. Therefore, if you register three months after you arrive, you will still be charged for those first three months.

If you use Dutch medical services during your stay, you may be entitled to reimbursement from your home country. Make sure that you keep all of your prescriptions and receipts.

If you are an EU citizen, you should apply for a European Health Insurance Card (EHIC) through the national health provider in your home country. This card makes it easier to access health care in European countries and means that you either do not have to pay for emergency treatment or you get health care charges refunding more quickly.

▶ See p24 for more information about the Dutch health system.

SAFETY AND CRIME

Serious crime in the Netherlands is relatively rare, although petty theft and pickpocketing is more common.

Always make sure that you keep a watchful eye out around train stations and in tourist areas. Thieves also target hotel rooms, so make sure you keep your valuables locked away or hand them to the hotel desk for security.

The Essentials

BIKE SCAM

There are countless criminal scams to watch out for in the Netherlands. One particularly devious one often fools even the most street savvy.

This scam usually happens in the evening. Once the potential victim has parked his or her bike, the would-be thief comes along and chains his or her own bike to it, making this seem like an innocent mistake.

But the apparent error isn't so innocent. The hope is that the victim will leave their bike overnight, thinking that the owner of the other bike will eventually come back and retrieve it.

What actually happens is that the bike thief returns in the early hours of the morning and, at a time when no one is watching, uses an electric saw to cut through the lock of the victim's bike.

The police are wise to this scam but can do nothing about it; they are not permitted to severe the bike lock on your behalf.

Just remember, if someone has chained their bike to yours, don't leave your bike overnight. It may not be there in the morning

Theft is especially common on trains to and from Schiphol airport, with laptops being a prime target.

Bike theft is becoming more and more common, particularly in town centres. Long-term drug users are often the culprits. A variety of scams exist to separate you from your bike (see box on p22).

Always remember to fasten the clips on your bicycle bags. There have been reports of thieves snatching items from the bags of cyclists who have stopped at traffic lights.

Make sure that you buy a good lock and always fasten it securely. There are many official bike racks around the country for this very purpose. Some of the more expensive bikes may have a serial number printed on the frame. It is a good idea to make a note of this number, so attempts can be made to recover the bike if it is stolen.

NATIONAL HOLIDAYS

The Netherlands celebrates 13 national days (see box on p23), although not all of these are public holidays. For those days that are not public holidays, the decision about whether to give time off rests with individual companies.

The Netherlands recognises many of the days commonly found in other western European countries, such as Christmas Day and Easter Day. Good Friday, though, is not a mandatory day off.

In addition, the country celebrates Remembrance of the Dead (a national holiday) and Saint Nicholas' Eve (not a national holiday).

Liberation Day, commemorating the end of German occupation in the second world war, is only given as a holiday once every five years. The next Liberation Day holiday will be on May 5, 2015.

If either Christmas day or the day after Christmas (*tweede kerstdag*) falls on a weekend, then no alternative day off is given in lieu.

There have recently been calls for the Islamic festival of Eid al-Fitr, which comes at the end of Ramadan, to be a national holiday. However, political opposition has prevented discussions on this going forward. Most companies, though, will now give this as a day off for Islamic employees.

NATIONAL HOLIDAYS IN THE NETHERLANDS

Date	Day	Notes
January 1	New Year's Day	
March / April	Easter Sunday	
April 30	Queen's Day / King's Day	Queen's Day is now celebrated on the birthday of the late Queen Juliana. If April 30 is a Sunday, the day is celebrated the day before. With the abdication of Queen Beatrix (p61), Queen's Day will become King's Day after 2013.
May 5	Liberation Day	Celebration of the Capitulation of German forces in the second world war. National holiday every five years.
40 days after Easter	Ascension Day	
7 weeks after Easter	Pentecost	
December 25-26	Christmas	

OTHER DAYS OF SPECIAL SIGNIFICANCE

The table below indicates other special national days for the Dutch. These days are not official national holidays, although some companies may give a day off.

Date	Day	Notes
January 6	Epiphany	
March / April	Good Friday	Banks and post offices are closed — but commercial companies often work.
May 4	Remembrance of the Dead	This day is to commemorate all those who died in the second world war.
November 11	Saint Martin's Day	
December 5	Saint Nicholas' Eve	
December 15	Kingdom Day	The signing of the 'Charter for the Kingdom of the Netherlands' in 1954.

Living & Working

VISAS AND PERMITS

Members of the EU, European Economic Area (EEA) and Switzerland do not require a **visa to visit or work in the Netherlands**.

Visitors from Australia, New Zealand, the United States and Taiwan do not require a visa for stays of less than 90 days, although they will not be able to work without a work permit.

The Dutch Embassy in your home country will be able to provide you with the latest information about visa requirements. If you are already in the Netherlands, questions can be asked at the local municipality (see box below).

If you are planning to visit the country for **longer than 90 days or work in the Netherlands** then you must register with the *gemeente* (see box below) in the area where you are living. Failure to do this could incur a fine of up to €400.

EU citizens automatically have the right to residency, but non-EU citizens do not. If you are not an EU citizen, but are married to someone from the EU (or in a recognised partnership), then you should be able to obtain a residence permit with little difficulty. Otherwise, your

---

GEMEENTE AND *STADHUIS*

Reading this chapter, you're bound to notice how often the term '*gemeente*' is used. In fact, if you are moving to the Netherlands, you will hear the word so many times that you will probably start using it directly in Dutch, rather than translating it.

The *gemeente* is responsible for managing the municipality of a particular town or city, and will be your main point of reference for most things that you need to know whilst living in the country. Here you can find out about such diverse things as parking permits, rubbish disposal, problems with your landlord and so forth.

Stadhuis refers to the town hall where the *gemeente* has its offices. Larger towns and cities may have a number of stadhuis locations.

Questions can often be answered by telephone, although staff aren't always happy to speak in English. A lot of information is available on the *gemeente* website, but most of it is in Dutch.

The following is a selective list of *gemeente* offices in the country:

- **Den Haag:** 🏠 Spui 70; ☎ 14 070 or 070 353 3000; 🖵 www. denhaag.nl; 🕿 Mon-Wed & Fri: 7.30am to 4.30pm, Thu: 7.30am to 8pm

- **Rotterdam:** 🏠 Stadhuis Coolsingel 40; ☎ 14 010; 🖵 www.rotterdam.nl; 🕿 Mon-Wed & Fri: 8am to 4pm, Thu: 8am to 1.30pm

- **Delft:** 🏠 Phoenixstraat 16; ☎ 14015 or 015 260 2222; 🖵 www.delft.nl; 🕿 Mon-Thu: 8am to 5pm, Fri: 8am to 8pm

- **Amsterdam:** 🏠 Amstel 1; ☎ 14 020; 🖵 www.amsterdam.nl; 🕿 Mon-Wed & Fri: 8.30am to 3pm, Thu: 1 to 7pm

best option for obtaining residency is to find a sponsor (p26).

The registration process is free, although from the moment that you register you will be liable for Dutch tax and you will have to take out compulsory Dutch health insurance (p38).

To register, you need proof of identity (such as a passport) and a proof of address (such as a tenancy agreement or property deed). If you are accompanied by your spouse you must also bring along your marriage certificate. Your birth certificate and those of any children that you have with you will also be required, but these can be provided at a later date. Original documents in English are usually accepted, although you may have to get them legalised by your home country. Some EU countries can provide a bilingual copy of your document free of charge.

Upon registration you will be issued with a proof of residency certificate called a *bewijs van bekendmaking*. This will include your unique identification number (*burgerservicenummer, BSN*, formerly called *sofinummer*). You will need this in situations where you have to prove your residency status, such as opening a bank account, registering with a doctor or accessing free legal help. You should also give this number to your employer. Visit 🖵 www.burgerservicenummer.nl for more info.

Non-EU nationals must also register with the **Immigration and Naturalisation Service (IND)**. Registration is recommended but not mandatory for EU citizens. Failure to register means that you are not entitled to social assistance and cannot apply for a government grant or loan. Many telecoms companies refuse subscriptions without evidence of such registration.

Childcare allowance and mortgages can also be harder to get if you don't register.

IND registration is free. Simply call ☎ 020 889 3045 to make an appointment. Note that the number given on the IND website — ☎ 0900 123 4561 — is a premium rate number.

During the phone call you will be asked what the reason is for your stay in the Netherlands. An appointment will be arranged at the IND office closest to your address. A confirmation letter and registration form will be sent to you. You must bring the following to your appointment:

- A copy of the filled-in form.

- Evidence of why you are staying in the country, such as an employer's declaration of the terms of your contract.

- Proof of sufficient financial means, such as a mention of your salary in the employer's declaration.

- Proof of health insurance.

- Passport or European identity card.

The IND website (🖵 www.ind.nl) has more information, including a small section in English.

A sticker will be placed in your passport as proof of your registration with IND. This sticker remains valid for the entire duration of your stay in the Netherlands. There is no need to extend or renew it.

If you only bring along your European identity card — rather than your passport — a separate document will be issued to confirm your registration.

Living & Working

COLLECTIVE LABOUR AGREEMENTS

Alongside your contract, companies or sectors also recognise a collective labour agreement or *collectieve arbeidsovereenkomst* (CAO). Each industrial sector has it's own CAO and the ones that don't recognise it will have to agree with the unions a different one. This contains supplementary rules for all employees on things such as payment, working hours, supplementary pension provision and sick leave.

You can obtain more information about CAOs from your employer, trade union or on the website 🖵 www.cao.szw.nl.

WORK PERMIT

EU citizens have the automatic right to work in the Netherlands. Non-EU citizens married to EU nationals can also seek work permits, once they are registered.

If you fall outside of these categories, then the best option for working in the country is to try and find an organisation that will sponsor you.

Under the country's Foreign Nationals Employment Act — Wet Arbeid Vreemdelingen (WAV) — employers must first try to recruit within the Netherlands and in other EU countries before seeking workers from elsewhere, although this provision does not apply to inter-governmental organisations.

A work permit can be obtained by your employer from Uitvoeringsinstelling Werknemersverzekeringen (UWV), which is also responsible for social benefits. Further information is available at 🖵 www.werk.nl.

You must be aged between 18 and 45 to be eligible for a standard work permit.

The maximum duration of a work permit is three years. Employees who have worked for three consecutive years in the Netherlands, with full residency status, will generally be granted an extension to this period. If you are allowed to work in the Netherlands, then your spouse or partner is usually allowed to work as well.

QUALIFICATION EVALUATION

If you intend to use qualifications obtained in another country in order to work or study in the Netherlands, you may first have to have them evaluated. The official centres that offer this service are Nuffic (🖵 www.nuffic.nl) and Colo (🖵 www.colo.nl). See 🖵 www.idw.nl for more information.

If you are unemployed and looking for a job, the UWV (🖵 www.werk.nl) will help you get your documents evaluated, free of charge.

You can also visit 🖵 www.professionalrecognition.nl for more information on practising a regulated profession in the Netherlands.

EMPLOYMENT STATUS

Your employment rights depend very much on which category of worker you fall into.

Working for a Dutch employer

Your employment contract will either be directly with your Dutch employer or with a temporary employment agency. If it is with the latter, then you may be able to work for multiple companies rather than just a single one.

There are different types of contract.

A **standard employment** contract includes conditions governing pay, working hours, holidays and leave. If you are employed by

LOOKING FOR A JOB?

The following websites are useful places to start:

- 💻 www.unique.nl
- 💻 www.undutchables.nl
- 💻 www.adamsrecruitment.nl
- 💻 www.anyworkanywhere.com
- 💻 www.escapeartist.com/netherlands/jobs.htm
- 💻 www.englishlanguagejobs.com
- 💻 www.bluelynx.nl
- 💻 www.kellyservices.com
- 💻 www.togetherabroad.nl
- 💻 www.werk.nl (only in Dutch)

a Dutch employer, you will automatically be insured against unemployment, illness and occupational disability.

When you start work, your employer will ask to see a valid identity document confirming your nationality, *burgerservicenummer* and work permit if needed. If you do not yet have a *burgerservicenummer*, proof that you are seeking one (such as confirmation of an appointment) should suffice.

Always ask for a written employment contract in your own language or in English and only sign the contract if you understand what it says.

The **nul uren contract** (zero hour contract) is a popular way of employing students and other temporary workers. It is very common in the food catering industry, supermarkets and other places where people are often needed to fill short-term gaps.

Under this type of contract, the employer is not obliged to call you for work but, if you are called, then you should be prepared to go (within reason, of course — he cannot simply call you at the last minute).

You are not compelled to go when called, but failure to do so could mean that you are not called in the future.

It is worth pointing out some basic rights that you have with this kind of contract, since employers regularly try to break the rules, especially for foreigners.

If you are called out, you cannot be asked to work less than three hours. After six months, if the employee is working a fairly constant number of hours each week, then he or she may be entitled to a more formal contract, indicating the minimum number of hours worked each week.

This is a flexible contact for both the employer and the employee. Either can terminate the contract without a formal notice period.

Another type of temporary contact is the **min/max contract,** which indicates the minimum number of hours to be worked each week. The employee gets paid for the number of hours that are written on the contract, even if he or she hasn't been called for work.

If four temporary contracts with the same employer have been agreed, with less than a three-month break between each of them, the employer is obliged to offer a permanent one.

Seconded as an employee to the Netherlands

You will have this employment status if you are working temporarily in the Netherlands for your own employer or for a temporary employment agency in your country of origin.

The terms and conditions of your contract must comply with the legal rules of your home country. However, certain Dutch rules will also govern your terms of employment. For

Living & Working

Living & Working

example, you must be paid at least the Dutch minimum wage and have a minimum holiday entitlement.

Employment conditions and work/rest periods must also comply with legal minimums (see 'Labour Law' section below).

You may choose to remain socially-insured in your home country.

Self-employed

If you are classed as self-employed then you can determine your own employment terms, such as the hourly wage you will receive.

There are two possibilities for carrying out self-employed work in the Netherlands.

You may be able to remain resident of your home country whilst working in the Netherlands, in which case you will be socially-insured back home.

Alternatively, you can establish a Dutch one-man-company, known as a *zelfstandige zonder personee* (ZZP) or 'self-employed without staff'. This means that you must be registered as a Dutch taxpayer and be socially-insured in accordance with Dutch legislation. As an independent contractor you are not automatically insured against unemployment, illness and occupational disability, although you can arrange private cover for this.

Being self-employed in the Netherlands gives you certain fiscal advantages.

The Dutch Chamber of Commerce (💻 www.kvk.nl) can provide further advice about being an independent contractor in the Netherlands.

LABOUR LAW

Leave

Every employee in the Netherlands has the right to paid holidays. You are also entitled to leave days, with either full or partial salary, in the case of unforeseen personal circumstances or certain family events (including pregnancy, maternity, marriages and funerals). For more details on the valid reasons for seeking leave, see 💻 www.szw. nl. Different or supplementary arrangements may have been agreed in a CAO (see box on p26).

The number of leave days that workers in the Netherlands are entitled to is equivalent to the number of working days per week multiplied by four. So, for those working the full five-day week, the minimum leave entitlement will be 20 days.

You will receive your full salary during your holiday. Workers are also entitled to a 'holiday allowance' of 8% of gross annual salary, which is paid out at least once a year (usually at the end of May or beginning of June).

Working hours

Dutch rules limit working hours for most employees to a maximum of 40 hours per week (eight hours

---

CIVIL CODE OF THE NETHERLANDS

The civil code of the Netherlands — the Burgerlijk Wetboek (BW) — is available online at 💻 www. wetboek-online.nl/wet/BW1. html). The sixth book of the BW is about contracts and obligations, so most of your questions about labour law can be answered if you look there. It is only in Dutch though.

MINIMUM WAGE

The Netherlands enforces a legal minimum wage.

If you receive less than this, you may appeal to your employer. If discussing a solution with him is not successful, you can then approach the Labour Inspectorate or local court. Employers who pay employees less than the legal minimum wage will be forced by the Labour Inspectorate to pay an immediate fine.

The minimum wage also applies to employees of a foreign company or temporary employment agency working in the Netherlands. You can find the latest details about the minimum wage at: 🖥 www.szw.nl (also in English).

The minimum wage that you are entitled to depends on your age. The following table provides details of the minimum wage as of January 2013.

Age	Monthly	Weekly	Daily
23+ years	€1,469.40	€339.10	€67.82
22 years	€1,249	€288.25	€57.65
21 years	€1,065.30	€245.85	€49.17
20 years	€903.70	€208.55	€41.71
19 years	€771.45	€178.05	€35.61
18 years	€668.60	€154.30	€30.86
17 years	€580.40	€133.95	€26.79
16 years	€506.95	€117.00	€23.40
15 years	€440.80	€101.75	€20.35

per day), although there are exceptions for professions such as the hospitality industry.

There is also the possibility of a four-day week, where employers can work up to 10 hours per day, but in such a case a specific agreement should be made with the employer in advance.

Employers are not allowed to force staff to work for longer than four and a half hours without giving them at least a half hour break, although this break does not have to be paid.

After a working day you have the right to at least 11 hours of consecutive rest. After a working week you have the right to rest for at least 36 hours.

If you are working at night, and your shift ends after 2am, then you have the right to at least 14 hours of rest before working again.

Working time rules do not apply to independent contractors, except where the safety of third parties is involved, such as in the transportation sector.

Illness

If you become ill, you are entitled to at least 70% of your salary for a maximum of two years. However, in order to get this payment you need to show that you are doing everything you can to get back to work as quickly as possible.

If you become ill in the Netherlands but want to recuperate in your own country, then you need permission from your employer. A doctor has to check that this will not delay your recovery.

If you are ill for more than two years, you may request an occupational disability benefit from the UWV: 🖥 www.uwv.nl. You need to show that you are at least 35% work-disabled to be eligible for this. If you also have the right to an occupational disability benefit in your home country, this will be deducted from the Dutch benefit.

The UWV may also be able to help if your employment contract expires during your illness and you are no longer covered by its social security provisions.

Unemployment

If you lose your job whilst a resident in the Netherlands, then you may be entitled to unemployment benefit from the UWV.

To be eligible for this, you must remain in the Netherlands and show that you are actively seeking work. You must also register with the national job-seekers' agency, which is part of UWV. The duration of your unemployment benefits depends on how long you previously worked for.

Whilst looking for work, you will be entitled to take 20 days off each calendar year, although you must notify the UWV every time you go abroad.

You can start procedures with the UWV as soon as you are given your notice (usually a month before you have to leave). However, you cannot claim your benefits until two days before you leave.

For further questions, contact the UWV offices that are closest to you. In The Hague, the UWV is to be found at 🏠 Verheeskade 187; ☎ 070 850 4300; ☎ Mon-Fri: 8.30am to 4.30pm.

Family allowance

Registered residents who have children under 18 are entitled to child benefit. For a single child, this will range from €188 to €269 per quarter, depending on the child's age.

You can apply for family allowance through the Social Insurance Bank (🖥 www.svb.nl). Your personal situation, or that of your partner, has an influence on the right to, or extent of, the family allowance.

Pension

People who pay tax in the Netherlands are insured under the national state pension system. For every year that you are insured, you will build up 2% of the full pension. Thus, if you have worked in the Netherlands from the age of 15 until the age of 65, you will get a full state pension. After this 50-year period, your state pension will not increase.

You may also accumulate a company pension through your work.

A supplementary pension-fund can be arranged through your pension fund agent. You can find more information about pensions at 🖥 www.svb.nl.

Maternity leave

Women are entitled to paid maternity leave for a maximum of 16 weeks. This period starts from between four and six weeks before the due date.

Women are entitled to their salary, capped at €174.

If the mother is sick after her maternity leave, she is entitled to 100% sick leave (p29).

Men are entitled to two days of paternity leave. Both parents can ask for additional unpaid parental leave.

Women who want to spend more time with their children, once their maternity leave has finished, are allowed to request to work part-time temporarily, with a return to full-time work later on.

ACCOMMODATION

Renting

There are two type of rental accommodation offered in the Netherlands — one by private landlords and the other through the country's social housing system. Social housing is significantly cheaper, but comes with a number of conditions attached (p34).

To give a rough idea of what to expect in terms of **private housing**, a one-bedroom apartment in the centre of The Hague might cost somewhere in the region of €775 (excluding charges). The same apartment outside the centre could cost €620. For a three-bedroom apartment, you'd be looking in the region of between €1,000 (outside the city centre) and €1,400 (within the city centre).

Accommodation tends to be slightly cheaper in other areas of the Netherlands, apart from Amsterdam, where prices are even higher.

You can rent accommodation from a private individual or from an estate agent.

Estate agents will typically show you properties for free, until you find one that you want. When you decide to take a property, you will usually be asked to pay a month's

FINDING A PLACE TO STAY

You might find the following web addresses useful:

Just for rent

- 🖥 www.kamernet.nl`
- 🖥 www.easykamer.nl (multilingual)
- 🖥 www.opmijnkamer.nl
- 🖥 www.kamer.nl

For rental and purchase

- 🖥 www.funda.nl
- 🖥 www.duinzigt.nl
- 🖥 www.wooncompany.nl
- 🖥 www.pararius.com

rent to the estate agent as a finding fee. In some fairly rare cases this fee may be paid by the landlord.

Some agencies, primarily targeted at expats, also charge a registration fee in order to help you find a property.

Estate agencies will not generally show you a property on the same day you ask for an appointment. Most of the time you will be given an appointment two or three days later, depending on how busy they are.

If you like the place that you have viewed, don't forget to let the estate agent know as soon as you can. The best places go within hours of being put on the market. Remember, once you have signed the contract, you still have three working days to change your mind.

You can always look for a property on your own as well (see box on p31 for some websites that can help).

Pay attention to the number of *kamers* (rooms) when looking for accommodation in the Netherlands. The Dutch include every

Living & Working

TENANT RIGHTS

There's some truth in the widely-held belief that Dutch landlords prefer expats as tenants (as long as they can show that they have a decent job). This is largely because many expats do not know their rights as tenants.

The basic rental contract is for an unlimited **duration**, with a minimum term of one year, and only the judiciary — not the landlord — can evict a tenant. A growing number of landlords are trying to get tenants to sign contracts that do not adhere to this standard, but such contracts are usually rejected by the courts.

The main situation where the courts could rule in the landlord's favour is if he or she has been living abroad and wants to return to the apartment, and can prove that this is the only house that he or she owns.

You should also be aware that there are strict limits about how much **rent** a landlord can charge you. The Huurcommissie (☎ 0800 488 7243; 💻 www.huurcommissie.nl) can assess, free of charge, whether what you are paying is fair (although you must request this within six months of the start of your contract). If you are found to be paying too much, the Huurcommissie can ask the landlord to return whatever you have overpaid. A court order is not needed for this. This is why the Huurcommissie is so feared by unscrupulous landlords. If you have a dispute with your landlord, just mention the Huurcommissie and see what happens!

The only exception to this 'maximum rate of rent' rule is if you are staying in an historically-listed building. In this case, there is no limit on the rent you can be asked to pay.

The Huurcommissie can also take action if you believe you are paying too much for utilities. In order to reduce their tax bill, landlords regularly lower the basic rent they are charging, whilst at the same time raising the charges. However, the landlord must always provide utility bills at least once a year, in order to justify the amount he is charging you. Few do, but if he doesn't — or if the amount you are paying is not reflected by the bill — then you could have a case to put before the Huurcommissie.

For any other problems that you have with your landlord, Juridisch Loket (☎ 0900 8020; 💻 www.juridischloket.nl) provides free legal advice for residents. It is possible to have a free 10-minute face-to-face consultation without prior appointment. If you want to discuss things by phone or schedule a longer consultation, calls cost 10 cents per minute.

Juridisch Loket can arrange basic solicitor services such as sending official letters to your landlord.

An alternative way of resolving disputes is to speak to the national tenants' association, Woonbond (☎ 0205 517 700; 💻 www.woonbond.nl), but you must be a member before they will take any action on your behalf. Personal membership costs €33.50 per year.

The Hague Law Centre (💻 www.haagsewetswinkel.nl), run by law students, also offers free advice.

room in their room counts, apart from the kitchen and bathroom. So a three-*kamer* property may only have two bedrooms.

The tenant has many more rights in the Netherlands than might be the case in other countries — refer to the box on p32 to make sure you are being treated fairly by your landlord.

If you are not sure how long you will be in the Netherlands, you can ask for a 'diplomatic clause' (*diplomatenclausule*) to be included in your contract. This clause — which isn't, despite the name, just for diplomats — states that, should a tenant be relocated for work purposes more than 50 km away, the tenant is allowed to terminate the contract prematurely, providing two months' notice is given. *Nota bene*, though, that the diplomatic clause works both ways — it also gives the lessor the right to terminate the agreement and reoccupy the property early.

CARETAKER ACCOMMODATION

Ad Hoc Apartments (💻 www.adhocbeheer.nl) takes care of apartments on behalf of clients and lets these places out for exceedingly little money (rent is often as low as €150 to €300 a month).

In the Netherlands, until very recently, squatters were entitled to legally occupy any apartment that was left temporarily vacant. And, once a squatting group had taken up residence in a particular apartment, it was almost impossible to remove them and would, at a minimum, require a court injunction.

Thus many property owners preferred to let someone else use the property, in return for an agreement that they could have it back whenever they wanted. Some of these properties are furnished, whilst others are not.

Before you are eligible to rent one of these apartments, you must have a recommendation from someone who is already using the system. Each person that enters the system is allowed to recommend a maximum of two people, and they can only recommend them if they have always been good tenants (i.e., if they have always respected the rules and paid the rent on time).

The significant drawback to this type of accommodation is that you can be asked to move at a moment's notice (often within a week). The Ad Hoc organisation will always provide you with alternative accommodation, but the conditions of the place can vary significantly. You could, for example, move from an eight-room villa to a tiny apartment, but still be paying the same rent. You can refuse the proposed change of apartment, but you can only do so twice. Refuse a third time and you have to leave the system.

The frequency with which you are asked to change apartment varies quite a lot. You can be lucky and stay in a property for years or end up choosing properties where the owners want them back fairly quickly.

This system is slowly changing. Already, these kinds of apartment are fairly limited. Now that squatters' rights are being curtailed, it is only a matter of time before the system dies away altogether.

Ad Hoc can also arrange office space.

A fixed-term contract will continue automatically — under what is known as a 'silent agreement' (*stilzwijgende*) — unless other provisions are made. So make sure that you give written notice to your landlord in advance of the end of contract, or you could face further unexpected rental charges.

You should carefully check the inventory when you move into a new rental property. Note any wear-and-tear that has not already been recorded. By law, you must return the place in the same condition in which you found it. Landlords can be unscrupulous in trying to charge you extra when you leave. Making a careful note of the condition of everything when you move in is a good first line of defence.

If you are on a low income, you can apply to stay in **social housing**, although there is a long waiting list for this (in some cases, as much as 10 years!) Expect to pay between €250 and €450 a month for a decent apartment.

Once you have been deemed eligible, you can apply for apartments by going to the relevant website for where you live:

- Amsterdam
  💻 www2.woningnet.nl
- The Hague
  💻 www.haaglanden.nl
- Rotterdam
  💻 www.woonnet-rijnmond.nl

The third type of housing is **accommodation managed by a private letting firm on behalf of a client**, who is usually overseas. This offers an incredibly cheap way of staying in some really nice places (see box on p33).

Buying

If you are planning to live in the Netherlands for some length of time, it might be worth buying a property rather than renting one. The general rule of thumb is that you should own a property for at least three years before selling it on. Any less and you may lose money because of the buying and selling fees.

One particular incentive for purchasing a house is that the interest from any mortgage is fully tax-deductible, although of course this is only an advantage to Dutch taxpayers. There is constant speculation that, in this age of austerity, the Dutch government may decide to lessen the tax benefit for mortgage-holders. However, the system currently proves too popular among Dutch voters for the government to make any overt movements in this direction.

Following the collapse of the financial markets in 2008, banks in the Netherlands (as elsewhere) have become more cautious about lending to first-time buyers. Most will let you borrow up to three and a half times your salary, although it will be difficult to obtain a mortgage if you do not have a permanent contract. You may be able to get around this by asking your employer to write you a letter saying that he intends to renew your contract once it has expired.

Many mortgage providers will include a clause that says you cannot rent out the property without their permission. The logic behind this is that, if you cannot keep up repayments on the mortgage, the bank wants to be able to repossess the house without dealing with difficult tenants. Breaching this clause, if it exists within the terms of your mortgage, could land you in court.

A *makelaar* can help with your property search. Fees vary. *Makelaars* either ask for a fixed or monthly fee, or a fee based on a

HOMEOWNERS' ASSOCIATIONS

In the Netherlands, the local homeowners' association is known as the Verenigingen van Eigenaren (VvE). If you buy an apartment that is part of a unit of apartments, then you will almost certainly have to deal with the VvE.

You will be expected to pay a certain amount into the VvE each month. This money is put into a bank account and used to pay for any communal repairs that might be needed.

The amount that you must contribute each month will be determined by the VvE, although the authorities can order the amount to be raised if it is considered too low to meet current needs.

Decisions with the VvE are taken by majority vote — for every decision, the approval or disapproval or each member of the VvE must be sought.

It is fairly common to employ a management company to carry out the administration of the VvE. Fees for this will be taken out of the communal pot of money.

Conflicts among tenants are common. VvE Balie is an organisation that has been set up by the authorities to help resolve any disputes. Each municipality has its own VvE Balie. The one in The Hague can be found at 🖳 Leyweg 813; ☎ 070 353 3281.

percentage of the price of the house that you end up buying (typically between 1% and 2%). There may be other clauses in the *makelaar's* contract — such as a limit on the number of houses that they have to find for you each month — so check well.

The alternative to using a *makelaar* is to simply rely on viewings through individual estate agents. If you are shown a house that you like, then you can make an offer through the estate agent and they will negotiate on your behalf with the owner of the property. Remember, though, that the estate agent generally represents the seller's — rather than the buyer's — interests, since it is the seller who pays the fees. For this reason, it is in the interests of the estate agent to get the highest price possible.

When you buy a property, you will have to pay a standard transfer tax. The government temporarily reduced this rate from 6% to 2% in June 2011, in order to stimulate the housing sector.

Dutch law requires a notary to be hired in order to perform the property registration process. Legal fees are negotiable, but usually work out at around 1% to 2% of the total property value, and includes the fees that you must pay for the deed of transfer.

UTILITY CHARGES

If you are a homeowner in the Netherlands, you will certainly have to deal with bills from time to time — this section explains what charges to expect.

If you are a tenant, your landlord may have included utility charges as part of your monthly rent. Your contract will tell you if this is the case. Be careful, though: many contracts will include a limit on this. If you go above this limit, then you may be asked to pay more. Note also that, even if charges are included as part of the overall rent, the landlord has an obligation to provide you with copies of all bills

Living & Working

— make sure that you are being asked to pay a fair amount in charges (see box on p32).

Water

Each geographical region has a water board (*waterschappen*), which is responsible for the management and treatment of water resources. In The Hague — and the rest of South Holland — this is Dunea (⌨ www.dunea.nl).

The regional water board will deal with your water connection and supply. A water meter in the home measures consumption, and you will have to pay the water board according to the amount of water that you use.

You will also have to pay an annual tax for being connected to the water supply (*watersysteemheffing*), which includes a waste water purification tax (*zuiveringscheffing*) and a maintenance fee for the dykes and water level. The level of the tax varies from household to household, depending on the property that you live in and how many people live with you.

If you are a tenant, this water tax will be split equally between you and your landlord.

Gas and electricity

Gas and electricity are generally supplied by the same provider. Since the privatisation of the Dutch energy market, numerous providers have sprung up and it pays to

shop around. Tariffs can vary considerably. Many companies also offer a 'green' option, where power is sourced from environmentally sound areas or drawn from clean renewable sources such as the sun, sea or wind.

Energy consumption is recorded by meters within your home, and you should always note the reading as soon as you move in to a new place. Your monthly bill will be based on the previous year's consumption, which means that if you have just moved into a place you may be paying more (or less) than you might ordinarily consume. Any discrepancies are resolved at the end of the calendar year.

Nuon is the only provider that offers the possibility of opting for a bill that accurately reflects your monthly consumption, but you will have to pay more for this service.

Reduced tariffs for electricity are available at night (from 11pm to 7am) and during weekends.

Note that some companies outsource customer relations to another company called Stedin (⌨ www.stedinmeetbedrijf.nl) so you may receive a letter from them requesting the current meter reading.

POWER CUTS

If you need to report a power outage, you can call the free national number ☎ 0800 9009 or visit the website ⌨ www.gasenstroomstoringen.nl. This service is available around the clock.

MAIN GAS/ELECTRICITY SUPPLIERS

E.ON	⌨ www.eon.nl
Eneco	⌨ thuis.eneco.nl
Energie Direct	⌨ www.energiedirect.nl
Essent	⌨ www.essent.nl
Greenchoice	⌨ www.greenchoice.nl
Nederlandse Energie Maatschappij	⌨ www.nle.nl
Nuon	⌨ www.nuon.nl
Oxxio	⌨ www.oxxio.nl

INSURANCE *(Verzekering)*

The Dutch are known for constantly fretting about what the future may bring. They generally appreciate predictability and certainty, and don't have much time for surprises, particularly the unpleasant kind. It should therefore come as no surprise that they are very attached to insurance products, many of which are compulsory for residents.

There are plenty of insurance companies to choose from. Some give discounts for couples, families or employees of particular organisations with whom they have special arrangements, so it pays to shop around.

Note that most insurance companies do not accept claims within the first three months of taking out a policy.

Personal indemnity insurance
(Aansprakelijkheidsverzekering)

Under Dutch law, you are legally required to compensate anyone who suffers harm through an accident that you are responsible for. In some instances, the monetary value involved in such compensation can be quite considerable, which is why many people opt to take out personal indemnity insurance. This insurance will cover most damage for which you, as a private individual, can be held liable, although it will not cover road accidents; for that you must take out additional insurance. Most AVP policies will also cover damage caused by your child or pet.

Legal insurance
(Rechtsverzekering)

In addition to personal liability insurance, you can also take out legal insurance, which will give you free

---

INSURANCE COMPANIES

Here is a list of the main insurance companies in the Netherlands:

- 🖥 www.cz.nl
- 🖥 www.deltalloyd.nl
- 🖥 www.anderzorg.nl
- 🖥 www.ohra.nl
- 🖥 www.vgz.nl
- 🖥 www.kiemer.nl
- 🖥 verzekeruzelf.nl*

To compare the different policies offered by various insurance companies, you can use a comparison website such as 🖥 www.independer.nl and select the type of insurance you need.

*Verzekeruzelf is a 100% online insurance company and therefore one of the cheapest.

---

access to legal advice should you need it, and often some access to solicitors or lawyers. Note, however, that you will usually be unable to make a claim under your insurance policy for three to six months after taking it out. This is to prevent people from taking out the insurance just because they know they are going to need legal help.

Homeowners' insurance
(Opstalverzekering)

If you own a property in the Netherlands, you should take out homeowners' insurance on the building. This will cover damage caused by things like fire, floods and theft. If you have taken out a mortgage to buy your property, then your bank will probably require you to have this insurance as a condition of the loan. Valuable items may need to be covered by a separate policy.

House content insurance
(Inboedelverzekering)

In the Netherlands, it is quite common to insure the content of your house. Certain items such as laptops and mobile phones are not generally covered by such insurance.

Glass insurance
(Glasverzekering)

If you live on the ground floor, you may also want to think of getting glass insurance. This is normally not included as part of standard homeowner's insurance. Smashed windows are a particular hazard during the anarchistic insanity of New Year's Eve (p87).

Vehicle insurance
(autoverzekeringen)

It is a legal requirement for all motorists in the Netherlands to take out, as a minimum, third party auto insurance, which is known as *'wettelijke aansprakelijkheid'*. More comprehensive insurance, which covers damage to your vehicle, is available but not obligatory.

Most insurance policies operate on a 'no claims' basis, meaning that, if you do not make a claim on your insurance policy, your premium will be less in subsequent years.

You must be a resident of the Netherlands in order to take out motor insurance in the country. Foreign cars may be insured with Dutch insurers if they are registered, or are in the process of being registered, in the Netherlands.

In the event of an accident, each person involved should fill in a claim report and send it to their own insurance company. The form is identical for each insurance company and it is advisable to keep it in the vehicle at all times.

Insurance documents must be carried in the car at all times.

Health insurance
(zorgverzekering)

It is now mandatory for all Dutch residents to take out a minimum level of basic healthcare insurance (*basisverzekering*). Residents of the country who do not have health cover could face a hefty fine.

As a foreigner, you have four months from registering with the authorities to sort out health insurance. However, it is important to note that the insurance company will charge you from the moment that you register with the *gemeente* — and not from the moment that you take out the insurance. As a resident of the Netherlands, you must take out Dutch health cover even if another insurance policy from abroad would cover you.

You are free to decide which company you take out insurance with, though. ⌨ www.kiesbeter.nl can help you choose.

The basic health insurance package is fairly similar across all providers, although costs might vary. Insurers that operate exclusively online tend to be far more economical than those that have a fixed office.

Expect to pay around €100 per month for the basic package. In addition to this, you will be asked to pay the first €350 of your medical expenses each year. This amount, known as *eigen risico* ('own risk') will be deducted from your bank account without prior notification within eight months of the end of the insurance year in which you sought medical treatment. The *eigen risico* amount increases each year.

No insurance company can refuse to insure you for basic health cover, regardless of your age, lifestyle or medical condition.

If your income is under a certain minimum level, you can apply for an allowance from the tax authorities to help you with healthcare insurance (*zorgtoeslag*). More details of this are available at 🖳 www.toeslagen.nl.

Basic insurance covers visits to your general practitioner (*huisart*), hospital stays and prescription medicine. Dental care is included for children up to the age of 18, but you must take out additional insurance if you want adult dental cover.

If you opt for this, make sure you check exactly what it covers, since policies often have limits on what you can claim for. Most insurers will require you to have a dental check-up before you take out the insurance policy.

If you want to take out more comprehensive health cover, you should shop around as the benefits and costs of different packages can vary quite significantly.

Some insurance companies will allow you to choose where to be treated and others will have a list of the establishments where you can go.

Once you are insured, you should register with a family clinic. If you want to see a specialist, you must have a referral from your family doctor, otherwise your insurance company will not pay for it. Specialists can be extremely costly in the Netherlands, so it is wise to know in advance how much you will have to pay before you go — and to make sure that your insurance will cover the cost.

If you have Dutch health insurance, the medical provider will invoice your insurer directly and you will not have to pay anything.

APPOINTMENTS

If you are more than 10 minutes late, the hospital or health clinic has the right to cancel your appointment and you may still be charged for this.

If you visit the doctor and exceed the time allocated, there is a good chance that you will either be asked to leave or to pay an additional fee.

Doctors have an unfortunate reputation for under-estimating the severity of medical conditions. In fact, there is an a saying about the Dutch health system that, no matter what ails you, a paracetamol is certain to set you right.

If you are employed, you may be entitled to enrol in a collective health insurance scheme, which could give you a discount.

You are only allowed to change your health insurance company in November.

If you need emergency treatment, you will be asked to show proof of Dutch insurance. If you cannot show this, then you will have to pay up-front and seek reimbursement from your home country afterwards, if you are entitled to do this.

If you don't have health insurance, medical treatment in the Netherlands can be extremely expensive. Even in an emergency, you may be forced to pay up-front registration costs, which could be as high as €200, before you are even seen by a medical professional. Even if you have travel insurance or a European medical health card that entitles you to reimbursement from your home country, the Dutch are meticulous in making sure you pay before you are seen.

Living & Working

The Stichting Mobiele Artsen Service Haaglanden (☎ 070 346 9669; 🖳 www.smashaaglanden.nl) offers medical support in The Hague and surrounding areas when general surgeries are closed (typically during weekends and weekdays after 5pm). Your health insurance will cover the costs of this service. If you don't have any insurance, the consultation fee is around €40. You will also have to pay any additional treatment costs, but registration is free.

COMMUNICATION

Internet at home

Internet in the Netherlands is generally fast and inexpensive. The Organisation for Economic Co-operation and Development (OECD), a group of countries committed to the market economy, ranks the Netherlands top of its members in terms of per-capita broadband usage.

Getting connected to the Internet is relatively painless. Your biggest challenge will be deciding which provider to go for, since there are a growing number in the country, each offering different deals and price structures.

Whilst dial-up providers still exist, the most popular ways of connecting to the Internet are via ADSL or Cable. Cable providers typically offer deals whereby you can get a television subscription and home phone number alongside your Internet connection.

Getting connected to the Internet can be done online (although the websites are usually only in Dutch), via telephone or in person at the relevant shop.

When subscribing to the Internet, check whether there is a limit to the data (*datalimiet*) you can download

INTERNET PROVIDERS

ADSL

- 🖳 www.sitebytes.nl
- 🖳 www.bbned.nl
- 🖳 www.canaldigitaal.nl
- 🖳 www.dataweb.nl
- 🖳 www.freeler.nl
- 🖳 www.hccnet.nl
- 🖳 www.is.nl
- 🖳 www.mxstream.nl
- 🖳 www.scarlet.nl
- 🖳 www.t-mobile.nl
- 🖳 www.tele2.nl
- 🖳 www.telfort.nl
- 🖳 www.vodafone.nl
- 🖳 www.xs4all.nl

Cable

- 🖳 www.t-mobile.nl
- 🖳 www.upc.nl
- 🖳 www.zeelandnet.nl
- 🖳 www.ziggo.nl

Fibre-optics

- 🖳 www.vodafone.nl
- 🖳 www.concepts.nl

or whether the amount is unlimited (*geen datalimiet*). Ask around for the best coverage in your area. KPN has a reputation for being the most reliable service provider, although it tends to be slightly more expensive than the others. Ziggo and Tele2 are also popular options.

Internet around town

There are a number of cafés throughout the Netherlands that offer wireless Internet. In The Hague, you could try one of the following:

- Bagels & Beans (🏠 Plaats 21; 🖳 www.bagelsbeans.nl)
- Café Madeleine (🏠 Valkenbosplein 10; 🖳 www. cafemadeleine.fr)

- Catootje (🏠 Reinkenstraat 103)
- Coffee Company (🏠 Korte Poten 21 and Noordeinde 54; 🖥 www. coffeecompany.nl)
- De Freule (🏠 Fahrenheitstraat 558; 🖥 www.defreule.nu)
- Vapiano (🏠 Buitenhof 45)

There are also a number of free wi-fi connections around the town. To find the one nearest to you, visit 🖥 www.wirelessdenhaag.nl.

Most libraries in The Hague also have free wi-fi. For locations, see 🖥 www.bibliotheekdenhaag.nl.

There are a fairly small number of dedicated Internet cafés in The Hague. See, for example:

- Central Library (🏠 Spui 68)
- Yildiz (🏠 Zusterstraat 26)
- Connexion (🏠 Stationsplein 1)

Television

There are 12 television stations that you can watch without a subscription — three public channels (Nederland 1, 2 and 3) and nine commercial stations. The government switched off analogue TV broadcasting in 2006.

More channels are available with a subscription. Popular foreign channels include the BBC, Rai Uno, CNN, the Discovery Channel, National Geographic, TVE and TV5.

For a wider selection you will need to purchase a satellite dish (*schotelantenne*).

Video-on-demand (VOD) is becoming increasingly popular in the Netherlands. To use this service, you need to purchase a compatible digital box — Samsung Smart TV is one of the most popular — and to be connected to the Internet. You will also need to open an account with a VOD provider. You will typically charge your account with a certain amount of money, and

the fee for watching a film will be deducted from this amount. Once you have opted to watch a film, it is usually available for the following 24 hours.

The French cinema chain Pathé is one of the largest VOD providers in the Netherlands.

For €15 a month, you can subscribe to Film 1 (🖥 www.film1.nl), which gives you access to a number of movies a month. You can cancel at any time, by giving one month's notice.

Landline

Getting a land connection shouldn't be a problem, though you will need to provide a valid ID and residence permit or employment contract. You may also need to pay a deposit, particularly if you are not an EU citizen.

The phone system is still owned by KPN, the previously state-run company. However, since privatisation, a number of other companies have also been given the right to operate telephone services over the KPN infrastructure.

The largest providers are KPN (🖥 www.kpn.nl), Ziggo (🖥 www. ziggo.nl), UPC (🖥 www.upc.nl), Tele2 (🖥 www.tele2.nl), Primus and Budget Phone (🖥 www. budgetphone.nl).

These companies offer very competitive rates, and sometimes include package deals that combine Internet and television with a telephone connection.

Mobile phones

There is a wide range of mobile phone operators available, each offering slightly different options: KPN (🖥 www.kpn.nl), Vodafone (🖥 www.vodafone.nl), Telfort (🖥 www.telfort.nl), T-Mobile (🖥 www.t-mobile.nl), Lebara

(💻 www.lebara-mobile.nl), Lyca-Mobile (💻 www.lycamobile.nl) and Simpel (💻 www.simpel.nl), Symio (💻 www.simyo.nl), and Holland-snieuwe (💻 www.hollandsnieuwe.nl).

Both subscription and pay-as-you-go services are available.

A subscription will offer you cheaper calls, but obviously you are then committed to paying a set fee every month.

In order to take out a mobile phone subscription, you must be legally registered in the country (p24). You will be asked to provide your BSN and IND numbers.

Lebara and LycaMobile only offer pay-as-you-go packages, but are particularly convenient for calling abroad. LycaMobile offers a 30-day Internet package at convenient rates, but note that after this 30-day period you will be automatically charged a set fee for each megabyte downloaded unless you renew your subscription.

Symio offers cheap rates within the Netherlands, even if you only take out a subscription on a monthly basis.

Only three mobile phone providers have designated shops in the Netherlands: Vodafone, Telfort and T-mobile. The rest are Internet-based, with facilities to subscribe and order SIM cards online.

For LycaMobile and Lebara, you can also buy SIM cards in many small independent stores — just look for their logos in the window.

SIM cards generally cost between €7.50 and €10, and tend to come with some credit. Additional credit is often awarded for registering the SIM card online.

Top-up cards can be bought in a wide variety of independent shops, the main supermarkets and pet-rol stations. Some companies also allow top-ups to be made online.

Postal and delivery services

The Dutch postal service is operated by TNT Post and is generally fast and efficient. Post offices (💻 www.postkantoor.nl) are typically open between 8.30am and 5pm, Monday to Friday. Some larger branches may also be open on Saturday mornings.

Post boxes are everywhere in the country. They are usually orange, although you may find some of the older-style red post boxes in rural areas. There are normally two slots into which you can put your mail — one for postcodes in the immediate locality, and the other for all other mail.

If you are not at home to receive a package, it will usually be delivered to your neighbour instead. A written message will be left to advise you of this.

If your neighbours are not available to take the package, another delivery attempt will be made on a subsequent day. Again, a message will indicate this. You can change the day of delivery by going online.

The postal service will attempt to deliver your package up to a maximum of three times. After the third unsuccessful attempt, the package will be sent to the nearest post office and you will have two weeks in which to collect it.

Sending mail or packages to addresses outside of the Netherlands is surprisingly expensive. To check the latest prices, go to 💻 www.postnl.nl.

Stamps for letters and small packages (which fit through a standard letter box) can also be bought online, although obviously you must be able to print them!

If you try to buy stamps at your local post office, you may find that they are only sold in books of six or 10. A few small post offices still sell single stamps, but they care a dying breed.

For urgent deliveries, you might like to consider using one of the main shipping companies that operate in the country: DHL (☎ 0800 0552; 🖥 www.dhl.com), TNT (☎ 0800 1234; 🖥 www.tnt.com) or UPS (☎ 0800 099 1300; 🖥 www.ups.com).

BUSINESS AND CULTURE ETIQUETTE

The Dutch are known for their **punctuality**. Try to be on time for business and personal meetings — missing appointments or failing to turn up when you say you will can ruin business relationships. At the very least, if you know you are going to be late and cannot avoid this, make sure that you call ahead and let people know.

The Dutch prize efficiency in all things. They tend to get down to business immediately and keep small talk to a minimum. People from other cultures might perceive this as impolite or unfriendly, but it is just the way they like to do things. It is not their intention to offend.

Similarly, the Dutch are often forthright in their dealings with others, saying what they mean rather than trying to sugar-coat things. Again, you should not take offence at this abruptness.

There is no fixed rule for when to give business cards. They can be presented at the beginning of the meeting as part of your introduction, or at the end as you are saying your goodbyes.

In many companies the **decision-making process** is slow and ponderous, involving wide consultation. Consensus is vital. The Dutch will keep talking until all parties agree.

However, once decisions are made, implementation is fast and efficient.

In the Netherlands, **commitments** are taken seriously and are honoured. Do not promise anything or offer something that you are not planning to deliver. A spoken agreement with others present has the same value as a signed contract.

If the Dutch express uncertainty about their ability to deliver something, this is usually not a negotiation trick or a polite attempt at refusal, but a honest warning. In fact, it may be a good indication that the other party will try to deliver, but may face some problems or delays. The Dutch usually err on the side of caution in such matters, to avoid making promises they cannot keep.

The Dutch find any form of ostentation embarrassing. A grand gesture of generosity will make them uncomfortable.

At business meetings, it is best to dress formally, unless you know you can get away with more casual attire.

Above all, remember that the Dutch, who historically have always been a trading people, are hard negotiators. State what you expect and be clear about what you want and need.

For more tips on cultural etiquette, see p74.

SCHOOLS AND EDUCATION

Education in the Netherlands is compulsory between the ages of four or five and approximately 16 (depending on the type of school attended).

Primary school (*basisschool*) lasts for eight years (from four until 12). At the end of school, pupils are required to sit a test that will tell them which type of **secondary education** (*voortgezet onderwijs*) they must attend.

There are three streams in all (see diagram). The VMBO/MBO stream offers vocational training. The HAVO/HBO stream offers pupils a diploma, without the need to go to university. The VWO/WO stream is more academic and the expectation is that those pupils who undertake these qualifications will go on to university.

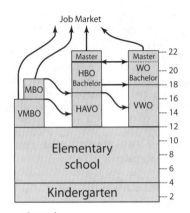

In this way, the Dutch education system appears to be mapping out the future of children from a very early age. However, there is the option to change streams. Students who can show they are capable enough can move to a more academic stream (although they may need to spend an extra year studying). Similarly, students who can't cope with the more academic stream in which they find themselves can ask to move to the more vocational stream.

Both private and state schooling exist in the Netherlands.

In the private sector most schools are Roman Catholic or Protestant but other denominations are also catered for. There are many non-denominational schools, too.

There is a strong emphasis on language-learning (mainly English) throughout all levels.

There are numerous international publicly-funded fee-paying schools at both primary and secondary levels. There are strict rules on who can attend international schools:

- Members of a non-Dutch family who are staying in the Netherlands for a limited period of time.

- Members of a Dutch family who have mostly been educated abroad.

- Members of a Dutch family who will be moving abroad (they can only enrol for one transitory year).

Below are details of the international schools in The Hague.

Lighthouse Special Education (🏠 Amalia van Solmsstraat 155; ☎ 070 335 5698; 🖥 www.lighthousese.nl) was established in 1998 as a primary school for children with special needs. It is open to children between the ages of five and 13. The school also runs an international pre-school group called 'Three Little Ships'. The school uses a special education programme conducted in English. The school is financed by a combination of government subsidies and parental contributions. As part of the admissions process, an assessment has to be carried out, which usually costs around €1,200. Once a child is enrolled, the parents are asked to sign an agreement regarding the amount of money they will contribute towards school fees. In principle, this contribution is voluntary but the expectation is that parents will pay €18,800 per year for pre-school education and €24,200 per year for primary school education.

The American School (🏠 Rijksstraatweg 200; ☎ 070 512 1060; 🖥 www.ash.nl) is located in Wassenaar, on the northern outskirts of The Hague. The school takes pupils from the age of three (pre-school) through to the age of 18 (high school). Just under a third of its 1,100 students are American, 10% are Dutch and the rest come from a wide range of other countries all over the world. The school follows an International Baccalaureate curriculum. Fees for the school are €11,275 for pre-school, €14,745 for elementary school, €16,755 for middle school and €17,985 for high school. In addition, there is a one-time enrolment fee of €3,900 and an annual capital levy fee of €2,725 per year.

The British School (🏠 Vrouw Avenweg 640; ☎ 070 315 4077; 🖥 www.britishschool.nl) follows the British curricula, and offers GCSE, A-level and International Baccalaureate qualifications. School fees are between €12,510 and €17,430 per year, depending on the age of the pupil. In addition, there is a one-time enrolment fee of €2,000, plus an annual capital fee of 7% of the tuition fees. Pupils at the school are aged from three to 18.

Haagsche Schoolvereniging (🏠 Nassaulaan 26; ☎ 070 318 49 50; 🖥 www.hsvdenhaag.nl) is a Dutch international primary school. The school has two other locations: at Koningin Sophiestraat 24A and Van Nijenrodestraat 16. School fees are €4,000 per year. The school has 360 pupils all in all, spread across the three locations. Teaching is in English.

Deutsche Schule (🏠 Van Bleiswijkstraat 125; ☎ 070 354 9454; 🖥 www.disdh.nl) is a German international school in The Hague, with all teaching done in German. The school follows the standard German curriculum. Fees are €7,000 to €10,500 per year, depending on age.

European School (🖥 www.europeanschoolthehague.nl) is a brand-new school in The Hague, catering for children from nursery-level up to the end of secondary school. However, the first secondary school classes will not start until August 2014. School fees are €6,500 per year.

Lycée Français Vincent van Gogh (🏠 Scheveningseweg 237; 070 306 6920; 🖥 www.lyceevangogh.nl) is a French school. Classes are taught in French and the curriculum followed is the standard French one. The school offers *primaire*, *collège* and *lycée* education. Fees are set at between €6,060 and €8,718, depending on the age of the student, plus a one-off registration fee of €200. There is also a branch of the school in Amsterdam.

The Windmill (🏠 Elzendreef 6-8; 🖥 070 327 2088; 🖥 www.thewindmill.nl) is an English-speaking pre-school for children aged between two and five. Fees are payable per term and calculated according to the amount of time that the child spends at the playschool. If he or she is enrols for five full days a week, then the fees are set at €4,250 per term. A one-off registration fee of €100 per child is applicable.

COURSES

There are a great many opportunities for taking courses in the Netherlands. This section lists some of the more popular places to study.

Volksuniversiteit (🖥 www.volksuniversiteit.nl) is a reliable school that offers a range of courses, including extensive language courses. The school has branches all over the country, and offers courses for 30 languages, including Dutch. Fees are reasonable. A 42-hour beginner's course in Dutch, for example, costs €298. Other courses that are taught include photography, food and drink, computing, and aromatherapy. A discount is available with a regional pass (p48).

Roc Mondriaan (🏠 Zuidlarenstraat 10; 📞 088 666 3795; 🖥 www.rocmondriaan.nl) has its headquarters in The Hague, with branches in Leiden, Delft, Rijswijk and Voorburg. The school is well known for its vocational catering courses, but it also offers classes in Dutch (up to intermediary B2 level). See box on p46 for more details.

Koorenhuis (🏠 Prinsegracht 27; 📞 070 707 1722; 🖥 www.koorenhuis.nl) is a school for the performing arts, based in The Hague, which specialises in music and dance. A discount is available for holders of the *ooievaarspas* (p48).

Taal in de Buurt is intended to help people in their neighbourhood learn Dutch. The lessons are held twice a week for at least 24 weeks, and are intended for everyone over the age of 18. For more details about these courses, including where they take place, see 🖥 www.denhaag.nl/en/residents/to/Taal-in-de-Buurt-Dutch-course.htm

If you want to find an **online language course**, a couple of good websites to check are 🖥 www.italki.com and 🖥 www.verbalplanet.com. You can check credentials and reviews of the teachers.

If you want to learn Dutch on your own, we recommend the language section of this book (p272),

COMPULSORY DUTCH EXAM

Most non-EU citizens wanting to take up residency in the country must pass a Dutch language exam (with some exceptions, such as people who are skilled immigrants — check 🖥 www.ind.nl to see if you have to pass the exam). For EU citizens, studying Dutch is option.

Up until the end of 2012, the Dutch government subsidised language courses in order to promote better integration of foreign nationals. However, cutbacks have changed this.

Non-EU citizens still need to learn Dutch and pass the exam, but courses are no longer free.

People can decide to study on their own and register for the exam at 🖥 www.duo.nl.

Alternatively, some of the schools that used to provide subsidised Dutch courses will continue to offer classes, but students will now have to pay for these. The whole process is still uncertain. For more information contact one of the schools: Capabel Taal (🖥 www.capabeltaal.nl), ROC Mondriaan (🖥 www.rocmondriaan.nl) or Sagenn (🖥 www.sagenn.nl).

complete with freely-downloadable audio files. You can also find self-study books at most libraries in the Netherlands. Recommended self-study books are: Teach Yourself Dutch (🖥 www.teachyourself.com) and Routledge Intensive Dutch Course (🖥 www.routledge.com).

There is also Assimil (🖥 www.assimil.com), a dialogue-based method with audio CDs. Rosetta Stone (🖥 www.rosettastone.co.uk) is an interactive picture-based method for the computer. For on-line self-study resources, check out:

- 💻 oefenen.nl (free)
- 💻 www.2bdutch.nl
- 💻 www.utwente.nl/tcp/selfstudy/ selfstudydutch.doc

OPENING A BANK ACCOUNT

To open a bank account, you will need to produce a valid ID, proof of residence and your BSN (p24). A current account (*lopende rekening*) allows you to withdraw and deposit money when you want. A savings account (*spaarrekening*) usually offers a better rate of interest, but you will be more restricted in terms of when you can take money out.

A bank account costs between €3 and €18 per quarter, depending on the type of package and the bank that you opt for.

The main banks are:

- **Abn Amro**: 💻 www.abnamro. nl; ☎ 0900 0024 (€0.10 per minute)

- **ING**: 💻 www.ing.com; ☎ 020 541 5411

- **Rabobank**: 💻 www.rabobank. nl; ☎ 0900 9890 (€0.10 per minute)

LIBRARIES

Public libraries are free to use for reference purposes. However, if you want to be able to take books home then you must subscribe. This is free for those under a certain age — typically 18, although this varies from region to region — and regional discount cards (p48). For those who are not eligible for free membership, costs vary from between €18 and €30, depending on location and age.

LOST CARDS

If you lose your bank card or have it stolen, you should call ☎ 0800 0313 (free of charge if you are calling from within the Netherlands) or ☎ 0031 30 283 5372 (if you are calling from abroad). This number works for whatever bank you have your account with, You are given a choice:

- Press one for ING
- Press two for Rabobank
- Press three for ABN Amro
- Press four for all other banks

Many of the larger libraries have books in languages other than Dutch, although this typically depends on the ethnicity of the neighbourhood in which they are located. English books and magazines are widely available in libraries. You can also find self-study coursebooks for Dutch and other European languages.

Libraries are good places to try if you are looking for Internet access. Many provide wireless connections, and some have computers that can be used on a pay-as-you-go basis.

Here are details of central libraries in some of the main cities:

- **Den Haag**: 🏠 Spui 68; ☎ 070 353 4455; 💻 www. bibliotheekdenhaag.nl; ☾ Mon: 12noon to 8pm, Tue-Fri: 10am to 8pm, Sat: 10am to 5pm, Sun: 12 to 5pm

- **Rotterdam**: 🏠 Hoogstraat 110; ☎ 010 281 6100; 💻 www. bibliotheek.rotterdam.nl; ☾ Mon 1 to 8pm, Tue-Sat: 10am to 8pm, Sun: closed

- **Delft**: 🏠 Vesteplein 100; ☎ 015 212 3450; 💻 www.

dok.info; ☎ Mon & Thu & Fri: 12.30pm to 6pm; Wed: 10am to 6pm; Sat: 10am to 5pm; Sun: closed

- **Amsterdam**: 🏠 Oosterdok-skade 143; ☎ 020 523 0900; ☎ Mon-Sun: 10am to 10pm; 🖥 www.oba.nl

The Royal National Library is found in The Hague at 🏠 Prins Willem-Alexanderhof 5 (🖥 www.kb.nl). Consultation is free. You can also get a year's pass for €15, which allows you to take out books and rent DVDs.

WASTE

General waste is put out for collection once a week in The Hague and twice a week in Amsterdam. Paper and cardboard items are collected once every four weeks.

Waste can only be put out on the street after 10pm on the evening before the day of collection.

To find out the days of collection in your particular area, see 🖥 huisvuilkalender.denhaag.nl.

Waste is not collected on public holidays. Putting rubbish outside on the wrong day can result in a fine — the authorities can be quite assiduous in working out to whom a particular bag of rubbish belongs.

If you go on holiday, and therefore cannot put your rubbish out on the designated day, you can either take it to another area or ask a friend to put it out for you.

Garden waste and very large items (*grofvuil*) cannot be put out on the street. Instead, you must call the *gemeente* on ☎ 070 366 0808 to arrange for collection. For garden waste, you will be provided with a special container. This container can be put out on certain days of the month, depending on your area, or you can arrange for collection on a particular day.

You can also take large items to one of the main waste and recycling stations around the city:

- Scheveningen: 🏠 Vissershaven-straat 2
- Zichtenburg: 🏠 De Werf 13
- Binckhorst: 🏠 Plutostraat 1

The opening times are Monday to Saturday 8.30am to 5pm

You must have an *afvalpas* in order to make use of these stations. If such a pass isn't sent to you automatically, then you can also request one online: 🖥 www.denhaag.nl.

Since 2012, the local authorities have been trying to improve the current waste collection system in The Hague by installing giant rubbish bins in the main areas of the city, where you can dispose of waste any day of the week. Although some progress has been made, most areas of The Hague do not yet have such bins. The waste-disposal improvement programme should be completed by 2014.

DISCOUNTS

Discount cards are a popular way of saving money in the Netherlands. Here are a few of the more common ones:

The Guest Card (🖥 www.thehaguestcard.nl) is a card aimed at expats. It costs €12 per year and entitles you to discounts on health insurance, wine shops, tickets to English theatre shows, among other things.

Ooievaarspas (🖥 www.ooievaarspas.nl) is available to residents of The Hague who are on a low income. The card, which costs €12.50 per year, entitles you to a free subscription to the library, half-price on cinema tickets at the Filmhuis (🖵 www.filmhuisdenhaag.nl) and discounts on a number of educational courses around the city. You can request the card online or by visiting the *gemeente* and filling in a form. The card lasts from January to January, and there is no reduction if you get it part-way through the year.

Voorwaarden Pathé Filmvoordeelpas (🖵 www.pathe.nl) gives you a 30% discount on the price of a cinema ticket at Pathé cinema — which, given the high price of movie tickets in the Netherlands, can represent a significant saving. The card costs €42 and contains six tickets. It is valid for one year. You can use it for a maximum of three people at one time. The card is regional, and can be used in any Pathé cinema within the region where you purchased it. Region One consists of Groningen, Eindhoven, Helmond, Tilburg, Breda, Arnhem, Zwolle, Alkmaar and Maastricht. Region Two consists of Amsterdam, Haarlem, Den Haag, Delft, Rotterdam and Zaandam.

Museumkaart (🖵 www.museumkaart.nl) gives you unlimited access for a year to more than 400 museums all around the country. The card costs €44.95 for adults and €22.50 for those younger than 18. You will also have to pay a one-off administration fee of €4.95 for the first year.

CJP Pas (🖵 www.cjp.nl) is available for people under the age of 30 and gives discounts for the cinema, festivals, concerts, travel and exhibitions. It costs €15 for a year.

Delftpas (🖵 www.delft.nl/delftpas) offers discounts on sporting and cultural activities, and provides free access to the library. The standard cost of the card is €60, although those on low income can get it for €5. The card can only be purchased in January or February and is valid for an entire year. It is available for residents of Delft and those who live nearby. People holding a Rotterdampas can also benefit from the Delftpas offers.

Rotterdampas (🖵 www.rotterdampas.nl) for Rotterdam offers the same benefits as the Delftpas, mentioned above. The pass costs €60 for adults, €12.50 for students and €5 for those on a low income.

Stadspas (🖵 www.stadspas.nl) is available free of charge for those living in Amsterdam. It gives you eleven coupons for use at more than 300 locations. The pass also gives discounts for the theatre, cinema, museum, circus, restaurants and sauna.

Significant discounts are available if you shop at the supermarket chain Albert Heijn by obtaining a **bonuskaart** (🖵 www.ah.nl/bonuskaart) Without this card, you will not be able to benefit from any discounts that are advertised in the stores. To make use of the card, simply hand it to the cashier to swipe and discounts will be applied immediately. Product discounts are typically between 10% and 50%. The card is free and you can ask for it at the customer service desk.

Air miles (🖵 www.airmiles.nl) is a popular Dutch system that awards you discount points when you shop at certain chains. These points can be used to get discounts on some products, some theme parks and flights with Transavia. The card costs €12.50. It can be bought online or at selected shops.

MOVING TO THE NETHERLANDS

The **Hague International Centre** (🖵 Spui 70; ☎ 070 353 5043; 🕓 Mon-Fri: 9am to 5pm) can provide a limited amount of

Living & Working

information for visitors to The Hague. The centre also provides a welcome pack for visitors, containing useful information about the city and a range of discount vouchers. However, cut-backs mean that this will be discontinued from the start of 2014.

Six times a year, the centre organises a day on which you can find out more about The Hague and meet other members of the international community.

The best part of this 'Welcome to The Hague' programme is a guided tour through the city's historic centre. Attendance is free and details of forthcoming tours are posted on the centre's website.

The centre can provide a range of information about services that are offered by the various municipal departments, such as issuing parking permits, marriages, registration of birth, converting driving licences, collecting rubbish and so forth. The centre also supplies basic information on areas, including topics such as health care and education.

The Hague International Centre is a joint initiative between the Municipality of The Hague, the Immigration and Naturalisation Service (IND) and ACCESS, a non-profit organisation that supports the international community in the Netherlands (⌨ www.access-nl.org).

There are a few websites that offer information about the Netherlands, including classified advertisements and the opportunity to meet fellow expats: **Expatica** (⌨ www.expatica.com) and **Just Landed** (⌨ www.justlanded.com). One of the most interesting aspects of the Expatica website is question-and-answer page, where experts reply to users questions on different topics — simply click on 'Ask The Expert'.

PAYING FOR THINGS

PIN is the preferred method of payment in the Netherlands, for everything from groceries to larger purchases. Most shops and ATM machines will also accept major foreign bank cards.

Chipknip   (⌨ www.chipknip.nl) is an alternative to the PIN system. To use this system, you must first preload your card with an amount of money, which is then debited every time you use it. The system is particularly useful for smaller payments in car parks, telephone boxes and any shop that display the *chipknip* sign. The downside to the system is that, if you lose your card, then all the money that you have preloaded on to it will also be lost. You can recharge your *chipknip* card at various recharge stations around the town, often found at train stations, large supermarkets and university campuses.

iDEAL (⌨ www.ideal.nl) allows customers to securely pay for things over the Internet by directly connecting with their online bank account. The system is only available on Dutch websites and you must have a Dutch bank account in order to be able to use it. You will need your bank debit card and a card reader, or internet banking access code.

There are a very few shops in the Netherlands that do not accept **cash**, insisting that you have to pay with a card instead (such as the supermarket Marqt). Many vending machines — such as the ones used at train stations to buy tickets, or to recharge your tram card — only accept cards. If you want to pay with cash, you have to queue at the counter and endure a surcharge. You should also note that, since shops do not accept one-or-two-cent coins in the Netherlands, the amount that you pay will often be rounded up or down to the nearest five cents.

Credit cards are not as widely accepted in shops as might be the case in other countries.

PayPal (⌨ www.paypal.com) is an increasingly popular way of paying for things online.

TAX, TAX RELIEF AND BENEFITS

DigID (⌨ www.digid.nl) is a digital signature that allows you to access many online services offered by the *gemeente*, including paying tax online. It is free to apply for this number. You will receive it in the post after a couple of days, along with your activation code. You must activate the DigID within 48 hours, otherwise it becomes invalid and you will need to go through the process all over again.

Financial support is available for those on a low income (*toeslagen*). You must be registered with your local *gemeente* in order to receive these benefits. Some politicians are trying to push through a law that would make it possible only for Dutch speakers to receive benefits. Although this is against the EU's freedom of movement legislation, it could still be applied for non-EU nationals.

For people who have difficulty paying their rent, the government provides financial assistance called *huurtoeslag*. To be eligible for this, your income should be no higher than €22,000 a year. If you have a partner, then your combined income should be below €30,000. Your rent must also be below a certain amount, typically €650.

You can also get financial support when you lose your job or when you cannot afford to pay in full your health insurance.

To apply for financial assistance, visit ⌨ www.toeslagen.nl.

HAVING A BABY

Pre-natal care

When planning to have a baby in the Netherlands, you may want to think about taking out more comprehensive health insurance, since many basic packages do not cover the services that you may need during your pregnancy.

Unless there are complications, it will be a midwife, rather than a gynaecologist, that supports you during your pregnancy. You should choose the midwife organisation that bests suits your needs. Some options in The Hague are:

- **LIFE** (🏠 Hobbemaplein 8; ☎ 070 767 0086; ⌨ www.verloskundigepraktijklife.nl)
- **Femme** (🏠 Lijnbaan 32; ☎ 070 427 7666; ⌨ www.femme-verloskundigen.nl)
- **Mundo** (🏠 Houtzagerssingel 65; ☎ 070 346 8288; ⌨ www.mundo-vroedvrouwen.nl)
- **ELLA** (🏠 Kaapstraat 84; ☎ 070 391 2042; ⌨ www.ella-verloskundigen.nl)

For other options, or to search in different areas, visit the national organisation of midwives (⌨ www.knov.nl).

Within each organisation, there are several midwifes. Any one of these midwives may assist you during your pregnancy, depending on who is available. You will be invited to meet all midwives once you register with a particular organisation.

In general, the first pre-natal visit takes place during the third month of pregnancy. Tests and examinations are not routinely performed. Genetic testing is only routinely

Living & Working

advised for women that are older than 35.

There are a number of companies and organisations that arrange pre-natal classes. Some are in English, whilst others are only in Dutch. Costs and lengths vary, but are typically between €180 and €250 for the duration of your pregnancy. The approaches that the classes use vary significantly, so check the one that best fits your needs:

DEN HAAG

- 🖥 www.bumpandbeyond.nl
- 🖥 www.greatexpectations.nl
- 🖥 www.access.nl.org

LEIDEN

- 🖥 www.comfortablebirth.com
- 🖥 www.yoga-nl.nu/zwanger

AMSTERDAM

- 🖥 www.aurora-holistic-center.nl

▶ See p30 for information about maternity leave.

Giving birth

It is very common practice for women in the Netherlands to give birth at home with the help of a midwife (*verloskundige*) rather than in a hospital, although this has started to change in recent years.

Remember that, if you opt for a home birth, midwives are not al-lowed to administer anaesthet-ics or medications that need a prescription.

Even if you give birth in a hospi-tal, it will still be the midwife who helps you. A gynaecologist will only give assistance if your medical condition requires it. Women who choose to give birth at a hospital will usually only be admitted within a day of delivery, unless there are complications.

The Dutch believe in keeping childbirth as natural as possible, so painkillers are not generally given. Pain management during a hos-pital birth may be requested but, because anaesthetists are not usu-ally available after normal business hours, epidurals cannot be guaran-teed. If pain relief is important for you, make sure you discuss this with your midwife or doctor well in advance of the birth so things can be properly planned.

Fathers are allowed to be with the woman during childbirth.

An alternative to a hospital or home birth is to give birth in a *kraamzorghotel*. This allows a wid-er number of options, such as the possibility of giving birth in water. There is no waiting list, but you must book two months in advance. *Kraamzorghotels* are not that com-mon. In South Holland, you can find one in The Hague - Wereld Won-der (🖥 www.wereld-wonder.nl) - and one in Rotterdam (🖥 www. kraamzorgrotterdam.nl). Remem-ber that this is not a hospital, so if there are any complications you may be transferred to one.

Post-natal care

One of the perks of giving birth in the Netherlands is the post-natal care that mothers receive.

A nurse will visit the mother and newly-born child at home immedi-ately after the birth, for a total of 49 spread across one or two weeks. The nurse will also give advice on the care of the newborn, including information about how to breast-feed and how to prepare meals for your baby.

The kind of help you will receive will partially depends on the person that comes to your home. Make sure you specify if you want some-one who speaks English. If you are not satisfied with your nurse, you can ask to change him or her.

This post-natal service can be booked in advance via 🖳 www.kraamzorg.nl. Health insurance will usually cover the cost.

From two weeks after the birth until the child turns four, a regional *consultatiebureau* will provide routine health check-ups and monitor development of the child.

Parents will be provided with a handbook that outlines a baby's first year of development and supplies important phone numbers. The handbook can also be used to record appointments at the clinic, vaccinations, and changes in the child's height and weight. You should always bring this book with you to your appointments.

For the nearest consultatiebureau, visit Mea Vita (🖳 www.meavita.nl; ☎ 070 379 5025) or Jong Florence (🖳 www.jongflorence.nl).

Registering your baby

Within three days of the birth, your baby should be registered with the *gemeente* at the place where he or she was born. This can be done by either parent, or by a third person who has been authorised by the parents to do so.

To register the birth, you will need to bring a proof of identity for both the child's mother and father and the statement the doctor or midwife provided at childbirth. If you are married, you should also bring along your marriage certificate (if the *gemeente* doesn't have it already). If you are not married, the father must legally recognise the baby before the childbirth with a deed of acknowledgement (*akte van erkenning ongeboren kind*). Couples living together can bring their *samen wonen* certificate.

You will then be provided with a Dutch birth certificate for the baby. An international birth certificate can be provided for an additional fee.

You should also register your child with your insurer within four months of the birth, otherwise your child may not be covered under the terms of your insurance.

Parents can decide whether to give their children the father's surname or the mother's.

If you are not married, your baby will only have automatic Dutch nationality if the mother is Dutch. If only the father is Dutch, a special application must be made during pregnancy. If neither parent is Dutch, they must consult their embassy or embassies to establish the nationality of the baby.

They will also have to inform their embassies before the birth.

You can apply for a residence permit for your child within three years of the birth, if the child already has a passport, and after three years if the child doesn't.

TRAVELLING ABROAD AND VACCINATIONS

The official website for compulsory and recommended vaccinations is 🖳 www.lcr.nl (Dutch only).

Most Dutch insurance policies will cover travel vaccinations up to a certain amount per year. You will have to pay first and then seek reimbursement (ask your insurance company for a form).

There are a number of places where you can get vaccinations in The Hague.

The municipal health service **GGD** (🏠 Westeinde 128) is located just behind the Westeinde Hospital. It offers consultation and vaccinations for both residents and non-residents. You can make an appointment online: 🖳 www.

wkmreizigerszorg.nl/ggddenhaag or by calling ☎ 070 353 7240. Appointments can be scheduled with short notice if there is availability. Appointments are only possible during weekdays from 8am to 5pm. Payment is only possible with debit card. Prices are lower than in private clinics.

At the **KLM Travel Clinic** (🏠 Hofweg 9; 🖥 www.klmtravel-clinic.nl), you can just turn up without prior reservation. If you want to make an appointment, you should call ☎ 0900 109 1096 (10 cents per minute). The clinic is open from Monday to Saturday, 8.30am until 4.30pm (until 8.30pm on Wednesday and Thursday). You can also make an appointment online, but only on the Dutch version of the website. There is also a branch of the clinic in Schiphol airport (open daily, 8.30am to 4.30pm).

Both places have a vaccination price list available on their websites.

LEAVING THE NETHERLANDS

If you are planning to leave the Netherlands, you should start the deregistration process at least a month before your departure date. Once you have deregistered with the gemeente, you are required to leave the country within 28 days.

When you deregister, you will be asked to provide contact details about where you can be reached.

In order to cancel any utility bills or other subscriptions that are under your name, you should obtain a uittreksel 60 paper from the gemeente that proves you are leaving. Bills for any outstanding charges

will be sent to the address that you have provided the gemeente with.

You will also have to notify your insurer and contact the tax authorities (🖥 www.belastingdienst.nl) to check that everything has been paid and to check your future situation if you own a house in the Netherlands.

If you own a car and want to take it with you, you should de-register your vehicle with the RDW (🖥 www.rdw.nl).

When moving, you should bear in mind that it is not easy to find cardboard boxes for free. Dutch people usually buy them at shops like Gamma, Karwei and Praxis.

FURTHER INFORMATION

If you have any specific questions about the Netherlands, then a good **multilingual forum** where to post them is 🖥 www.leforum.nl. People post in English, Italian, Spanish and French, although the French users are most active.

Blue Umbrella is a private organisation authorised by the Dutch Tax Authority, which helps expats with making requests for benefits and understanding paperwork that is written in Dutch. It can provide advice on a variety of different matters. It isn't free, but it can be useful in negotiating the often confusing plethora of information that permeates Dutch officialdom. For more information, consult their website 🖥 www.blueumbrella.nl.

Educaide (🖥 www.educaide.nl) is an organisation based in The Hague that offers advice for parents and companies about education in the Netherlands.

About The Netherlands

The Netherlands has something of a reputation for being a neat and orderly place.

After spending only a few days in the country, it is not difficult to see why: the streets are clean, everything works (most of the time) and it is easy to travel around.

The Dutch are also known for their tolerance. Walk through the red light district of Amsterdam or venture into the cloying air of one of the country's many coffee shops and you'll soon start to notice this.

However, you should remember that such apparent tolerance is tempered with a deeper sense of pragmatism.

Many Dutch are acutely embarrassed about the reputation they have as a sexually-liberal drug-using nation. Most of the people that you see paying for sex or taking drugs will, in actual fact, be foreigners.

When people refer to the Netherlands' penchant for liberalism, the Dutch simply grin and bear it, because they know that it's better to have things out in the open, where they can have full control, rather than sweeping everything under the carpet. As you will quickly find once you step into this country, there is a great deal more to be found than sex and drugs.

The Dutch are famous for their dedication to work and their high-level of productivity. But living in the Netherlands does not have to mean a stressful life. Its dreamy canals, bike-clogged streets and fairy-tale villages take one away from all the hustle-and-bustle of working life.

Because there are few hills, and because of the serenity of the countryside, the Netherlands is ideal cycling country.

Windmills are a prominent feature of the landscape, many of which are now open to the public. Some are still in operation.

The country is also widely associated with tulips, which start to bloom in the Spring and throw the entire country into an orgy of colour.

Clogs, that other internationally-recognised symbol of Dutchness, are also to be found all over the Netherlands — but usually only in tourist shops. They have had their day as footwear of choice, swept away by synthetic alternatives. Still, you may find the occasional farmer in more rural areas availing of them. They have not yet died a complete death.

The Netherlands is also famous for its art and architecture. Most large towns lay claim to at least one world-renowned painter, many of whose works are displayed in the local galleries.

GEOGRAPHY AND CLIMATE

Take a train across the Netherlands, and you will pass miles upon

THE NETHERLANDS AT A GLANCE

(adapted from the Central Intelligence Agency World Fact Book)

Capital:	Amsterdam
Official language:	Dutch (Frisian only in Friesland)
Government:	Constitutional Monarchy
Prime Minister:	Mark Rutte
Deputy Prime Minister:	Lodewijk Asscher
Constitution adopted:	1815; revised 1848 and 1983
Currency:	Euro (€)
GDP:	€580.35 billion (2011 est.)
GDP real growth rate:	1.3% (2011 est.)
GDP per capita:	€34,750 (2011 est.)
Main exports:	Machinery and equipment, chemicals, fuels, foodstuffs
Time zone:	GMT+1, Daylight Saving Time
Internet domain suffix:	.nl
Country dialling code:	+31
Land area:	41,543 km^2
Land boundaries:	1,027 km
Coastline:	451 km
Population:	16,730,632 (July 2012 est.)
Population growth rate:	0.452% (2012 est.)
Birth rate:	10.89 per 1,000 population (2012 est.)
Death rate:	8.39 per 1,000 population (2012 est.)
Total fertility rate:	1.78 per woman (2012 est.)
Life expectancy at birth:	80.91 years (2012 est.)
HIV/AIDS adult prevalence rate:	0.2% (2009 est.)
Ethnic groups:	Dutch 80.7%, EU 5%, Indonesian 2.4%, Turkish 2.2%, Surinamese 2%, Moroccan 2%, Caribbean 0.8%, other 4.8% (2008 est.)
Religions:	Roman Catholic 30%, Dutch Reformed 11%, Calvinist 6%, other Protestant 3%, Muslim 5.8%, other 2.2%, none 42% (2006 est.)

About The Netherlands

miles of utterly applanate fields. There is not even the attempt of an incline towards the horizon.

Things are slightly different in the south and east of the country. In the east, the gently rolling lowlands start to rise to meet the low hills of Germany. In the south-east quarter of the country, near Maastricht, you will find the beginnings of The Ardennes, a range of hills that sweep into Belgium.

It is here that you will find the Netherlands' highest peak: Vaalserberg, rising to a rather modest 322.7 metres.

The Netherlands is situated in the north-west of Europe. It shares land borders with Belgium (to the south) and Germany (to the east). It also has access to the North Sea and Wadden Sea.

The Netherlands is often mistakenly referred to as Holland. In reality, North and South Holland are two separate provinces within the country. Whilst many people in these provinces will forgive the odd slippage, if you refer to the country in the wrong way, those that live in the outlying regions — especially Groningen, Friesland and Zeeland — might feel a bit put out that visitors to the country can't get the basic name right. The Netherlands itself consists of 12 provinces.

The topography of the Netherlands is characterised by the country's centuries-long battle against the sea. In fact, about a fifth of the land (nearly 7000 km^2) has been reclaimed from below sea level.

Perhaps the most famous example of this is Flevoland, in the centre of the country. Until 1986, this province didn't exist. It was created when the Zuiderzee, an inland sea, was closed off from the Wadden Sea by the construction of the Afsluitdijk. The Zuiderzee is now called IJsselmeer (lake at the end of the river IJssel).

The composition of the soil is a mixture of clay (in the north) and sand (in the south). Over the centuries, this has made cultivation of the land something of a challenge.

Banks of sand dunes stretch along the coast, varying in width from a few hundred metres up to several kilometres.

The Netherlands has a temperate climate with four distinct seasons. Its weather is influenced by the ocean. Winters are fairly chilly. Summers are warmer, but even then the weather can be unreliable. Rainfall is distributed throughout the year. The wind, particularly in the coastal regions, can make days feel all the colder.

The average temperature throughout the year is 9.6°C. The hottest months are July and August, when the average temperature is around 22°C. The coldest months are January and February, with an average daily temperature of −1°C but it can easily dip to -6°C.

The Netherlands receives an average of 766 mm of rainfall a year. The wettest month is August, which receives an average of 95 mm. The driest months are between February and May, receiving an average of 50 mm rainfall.

Since the Netherlands is a fairly small country, don't expect the climate to vary significantly within its borders — although, in the north, you'll find things to be slightly colder.

THE PEOPLE

Pin-pointing exactly who the Dutch are is not an easy thing to do.

Whilst the stereotypical Nederlander is tall with blond hair and light eyes, it would be wrong to

About The Netherlands

label the entire population as a single homogeneous group.

Over the millennia, different cultures have all left their mark on Dutch ethnicity. Centuries of conquest saw the Romans, Saxons and Franks all vying for control of the region. More recent immigration has been altering the ethnic make-up of the country.

Most of the Dutch derive a large part of their heritage from Germanic tribes, which became heavily involved in the region from the 5th century AD.

Historically, the Dutch in the east were Saxons, whilst those in the west and south were Franks, although internal migration long ago disrupted this neat cut-and-dry picture of the country.

The Frisian people in the north, which have a history of fierce independence and have successfully resisted centuries of foreign domination, are also Germanic, tracing their origin back to the expansion of tribes from the West around 700 BC.

Remnants of another race are to be found in Zeeland, in the south of the country. This small collection of islets, which are now connected by man-made bridges (the so-called Deltaworks — p269), were largely cut off from the rest of the country during the wars between the Romans, Saxons and Franks. They therefore managed to escape the annihilation or assimilation that was the fate of many other tribal communities.

Originally from central and eastern Europe, these people tend to be shorter than the stereotypical Dutch, with darker eyes and darker hair.

There was a particularly large influx of immigrants from Indonesia in the 1940s and 1950s, shortly after the former colony gained its independence (1948). The descendents of these families now make up a significant portion of Dutch ethnicity.

More recently, Dutch immigration has been characterised by asylum-seekers — largely from the Middle East and north Africa — and migrant workers from eastern Europe, who, under EU rules, can now legally seek employment in the country.

For more in-depth information about Dutch culture, see p74.

FLORA AND FAUNA

Centuries of farming and over-cultivation of the land has put huge pressure on the Netherlands' natural ecosystems.

It is only since the early 1980s that the government has started to take concrete steps towards reversing some of the damage that has been caused by humans.

After the authorities drained the Zuiderzee, in order to reclaim what is now known as Flevoland, they discovered the remains of vast numbers of animal species that were no longer to be found in the country: bear, reindeer, wild horse, bison. All animals that had been driven from the Netherlands by the hand of man.

Over the past few decades, the Dutch authorities have been making an effort to reintroduce animals into the wild. Many animals have been imported from eastern Europe where they still roam free — animals like bison, red deer and wild horse. The authorities are thinking of importing elk, too, and there are signs that wolves, which are already in parts of Germany, could return (although farmers are showing strong opposition to this).

There are three main types of ecosystem in the Netherlands.

Sandy soils are found in the west of the country, as well as in parts of Drenthe and other eastern provinces.

In Zeeland, and along the rivers that thread their way through the centre of the country, is to be found clay. There is also clay in the north of the country.

The third distinctive ecological system is that of peat, which was extensively mined in the 17th century and sold as fuel. The largest areas of peat are in North Holland, around Amsterdam, and in the south of the country. The over-mining of peat caused the lowering of land in certain areas, leading to the formation of new lakes and an increased risk of flooding. This is why Schiphol airport is now seven feet below sea level, rather than seven feet above, as would have been the case if the peat hadn't been taken away.

Each of these soil types have contributed to the establishment of different natural habitats, although over the centuries they have been all but destroyed by man. Only now, thanks to conservation efforts, are they starting to reassert themselves.

In the south-west of the country, the delta system of Zeeland remains a bird-lover's paradise, but the natural ecosystem has had to cope with all sorts of man-made ailments. In particular, a series of dams have cut the islands off from the sea, robbing the region of its salinity. Moves are afoot to change this, and to make some of the dykes more permeable, so that salt water can be let into the region. One of the islands in the delta, Tiengemeten, has now been given entirely back to nature.

The sand dunes, which run all the way up the western coast, are well preserved and, unlike in Belgium where urban development has eroded them, provide an important defence against the vagaries of the sea.

Further north lie the Wadden Islands, one of the most rewarding areas for nature-lovers to explore, and an important breeding ground for birds.

In Flevoland, the part of the Netherlands that was recently reclaimed from the sea, a massive conservation campaign has seen the return of a number of species that had previously been driven out of the area. If you visit Oostvaardersplassen nature reserve, you can now see wild horses and cows by the thousands (p262).

In the centre of the country, around Arnhem, there is a large wooded area, containing all manner of interesting animals, including wild boar, fox and badger. This forms De Hoge Veluwe, the largest national park in the Netherlands.

If you want to get a glimpse of what the Netherlands looked like hundreds of years ago, then head up to northern Friesland. Here you will find the landscapes of old that the likes of Filips Koninck and Jacob van Ruisdael became famous for painting.

Great natural beauty is to be found along the banks of the rivers that run through the southern part of the country, between Dordrecht and Nijmegen. Here, attempts to raise the banks of the river, so as to prevent it from flooding, have helped turn agricultural farmland back into nature spots.

The best example of this is around Nijmegen, where a fairly recent conservation project provides the perfect example of how nature can exist so close to a major urban settlement. Thousands of birds flock to the area, and wild cows graze just on the outskirts of the city.

About The Netherlands

There are a few websites that can help you in the pursuit of natural beauty in the Netherlands.

If you want information about the birds that can be seen around the Netherlands, 🖥 www.sovon.nl is a website maintained by a group of volunteers that help create inventories of birds in the country.

The website for the organisation that manages most of the natural reserves in the country, and can therefore provide good information on them, is 🖥 www.natuurmonumenten.nl.

For more information on the various natural reserves, visit 🖥 www.staatsbosbeheer.nl.

THE ECONOMY

According to the International Monetary Fund (IMF), the Netherlands is the 18th-largest economy in the world.

Nearly two-thirds of the economy is based on foreign trade, with the main industrial sectors being food processing, chemicals, petroleum refining and electrical machinery.

Services account for about three-quarters of the national income and are primarily in transportation, distribution, logistics, and financial areas such as banking and insurance.

The Netherlands has some oil reserves in the North Sea, but these are of little consequence and produce no more than 70,000 barrels per day.

Of far more interest are the vast amounts of natural gas that the country produces — 64 billion cubic metres a year, making it the second-largest producer in the EU and seventh largest in the world.

The Netherlands is home to some of the world's largest corporations, including Royal Dutch Shell, Unilever and Heineken.

The Dutch have been among the strongest supporters of the single European currency.

The strength of the Dutch economy means that the country has not suffered some of the adverse conditions that membership of the euro has brought about — in Greece and Ireland, for example.

Nonetheless, some economists argue that the fact that the Dutch cannot independently revalue their currency has harmed competitiveness.

This is one of the reason that large firms have been keen to keep a lid on wage increases, but demands from trade unions and a shortage of labour have made this difficult.

Since the 1980s, the Dutch government has progressively reduced its involved in the management of the economy, shying away from new legislation and leaving the tax system alone.

But the financial crisis that began in the summer of 2008 hit the country hard, and forced the government to reconsider its *laissez-faire* attitude towards the economy.

The government responded to the crisis by launching three economic stimulus packages, worth a total of €12.5 billion. These packages were largely aimed at bolstering the lending and exports sector.

Like countries all over Europe, the Netherlands is weighed down by an unsustainable public deficit — currently 5.7% of GDP (€27 billion).

The country is now looking at ways in which it can cut spending. The target is to reduce the deficit by €18 billion by 2015. Measures will include raising the retirement age (from 65 to 67), reducing military spending, increasing taxes and cutting government programs.

POLITICS

The Netherlands is a constitutional monarchy. The first independent monarch, William I, was installed in the country in 1815, after the expulsion of the French.

As we were going to press, the serving monarch, Queen Beatrix, announced that she would be stepping down on April 30, 2013. Her eldest son, Willem-Alexander, will be inaugurated as king.

These days the role of the monarch is largely ceremonial. His or her principal political involvement is in forming the government, including appointing the prime minister. The choice of the prime minister will usually be the head of the party that wins the most seats during the election. The current prime minister is Mark Rutte from the VVD.

Politics in the Netherlands used to be much more decentralised than it is today. Until 1966, society was divided into four segments known as pillars: Calvinist, Catholic, socialist, and liberal. Each of these pillars had their own organisations, including political parties. It is from these pillars that many of the parties that exist today have emerged.

Political decisions were reached at the top-level by consensus and agreement, known as consociationalism.

These days, the Netherlands has a system of proportional representation, which allows even fairly small parties to have considerable influence in government. This prevents politics being dominated by the two main parties, but has also created some controversy as right-wing fringe parties have gained a foot in the door.

Main parties often have to form coalitions with smaller ones. Geert Wilders, head of the PVV (p62), became particularly important in the 2010 election, as Mark Rutte's government sought to cosy up to him.

Wilders involvement in government became short-lived, though. In April 2012, he withdrew his support from the coalition in protest of austerity measures. In the ensuing national election, held that September, the PVV did far less well than previously, meaning that it was no longer in a position to hold together the government.

Since 1994, the government has largely been governed by some combination of liberal and social-democrat parties, with other parties coming on board whenever their support was needed. This is often referred to as the 'Purple Coalition' because of the colour that results from mixing liberal blue with social democrat red.

HISTORY

The history of the Netherlands is characterised by foreign occupation and invasion. In fact the borders of the area, which was known as the Low Countries and encompassed Belgium and Luxembourg, have been continuously redrawn during the region's tumultuous past.

It was not until 1830 that what is now known as the Netherlands took on its present form, following an uprising by the Belgians in the south. From this area was carved out modern-day Belgium, Luxembourg and the Netherlands — the Benelux countries.

The potted history that follows focuses principally on the events that transpired in the area that now makes up modern-day Netherlands, but inevitably touches on the history of all three Benelux countries.

Early human activity

Early archaeological evidence suggests that there was human

About The Netherlands

MAIN POLITICAL PARTIES

The **People's Party for Freedom and Democracy (VVD)**, a conservative right-wing liberal party, is the senior partner in the current coalition government and its leader, Mark Rutte, is prime minister. The party attaches great importance to individual and economic freedom.

The centre-left **Labour Party (PvdA)** is the second-largest party in the Netherlands and the other half of the current coalition. Historically, it has been committed to developing the country's social welfare system, but more recently it has worked towards combining the welfare state with private enterprise.

Christian Democratic Appeal (CDA), a centre-right Christian Democratic party, was in power until 2010, when the country's involvement in Afghanistan brought down the government and forced fresh elections.

The **Socialist Party (SP)** has its origins in radical communism, but is now a mainstream socialist party, leaning to the left of the PvdA on many issues. Its core preoccupations are social welfare and employment.

The **Party for Freedom (PVV)** was founded by Geert Wilders in 2005 and enjoyed a brief spell in government between 2010 and 2012, as junior partner of the VVD-led coalition. However, its failure to win sufficient votes in the 2012 election means that it is now in opposition. Its stand against immigration, and anti-Islamic rhetoric, has made the party one of the more controversial.

Democrats 66 is generally left-wing, and supports liberal policies on abortion and euthanasia, as well as reform of the welfare state.

The **Green Left** combines environmentalism with left-wing ideals.

The **Christian Union (CU)** is made up largely of orthodox Protestant Christians. The party is often viewed as centre-left, but it has conservative stances on abortion, euthanasia and gay marriage.

The **Party for the Animals** is the smallest political party in government, with just two seats (out of 150) in the House of Representatives. It claims to be a single-issue party, fighting for animal rights.

The **Political Reformed Party (SGP)** is the country's oldest political party. It is a right-wing Christian party and has strongly orthodox views. The party opposes feminism and, until 2006, women were not allowed to be members. The party does not seek to be in government, but instead uses parliament to express its principals. In this sense, it is known as a testimonial party.

activity in the Low Countries at least 200,000 years ago.

The first people almost certainly survived as hunter-gatherers, living in makeshift tents. As the ice receded, and the weather turned warmer, the newcomers to the land found that they needed to travel less in search of food, and ended up settling in the country.

Much as is the case today, the Low Countries of the prehistoric period formed a meeting point between east and west, north and south. This attracted a melting pot of different tribes and cultures, who ended up in the Low Countries on their way to somewhere else.

It is still possible to see some of the remains of these early Dutch dwellers in the northeast of the country, where megalithic stone structures, known as *hunebedden*, lie scattered around the province of Drenthe (p238).

These intriguing structures were built by a particular group of people known as the Funnelbeakers (Dutch: *trechterbekercultuur*), named after the pottery that once fashioned, between roughly 5300 and 2000 BC.

The *hunebedden* are thought to be the remains of burial chambers. Carvings adorn some of the stones, believed to identify the rank and position of those buried in the area.

The Funnelbeakers began to cultivate the land, but only in the south. The inhospitable north did not immediately lend itself to cultivation.

It would take the arrival of the Bellbeaker people, around 2500 BC, before agriculture started to expand and the rearing of livestock became common.

The Bronze Age started around 2000 BC. Intriguingly, bronze is not a metal that is readily found in the Netherlands and so was probably imported.

The discovery of iron, around 700 BC, brought renewed prosperity to the Low Countries. Iron ore was found in the north as well as the centre of the country. Smiths started manufacturing new tools, out of both bronze and iron, which could be used or traded.

In the centuries that followed, an ever-growing number of Germanic tribes moved into the area to settle, such as the Tubanti, the Canninefates, and the Frisians. A few Celtic tribes also established themselves in the country.

The Roman era

Around 58 BC, Roman forces, under the command of Julius Caesar, conquered the southern part of the Low Countries.

The Romans initially settled south of the Rhine, which became the northern limit of the Roman Empire.

Caesar did not press on further north, to where the Frisians lived. That fell to his successor, Emperor Augustus, who wanted to take the borders of the Roman Empire up to the river Elbe. This would then bring the Frisian people under Roman control.

At first, the Frisians co-operated with the Romans. Rather than fight the invading forces, they agreed to pay regular taxes in the form of cowhides.

But under Tiberius, who followed Augustus, the taxes became too high. In 28 AD, the Frisians launched a rebellion against the Romans, even going so far as to lynch and hang the taxman.

Since the Roman Empire had other problems at the time, there was no reprisal upon the Frisians. The Romans retreated south of the Rhine, and the two sides settled into an uneasy agreement to respect one another's borders.

The Romans built the first military forts and cities in the country. The remains of these encampments can still be seen at present-day Valkenburg, Utrecht and Nijmegen.

Of all the Roman cities, Nijmegen was probably the most important to the Empire. It was chosen as a military camp for its strategic location overlooking the Waal and Rhine valley. These days, Nijmegen is regarded as the oldest city in the Netherlands (p236).

In the area south of the Rhine, the Romans enjoyed a generally convivial relationship with the original inhabitants, who began to prosper with the introduction of Roman technology and better agricultural methods.

About The Netherlands

One significant rebellion, which was stage around 69 AD by the Batavians, an ancient Germanic tribe, was quickly put down.

The 1st and 2nd century AD saw a period of peace and relative prosperity in the region.

This lasted until the 3rd century, when Germanic tribes from the east began to make ever-more frequent incursions into the Roman-held land.

In 406 AD, a devastating invasion from the Gauls, to the south of the Low Countries, finally put an end to Roman rule, which had already been weakened by German attacks.

The Franks and the Saxons

As the Romans withdrew from the Low Countries, a loose-knit collection of Germanic tribes, known collectively as the Franks, moved in to take their place.

It was the Franks that introduced Christianity into the Low Countries, often converting the local population by force if necessary.

From the middle of the 5th century AD, the ruling Frankish dynasty in the Low Countries was the Merovingian family. In practice this dynasty consisted of numerous fiefdoms representing different branches of the family, usually at war with one another.

Missionaries roamed the land, and churches were built on the ruins of old Roman forts. The first church was built in Utrecht in 629 AD, although the Frisians later destroyed it. Despite the onslaught of Christianity, the hard-headed Frisians in the north continued to cling to their old beliefs.

It was Willibrord, an English monk from Northumbria (later to become a saint), who is best remembered for his work among the northern heathens. His tireless work earned him the title of 'Apostle to the Frisians' and he was later made Bishop of Utrecht. Stories tell of how Willibrord destroyed Frisian pagan sanctuaries and temples in an effort to convert them. He was helped in his work by the missionary Wynfryth, later to become Saint Boniface, who was eventually murdered in 754 AD by a group of disenchanted Frisians.

By 800 AD, there is some evidence that the ruling Frisian elites had been converted to Catholicism. However, the vast majority of the population still practiced their former beliefs.

The Merovingian dynasty ended in 751 AD, when Pepin III, of the Carlovingian family, deposed the last of the Merovingian kings and proclaimed himself ruler.

He did so with the Pope's support and was anointed king by the missionary archbishop Boniface. After the latter's death, he embarked on a struggle against the Saxons, who were resisting Frankish domination under the leadership of a Saxon noble called Widukind.

It was Pepin III's son, Charlemagne, that brought Widukind to his knees. In 785 AD, Widukind capitulated and swore allegiance to the Franks.

The Holy Roman Empire

Charlemagne aspired to model his kingdom on the Roman empire and in 800 he had the Pope crown him Holy Roman Emperor. His 47-year-long reign was a period of administrative reform and cultural renaissance. At the height of his power, he ruled over an area that extended from the river Elbe to the Pyrenees and from central Italy to the North Sea.

Between 800 AD and 1000 AD, the Low Countries suffered from

countless Viking raids. At the time, the German and French powers were at war with one another and couldn't offer any sort of resistance to the Vikings. What resistance there was tended to come from local nobles, who gained in status as a result of successful victories against the Vikings. Many urban centres started to construct walls to keep out these raids, remnants of which can still be seen in some Dutch cities, such as Deventer.

Around the turn of the millennium, there were several agricultural developments that allowed the country to produce more food. Better technology allowed the exploitation of regions not previously cultivated, such as the sandy soils of the east and the south, and the salty marshes of northern Friesland.

This revolution in agriculture increased economic development. As production exceeded local needs, an export industry sprung up, aided by the introduction of hard coinage. In turn, this encouraged urban expansion and a merchant middle class began to emerge.

With this new wealth, cities started to become more independent. Local rulers turned their counties and duchies into private kingdoms, and the Holy Roman Empire found that it could no longer maintain political unity.

In the north, Friesland continued to maintain its independence and resisted the imposition of the feudal system. But this couldn't last forever, and in 1498 Albert III, the Duke of Saxony, successfully vanquished the Frisians.

The decentralisation of power away from the Holy Roman Empire meant that, by the beginning of the 15th century, a few largely autonomous lords controlled most of the region. The most powerful fiefdoms at the time were Holland, Brabant,

Utrecht and Gelre. These feudal states were almost continually at war with one another.

Some attempt to unify the region was made by Philip III, who became Duke of Burgundy in 1419. An adept political leader, he managed to gain control over a large part of the Low Countries, including Holland, Zeeland, and Brabant. He established a strong administration in Bruges, in present-day Belgium, and stripped many of the towns of the rights that were enshrined in their charters.

In a bid to consolidate Burgundian power, Mary, the granddaughter of Philip III, was married off to Maximilian I of the Habsburg dynasty in 1477.

Far from strengthening the house of Burgundy, however, the marriage elevated the prominence of the Habsburgs. Mary was killed in a riding accident in 1482, leaving Maximilian to govern Mary's inheritance.

Maximilian, who became Holy Roman Emperor in 1486, continued the policy of centralisation that had been begun by Philip III.

By the 16th century, all of the Low Countries had fallen under control of the Habsburg dynasty.

Europe's reformation movement, which pitted an emerging Protestant religion against the Catholic establishment, proved to be the biggest threat to the rule of the Holy Roman Emperor in the Netherlands.

These protestant reformers protested against doctrines imposed by the Catholic church, and moved to set up their own Protestant churches.

In the Netherlands, the discontent with Catholicism manifested itself in the Eighty Years' War, which began in 1568 as a revolt against Philip II of Spain (to be distinguished from Philip III of Burgundy, mentioned above), who was then the ruling sovereign of the Netherlands.

Although the armies of Philip II managed to gain control over most of the rebelling provinces, the north was able to resist the insurgency and, under William I, established its own republic independent of the Spanish throne (see box).

The Dutch Republic was a federation of seven provinces: Holland, Zeeland, Friesland, Groningen, Utrecht, Gelderland and Overijssel

The war between the Spanish and the newly-founded republic continued until 1648, when a treaty between the two sides was signed that formally recognised the Dutch Republic as an independent country.

The Golden Age

Despite war with Spain, the end of the 16th century was characterised by a high level of prosperity in the Dutch Republic, along with a flourishing of science and art. This was the beginning of the Golden Age in the Netherlands.

Overseas trade became particularly important.

In 1600, the first Dutch ship returned from a trip to India, bringing back a cargo of spices and other highly-prized cargo. Two years later, in 1602, the Dutch East India Company was formed.

Thanks to more efficient cost structures, the Dutch East India Company was able to muscle in on the shipping routes traditionally dominated by Portugal and Spain. It rapidly became the world's largest trading enterprise.

Its sister company, the Dutch West India Company, was granted a charter in 1621 for a trade monopoly with the Americas. It also established key trading posts along the coast of Africa. The company

> ## FATHER OF A NATION
>
> William of Orange — sometimes known as William I (not to be confused with Willem Fredrik, who became the first king of an independent Netherlands in 1815) or William the Silent — was born in 1533. He came from a noble family, and for a time served the Habsburgs as a member of the court of Margaret of Parma, governor of the Spanish Netherlands.
>
> But he eventually fell out with his paymasters, principally over attempts to centralise political power and move it away from the local estates.
>
> His stance against the Spanish prompted the Eighty Years' War, which culminated in the forming of an independent nation in 1648, with the House of Orange at the helm.
>
> William I died in 1584.

was eventually given jurisdiction over the African slave trade, which also helped to support the Dutch economy.

The Dutch West India Company became important not only in the Dutch colonisation of the Americas, but in the discovery and eventual settlement of New Zealand, Tasmania and parts of south-eastern Asia.

Increased trade and commerce gave rise to another important industry that was to help the Dutch economy develop: finance.

With the expansion of trade by sea, Dutch merchants started to look for a way that they could decrease their reliance on cash. The result was a slip of paper, known as a bill of exchange, which required the debtor to pay a debt at a specific time and place. This was an idea borrowed from the Italians, who had already been using it for a few hundred years.

In an effort to standardise this practice, the Dutch government established an exchange bank in 1609 and required all trades to be processed through this institution. The bank flourished because of its ability to handle deposits and transfers, and to settle international debt.

Thus was born the concept of finance in the Netherlands, and it didn't take long for some merchant families to turn away from overseas trade and begin trading in financial transactions.

A stock exchange and financial centre started to grow up around this.

As the wealth of the country grew, so did the arts and the sciences.

Frans Hals became well known for his group portraits, often of wealthy citizens; Hercules Seghers was a well-known landscape artist; Hendrick Avercamp also painted landscapes; Jan Vermeer, who depicted domestic life in many of his paintings, is perhaps now best remembered for his painting of a *Girl with a Pearl Earring*; Rembrandt Harmenszoon is widely acknowledged as one of the greatest Dutch painters, renowned for both his portraits and depictions of scenes from the Bible.

Prominent scientists of the time include Jan Leeghwater, a hydraulic engineer who pioneered technology to drain lakes, Christiaan Huygens, an astronomer who discovered Saturn's rings, and Cornelis Corneliszoon, inventor of the saw mill.

The French philosopher René Descartes, most famous for his line "I think, therefore I am", ended up spending the last two decades of his life in the Netherlands during the Golden Age.

Despite this rising prosperity, though, war was never very far away.

As the Dutch Republic started to rival England's dominance of the seas, the two powers clashed more and more frequently.

From the middle of the 17th century until the end of the 18th century, several wars were fought between the Dutch Republic and England.

The last Anglo-Dutch war took place between 1780 and 1784, and occurred because of the Dutch Republic's support for American independence.

It was this last war that proved most costly for the Dutch, and was to lead to a permanent decline in the country's global influence.

It was not just wars with England that weakened the Dutch. There was also political unrest within the country.

Conflict was starting to emerge between those loyal to the House of Orange, who wanted the ruling elite to have more power, and the republicans, who wanted power to be decentralised to the towns and cities.

Such political turmoil provided the French with the perfect opportunity to seize control of the country, which it did in 1795, in the wake of the French revolution.

French Rule

The toppling of the House of Orange was very much a by-product of the French revolution, and reflecting the strong anti-monarchy feeling that was sweeping Europe at the time.

The French revolution began in 1789 and, by 1792, the country was under the command of revolutionary forces.

An armed insurrection, inspired by the revolution in America, had already been launched against the House of Orange in 1785. It was brutally suppressed with the backing of Britain.

The heavy-handed response to this revolution created an environment that was perfect for the arrival of the French, which looked to export the success of their revolution. William V was quickly ousted and fled to England.

The Dutch Republic was renamed the Batavian Republic, after the ancient Germanic tribe who lived in the region during Roman times. Officially, the country remained independent of France, although in practice little took place without the say-so of Paris.

Napoleon Bonaparte was proclaimed ruler of France in 1799. In 1806, he renamed the Batavian Republic the Kingdom of Holland and appointed his brother, Louis Bonaparte, as king.

But Louis proved not to be the loyal French subject that Napoleon would have hoped for. Thus, four years later, he decided to remove him from office and absorb the Netherlands into the French Empire.

But Napoleon was unable to retain control of the Kingdom of Holland. Following his devastating defeat in Russia in 1812, Napoleon was forced into exile on the Italian island of Elba.

Although Napoleon was to return from exile a year later and regain control of France, his temporary exit from the political stage gave the Netherlands the opportunity to reassert its independence and invite William VI, the son of William V, back from exile. He landed at Scheveningen, which is now part of The Hague, in 1813. Two years later, he was crowned King William I.

Kingdom of the Netherlands

Following the defeat of Napoleon, and the return of the House of Orange to the throne, the Kingdom of the Netherlands was reunified with the region's southern lands — roughly what is now Belgium and Luxembourg.

William set about overturning the old order of things. In particular, he took issue with the privileges that the Catholic Church had enjoyed over the centuries — especially its favourable tax treatment — and insisted that all of his subjects enjoyed the same civil and political rights.

Whilst William appeared to be an enlightened monarch, who worked towards economic modernisation and promoting equal rights for all, the years of his reign (1815 to 1840) resulted in greater centralisation of power.

The first 15 years of his rule showed marked economic growth and prosperity, as industrialisation started to take off in the south and overseas trade resumed in the north.

But all was not well in the fractious kingdom, and cracks started to appear between the Dutch-speaking north and the French-speaking south.

In the predominantly Catholic south, William's policies were not popular. His attempts to make Dutch the universal language of the kingdom were strongly resisted. Southerners also complained of under-representation in the northern legislature.

In 1830, things came to a head, when revolution broke out among the southern provinces.

At first, William harboured ideas to regain control over the break-away south. However, the southerners proved too stalwart in their resistance. Moreover, foreign powers that might have backed William decided to side with the revolutionaries.

In 1831, Franco-British intervention forced William to withdraw his forces from the south. In 1833, an armistice was concluded that formally granted Belgium independence from its northern neighbours, although William did not recognise the secession until 1839.

A year later, William abdicated so he could marry a Belgian and was succeeded by his son, William II, who in 1848 rewrote the country's constitution. This constitution introduced a system of parliamentary democracy, and remained largely unchanged until 1983.

The war years

When war broke out in 1914, the Netherlands declared its neutrality.

However, it was difficult for the country to remain completely outside the war effort.

During the war years, the Dutch continued to maintain trade links with the rest of the world, including Germany.

This irked Britain and the other Allies, who maintained a strict naval blockade against the Germans. The Allies tried to prevent all trade between the Netherlands and Germany, but this proved difficult.

For its part, Germany saw no advantage in invading the Netherlands and therefore the country was able to remain unoccupied throughout the war.

However, when Germany occupied Belgium, the Netherlands opened its doors for Belgian refugees.

The Netherlands even granted asylum for the German Kaiser Wilhelm II, who was forced to abdicate in 1918 after it became clear that Germany was losing the war.

The Netherlands' experience of the second world war was completely different. Although once again the country declared neutrality, it was ultimately overrun by German forces in 1940.

Germany viewed the Netherlands as of secondary importance to its war strategy. Its real prize in western Europe was France, but German tacticians believed that the sooner they took out the Netherlands, the sooner they could concentrate all their resources on France.

The Germans decided to launch a ferocious attack on Rotterdam, the country's industrial hub, in the belief that this would quickly bring the country to its knees. Germany had hoped to be in control of the Netherlands in a single day. It took three.

The Dutch army, taken by surprise, did not put up any real resistance. The Great Depression had resulted in large cuts to the budget of the armed forces, and the country's military might was not what it used to be.

Following the sudden occupation of the Netherlands, the Dutch government fled to London, where it directed the country's war effort from exile.

Following the Japanese bombing of Pearl Harbour in 1941, the Dutch government declared war on Japan. Although the Dutch army had been decimated, and the government was no longer in control of the country, Dutch overseas territories were still able to participate in the war effort.

Initially, the Germans were less repressive in the Netherlands than in other occupied countries, possibly because they considered the Dutch to be fellow Aryans.

However, as the war proceeded, Germany tightened its grip on the country. Tens of thousands of Jews

About The Netherlands

were rounded up and shipped to concentration camps in Germany and East Europe.

Heart-wrenching tales of Jewish courage and loss abound in the history of the Netherlands. Perhaps the most famous tale is the one of Anne Frank, a young Jewish girl who kept a detailed diary of her time in hiding (see box).

Whilst the exiled Dutch government were trying to manage things from abroad, the underground resistance within the country was proving increasingly important in disrupting the German occupation.

Resistance was generally covert and involved sabotaging phone lines and railways, and disrupting German supplies. Resistance operatives also forged money and documents, and engaged in intelligence-gathering. One of the riskiest activities was hiding and sheltering Jewish families and enemies of the Nazi regime.

Whilst the resistance was largely covert, one important event took place on 25 February 1941, when the Communist Party of the Netherlands called for a general strike in response to the first Nazi raid on the Jewish population. The strike was largely symbolic, and was forcefully put down by German soldiers, who fired on the civilian population. Future efforts to resist German occupation would be much more discreet.

Liberation began in the autumn of 1944, when US troops managed to take control of a small part of Limburg in the south. Capitalising on this success, the British and Americans used air strikes to establish a corridor to Nijmegen in a military operation that came to be known as Operation Market Garden.

Allied forces wanted to press on further, up to Arnhem, which could have provided the necessary

ANNE FRANK

Of all the victims of the Nazi holocaust, it is Anne Frank that has most captured the popular imagination.

Anne was born in Frankfurt am Main, in Germany, in 1929, but a few years later her family moved to Amsterdam in the Netherlands.

In 1942, after the Germans had begun their persecution of the Dutch Jewish community, Anne's father, Otto, arranged for the family to go into hiding.

For much of the war, the Frank family lived in rooms that were concealed behind the main offices of the family company. It was here that Anne began to keep a detailed diary of her time in hiding, in a book that she had received for her 13th birthday.

Loyal employees kept their location a secret, but they were ultimately betrayed by someone who has never been identified. In August 1944, German security police raided the hiding place and arrested the Frank family.

The Franks were deported to concentration camps. Anne was initially sent to the notorious concentration camp in Auschwitz, although she was later relocated to Bergen-Belsen camp in Lower Saxony.

It was here that she contracted typhus and died in March 1945, just months before the end of the war.

Her father, Otto, was the only member of the family to survive the camps. After the war had ended, and he was freed, he returned to the Frank house and discovered the diary that Anne had kept.

In tribute to his daughter, he decided to publish the diary, which quickly became a worldwide best-seller.

You can visit the Anne Frank museum in Amsterdam (p254).

About The Netherlands

turning point in the war that they were hoping for. However, German opposition proved much stronger than had been anticipated, and the Allies failed to advance any further.

Despite this setback, the Allies continued their operation against German forces in the Netherlands. During the last few months of 1944, a battalion of Canadian troops managed to liberate Zeeland in order to gain access to the harbour at Antwerp. From here, the army was able to push on up through the Netherlands and, on 5 May 1945, German forces finally surrendered at Wageningen.

Post-war years

Like everywhere, the second world war had exacted a terrible toll on the Netherlands.

The material damage to the country was estimated at between 10 and 15 billion guilders (roughly €120 to 180 billion in today's money). About a third of all industry had been wiped out. Most of the transport system was in ruins, and large numbers of houses had been destroyed.

The industrial city of Rotterdam had been particularly badly hit, since this was the initial focus of the German invasion of the country.

The years immediately after the war saw a massive reconstruction campaign. This involved not only rebuilding those areas that had been devastated by the war, but also expanding and modernising cities.

The Netherlands wanted Germany to pay for this effort, but the Allies rejected this on the grounds that the country should not be forced to pay monetary compensation. The Netherlands then proposed annexing parts of West Germany as compensation — including Cologne,

Aachen, Münster and Osnabrück. But the Allies again objected, this time on the grounds that such annexation could create instability in the region.

What really helped the Netherlands in their reconstruction effort was the economic assistance provided by the Marshall Plan, launched by the US in 1948 in order to rebuild Europe. The Netherlands received more than $1 billion (roughly €9 billion in today's money) in aid from the US.

Shortly after the end of the war, attempts were made to overturn the old political order. In particular, a new unity movement was founded to counter the pre-existing divisions of politics and society along religious lines.

Pillarisation, however, was so ingrained in the Dutch way of life that it could not be so easily defeated. The results of the 1948 election came as a shock to everyone, and the country voted overwhelmingly for the old parties.

Meanwhile, the Netherlands was starting to suffer from problems in its overseas territories.

During the war, much of Indonesia was occupied by the Japanese. Some in Indonesia viewed the Japanese as liberators from Dutch colonial rule. Others viewed them as aggressors.

By the end of the war, Japan's occupation of the archipelago had given rise to an independence movement led by Sukarno Partai. With the Japanese retreating, he wasted no time in declaring independence from foreign occupation.

Back home, though, there was a strong feeling that Dutch colonial rule should be restored. This led, in 1947, to the start of a military operation against Indonesian nationalism.

The campaign was a disaster, and resulted in many deaths on all sides. Eventually, the United Nations became involved and ordered hostilities to desist. The Dutch reluctantly capitulated, and their Asian colonies were incorporated into Indonesia in 1950.

The involvement of the Netherlands in the second world war marked the end of Dutch neutrality, which had been a hallmark of the country's foreign policy ever since 1839.

The Netherlands realised that it had to protect itself against future invasions, and made a point of joining the North Atlantic Treaty Organisation (NATO) as soon as it was founded in 1949.

In 1957, the Netherlands was also one of the founding members of the European Economic Community (EEC), later to become the EU, which it believed was important for the future of European stability.

Political change

The 1960s and 1970s was a time of social and political upheaval in the country.

Student and left-wing movements sprung up, seeking to distance themselves from the ruling political establishment. A more liberal attitude towards drugs and sex started to emerge. The young began to push for gender equality, demilitarisation and protection of the environment.

One particular counterculture movement that captured the popular imagination sprung up out of Robert Jasper Grootveld's campaign against the cigarette companies.

The Provo Movement, as it became known, provided an outlet for angry and alienated young people. The movement used pranks to provoke the police into action — and usually overreaction.

The central philosophy behind the movement was that the police response to nonviolent protest would provoke outrage and panic, thereby inspiring revolt.

The Provos gained worldwide prominence with their protest over the lavish wedding of Princess Beatrix in 1966.

The Dutch royal family were already unpopular, but the announcement that Princess Beatrix was to marry a former member of the Nazi youth movement sent support for them even lower.

In the run-up to the wedding, more and more youths joined in with the Provo protests and the police became increasingly jittery. Provo's tactics worked: the more force that the police responded with, the more the public condemned the authorities. In the end, an independent inquiry into the policing of the event resulted in the sacking of the police commissioner and subsequently the mayor of Amsterdam.

But the protests did not dampen Princess Beatrix's enthusiasm for marrying a German and on March 10, 1966, she was wed to Klaus von Amsberg.

Accepted into mainstream culture, the Provo movement was able to win a seat in the 1966 Amsterdam municipal elections.

However, a year later, the movement was disbanded. The libertarians that were behind it believed it had now become too institutional. Furthermore, with the ousting of the police commissioner and mayor of Amsterdam from office, the movement had managed to get rid of two of its main enemies.

One of the consequences of these movements was a backlash against the pillarisation of society, which under these new anti-establishment ideals start to fall apart. New political parties, such as D66, began to emerge in order to accelerate the process and herald in a new political order.

Although many of the old political parties still remained and continued to follow the same religious and political ideals, the shape of Dutch politics had changed for good.

Into the 21st century

The Netherlands has a long-standing reputation as a liberal and overtly tolerant country, but events in recent years have shaken this foundation and prompted a collective rethinking of the country's social consciousness.

The creation of the Purple Coalition in 1994 — which brought together the PvdA, D66 and VVD (see p62 for a reminder of Dutch political parties) — sparked a new era in Dutch liberalisation.

Promoting liberal values, and ignoring opposition from the orthodox religious establishment, the Coalition took steps to legalise abortion, euthanasia and gay marriage. It also took a more liberal stance towards immigration than governments from some of the neighbouring countries.

These liberal values, however, were threatened by the assassination of two public figures at the beginning of the 21st century.

The first assassination came in 2002, when Pim Fortuyn, a controversial politician, was gunned down in a parking lot by animal rights activist Volkert van der Graaf.

The shooting came just days ahead of the general elections, and was as a direct result of Fortuyn's stance towards immigration. With persuasive charisma, Fortuyn forcefully argued that no more immigrants should be allowed into the country, that the Netherlands was effectively full. In his trial, van der Graaf said he had murdered the politician to stop him exploiting Muslims as 'scapegoats'.

Fortuyn's murder prompted an immediate swing to the right. Rather than dissuade politicians from espousing anti-immigration rhetoric, the assassination wrenched voters away from liberal ideals.

The other murder that rocked the country was that of Theo van Gogh, a controversial Dutch film director.

The van Gogh film that caused most consternation was Submission, which he co-produced with Somali-born writer Ayaan Hirsi Ali. The 11-minute film, which was broadcast on 29 August 2004, took a highly-critical look at how women were treated under Islam.

When the film was broadcast, it caused a furore among the Islamic community — not just in the Netherlands but around the world.

Van Gogh was shot on the morning of 2 November 2004 by Mohammed Bouyeri, a Dutch-Moroccan. A note was found pinned to the body of van Gogh, threatening western countries and Jews.

The murder of van Gogh sparked a storm of outrage throughout the Netherlands and further polarized the debate over immigration in the country.

It is probably fair to say that the biggest legacy of these two assassinations is a questioning of fundamental Dutch values, which is still going on.

Such tragic incidents have given voice to those right-wing politicians that would stamp out immigration altogether. The controversial Geert Wilders from the PPV, who gained a prominent position in coalition government in 2010 only to lose it again two years later (p61), is just the latest in a line of populist politicians that seek to garner votes through xenophobic rhetoric. There will almost certainly be more.

About The Netherlands

Culture

Foreigners may find it hard to adjust to Dutch culture for two principal reasons.

Firstly, the Dutch can appear a little stand-offish and reserved. It is rare that someone from the Netherlands immediately accepts you into their circle of friends, without getting to know you quite well first. When you receive your first invitation to dinner at their home, you'll know you've taken that first step.

No offence is intended in this — it is just that they prefer to keep themselves to themselves, and not intrude into anyone else's space unless invited.

Secondly, the Dutch tend to be very direct in their way of speaking. They seek to avoid all misunderstandings from the outset but seem to pay little heed to people's sensitivities. Clumsy translations from Dutch into English make this directness all the more pronounced.

You shouldn't be offended by either of these cultural traits. The Dutch are just being themselves.

GREETINGS

When meeting people for the first time, hold out your hand and say your name. In formal situations, the older or more senior person may extend their hand first, although the younger or more junior will say their name first.

Dutch acquaintances who haven't seen each other in a while will shake hands. If you meet someone on a regular basis (for example, a colleague), it is unlikely that you would shake hands every time; a verbal greeting would be sufficient.

Family and close friends may greet each other with three kisses, starting from the left side. This is the opposite side from where you would start in most other European countries, including France and Italy. Kissing between men is not so common, although family members or close friends sometimes do.

At a dinner party, it is usual to greet all guests in turn (and say goodbye to each one afterwards), unless the group is particularly large.

People that know one another well might call out '*dag*' as a way of saying both 'hello' and 'goodbye'. '*Hoi*', meaning 'hi', can also be used when meeting someone or taking leave. The word is usually said twice when leaving, as in '*hoi hoi*'.

Another informal greeting is '*doei*', often shouted over the shoulder upon departure, with a shifting inflection a little like a bird's warble.

When entering a restricted gathering — such as a small meeting of friends — it is considered impolite if you do not venture a greeting such as '*goedemorgen*' ('good morning') or '*goedenavond*' ('good evening'). When you leave, you should say '*dag*' (informal) or '*tot ziens*' (formal).

Such greetings are often exchanged in waiting rooms, on buses with the driver (at least when you enter from the front) and in lifts.

VISITS AND APPOINTMENTS

Dutch people plan things well in advance, even when meeting a friend. This can make arrangements feel a little overly-formal at times, as a friend whips out his or her agenda to check availability for a casual drink.

When you want to meet a Dutch friend, it is normal to schedule this a week or two in advance. Invitations for birthday parties or gatherings should also be sent well in advance.

The Dutch are usually very punctual. If a meeting is arranged at a precise time, being more than 10 minutes late is considered impolite. Arriving late for work, for meetings or for classes is even less tolerated.

It is unusual to turn up at someone's place without having a prior appointment. This is generally only done between people that know each other very well, and on the understanding that offence is not taken if the other person is too busy to meet.

This even applies amongst close family; even parents don't generally turn up without prior arrangement.

EATING AND HOSPITALITY

Once you get to know the Dutch, they can be extremely hospitable. But initially you are likely to find them quite reserved.

If you've just moved into a new area, don't wait for your neighbours to come and introduce themselves — they won't. You must make the first move.

If you want to get to know your neighbours — and in general they won't be offended if you don't — then, within a few weeks of moving into your new place, you should extend an invitation to them.

Such an invitation usually consists of a drink rather than dinner, which would be considered too forward. The drink could consist of afternoon tea and cookies offered at around 4pm. This is a particularly good idea at the weekend. Alternatively, invite your neighbours around for an early pre-dinner drink. Don't forget that the Dutch tend to have their dinner fairly early and so an invitation shouldn't be for much later than 6pm.

If you are going to invite someone to your house, make sure that you specify whether or not the invitation will include a meal. Simply suggesting there will be 'food' may imply nibbles or snacks, and your guests might decide to eat before they arrive.

If you are invited to a Dutch household, you will usually be told whether it is a dinner invitation or just for drinks. If your hosts do not specify, assume that the invitation is just drinks.

If you want to bring a present for your host, flowers or chocolates are appropriate. Bringing a bottle of wine might also be a good idea, depending on what kind of invitation has been extended.

Food in the Netherlands does not have the same social significance that it does elsewhere. It is very much seen as a necessity rather than a luxury. Therefore, many social gatherings and business meetings take place over a cup of coffee or a glass of wine, rather than a formal dinner.

Most Dutch eat three meals a day. **Breakfast** is eaten first thing in the morning, typically consisting of cereal or bread and cheese. **Lunch** is eaten around mid-day, and may simply be sandwiches or a salad. **Dinner** is the most important meal of the day, sometimes consisting of three courses with soup as the starter. The Dutch generally eat early (between 5 and 7pm), which is important to bear in mind when booking a restaurant. Even in the larger cities, many restaurants do not take reservations after 9pm. In more rural areas the last booking can be even earlier, with reservations taken no later than 7.30 or 8pm.

Besides these three meals, most Dutch also have a morning coffee break at 11am and then another

Culture

break (usually for tea) in the afternoon, around 4pm.

The Dutch **borrel** is an informal gathering of people for an alcoholic drink, such as beer or *jenever*, along with some savoury snack, such as *bitterballen*. It is generally taken just before dinner, and is particular common after work on a Friday.

DRESS

The Dutch tend to dress conservatively with little eye for flair or flamboyance. Ostentatious displays of wealth are rare, and showing off how rich you are is unlikely to go down well. In fact, the affluent often tone down their outward appearance when out in public.

This is not to say that the Dutch don't have a certain elegance in their dress. They do, particularly the older generation. But such elegance is rarely an excuse for showing off the finest jewellery.

Unless otherwise specified, smart casual is the norm for dinner and cocktail parties. This might consist of smart trousers or even jeans, plus a comfortable shirt. T-shirts are not usually worn to dinner parties. Women may prefer to wear a skirt or dress instead of trousers.

Business attire consists of smart trousers and a shirt. Women may choose to wear a skirt or dress instead. A tie is not usually required, except for certain professions; top-level managers, financial professionals and government officials may feel obliged to wear one.

Many regions of the Netherlands have their own distinctive traditional dress. Such costumes are still brought out on special occasions, such as during the famous cheese market in Alkmaar (p226).

Wooden clogs have become synonymous with traditional Dutch attire, and countless shops throughout the Netherlands sell this type

THE ROYAL ATTITUDE TO TIES

Prince Claus, the late husband of Beatrix — who stepped down as Queen at the start of 2013 — once caused a stir in the Netherlands by publicly ripping off his tie and calling it a "snake around my neck". He was opening the 1998 African fashion show in the country. The tie landed at the feet of his wife and, to the surprise of many that attended, he received a standing ovation.

of footwear for the tourists. Nowadays, clogs are rarely worn by the locals, although some farmers are still to be found clomping around in them, reporting that they remain a comfortable and practical choice of footwear. Clogs have even been certified by the European Union as safety shoes.

WEDDINGS

Before couples can wed, they must formally state their intention to do so. They do this at the town hall (*stadhuis*), in a process known as *ondertrouw*. This should take place at least two weeks and no more than a year before the wedding.

Once the *ondertrouw* has been completed, the legal process of getting married takes place within the *stadhuis*.

Sometimes a church wedding will be added on to this formal procedure (but only once the civil part of the ceremony has been completed).

If a church wedding is included, then the formal marriage process in the *stadhuis* will be fairly short. The exchange of vows and signing of the marriage certificate will take place in the church.

Recently there has been a noticeable decline in the number of Dutch couples choosing to get married in a church.

Gifts are usually given to the married couple after the ceremony has finished and photos have been taken.

A gift list is normally sent out along with the invitation. Sometimes the marrying couple may express a preference for cash rather than a gift.

The ceremony is commonly followed by a dinner or reception (sometimes both). Depending on the preference of the married couple, it may be only close friends and family that are invited to this post-wedding event.

At more traditional weddings, guests may be presented with a small package of sugary sweets, known as '*bruidssuiker*' ('bride's sugar'). These sweets represent the five wedding wishes of love, happiness, loyalty, prosperity and virility. A spiced liquor, known as '*bruidstranen*' ('bride's tears'), may be served before the dinner or at the reception.

BIRTHDAYS

In general, the Dutch are careful to remember people's birthdays, and often have a calendar (quite typically on the back of the toilet door) just for this purpose. They will either call, visit in person or send a card.

A birthday party may be held in a bar rather than at home, with friends and family invited for drinks. The person having the birthday may also arrange for some bar snacks and nibbles to be provided, but guests will usually have to buy their own drinks. If the birthday party is held at home, then chairs will typically be placed in a circle for ease of conversation.

It is normal to give a present to a friend or colleague that is having a

---

THE DUTCH HAPPY BIRTHDAY SONG

*Lang zal ze leven
Lang zal ze leven
Lang zal ze leven in de gloria
In de gloria, in de gloria*

*Hieperdepiep Hoera
Hieperdepiep Hoera
Hieperdepiep Hoera*

---

birthday. The present doesn't have to be too extravagant — perhaps a book or magazine, flowers or chocolates. The important thing is to at least offer something.

Gift vouchers — known as *cadeaubon* — are usually well-received as a present. Another common and inexpensive gift are lottery tickets. When you buy them, you can ask for them to be sealed in a special gift envelope.

To wish someone 'happy birthday', shake hands and say '*gefeliciteerd*' ('congratulations'). This explains why a Dutch acquaintance might say 'congratulations' on your birthday instead of 'happy birthday'.

Well-wishers will also typically congratulate the close family of whoever's birthday it is.

The Dutch have their own version of 'Happy Birthday' (see box), which is sung to a slightly different tune to the English rendition. At the end of the song, the well-wishers will exclaim '*Hieperdepiep Hoera*' ('hiphip hooray!') three times.

If you are working on your birthday, it is a good idea to bring something small to eat in order to celebrate with your colleagues. Children often bring treats for their classmates.

FUNERALS

A *rouwkaart* is a card that comes in a white envelope with a black or grey border. When you receive it, it

Culture

means that someone you know has died.

Black, or a suitably dark colour, is the normal dress style at funerals. Wearing white is considered inappropriate.

A funeral may or may not include a church service, depending on the wishes of the deceased's family. If it doesn't, then the service will normally take place at a funeral home or crematorium. After the service, there will usually be a small reception where drinks and sandwiches are served.

Funerals are usually attended by invitation only, although invitations may sometimes be in the form of a newspaper advertisement.

Your presence at a funeral will be very much appreciated, but if you do not wish to attend simply send the card back along with an expression of condolence.

Gifts are not customary at funerals. Some people bring flowers to leave on top of the coffin, although it is quite common to send them instead.

NEW HOUSE

When someone buys a house, it is usual to congratulate them by sending a card or giving a plant as a present.

BABIES

Proud parents announce the arrival of a new baby by sending out cards. The typical response to this is to pay a visit or to send a card or small gift.

The parents of the newborn will often provide a type of toast called '*beschuit*' with coloured sprinkles on. The colour of these sprinkles depends on the sex of the baby: pink and white for girls, blue and white for boys.

ENGAGEMENT, MARRIAGE AND FAMILY

An engagement is announced to friends by sending cards. If you are invited to the reception, flowers or a small gift are the norm.

For weddings, the tradition is for the parents of the couple to send out invitations.

The definition of marriage in the Netherlands has undergone major changes over the past few decades, and can now mean 'living together' without a formal marriage certificate. Same-sex marriage is acceptable, and people of the same sex are legally allowed to adopt children.

Traditional Dutch family units tend to consist of a mother and father plus their children.

Grandparents and extended family may live nearby; recent studies suggest that 50% of children live within 10 km of their parents once they leave home.

Families tend to be small, usually consisting of no more than two children. Divorce is on the rise in the Netherlands, and this has resulted in more single-parent households or children living with only one parent plus new partner.

The majority of Dutch women stay at home to look after the children when they are young or, if they do have a job, tend to only work part-time.

Family ties are close in the Netherlands, and special occasions are often marked by large numbers of family members descending on a central household.

The Dutch attitude to bringing up kids is noticeably liberal. From a fairly early age, children are allowed to do what they like and are not often disciplined. The belief is that they should be free to discover the world for themselves. This results in children maturing earlier than in other countries where parents take tighter control over their children's lives.

Publicly disciplining children is almost unheard of. If a child is misbehaving in public, the behaviour will be tolerated and rarely remarked upon. It would be unthinkable for anyone apart from a close relative to tell the child off.

It is equally unacceptable for someone to give advice to parents about how they should or should not bring up their kids. Family life is considered very much a private affair.

Hitting kids is now illegal in the Netherlands.

NEW YEAR

The experience of New Year spent in a Dutch city will not be one you quickly forget.

There is no real tradition of a New Year's Eve meal with family and friends. Rather, the Dutch usually eat something quick — even just a sandwich — whilst getting ready for the evening party.

For the Dutch, New Year's Eve is mainly about fireworks and alcohol. From early morning of the 31st until very late into the evening, the Netherlands will be an explosion of loud bangs, flashing lights and petrified pets.

Although strong fireworks are illegal in the Netherlands, many are smuggled over the border from Germany or Belgium and sold on the black market. For the Dutch, the bigger the bang the better.

In certain areas, users of fireworks can be particularly reckless and so you may be better off staying indoors. Things are slightly better in the well-lit central areas, and so you should be able to walk around fairly safely.

Shops in the Netherlands are only allowed to sell fireworks a few days before New Year's Eve — for the rest of the year, they are not sold.

People that wish to purchase them need to reserve them in advance.

Most shops and restaurants will close by 6pm. Bars will stay open much later.

It is strongly advised to tape up your letter box on New Year's Eve, lest a burning firework ends up in your living room.

New Year's Eve is also where glass insurance (p38) comes in handy. Your researchers speak from experience.

On New Year's Day, at 12noon, the tradition is to charge into the bitingly cold North Sea waters off the coast of Scheveningen. It's a terrific hangover cure. It costs a couple of euros to participate in this folly, and you should make sure you get there early because only a limited number of people are allowed on the beach.

SINTERKLAAS AND CHRISTMAS

Sinterklaas — Saint Nicholas in English — is celebrated in the Netherlands on December 5, which is officially Saint Nicholas Eve. Other countries — Belgium, Germany and France — have their celebrations and present-giving the morning of the following day.

Saint Nicholas was actually the patron saint of children. The tradition played out in the Netherlands is that he sails by steamboat from Spain, arriving in the country in mid-November (usually on a Saturday). It is slightly unclear as to where this tradition originated from. One story has it that Saint Nicholas was interred in Bari, which at the time the tradition started evolving was under Spanish rule. Another fable is that Spain was an important trading partner of the Netherlands, trading amongst other

Culture

things oranges — one of the gifts that Sinterklaas would traditionally bestow upon good children.

Every year, hundreds of people gather around the harbour in Scheveningen to witness the arrival of Sinterklaas, accompanied by his Zwarte Piet (lit: Black Pete) helpers. Sweets are thrown to the expectant crowds, concerts are organised and street entertainers weave through the crowds. See ⌨ www.sinterklaasindenhaag.nl for more details.

The arrival of Sinterklaas into town is a huge event and is broadcast on national television.

Once Sinterklaas arrives, the whole country is alive with news of his activities. Even national news programmes enthusiastically cling to the Sinterklaas-mania, often dedicating a few minutes each day to talk about him. Questions are even asked about Sinterklaas during debates in the Dutch Parliament

Traditional Sinterklaas treats for children include big chocolate letters, gingerbread nuts, chocolate coins and marzipan figures.

Presents may be exchanged either on Sinterklaas Eve (December 5) or on Christmas Day — better-off families may even give gifts on both!

Gift-giving for Sinterklaas is done in a particular way. Rather than everyone buy presents for everyone else, each person typically buys just one present for a chosen member of the family. These presents are then put in a sack and pulled out one by one, so that nobody knows who has given a particular gift.

The presents are often wrapped in inventive ways, to disguise what they really are. It is also traditional to include a humorous poem with the present, often poking fun at the recipient for his or her well-known bad habits or other character deficiencies.

On Sinterklaas Eve, presents for children — or at least those young enough to still believe in the steamboat-owning philanthropist — are given earlier in the evening. Once the children have been put to bed, then adults exchange presents.

There is no special gathering on Christmas Eve, but on Christmas Day close family will generally meet for lunch.

December 26 is known as *tweede kerstdag* ('second Christmas Day'). It is a bank holiday, but many shops will be open according to Sunday opening times (12noon to 6pm).

DUTCH HOMES

Dutch homes are generally neat and orderly — reflecting, no doubt, the Dutch penchant for leading a largely organised and pragmatic lifestyle.

Many older-style houses are impossibly narrow, consisting of several floors. This is a consequence of ancient tax laws, which were based on surface area of the house.

Modern houses are often wider, although in the cities not by much; living space is still at a premium.

Dutch staircases can take a little getting used to. Undeniably steep, with steps of miserly proportions, they do require some work to climb.

For such a private group of people, it may seem slightly odd that many of the Dutch leave their curtains wide open — or sometimes don't have them at all. This is even true on the ground floor, which looks out onto the street. As an outsider, it can be difficult to resist peering inside, to catch a glimpse of people eating or watching TV. However, this is considered bad form; the Dutch do not feel the need for curtains because they do not think that people will be looking into their home.

The room at the front of the house, overlooking the street, is generally the living room. Although the Dutch assume that others will not be peering into their house, they are aware that the front room is still very much on display and therefore will take a great deal of care over its presentation. It will usually be spectacularly neat and tidy, often with lots of books, a sofa and a television.

The Dutch like open spaces, favouring largish dining and living areas. The kitchen is often one of the smaller rooms in an apartment, and doesn't generally have an oven (something to bear in mind if you are planning on renting a furnished apartment).

The walls in an apartment, particularly in newer buildings, are relatively thin and don't insulate sound as well as they might. Dutch law imposes a noise curfew from 11pm. Neighbours will not hesitate to call the police or bang on your door if they believe the noise you are making is excessive.

SEX, DRUGS AND ROCK 'N' ROLL

Over the decades, the Dutch have gained something of a reputation for having a liberal attitude towards drug-taking and sex.

The red light district of Amsterdam is world-famous, and a trip to see the scantily-clad women on display in the windows is on the list of most tourists' itineraries (p251).

Marijuana-smoking has become so ubiquitous that, if you live in a Dutch city for any length of time, you will think nothing of catching a pungent whiff of the drug as you're walking through the streets.

But such liberalism is not universal. In fact, many Dutch feel acutely embarrassed about the perception people have of them as a drug-using, openly promiscuous society.

Such a backlash against the drug and sex culture is reflected in the

THE LOW-DOWN ON PROSTITUTION

Prostitution occurs in various forms: 'window' and street prostitution, clubs, escort agencies and home-based prostitution. All are legal in the Netherlands.

Window prostitution is the most easily-identifiable type of prostitution in the Netherlands and occurs in a dozen or so cities across the country, Amsterdam's red light district being the most famous.

A quarter of an hour with a prostitute in one of the country's red light districts will typically cost €50. Brothels and sex clubs all have their various prices and conditions.

Whilst the openness of the sex trade in the Netherlands may contribute to a safer environment for women, you should bear in mind that the industry still has some unsavoury characteristics.

There is good evidence that human trafficking takes place in order to feed the appetite for prostitution — and the UN's Office on Drugs and Crime (UNODC) has highlighted this as a significant problem. A growing realisation that this is what is going on has resulted in a gradual down-sizing of some red light districts, including the one in Amsterdam.

A number of brothels and sex clubs have also often been used as a front for criminal activity and closed down as a result.

Culture

CANNABIS

Cannabis is the generic name of the plant from which both marijuana (otherwise known as weed) and hashish come. Marijuana is the dried flowering top of the cannabis plant, and looks a little like dried moss. Hashish is the pure resin that is separated from the dried flowers. Hashish tends to be stronger and comes in small cubes that need to be crumbled before they can be used.

Cannabis can be taken in many different ways: smoked, dissolved in tea or baked into a cake. Most regions of the Netherlands have now banned space tea and space cakes, since many consumers didn't know how much of the drug they were taking and so ended up in hospital. However, you will still find both of these in the more liberal city of Amsterdam.

Establishments selling cannabis are known as 'coffee shops'. You can either choose to consume the drug on the premises, or take it away for private consumption later.

Coffee shops in the Netherlands are very relaxed places, and staff are usually happy to provide advice about the drugs that they sell. You must be 18 to enter a coffee shop, which is also the legal age from when you can start taking cannabis.

When you enter a coffee shop, you will normally be presented with a menu of different types of cannabis from which to choose. Whilst it may appear that there is little to distinguish the different varieties, true connoisseurs of the drug will tell you that choosing which one to smoke is a little like selecting a fine wine. Not only is the strength noticeably different but the taste is too.

Some of the more popular names you might encounter include White Widow, Night Shade, Super Skunk and Morning Glory. Many of the overseas varieties are stronger than the homegrown ones.

Cannabis is sold by the gram. The price varies significantly, depending on the type of drug, quality and strength. It would be reasonable to expect to pay between €8 and 10 for a gram, which should make a few joints. Cannabis is usually rolled with tobacco or with dried herbs. You can also buy pre-rolled spliffs, although they tend to be significantly more expensive.

It is unusual to find coffee shops selling both beer and cannabis — since it is not recommended to take the two together — although they do exist. Cremers in The Hague (🏠 Prinsestraat 84; ☎ 070 346 2346; 🏠 www.cafecremers.nl) is one example.

Although cannabis is decriminalised in the Netherlands, and easy to get hold of, as with any drug you should exercise due caution. If you have never experienced it before, make sure that you select a lower-strength variety and if you feel unwell stop using it. There is good scientific evidence that prolonged use of cannabis can have serious long-term health implications.

It is not permitted to smoke cannabis outside official establishments.

Culture

MAGIC MUSHROOMS AND TRUFFLES

Magic mushrooms were actually banned in the Netherlands in 2007 and given the same drug classification as cocaine.

However, a loophole in the law means that the ban did not extend to the sclerotium fungi, which is formed from the same organism that mushrooms come from and therefore has similar effects.

Sclerotia, more commonly known as magic truffles, are widely available in smartshops (a particularly Dutch establishment that specialises in the sale of items related to altering one's state of mind) throughout the country. You can find the only smartshop in The Hague at 🏠 Schoolstraat 11.

Like magic mushrooms, they are hallucinogenic. However, real hallucinations, in the sense that the user no longer knows the difference between perception and reality, are unlikely to occur. Typical effects include more intense colours and occasional kaleidoscopic visions. Objects can seem as if they are made of rubber. Distortions in time can also occur — a second may seem like an hour and vice-versa. Other distinguishing characteristics of a truffle trip are uncontrolled floods of laughter and intense joy.

Most people recommend taking magic truffles in calm and serene surroundings. In the middle of the countryside is usually preferable to the heart of the city. Do not take magic truffles if you are stressed, wound up or unhappy. Retailers recommend consuming half a box and then waiting to see what happens. Once the effect of the truffles kicks in, then you can decide whether you want to take any more. It usually takes 30 to 45 minutes for the effects of the drug to begin.

As with cannabis, there is a wide range of magic truffles to choose from, attached to such exotic names as 'Dragon's Dynamite', 'Atlantis', 'Mexicana' and 'Tampanensis'. Each variety comes with its own precise effect and intensity. Effects are also strongly personal. Different people may experience trips in different ways.

Smartshops also sell seeds for growing magic mushrooms and magic truffles. It is not illegal to grow magic mushrooms yourself.

As with any drug, use appropriate caution when sampling magic truffles and, if it is your first time, choose a less potent variety.

Culture

periodic attempts by politicians to curb the industries.

There is actually a darker side to prostitution than at first meets the eye, and there is good evidence that criminal gangs operate throughout the industry (see box on p81).

In terms of drugs, there are periodic calls for controls to be tightened up. Contrary to popular belief, smoking marijuana has never officially been made legal. The authorities simply turn a blind eye to the industry, thinking it is better to have it out in the open, where they can at least have some control over it.

There have been some moves to tighten up the drug trade. Most recently, parliament has passed a law giving regional authorities the power to ban the sale of marijuana to non-residents. There had been concerns that the legislation would automatically apply across the whole country, but by giving the local councils the final say, the government has made sure that drug tourism will not die out altogether. Amsterdam and The Hague have said that they will continue to allow foreigners access to coffee shops, whilst the southern cities of Maastricht and Tilburg will not.

In general, the sex and drug culture of the Netherlands is more appealing to foreigners than to the local Dutch. There is little evidence that the Dutch take more drugs or visit prostitutes more frequently than people from other countries. In fact, many of the people, including a growing number of the young, associate casual drug-taking with a 'loser' mentality and tend to stay clear of it.

When it comes to sex, the Dutch are quite comfortable discussing the topic in the open, even among family members. For many Dutch, it is also irrelevant whether sex takes place between a man and a woman, or members of the same sex.

It is this liberalism that people have come to respect and like the Dutch for.

SOCIALISING

Since the Dutch tend to be fairly reserved, it is not always all that easy to find new friends among them. Learning the socialising habits of the Dutch can help, though.

One of the ways that the Dutch love to socialise is through social clubs. In the main cities, there are clubs for just about every activity that you might fancy trying. Sports clubs are particularly popular.

The Netherlands also has a thriving bar culture. *Bruin cafés*

(literally: brown cafés) are a particularly Dutch place to hang out. Their curious name is taken from the dark brown wood panelling that many of the interiors are constructed from. *Bruin cafés* are welcoming and cosy — what the Dutch might refer to as '*gezelligheid*'.

Most *bruin cafés*, especially in the larger cities, are open until the early hours of the morning. You'll be able to get something to drink at *bruin cafés*, and quite often something small to eat as well.

RELIGION

Religion has had a far-reaching impact on the development of Dutch society and culture.

For centuries, the country was part of the Holy Roman Empire (p64), which allowed Catholicism to take hold, at least in the south.

Then came the Reformation (p65), which pitted Calvinism — a branch of Protestantism — against the dominant Catholic religion.

This led to a 'pillarisation' of society, whereby political and social groupings were often determined by religious affiliation.

Formal pillarisation has long since disappeared, brought down by the youth movements of the post-war years, but evidence can still be seen of it in many of the institutions that are around today — including newspapers and political parties.

These days, the Dutch are far less inclined towards formal religion than in the past.

According to the latest data from the national statistics bureau, only 39% of the population claim to be affiliated to a religion, whilst fewer than 20% visit church regularly. The largest religions remain Catholicism (26%) and Protestantism (11%). In recent years, Islam has also been on the rise, largely because of immigration. It now accounts for an estimated 6% of the population.

Today, the Netherlands is very much a secular society. However, whilst there has been a sharp decline in church attendance, it would be wrong to label the Dutch as an irrefutably heretical group. On the contrary, recent studies suggest that more than 60% believe in a higher power.

This spiritual belief translates into the way the Dutch conduct themselves in the real world — specifically through pragmatism and a heavy sense of responsibility.

Interestingly, despite the prevalence of the Catholic Church in the country, the Dutch have largely resisted the Catholic doctrine that has taken hold elsewhere. For example, prostitution, euthanasia and abortion all remain legal (although not everyone in society thinks that they should).

Religion is not a taboo subject as it is in other countries, and conversations often end up dwelling on the subject.

Whilst the Dutch remain tolerant of other religions, they are often perplexed by the seemingly insular nature of Islam. The murder of controversial film director Theo van Gogh in 2004 (p73) has deepened scepticism towards the religion.

Most Protestant and Catholic churches run services throughout the week, particularly in the larger cities, although Sunday congregations remain the largest.

POPULAR CULTURE

Art

Some of the truly great names of art have, at one time or another, entered into Dutch history: Frans Hals, Vincent van Gogh, Rembrandt van Rijn, Johannes Vermeer, MC Escher, to name but a few.

It is no wonder, then, that art has become such an integral part of the Dutch cultural mind-set. Almost every major town in the Netherlands lays claim to a prominent Dutch artist, whose works are usually proudly displayed in the local art gallery.

The majority of visitors to these galleries are actually Dutch, although the occasional foreigner will flit by (particularly to see the more famous masters).

The Dutch are eminently proud of their artistic heritage, and the country is full of avid art-lovers, who delight in being able to spend a Saturday or Sunday afternoon ambling around local art galleries.

The wealth of pictures on display, even within a single gallery, can be quite staggering.

Art in the Netherlands really began to blossom in the 17th century, with the arrival of the Golden Age. Before that, Dutch art was influenced by Romanesque and Gothic styles, which Flemish painters chose to refine.

It is during the Golden Age that the likes of Rembrandt van Rijn, Jan Vermeer, and Frans Hals took up their brushes and created what are now considered some of the finest works in the world.

During the 18th century, Dutch art was heavily influenced by French baroque and neoclassical artists.

Post-impressionism entered the country in the 19th century, a period that was typified by the great classic painter Vincent van Gogh

During the 20th century, Dutch painting was strongly influenced by cubism and expressionism. This later gave way to more abstract expressionism, with a group

Culture

of avant-garde artists, such as the illustrious Piet Mondriaan (p151).

Graphic artists, including MC Escher, also started to emerge at this time.

Music

You will encounter a wide range of musical styles and tastes, reflecting many different cultural influences from all over the world.

Popular music — often dubbed 'Nederpop' — has been heavily influenced by the popular European and American rock bands of the 1960s and 1970s. You will find it more 'rocky' than pop music from the UK, for example. For commercial reasons, many Dutch bands sing a lot of their songs in English, although there are also some well-known bands that continue to sing in Dutch.

The Netherlands has a long tradition of folkloric songs, which you may hear whilst in the country, particularly during special occasions.

One of the best known styles of folkloric music is so-called 'levenslied' music, which can be literally translated as 'songs about life'. Such songs were traditional for the working-class man, and dealt with topics such as romance, death and loss.

These songs are still sung on special occasions, or in certain venues, but they are less common than they used to be, swept away by the tide of popular music that emerged out of the 1960s.

Jazz is also very popular in the Netherlands and many of the cafés that play life music will hold jazz sessions. The Netherlands also hosts the annual North Sea Jazz Festival, which is one of the largest such festivals in the world.

Television

If the Netherlands has one claim to worldwide television fame, it is that this is the country in which the reality TV show Big Brother originated.

In general, the Dutch are big fans of game shows, and producers pride themselves on being as inventive and whacky as possible. The latest game show to cause waves in the Netherlands — Weg van Nederland — pits failed asylum seekers against each other in a quiz about Dutch culture, history and language. The winner is awarded €4,000.

Dutch are also big fans of American comedy shows and films (less so of the British). American programmes are usually aired in English with Dutch subtitles — one of the reasons that the Dutch grow up speaking the language so well, albeit with an American accent.

Sex is not something that Dutch television programmes shy away from. Be attentive with younger children after 9pm, when many channels will show advertisements for sex chat lines, featuring naked or semi-naked women.

Film

The Dutch film industry is relatively small, and there has so far been little international interest in Dutch films. Most national film-makers rely on government grants to make ends meet.

This said, though, there have been some Dutch successes that are starting to get recognition abroad. For example, the 2008 Dutch war film Oorlogswinter won an award at the Rome Film Festival and was short-listed at the Academy Awards for Best Foreign Film.

A number of Dutch film directors have become well-known for working in the industry outside of

Culture

their country of birth. Paul Verhoeven (*Robocop*) and Jan de Bont (*Speed* and *Twister*) are two obvious examples.

It is difficult to succinctly categorise Dutch films. Many of the more successful movies, which end up being screened in cinemas across the country, tend to either be dramas that end in tragedy or off-beat comedies with copious amounts of drunkenness, sexual innuendo and slapstick.

Sport

Sport is a hugely popular pastime for the Dutch, and there are countless sports and fitness clubs spread throughout the country.

Football is the most popular sport in the Netherlands, with Oranje being the national team (named after the royal House of Orange). During major international matches, you are likely to see the streets of the Netherlands flooded with orange banners (📷 #59).

Other popular sports include hockey, ice-skating, cycling and volleyball.

BIKES

Bikes are everywhere in the Netherlands, so it pays to spend some time thinking about Dutch cycling etiquette.

When cycling along a designated bicycle lane, it is perfectly acceptable to ride side-by-side with another cyclist. If you hear a bell or horn behind you, the cyclist on the left-hand-side should move as quickly as is safely possible out of the way, either in front of or behind his cycling companion.

The Dutch cycle very fast, and quickly get frustrated with foreigners who have not learnt the unwritten code of Dutch cycling etiquette.

A quick word about the bikes themselves. Since the country is so flat, many bikes have no more than three gears and some may not have gears at all. As for brakes, not all bicycles have them on the handlebars. A large number of bikes, including the ones you are likely to rent at stations, have back-pedal brakes, where you pedal in reverse in order to slow the bike. This can take a great deal of getting used to.

TIPPING

The price of restaurant meals in the Netherlands always includes a service charge, and therefore tipping is not obligatory. However, it is always appreciated. Waiters often get close to the minimum salary and so a few euros here and there can really help them.

Restaurant-goers tip mainly in the evening and at weekends, less so at lunchtime.

For other services, such as hotels and taxis, tips are not generally given — although you might want to give a few euros to hotel staff that help carry your bags up to your room.

Watch out for taxi drivers, who often seek additional tips by claiming not to have any change.

TOILETS

The Dutch are pioneers of the underground toilet. In the early hours of the evening, you'll find dozens of urinals rising up out of the ground to service the needs of men that might be caught short after a few pints. This has improved street cleanliness no end.

Incidentally, whilst on the subject of toilets, the Dutch were also pioneers of the 'urinal fly'. This is a small insect that is embossed on certain urinals to help improve men's aim. And it works! Just look for them at Schiphol airport.

Culture

Transport

The Dutch public transport system has a reputation for being efficient, clean and relatively cheap.

In fact, the Netherlands is so well-served by the public transport system that there should be no problem getting by in the country even if you do not have your own private vehicle. If you do need to use a car, but do not own one, there are car-sharing schemes to help you out.

The cheapness and relative efficiency of the Dutch public transport system is made all the more attractive when one considers the current price of petrol in the country; averaging €1.68 per litre (at last check), the third most expensive in Europe. Diesel is cheaper, averaging €1.38, the 14th most expensive in Europe.

DRIVING

Driving in the Netherlands is on the right-hand side of the road. Whilst drivers tend to be reasonably civilised in their use of the roads, the high density of the population in the Netherlands means that the roads are fairly congested, especially in the west of the country around the main cities of Amsterdam, Rotterdam and The Hague.

When driving in the Netherlands, always pay attention to bicycles. If turning off the road, make sure you check and double-check what is behind you. Bicycles are very thin and cannot always be easily seen. If you hit a bicycle whilst driving in the Netherlands, you will always be to blame – even if it was the cyclist that did something really, really silly.

The legal age for driving in the Netherlands is 18. This applies to both cars and motorbikes, although for scooters that travel less than 40 km/h the age limit is 16.

If you have a driving licence issued outside of the EU or European Free Trade Area (EFTA), you can normally drive in the Netherlands for 185 days (roughly six months) before having to apply for a Dutch licence. Those on an EU or EFTA licence should be able to continue driving with a foreign licence for up to 10 years.

It is a straight forward procedure for nationals from the EU and EFTA to get a Dutch licence; they simply have to exchange their current one. Others are required to take a CBR theory and driving test. The theory test costs €34.57, whilst the practical test costs €97.15. This test is also available in English, although may cost slightly more.

For more information on the licence, see 🖳 www.cbr.nl.

Exemptions are made for those working for inter-governmental organisations or embassies, and their immediate family. They do not need to exchange their foreign driving licence for a Dutch one.

The **Rijksdienst Voor Het Wegverkeer** (RDW) is the national authority for road traffic, transport and vehicle administration. All legal residents are required to register any vehicle that they own and use. All cars must have an up-to-date MOT, paid-up road tax and minimum liability insurance. Full details of these are available at 🖳 www.rijbewijs.nl. Your Dutch munici-

DRIVING RULES

Alcohol The drink-drive limit in the Netherlands is 0.05%. Driving with any more alcohol in your system could result in a hefty fine and/or imprisonment.

Children A proper child restraint system must be used in the back for children under three, and in the front for children who are younger than 12 or less than 1.5 metres tall.

Documentation When driving, you must carry your driving licence, identification card or passport, vehicle registration document (V5) and certificate of motor insurance.

Fines On-the-spot fines are issued for the infringement of all traffic regulations. Ensure an official receipt is issued by the officer collecting the fine. For parking fines, a ticket will be left on your car that you will either have to pay by bank transfer or directly with cash or card at the office of the local parking authorities. More serious infractions may see you being arrested.

Fire extinguisher Advised but not compulsory.

First aid kit Advised but not compulsory.

Mobile phones It is illegal to talk on the phone whilst driving, unless you make use of a hands-free kit.

Motorbikes It is compulsory to wear a crash helmet when driving motorbikes that have more than 50 cc of engine power. You can ride less powerful bikes without a helmet, provided that their speed has been limited to 40 km/h. Such bikes may also use the cycling lanes (*fietspad*).

Right of way Traffic coming from the right has priority over traffic coming from the left unless otherwise indicated (shark's teeth on the road means that you must also give way to traffic coming from the left).

Speed limit Unless otherwise indicated, the speed limit in Holland is 130 km/h for motorways, 100 km/h for A-roads, 80 km/h for areas outside towns and cities and 50 km/h for built-up areas.

Warning triangle Advised but not compulsory.

pality can also provide you with relevant information.

Given that the Netherlands is so densely populated, it should come as no surprise that parking, particularly in the larger towns and cities, can be difficult. If you are just visiting a town, it may be easier to park on the outskirts and take a bus or tram in.

Roads in most town centres demand payment for parking (unless you are a resident). This is usually between €1 and €3 per hour (€5 in the centre of Amsterdam). Payment is made through a parking meter. Failing to buy or display your ticket will result in a fine of €51, as well as the standard parking charge.

If you don't want to park on the street, you can usually find a **covered parking garage** to use (also costing between €1 and €3). Two companies operate most of these garages: Q-Park (⌨ www.q-park. nl), which has a free mobile phone application to find the nearest garage, and APCOA (⌨ www.apcoa.nl).

Residents are entitled to a **parking permit**. This can either be for residents' use (*parkeerverguning*) or for guests (*bezoekers vergunning*).

To apply for a parking permit, you will need your national BSN number (p24), proof of address and your car registration document, which must be in your name.

You can apply for a permit online via the website of your *gemeente*. Search for '*parkeervergunning voor bewoners*'.

The cost of the permit varies from city to city. In The Hague, a year's individual permit costs €65, whilst a guest permit costs €15.

A guest permit comes with a maximum 115 hours of parking (the exact amount depends on the area in which you live: busier areas may have less). Once all these hours have been used up, your guests will have to buy a normal ticket.

In some areas, it is possible to ask for a **second resident parking permit**, although this tends to be quite costly.

The guest card can be displayed in any vehicle, but must be activated before use. The permit can be deactivated when it is no longer required, although it will automatically be deactivated at the end of the normal paying period and you will have to reactivate it for use again the following day.

The permit comes with a map that shows the exact area in which you can park, as well as the freephone number that you can call when you need to activate or deactivate the card.

Since the activation of the card is all in Dutch, non-native speakers may find it easy to make a mistake.

When you call the freephone number, you will be asked to enter the number of your permit, followed by the '#' symbol, and then your PIN number, also followed by a '#'. Confirm your selection by pressing '1'. Unless you follow the instructions very carefully, and wait for a voice that confirms the successful activation of the permit, you risk incurring a fine. You can also activate via their website.

Conditions are similar in most of the Dutch cities. Note, however, that in Amsterdam parking permits are more expensive and take much longer to obtain. It is also not possible to apply for more than one permit per household.

You can request a parking permit online or in some cities by going to the office in person. In The Hague: 🏠 Loosduinseweg 13-17; ☎ 14 070; 🕑 Mon-Fri: 7.45am to 4pm.

An alternative to owning a car in the Netherlands is to subscribe to the Greenwheels **car-sharing** scheme (⌨ www.greenwheels.nl). This is particularly useful if you are based in one of the main cities such as Amsterdam or The Hague.

To use Greenwheels, you pay a flat subscription fee every month (usually €10 to €12.50, depending on offers). On top of that, you pay an hourly rental charge (from €2.50) and a small fee per kilometre driven (around €0.10). You also need to provide a €225 refundable deposit in case of accidents. You can pick up and drop off a Greenwheels car from points all over the city. Those holding a national rail card get a small discount off the standard Greenwheels price.

The Greenwheels cars are red with a splash of green paint on the side. You can reserve a car around the clock on the website or by calling ☎ 0882 100 100.

Transport

BUSES AND TRAMS

The cheapest way of getting about by bus and tram is to obtain an *OV-chipkaart*. This is a new system that has been slowly replacing the antiquated *strippenkaart*, which are now in use only in the remoter parts of the country (see box on p92).

On most trams and buses, you can also purchase tickets directly from the driver, although this tends to be considerably more expensive and you can only pay in cash.

This is not possible on the newer blue-and-white **Randstad-Rail trams** (🖥 www.randstadrail. nl), though. Here you must buy a ticket from a machine within the tram, which only accepts the exact change. *Randstadrail* connects the residential areas of The Hague, Rotterdam and Zoetermeer. There are plans to extend it to other parts of the country too.

Day tickets in The Hague are available for bus and tram travel but are surprisingly expensive, considering the compact nature of The Hague – between €6.40 and €8.80, depending on the area.

If you are travelling off-peak, then buying an **off-peak return ticket** can be more attractive than the *OV-chipkaart* in some cases.

HTM

The Hague's public transport system is administered by HTM (🖥 www.htm.nl). The customer service number is ☎ 0900 486 4636. Calls cost €0.10 a minute.

These tickets can be used during the week between 9am and 4pm, and after 7pm. They can also be used at the weekend and on public holidays. The tickets can be bought from customer service stalls, in some shops and, for a slightly higher cost, directly from the drivers.

With a 'personal' *OV-chipkaart*, it is possible to arrange for a monthly or yearly **subscription**. The subscription is divided into zones. You should arrange for a subscription for all zones that the public transport you normally take will pass through. Be careful. If you take out a subscription for certain zones, and then one day happen to take a bus or tram that passes through a zone for which you do not have a subscription, you will be charged extra. Even if you have a subscription, you still need to check in and check out with your *OV-chipkaart*. In The Hague, subscription costs are based on the number of adjoining zones you wish to travel

Transport

SUBSCRIPTION COSTS

Type	Monthly*	Yearly*
Central zone (5400)	€46,40	€464
Central zone + one adjoining zone	€76,20	€762
Central zone + two adjoining zone	€113	€1,133
Central zone + three adjoining zone	€150,70	€1,507
Central zone + four adjoining zone	€187,70	€1,877
Central zone + five adjoining zone	€225	€2,250

* Student and senior discounts apply

THE *OV-CHIPKAART*

The *OV-chipkaart* is fairly essential if you plan to rely on public transport during your stay in the Netherlands.

The card can either be 'anonymous' - meaning that it is not registered to an individual and so can be used by anyone - or 'personal' with a photo on.

The card costs €7.50 (nonrefundable). It can be purchased at train stations and HTM customer service counters. You can pay for credit to be preloaded on to the card at time of purchase.

The card can be recharged at the blue-and-yellow machines found at railway stations or at the yellow machines often found in supermarkets and some local shops (see photo on p95).

It is possible to purchase credit online, but in order to transfer the credit to the card you must first activate it at the yellow-and-blue machines you find at railway stations. You can also arrange for the card to be automatically recharged from your bank account when it falls below a certain level, but this carries extra risk in case the card is stolen.

The *OV-chipkaart* can be used to travel on public transport all over the country, although only 'personal' cards with preloaded credit of at least €20 can be used for train travel.

THE STRIPPENKAART

Until quite recently, the most convenient and economical way of paying on trams and buses was to use the *strippenkaart*. This was a single strip of card, with 15 or 45 units marked on. A validation machine, at the entrance of trams and buses, was used to mark off the required number of units, according to the number of zones that you will be travelling through.

The strippenkaart is now obsolete in most parts of the country, but it is fondly remembered by many that have a long-standing connection to the Netherlands.

One frustrating thing with the bus and trams is that, if you forget to check out with your *OV-chipkaart*, then you will be charged the maximum fare. If you have made a genuine mistake, you can get your money back by going to one of the local HTM offices. In The Hague, go to 🏠 Wagenstraat 35.

METRO

The Hague doesn't have a metro system, but nearby Rotterdam and Amsterdam do. The *OV-chipkaart* can be used on the metro. Alternatively, you can purchase tickets from ticket machines at metro stations.

TAXIS

You will often find taxi ranks outside stations, airports and tourist attractions. However, it can be better to request a taxi by telephone (see box on p93), since this avoids some of the traps that tourists often fall into.

Officially, taxis are required to run the meter, using an official tariff for all journeys. This is an initial

through, in addition to the central zone (see box on p91).

Wherever you want to travel in the country by tram or bus, you can **plan your journey** by going to 🖥 www.9292.nl. The website is in both English and Dutch, although the English version doesn't always work as well.

Transport

TAXI NUMBERS

The Hague

- **Taxi Centrale Haaglanden** (🖥 www.tch.nl; ☎ 070 390 6262)

- **De Hofstad Taxicentrale** (🖥 www.hofstadtax.nl; ☎ 070 346 2626)

- **Haagse Taxi Mobilofoon Centrale** (🖥 www.htmc.nl; ☎ 070 390 7722)

Leiden

- **Taxi Loyaal** (🖥 www. taxiloyaal.nl; ☎ 071 888 1869

- **Taxi Centrale Leiden** (🖥 www.taxicentraleleiden.nl; ☎ 071 210 0210)

Zoetermeer

- **Taxicentrale Zoetermeer** (🖥 www.hotax-zoetermeer.nl; ☎ 079 331 3131)

- **Taxi Zoetermeer** (🖥 www. zoetermeertaxi.nl; ☎ 079 888 6588)

Rijswijk

- **Taxi Service Point** (🖥 www. taxirijswijk.nl; ☎ 070 303 0000)

Delft

- **Deltax** (🖥 www.dtdeltax.nl; ☎ 015 219 1919)

- **A Taxi Delft** (🖥 www. ataxidelft.nl; ☎ 015 261 2121)

Amsterdam

- **TCA** (🖥 www.tcataxi.nl; ☎ 020 777 7777)

Rotterdam

- **Rotterdamse Taxi Centrale** (🖥 www.rtcnv.nl; ☎ 010 462 6060)

- **St Job** (🖥 www.st-job.nl; ☎ 010 425 7000)

fare (typically €2.66) plus a per-kilometre charge (at most €1.95) as well as a per-minute charge of €0.32. There is no charge for luggage, taxi call or night shift.

Using the meter, a journey from either of the main train stations in The Hague to the city centre should cost no more than €10 to €15 – but sometimes taxi drivers ask twice this amount!

If, when taking a taxi at the station, the driver refuses to use the meter, despite your insistence, you can try to take a taxi from the back of the queue instead. Since they know they will have to wait long-er for custom, they may be more willing to use the meter.

If going to the airport, fees are often considerably lower if the service is booked online or by telephone. It is usually more convenient to go for a fixed rate than to use the meter. Prices vary from company to company. From centre of The Hague to Rotterdam airport, expect to pay €36 to €45. To Schiphol airport, budget for €57 to €67.

When travelling to and from a station, a cheaper way to travel is to use the *trein-taxi*. This is a shared taxi that costs €4.70 per person regardless of the distance travelled within the city centre.

Transport

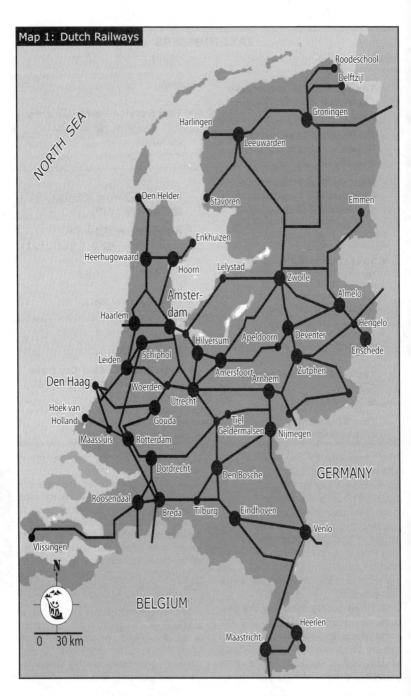

Map 1: Dutch Railways

You can purchase the ticket for the *trein-taxi* either at a train station or direct from the taxi driver, although this latter option is more expensive (€5.50). The taxi only leaves when it is full. There are 36 stations that offer the *trein-taxi* service. This does not include the major cities of Amsterdam, Rotterdam and The Hague.

PUBLIC TRANSPORT FARES AND ROUTES

- 🖥 www.htm.nl (The Hague, Leiden, Zoetermeer)
- 🖥 www.gvb.nl (Amsterdam)
- 🖥 www.ret.nl (Rotterdam)

TRAINS

For long-distance journeys, trains are by far the most convenient way of getting around. By and large, they are relatively inexpensive and efficient, although they don't tend to cope so well with harsh weather conditions or large events. During heavy snowfalls and major football tournaments, it is not unknown for the railway system to grind to a halt, leaving many people stranded. This is largely to do with the fact that there is little spare capacity in the scheduling of trains, so a problem with one part of the line can have serious knock-on effects elsewhere.

There are also regular engineering works at weekends, which can cause delays.

Train tickets can be purchased at the same blue-and-yellow machines where the *OV-chipkaart* (p88) can be recharged. Most machines only accept payment by debit and credit card (the latter with a surcharge). If you want to pay with cash, then you must make the purchase at one of the counters.

If you want to buy a ticket for a destination outside the Netherlands, other than Belgium, you will also need to go to the ticket counter.

Purchasing tickets at the counter incurs a surcharge of 50 cents for national destinations and €3.50 for international journeys.

TICKET MACHINES

Used to check in and check out on public transport

Machine for re-charging your *OV-chipkaart*

Machine for validating daily tickets

BUYING A BIKE

In a country with so many bikes, you would expect to be able to find them at a reasonable price, but this isn't the case.

Since they use bikes so much, the Dutch generally look for ones that are solid and can be used in all sorts of weather.

The Dutch see a bike as an investment that will be made over a long period of time, so they are quite happy to pay seemingly astronomical prices. A city bike, with only a fairly limited number of gears, might cost between €700 and €1,200. The most expensive bikes have a metal frame with a unique number engraved on it. This allows the bike to be traced, should it be stolen, and encourages would-be thieves to think twice before stealing it.

It is difficult to find a new bike for less than €200, although shops like Praxis, Gamma and Kijkshop sometimes have temporary reductions.

Even second-hand bikes can be pricey, rarely costing much less than €120. A second-hand bike that appears unusually cheap could be stolen.

Second-hand bikes can be found in charity shops. Most bike shops also sell second-hand bikes. The local *fietsdepot*, which stores bikes that have been illegally parked, sells second-hand bikes that have not been claimed for at least a year. They charge around €75 and will give you a receipt that you must keep in case someone claims to be the owner of the bike.

Markets also sometimes sell bikes, but make sure you ask for a receipt that proves the bike is not stolen.

Websites such as 🖵 marktplaats.nl advertise bikes for sale. Once again, be careful of stolen bikes.

When the ticket office is closed or doesn't exist, then you can buy the ticket from the controller on the train (although you should look for him or her as soon as you board).

Bikes are allowed in most trains during off-peak hours. There is no charge for carrying bikes that can be folded away, whilst other bikes incur a daily charge of €6. Tickets for bikes can be purchased at the same time as the ticket for travel.

If you are planning to stay in the country for some time, you might consider applying for a **discount rail subscription** called a *dal voordeel*, which entitles the user to a 40% discount on trains that are taken at off-peak times (9am to 4pm and after 6.30pm during the week and any time during weekends). The discount card costs €60 for the year. For an extra €20, you can also extend this discount card to include 20% off foreign train journeys to Belgium and Luxembourg. Up to three people can travel on the same card. Just select '*samen korting*' when purchasing your ticket at the machine.

You must have a Dutch bank account in order to apply for the card. The subscription fee will be taken automatically from your account annually unless you explicitly cancel this. The money is taken automatically, but you must remember to activate your subscription every year at the blue-and-yellow ticket machines.

Other types of subscription are also available.

Dal vrij: unlimited off-peak travel for €95 per month.

Weekend vrij: unlimited weekend travel for €40 per month.

Altijd voordeel: 20% discount during peak time and 40% discount during off-peak hours for €20 per month.

BIKE SIGNS TO LOOK OUT FOR

 Cycle route

 No bicycles allowed

 Cycle path

 Cycle and motorcycle route

 No bicycles or motor-cycles

 Except for bicycles

Kids vrij: free journeys for kids from four to 11 for €15 per year.

Altijd vrij: unlimited travel anywhere in the Netherlands at any time for €295 per month.

To find out more, or to see the timetables of the national rail system, go to 🖥 www.ns.nl.

If you have a smartphone, there is a very handy **application** (called NS Reisplanner) that can be downloaded from the website, which allows you to check departures, arrivals and delays.

CYCLING

It is difficult to think of the Netherlands without the country conjuring up images of pedalling your way through quaint little villages or alongside the shimmering waters of dreamy canals.

Cycling is probably the most popular way of getting around – not just in villages and the countryside, but also in the main cities.

An extensive network of cycle lanes and the flatness of the country make the bicycle such an attractive mode of transportation. Moreover, laws in the country generally benefit cyclists rather than motorists. Bikes are also able to travel both ways down many one-way streets, significantly speeding up journeys within cities.

Renting a bike is convenient and relatively inexpensive. There are private bike shops all over the country. Expect to pay between €7 and 10 for a day's rental of a standard bike. Some rental places will insist that you return the bike before they close, which might be as early as 5.30pm. Others, particularly in the countryside, will be more laid-back and happy for you to return it after closing hours, posting the keys through their letter box.

BIKE THEFT

Bike theft is unfortunately common, so make sure you invest in a good lock. Many Dutch bikes come with a wheel lock. This is good if you want to leave the bike for a short time — if you are popping into a shop to buy something, for example — but for any longer you should additionally lock the bike with a chain.

Deciding whether to leave the bike overnight depends on the area and the value of your bike.

Leaving your bike outside stations and in poorer neighbourhoods is not generally advisable. You might consider using a *fietsstalling* (see main text on p100).

You may have to pay a deposit (typically around €50) or leave your passport when renting a bicycle.

If you are going to be renting a bicycle regularly, then consider subscribing to the ***OV-fietskaart***. This incurs a once-off payment of €11 – although you do not have to pay this if you already have a discount train card (p95) – plus a subscription fee of €9 per year. The card then allows you to rent bikes at most stations in the country for just €3. You can still rent bikes without this card, but you will have to pay €7.50 a day and stump up a deposit of €50.

The *OV-fiets* subscription only entitles you to single-geared Dutch bikes. These have back-pedal brakes, which can take some getting used to. Slowing the bike by pedalling backwards, rather than squeezing the brakes on the handlebar, has the advantage that your hands are always free.

It is also possible to use your *OV-fietskaart* to rent scooters

CYCLING RULES

Riding a bicycle as a way of transportation comes with rules and the Dutch often get frustrated by the lack of knowledge displayed by tourists and foreign residents regarding two-wheeled etiquette.

- You cannot cycle in pedestrianised shopping areas during normal working hours. In The Hague this includes Noordeinde, Spuistraat and Venestaat. You should wheel the bike through these zones.
- Bicycles — even if being wheeled — are not allowed to enter markets.
- Cyclists are liable for any damage caused to property or people. You may want to get personal indemnity insurance in case of any accidents (p37).
- Parking the bicycle is not allowed outside officially-designated spots. Authorities usually turn a blind eye to this, but there are some areas where they will take action.
- You must turn your bike lights on when cycling at night, otherwise you risk a €40 fine (per light!).
- Cycling on the pavement is not allowed and could incur a fine.
- Motorbikes (under 50 cc) are permitted on many cycle paths, so watch out for them as a cyclist. Always indicate with your hand when you are turning.
- Helmets are not compulsory and are hardly ever worn by cyclists.

Transport

LONG-DISTANCE CYCLE ROUTES

LF signs to follow	Distance	Destination
LF1 Noordzeeroute	310 km	Den Helder – Sluis
LF2 Stedenroute	340 km	Amsterdam – Brussel
LF3 Rietlandroute	170 km	Holwerd – Kampen
LF3 Hanzeroute	135 km	Kampen – Millingen
LF3 Maasroute	230 km	Arnhem – Maastricht
LF4 Midden-Nederlandroute	290 km	Den Haag – Enschede
LF5 (connecting route)	20 km	Thorn – Roermond
LF6 (connecting route)	40 km	Maastricht – German border
LF7 Oeverlandroute	385 km	Alkmaar – Maastricht
LF8 (connecting route)	100 km	Ommen – Winterswijk
LF9 NAP-route	455 km	Nieuweschans – Breda
LF10 Waddenzeeroute	275 km	Callantsoog – Nieuweschans
LF11 Prinsenroute	125 km	Den Haag – Breda
LF12 Maas – en Vestingroute	220 km	Maassluis – Nijmegen
LF13 Schelde-Rheinroute	290 km	Vlissingen – Venlo
LF14 Saksenroute	240 km	Lauwersoog – Enschede
LF15 Boerenlandroute	260 km	Alkmaar – Enschede
LF16 Vechtdalroute	230 km	Zwolle – Darfeld (Germany)
LF17 (connecting route)	60 km	Gorinchem – Wijk bij Duurstede
LF18 (connecting route)	50 km	Ommen – Denekamp
LF19 (connecting route)	35 km	Deventer – Holten
LF20 Flevoroute	265 km	Haarlem – Groningen
LF21 Zuiderzeeroute	155 km	Amsterdam – Afsluitdijk
LF22 Zuiderzeeroute	135 km	Afsluitdijk – Kampen
LF23 Zuiderzeeroute	115 km	Kampen – Amsterdam
LF30 Schelde-Deltaroute	50 km	Breskens – Sas van Gent
LF51 Kempenroute	110 km	Eindhoven – Antwerpen (Belgium)

Transport

(€7.50 for three hours or €15 for 20 hours).

Bicycle stands are provided throughout the country for **parking** your bike. They are particularly common in shopping areas, and you can leave your bicycle there without charge. Train stations also provide ample parking space, again free of charge. Such parking may be located outside or on the first or second floor of the station – just look for the sign pointing to *fietsstalling*.

An alternative, which is possible in many areas, is to chain your bicycle to a post and just leave it there. However, this is not permitted in certain areas such as outside major stations, leaving your bike outside an official parking lot is not permitted. If you leave your bike in such an area for longer than 20 minutes, then the authorities are likely to cut the lock and have it taken away. Bikes can be reclaimed from the central *fiets* depot for a charge – around €25 – as long as ownership of the bike can be proved – for example, by producing the key to the padlock. Confiscated bicycles are kept for one year before being resold. In The Hague, the central *fiets* depot is at 🏠 Junostraat 24 (🖥 www.fietsdepothaaglanden.nl).

Although parking is generally free for bicycles, you might want to use the official *fietsstalling*, which typically costs between 20 and 60 cents. These lots are useful if you can't find any other parking space. Moreover, they are supervised and therefore more secure. Note, though, that supervision usually only lasts until around midnight – after that, anyone will be able to enter the parking lot. These lots are generally located near markets and in the centre of town.

Stations also often have secure paying and parking facilities,

SIGNS TO LOOK OUT FOR

Distance and direction signs

Mushroom (*paddestoel*) signs provided by ANWB

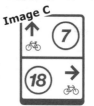

Intersection numbers (*fietsknooppunt*)

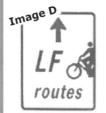

LF routes or long-distance routes

but only if you take out a weekly, monthly or yearly subscription.

Bicycles can be taken on trains during off-peak times (p95). This costs €6 per day. Tickets ca be bought at the automatic teller machines.

Cycle lanes are red with a picture of a white bike at intervals. They often run alongside pavements, which frustratingly means that many pedestrians mistakenly consider them as such. It is considered bad form – not to say dangerous – to walk in a cycle lane when there is a pavement just next to it.

It is acceptable for two bikes to be cycling next to each other, as long as they fit in the cycle lane. The sound of a bell or horn behind you indicates that you should give way and temporarily move over.

CYCLING AROUND THE NETHERLANDS

Maps

Generally the Netherlands is very well signposted for bikes, although there are some areas where signposts suddenly seem to disappear, so it is still worth taking a map if you are embarking on a long-distance trip.

The minimum scale recommended for a bike map (*fietskaart*) is 1:100,000. Better maps are to a scale of 1:50,000. However, they cover smaller areas so, depending on how far you are going, you may need to buy more than one.

Nederland Fietsland (🖵 www.nederlandfietsland.nl) publishes a good country-wide bike map. Falk (🖵 www.falk.nl) and ANWB (🖵 www.anwb.nl) both publish regional *fietskaarten*.

Garmin (🖵 www.garmin-winkel.nl) offers digital satellite-based (GPS) bike maps – €119.50 for the whole of the Benelux countries. Onroute (🖵 www.onroute.nl) also offers bike maps of the Netherlands for Garmin devices, for €89.

You can download a free open-source map for your Garmin device (🖵 www.openfietsmap.nl). It has been developed by cycling enthusiasts and is therefore not bad at all.

The Dutch Cyclist Union (🖵 www.fietsersbond.nl), which campaigns for safer cycling, has a really neat route-planner online. You can choose fast or scenic routes, and there are lots of ways in which you can refine your search. The tool is in multiple languages. You can print out the track or save it as a file for your map-reading software.

A selection of other route planners:

- 🖵 www.nederlandfietsland.nl
- 🖵 fietsen.123.nl
- 🖵 route.anwb.nl

A free smartphone application for monitoring your cycling progress is available at 🖵 www.fietstijden.nl.

Signposts

Cycle routes in the Netherlands are generally very clearly marked (see box on p100).

White-and-red signposts indicate the direction and distance to nearby cities (image A).

The Royal Dutch Touring Club (ANWB) has also installed a series of distinctive mushroom signs (image B), which also indicate distance and direction to nearby towns.

Each section of the cycle network is marked with a number, known as a *fietsknooppunt*. Signs along the route indicate which direction you have to cycle to reach the next number (image C). Regional maps showing these numbers are displayed at intervals along cycle routes.

If you are travelling between cities, then you may want to follow the cross-country **LF routes** signposts (image D). These are generally the fastest and most direct way of travelling between two particular points, although the route may not always be the prettiest. See p99

Transport

for the full list of LF routes in the country.

Cycle accommodation

Cycle paths are never very far away from accommodation, such as campsites and B&Bs. Many of these are marked on cycle maps, although a great number are not.

One organisation that is worth knowing about is the foundation Vrienden op de Fiets (🖳 www.vriendenopdefiets.nl). This is a widespread network of people offering a room and breakfast for fellow cyclist for €19 or less. It costs €10 to join the foundation.

WALKING

Most cities can be easily navigated on foot.

In general, since cycling is so popular, few people walk very far unless it is for recreational purposes.

There are many picturesque walks around the country: across sandy dunes, in national parks and even knee-deep in mud (p257).

The official Dutch walking association is the Stichting Wandelplatform-LAW (🖳 wandelnet.nl). They have mapped out a series of walks across the country, which can be joined and exited at various points. Their website suggests walking itineraries.

The ANWB (🖳 www.anwb.nl) also has a book of walks in the Netherlands, available for purchase.

Every summer, the Netherlands hosts one of the largest walking events in Europe, a four-day march that begins and ends in the eastern city of Nijmegen (p236).

WATER TRANSPORT

The Netherlands is a country built on water. There are several natural waterways that snake their way through the country. Over the decades and centuries, these have been inter-connected by man-made canals, which became a crucial component in the development of the Netherlands' trading system.

Ferries are a common way of crossing rivers in the more rural areas, such as the Biesbosch. Such a ride usually costs no more than a euro or two (including bike), more when crossing by car.

It is also possible to use a ferry to reach Belgium. Regular ferries run between Vlissingen and Breskens, both in the southern province of Zeeland. From Vlissingen, connecting buses run to the Belgian towns of Bruges and Knokke-Heist. The ferry ticket costs €2.85 (one way) and it is possible to pay with *OV-chipkaart*. Check the website 🖳 www.veolia-transport.nl for ferry times. There is a train station just next to the ferry terminal in Vlissingen.

Eating & Drinking

The Netherlands doesn't tend to feature in the culinary lexicon of most food-lovers.

There is some truth in the fact that the Dutch are less preoccupied with the delights of cooking than their Mediterranean cousins, and this has unfortunately contributed to the disappointing quality of restaurants that are on offer in the country.

Many traditional Dutch dishes tend to be fairly heavy — good for stocking up on energy in anticipation of the winter months.

The colonial history of the country has had a strong influence on the country's cuisine. Most significantly, Indonesia and Suriname have leant a lively blend of dishes to the Dutch kitchen.

There is a wealth of Surinamese and Indonesian restaurants throughout the country. Very often these styles of cooking are confused with one another. This is understandable, since, despite being on opposite ends of the world, the two countries share similar influences. At the same time, though, there are many distinctions to be made.

Suriname is a small country on the east coast of Latin America. Despite its location, the biggest influences on its food have come from West Africa and India. This is because of the cheap labourers that the Dutch brought over to the country when they began to colonise it. As a result, you will find Suriname cooking a tasty blend of spices and herbs, which might put some in mind of Indian curries.

INDONESIAN DISHES

Nasi goreng — stir fried rice, which can include a variety of other ingredients including egg, chicken and prawns.

Gado-gado — vegetable salad served with a peanut sauce dressing.

Saté — chunks of meat (most commonly chicken, pork or beef) threaded on a skewer and coated in peanut sauce.

Rendang — a spicy coconut stew, usually made with beef.

Sambal — a sauce made from chili peppers, usually used as a condiment.

Loempia — Indonesian-style spring rolls.

Soempia — fried and crispy egg rolls.

Ketjap — the Indonesian version of soya sauce, usually sweet, rich and syrupy. Indonesian restaurants often serve a variety of *ketjap* dishes. *Babi* (pork) *ketjap* is very popular.

SURINAME DISHES

Pom — a type of root, similar to yam. It is often served in a stew with chicken or shrimps, and flavoured with citrus fruit.

Pastei — a creole-style chicken pot pie.

Dhal — a lentil stew with strong Indian influences.

Roti — grilled flatbread, also from India.

Soto — a traditional soup that consists of broth, meat and vegetables.

Bakbana — fried plantain with peanut sauce.

Goedangan — mixed vegetable salad with coconut dressing.

Bojo — a cake made with coconut and cassava.

CAT FOOD?

There are certain similarities between the British and Dutch kitchens. But there are big differences, too.

In the UK, a particular delicacy is a type of small fish called whiting. The Dutch, though, would never be caught eating such a fish — though they will happily guzzle whole herrings in a single slurp.

In the Netherlands whiting is actually reserved for cat food.

Indonesian cuisine also has some influence from India, though with strong Asian overtones. The style of cooking is similar to that found in places like China and Cambodia, which are nearby. The staple of Indonesian cooking is rice.

As an aside, you will notice that many Chinese restaurants in the Netherlands label themselves as 'Chinese and Indonesian'. This is to broaden their appeal, and an indication that the two types of cooking share much in common.

A particular favourite of Indonesian cuisine is the *rijsttafel* (rice table). This is a tray of many different dishes, accompanied by rice, and is a great way of exploring the wonderful tastes that the country has to offer.

DRINKS

The Dutch are big drinkers of beer. If you go in to a bar and ask for a beer (*een biertje*), you will almost certainly be served a lager (*pils*) of some description.

Without a doubt, the country's most successful export beer is Heineken. But there are other popular beers, too, such as Amstel, Grolsch and Hertog Jan. Jupiler, a Belgian beer, is also widely available.

Although the vast majority of beers consumed in the country are produced by only a few breweries — Heineken and Grolsch being the largest — some independent breweries offer beers with a more distinctive taste.

For something a bit stronger, you could try a Trappist beer, brewed by monks. There is only one Trappist brewery in the Netherlands, located not far from Tilburg in the south (p233). Six other Trappist breweries exist across the border in Belgium.

Other popular alcoholic beverages in the Netherlands include *advocaat* and *jenever*.

Advocaat is made from eggs, sugar and brandy. It is often eaten as a desert, sometimes as a substitute for custard. It goes well with ice-cream or Dutch pastries. Alcoholic content is usually around 15%.

Jenever is a much stronger alcoholic drink, with alcohol content of around between 35 and 40%. Distilled from grain and flavoured with juniper berries, it is thought to be where gin comes from. The rather charming legend to the drink is that it was originally intended as a medicine, but proved to be so vile — distillation having not evolved to the standard of today — that it had to be flavoured with herbs in order to mask the flavour. *Jenever* is often served ice-cold from the refrigerator, but can equally be enjoyed at room temperature.

In terms of non-alcoholic drinks, the Dutch are great tea-lovers, but don't usually add milk (as the English do).

Interestingly, though, the Dutch do consume a lot of milk outside of their tea. This is often their drink of choice for accompanying lunch or dinner and it is quite normal to order it in a café or eatery, when it

TYPICAL DUTCH FARE

If you are looking for something traditionally Dutch to try, then the following tasty titbits are on offer:

Bitterballen (📷 #74)— fried balls of meat and flour, usually served with mustard. Great as a bar snack with beer.

Kroketten (📷 #69) — like bitterballen, they are also made with a meat ragout and fried. The difference is that they are of an oblong shape (rather than round) and have a variety of different fillings, such as saté or goulash.

Patat / friet — Dutch chips, universally popular and often eaten with mayonnaise. In fact, if you ask for *patat met* (literally 'chips with') it will be assumed that you want them with mayonnaise. *Patatje oorlog* ('war chips') are chips smothered in a combination of mayonnaise, ketchup and raw onions.

Other fried food — the Dutch are big lovers of fried food, widely available at stations and in snack bars. Popular options include *frikandel* (a kind of fried hotdog), *bereklauw* (a fried meatball on a skewer), and *kaassoufle* (a fried cheese parcel).

Stamppot — mashed potato mixed with a seasonal vegetable such as kale, and usually served with a *rookworst* (sausage). A little like the British bubble-and-squeak.

Haring (📷 #70) — a herring fish, usually eaten raw with onions. The best time for enjoying herring is at the end of spring and the beginning of summer.

Pannenkoeken (📷 #71) — Dutch pancakes, more like French *crêpes* than the English variety. Served with a variety of savoury and sweet fillings. Even when eating a savoury *pannenkoek*, you are likely to be offered sweet syrup to accompany it.

Poffertjes — mini-pancakes, slightly spongy in texture. Often eaten with a coating of sugar or syrup.

Oliebollen (📷 #69) — deep-fried dumplings, usually served with a coating of sugar. A popular traditional dish for New Year's Eve.

Stroopwafel (📷 #69) — two wafer-like biscuits with a layer of treacle or syrup in the middle. Popular with tea. If you leave the *stroopwafel* on top of your cup of tea for a few minutes, the syrup will melt.

Dropje — Dutch liquorice, available in both sweet and salty form.

Uitsmijter — the Dutch fried egg and ham, sometimes served with cheese.

Erwtensoep — pea soup, popular in the winter.

Rookworst — Dutch smoked sausage.

Kibbeling (📷 #68) — deep-fried pieces of cod, eaten as a snack.

Frikandel — a deep-fried sausage.

BITTERBALLEN

These days, bitterballen are usually bought frozen from the supermarket or else ordered as a snack in a bar. But if you feel like a challenge, or want to be more certain of what goes into them, you could try making them yourself.

Ingredients

60 g butter or margarine
250 g minced beef
1 carrot, finely diced
1 onion, finely chopped
salt and pepper
1/2 tsp freshly-ground nutmeg
1 tbsp fresh lemon juice
2 tbsp parsley
100 g flour
75 g breadcrumbs
250 ml beef stock
1 egg, beaten
oil for frying

Method

Melt 15 g of the butter in a large frying pan over a moderate heat. Add the meat, carrots and onions. Once the meat is browned and the carrots are tender, drain in a colander. Place in a mixing bowl. Season with salt pepper, nutmeg, parsley and lemon juice. Stir to combine. Set aside. Melt the remaining butter in a saucepan and gradually stir in the flour to make a roux. Add the beef stock. Bring to the boil, then add to meat mixture. Stir to combine thoroughly. Chill the mixture for at least two hours. When the mixture has solidified, roll it into balls about 2.5 cm in diameter. Coat the balls in breadcrumbs, then egg. Fry the balls in a deep-bottomed pan for a few minutes, until golden brown. Drain on paper towels and serve immediately.

will almost always be fresh (rather than long-life).

Rooibos tea, a herbal drink, is especially popular, particularly in winter. Fresh mint tea (often with honey) is also widely drunk and available in cafés.

The Dutch version of caffè latte is *koffie verkeerd*, which literally means 'wrong coffee', since it is served with more milk than coffee.

MEALS

Breakfast

Breakfast is eaten first thing in the morning, shortly after waking up.

Bread is a popular component of breakfast, and is served with a variety of different toppings. It is not usually toasted. Cheese, cold meats such as ham, jam, honey and syrup are popular accompaniments.

A uniquely Dutch topping is *hagelslag*, which is very similar to the hundreds-and-thousands that the British sometimes use to decorate cakes. The Dutch will simply sprinkle these over a slice of bread, often with butter on to prevent the sprinkles from falling off.

Another type of food that is popular for breakfast is the *beschuit*, a hard and dry cookie that sailors used to take with them on long sea voyages during the 17th century.

Cereals with milk are also a popular way of starting the day.

For drinks, coffee and tea are both popular.

Lunch

The Dutch do not generally consider lunch a particularly significant meal. Since the Dutch tend to eat dinner fairly early (see next section), they prefer to have something lighter for lunch. This may be a soup, sandwich or salad — usually something easy to prepare and often uncooked.

One Dutch lunchtime favourite is *broodje met kaas* (which is simply a white or brown bread roll with a slice of cheese inside).

Herring or croquettes (see box on p105) are also often eaten at lunchtime. Croquettes are almost never home-made, even when ordered in a restaurant. They usually come from the best-known croquette producer, Van Dobben, and restaurants will often indicate this on the menu to show 'quality'.

In restaurants, croquettes will usually be sandwiched between two slices of bread. But they are also available on their own from vending machines, commonly found at railway stations.

The Dutch *tosti* is a popular light lunch or pub snack. This is typically a slice of ham and cheese between two slices of toasted bread.

A particular favourite for a hot lunch is an *uitsmijter* (see box p105).

The Dutch food culture explains why so many places sell sandwiches at lunch, but rarely offer the cheap lunchtime deals you might find in other countries.

Dinner

The Dutch dine early, with many families sitting down to supper by 6pm. Dinner is typically the main meal of the day for the Dutch, and so will usually be heavier than lunch, perhaps consisting of some sort of meat with an assortment of vegetables. *Stamppot* and hearty vegetable soups such as *erwtensoep* (see box on p105) are also popular for dinner. Dinner is often followed by a dessert and / or a cup of coffee. A popular dessert to finish off with is yogurt accompanied by fruit compote.

EATING OUT

With most Dutch leading such busy lives, it is not surprising that eating out has gained such popularity in recent years. Along any major high street or town centre, countless restaurants of varying quality jostle for customers. Although food from all over the world is on offer, there are some particularly Dutch eating and drinking establishments to look out for.

A Dutch **eetcafé** (pronounced 'ate café") is a little like a French bistro, usually serving reasonably-priced food in informal surroundings. Many *eetcafés* serve traditional Dutch fare, such as *erwetensoep* and *uitsmijter*, whilst others are seeking to redefine themselves as a more classy establishment.

STAMPPOT

Traditionally served as peasant food, this is nonetheless a hearty meal, great for those winter evenings.

Ingredients

1 kg potatoes, peeled and diced
350 g kale (or other leafy green), trimmed and sliced
250 g lardon (cubed bacon)
2 onions, peeled and finely diced
1 bay leaf
salt and pepper
1 smoked sausage (optional)
120 ml milk
15 g butter

Method

Put the potatoes, bay leaf and a pinch of salt in a large pan. Add just enough cold water to cover (but no more). Bring to the boil. Cover and leave to simmer gently for 25 minutes. Meanwhile, steam the smoked sausage over a pan of water. Alternatively, if the sausage comes in a vacuum-sealed package, you can simply add this to the water that the potatoes are boiling in. Once the potatoes are cooked, remove the bay leaf. Drain and reserve 250 ml of the water. Return the potatoes and reserved water to the pot. Add the kale and continue cooking for a further 7 to 10 minutes, until the kale is soft and turns a dark green colour. Remove the pot of vegetables from the heat. Add the lardon mixture, milk, butter, salt and pepper to taste and mash. Slice the smoked sausage (if using) and serve alongside the *stamppot*.

A **brown café** (*bruin café*) has more of a pub feel to it, serving beer and other drinks, as well as snacks like *bitterballen* and occasionally fuller meals. Brown cafés are so called because of the dark wood that traditionally furnishes the place. These establishments tend to have a friendly, laid back atmosphere. They frequently stay open late, sometimes until well past the early hours.

Market stalls are popular places to eat fried seafood snacks, the most popular being Kibbeling or herring guzzled whole (📷 #70).

A **frituur/snack bar** sells chips, as well as other fried titbits such as *frikandel* and *kroketten*.

Food vending machines (*automatiek*) are found throughout the Netherlands, particularly at stations (📷 #72). The Dutch often refer to them as '*uit de muur eten*' ('food from the wall'). Bizarrely, many of them are not physically attached to a particular shop, so you don't usually know where the food comes from. Hot fried snacks, such as *kroketten*, are often sold in this way.

FINDING A RESTAURANT

The authors have spent a long time researching restaurants for this guidebook, and have taken care to only include those restaurants that offer decent service or value for money, or are a little bit special.

If you want to find out about the quality of a new restaurant, or one that is not mentioned in this guidebook, two websites that are worth consulting are 🖥 www.iens.nl and 🖥 www.eet. nu (both in Dutch).

PRICE CLASSIFICATION

The price classification that is used in this guidebook is based on the average cost of a main course, compared to other restaurants in the country:

💲	Cheap (if a main course is less than €10).
💲💲	Moderate (if a main course costs between €10 and €20).
💲💲💲	Expensive (if a main course costs more than €20).

CHEAP EATS

With a little bit of planning and patience you can eat well for half of the price. In the last couple of years, the website 🖥 www. groupon.nl (only in Dutch) has really taken off. It offers a deal every day, with at least a 50% discount. The offer must be bought on the day that it is offered and can be used any time afterwards, up until its expiry date.

Dutch **sandwich shops** (`broodjeszaak`) are all over the Netherlands, particular popular at lunchtime.

Many restaurants offer **take-away services**, but you will often pay the same price as you would to eat in (plus delivery). To find restaurants that offer take-away, consult one of the following websites: 🖥 www. thuisbezorgd.nl and 🖥 www.justeat. nl.

Catering in the Netherlands is much more common than in many other European countries. The Dutch make widespread use of catering for small parties at home and to celebrate special days like Christmas and Sinterklaas. Consequently, many restaurants in the country offer some form of catering service.

Remember that the Dutch eat early and therefore the kitchen of many restaurants will also close early. Making reservations for restaurants is common. If you turn up after 7pm without a reservation, you may not get served. You may also find it harder to book a table after 9pm.

WHERE TO SHOP FOR FOOD

Dutch supermarkets are well-stocked and sell a wide range of products, including many from abroad. Meat and fish, though, can be very disappointing. If you are happy to spend a few euros more, you are much better off finding a local butcher for meat. Fish is often of better quality, and cheaper, if you go to the market. Supermarket fruit and vegetables are okay, but you will find much more variety and prices will drop dramatically if you go to the market.

For a list of markets, see the relevant town sections in this book or check 🖥 www.hollandsemarkten.nl.

More tips about shopping can be found on p128.

With a population of a little more than half a million, The Hague is the third-largest city in the Netherlands (after Amsterdam and Rotterdam).

The Hague has the unusual distinction of being home to the Dutch government and parliament, despite not being a capital city. The Supreme Court of Arbitration, the Council of State and most embassies also reside within the city. The Dutch royal family have one of their official residences here, too.

International organisations with offices in The Hague include the International Court of Justice, the International Criminal Court, Europol, Eurojust, and the European Patent Office, as well as big companies such as Aegon, Shell and ING

Despite the size of The Hague, and its importance as the decision-making centre of the country, the city has a surprisingly calm, relaxed and unhurried feel to it.

The city is home to a scattering of educational institutions — such as the Royal Conservatory for Music and Dance, the Royal Academy of Art, the University of Applied Sciences and a branch of Leiden University's law school — but it doesn't give you quite the same feeling of liveliness that you would experience in the university towns of nearby Leiden and Delft.

The Hague makes a valiant effort in terms of nightlife, although it is never going to compete with the crazy insanity that afflicts Amsterdam. There is a wide range of bars and clubs throughout the city, each pulsating with their own particular vibe and energy.

One main attraction of The Hague is the easy access to beautifully sandy beaches, such as

Scheveningen in the northwestern part of the city and Kijkduin to the west.

The official name of The Hague is 's Gravenhage. This is a contraction of *des Graven Hage*, which means 'the count's wood' and was the term used to refer to the city from the 15th century onwards. Although 's Gravenhage may be the town's official name, it is rarely used other than in official documents and most people know the city simply as 'Den Haag'.

The Hague has two main railway stations. **Den Haag Centraal** (CS) is located northeast of the city, whilst **Den Haag Hollands Spoor** (HS) is located to the east. The two stations are about a 20-minute walk from one another, and are close to the city centre.

Intercity trains calling at The Hague will usually stop at one of the two stations, although not generally both. The stations have good public transport connections. Trains and trams shuttle frequently between the two.

Den Haag Centraal is located in a nicer area, but Hollands Spoor has the advantage that trains run throughout the night to both Schiphol airport and Amsterdam — useful for that early-morning flight or late-night revelling.

Other stations are **Den Haag Laan Van Noi** — located between The Hague and Voorburg, about 2.5 km from Centraal — and **Den Haag Mariahoeve** — just next to the headquarters of Dutch insurance company 'Aegon', about 4.5 km from the city centre.

The real heart of the city is the area around the **Binnenhof**, which in Dutch means 'inner court'. This

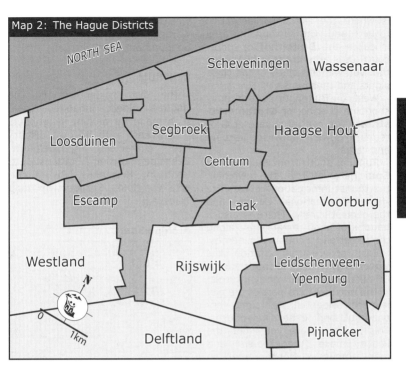

is where the Dutch Parliament is to be found. The surrounding area is called the **Buitenhof** or 'outer court'. It is around these two areas that you will find many of the city's sights and museums.

West of Buitenhof is the busy shopping precinct of **Grotemarktstraat**. The central square of Grotemarkt is well-known for its bars and cafés.

Running south from Buitenhof is **Spui**. Here you'll find the town hall, the tourist information centre, The Hague International Centre, and the central library. There is also a handful of good restaurants along the street and a couple of cinemas.

East of Centraal Station lies **Voorburg**, where the International Criminal Court is currently located.

The northwestern part of the city is more residential, with some very beautiful and expensive houses. This is also where you'll find the Peace Palace (*Vredespaleis*) and many embassies. Not the American or British ones, though — these are located closer to the centre (p295).

The Hague is divided into eight districts (Map 2, p110): Centrum, Scheveningen, Haagse Hout, Escamp, Laak, Loosduinen, Segbroek, Leidschenveen-Ypenburg. Each of these is divided into a number of neighbourhoods (Map 3, p111).

The Hague is also considered to be part of a contiguous block of eight other municipalities, which are together known as Haaglanden: Zoetermeer, Westland, Delft, Leidschendam-Voorburg, Pijnacker-Nootdorp, Rijswijk, Wassenaar and Midden-Delfland. An efficient public transport system means that people often work in one of these municipalities whilst living in another.

Generally speaking, the most prosperous neighbourhoods are in the northwest of the city. Other wealthy ones include Statenkwartier, Belgisch Park, Marlot, Benoordenhout and Centrum.

CENTRUM

The district Centrum is The Hague's oldest inhabited area. It is made up of nine neighbourhoods, each with its own distinctive character: Archipelbuurt, Zeeheldenkwartier, Stationsbuurt, Centrum, Kortenbos, Rivierenbuurt, Voorhout, Schilderswijk and Transvaal.

Archipelbuurt

The residential neighbourhood of Archipelbuurt took shape between 1880 and 1900. It was here that many former colonialists took up residence when they returned home after serving abroad for many years. You will find, therefore, that many of the streets in the area have been named after some of the thousands of islands that make up the Indonesian archipelago, which was the country's most important colony.

Much as you'd expect, Archipelbuurt is typified by its wide avenues lined with large houses. Many of these buildings are now offices. More modern ones have also been built on the south side of the area.

Archipelbuurt is generally a well-off area, and the majority of inhabitants live in luxury apartments or town houses, many of which are in neo-renaissance style.

These dwellings are located not far away from shops and restaurants, making for an exciting cosmopolitan atmosphere whilst retaining the shy charm of suburbia.

The neighbourhood's history is preserved in many landmarks, including the Jewish and Roman Catholic cemeteries on the southwestern edge of town.

The beautiful green Scheveningen wood (p162) borders the area. The Bankastraat is one of the busiest streets in Archipelbuurt, full of shops, restaurants, and bars. Surinamestraat is one of the neighbourhood's oldest streets and retains a lot of its original buildings.

Zeeheldenkwartier

Zeeheldenkwartier is a favoured region of the city for well-off Dutch and expats. It is also home to a thriving and artistic ecclesiastical community.

The neat squares and pristine streets are full of cafés, restaurants, foreign food stores, studios and art galleries.

The area is well-served by public transport, which run to both main train stations.

In July each year, Zeeheldenkwartier plays host to a popular family-friendly community festival (💻 www.zeeheldenfestival. nl), which is held in the Prins Hendrikplein.

In the summer, Anna Paulownaplein becomes a favourite spot for after-work drinks. Piet Heinstraat and Prins Hendrikstraat are the places to go for foreign shops and restaurants. For particularly pretty residential streets, take a look at Trompstraat and Hugo de Grootstraat.

Stationsbuurt

Despite attempts to improve the area, Stationsbuurt still suffers from high unemployment and a below-average level of income.

This is the location of the Hollands Spoor mainline railway station, dating from 1843. It is also where you'll find the city's red light district.

The neighbourhood is definitely not the prettiest part of the city, and is not particularly family-orientated.

It's true that Stationsbuurt has a reputation for being somewhat unsavoury, particularly late at night or in the early hours of the morning. But the area is good for those on a budget, and handy for being in close proximity to the heart of the city.

There are a couple of prettier locations, with canals and good bars, such as De Paas (p182) on Bierkade. There are some nice bakeries along Stationsweg.

Centrum

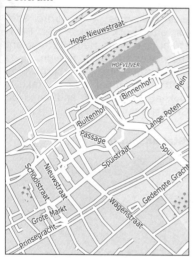

The true centre of The Hague is both residential and commercial; houses and apartment buildings mingle with shops, department stores and offices.

Visitors are drawn to the area for the lively atmosphere, the number of shops and other amenities (the town hall, the central library and The Hague International Centre) and an abundance of decent restaurants. It is also the place where you'll find many of the city's most interesting buildings, centuries-old structures nestling in-amongst the new.

Grote Markt, with its many bars and terraces, is one of the main meeting points for drinks. Plein, on the eastern edge of the area, is another.

Spuistraat, Grotemarktstraat and Wagenstraat are popular for shops. Wagenstraat is where you will find Chinatown.

De Passage (📷 #30) is one of the oldest covered malls in Europe and home to many specialist shops. It is the only remaining example of a neo-renaissance glass-roofed mall in the country.

Another interesting building in the area is the Snoeptrommel, or 'The Sting' (📷 #29), a round and colourful edifice that is now home to a clothes shop and café.

Kortenbos

Kortenbos was once dominated by the South Holland Brewery, whose manufacturing plant sprawled across the district. But the brewery was demolished in the 1970s, and new social housing sprang up to takes its place.

In Kortenbos's wealthy Hofkwartier section you will find Noordeinde Palace, the official place of work of the reigning monarch. The Hofkwartier lies between large commercial and residential streets: the Hoogstraat and the Prinsestraat. It is a busy area with boutiques, speciality shops, bars, restaurants and cafés.

Other areas of interest include Annastraat, with its many art nouveau buildings, and the Groenmarkt, with much older-style architecture and home of the former city hall. Hartogstraat is also interesting, with its neat 17th century houses, is another interesting place to visit.

Kortenbos is also where you will find Hofje van Nieuwkoop (📷 #13), one of the most impressive *hofjes* (149) in the city.

Noordeinde is an upmarket shopping street with art galleries and cafés.

Rivierenbuurt

Hemmed in-between railways and thoroughfares, Rivierenbuurt is a surprisingly quiet part of the city. Most of the buildings date from the early 20th century, and are built in the neo-renaissance style with brick façades and arched windows.

Some of the older buildings, though, have recently been demolished to make way for new ones — part of an urban renewal effort that is driven by private residents' own initiatives.

One of the chief advantages of this area is that it is close to both the city centre and the two main railway stations.

Voorhout

Voorhout is one of the oldest parts of the city centre, with evidence of a thriving settlement going back as far as the 13th century.

These days, the area has some lovely old buildings, a couple of nice Dutch bars, the Diligentia Theatre (p166) and the 14th century Kloosterkerk. Just next to the Kloosterkerk is the distinctive 15th century Pagehuis, which once accommodated young men training to be attendants to the royal family.

You'll also find the Escher Museum (p139) here, housed in the beautiful former palace of Queen Juliana.

There are a scattering of embassies in the area, including the British, American and Swiss ones.

One of the prettiest streets in the city is located here — Denneweg — with its beautiful buildings, atmospheric restaurants and charming cafés. This is principally the domain of well-off Dutch and expats.

You'll find many independent and interesting shops nearby. Frederikstraat is full of upmarket shops.

Orientation

In the summer, Voorhout is a popular place for outdoor sculpture exhibitions (p140).

Schilderswijk

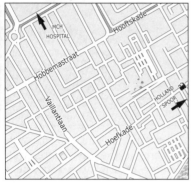

Schilderswijk is one of the largest neighbourhoods of The Hague's city centre.

The area used to have a poor reputation. Recently, though, the nearest neighbourhood to the centre, called Schilderbuurt-West, has visibly smartened itself up, and an increasing number of well-off Dutch and expats are deliberately choosing to live here. Good bakeries and cheap barbers can be found along Valliantlaan.

A city farm, plus a few children's playgrounds, are to be found in the area.

Well-stocked Turkish supermarkets and The Hague's main market are located nearby.

Schilderbuurt-West is conveniently close to the centre of the city and well-served by public transport, yet it is cheaper than the more up-market areas surrounding it.

The area is very near to MCH Westeinde, one of the main hospitals of the city.

Transvaal

Transvaal is a mostly residential area, although it is also the location of The Hague's main market (p133). You'll also find some cheaper supermarkets here, such as Lidl, and Hobbemanstraat, which boasts many independent shops, hairdressers and supermarkets.

Transvaal's population largely consists of ethnic minorities from Suriname, Turkey and Morocco. There are only a few green spaces and the residential buildings here are mostly social housing.

The area is generally safe during the day, but has a bad reputation for levels of disturbance and petty crime.

HAAGSE HOUT

Haagse Hout means 'The Woods of The Hague'. True to its name, the area is green and wooded. It enjoys a low crime rate, a higher-than-average income and a greater proportion of older residents. This area is popular with families who want to raise children in safe surroundings, with lots of green spaces and good schools. Haagse Hout is divided into four municipal sectors: Benoordenhout, Bezuidenhout, Mariahoeve en Marlot and Haagse Bos.

Bezuidenhout includes the Beatrixkwartier financial district and the Centraal Station. It has plenty of green areas nearby. One of the main thoroughfares, Theresiastraat, is a pleasant and lively street, full of shops and restaurants. The British School of The Hague is located here. Laan van Nieuw Oost-Indië, which reaches Voorburg (p189), is also a very pleasant area in which to live, well-connected to the city centre by tram and bus.

Benoordenhout is a fairly quiet neighbourhood, and one of The Hague's more expensive ones. It is close to the city centre, with residential buildings nestling in wooded areas.

There are six areas: Nassaubuurt, Uilennest, Duinzigt, Waalsdorp, Arendsdorp and Van Hoytemaplein.

The area is popular with members of the international community.

One of the neighbourhood's most attractive spots is Clingendael Park. It has a distinctive English feel but it is known for its Japanese garden (p153).

Prominent buildings in the neighbourhood include the Shell complex and the Esso tower.

Haagse Bos extends from the centre of The Hague near Malieveld to the city of Wassenaar (p193). The neighbourhood contains the remnants of a forest that once stretched all the way to Alkmaar in the east of the country. Haagse Bos is situated conveniently close to the A12 motorway, providing a speedy exit from The Hague for commuters.

Mariahoeve en Marlot is known for its expansive parkland. It is divided in to two areas.

Mariahoeve has a broader income-range, reflected in the variety of homes there, and you'll see both stylish villas and apartment buildings jostling alongside one another. There are office buildings and a shopping mall close to the residential area.

Marlot is the more prosperous part of the neighbourhood; the houses here are villas, large farmhouses and other expensive residences.

SCHEVENINGEN

Scheveningen (see Map 6 on p126) has been famous as a seaside resort ever since the early 19th century.

Its sandy beach slopes down towards the North Sea, and locals and tourists alike enjoy walking along the shore or the long promenade. You can also visit a lighthouse or you can stroll through the magnificent windswept dunes.

A number of popular events take place in the area, including the winter swim held on New Year's Day (p87), Flag Day (p160), the arrival of Sinterklaas (p79) and firework displays throughout the summer. There are also regular water-based events, ranging from fishing to windsurfing and sailing.

Scheveningen is divided into several areas: Scheveningen, Duinoord, Statenkwartier, Belgisch Park, Oostduinen, Duindorp, Zorgvliet, Van Stolkpark and Westbroekpark.

The neighbourhood of **Scheveningen** is right behind the seawall. This area includes the central Scheveningen village, the old port of Havenkwartier and Seinpostduinkwartier on the beach.

In the summer months, bars and restaurants open all along the edge of the beach.

Some houses date from the early 20th century when development began, but newer apartments and buildings have also gone up over the years. Plans for the redevelopment of the area, particularly in the Havenkwartier, include the demolition of several social-housing

Orientation

estates, making way for more up-scale residences and commercial concerns.

Statenkwartier is situated between the sandy beaches of Scheveningen and the city centre. Stately mansions in the art nouveau style stretch along wide, tree-lined avenues. The largest houses can be found on the edge of the district, along with broader streets and larger squares. Other neighbourhoods have narrower streets and smaller houses.

Many of the larger houses have been made into offices, although their external appearance has not changed.

The area has a distinctly youthful population, and a large number of expatriate residents. There are many trendy bars and restaurants here. This is also where you'll find the miniature model city of Madurodam (p152).

The main streets in the neighbourhood are the Frankenslag and Frederik Hendriklaan, a prominent shopping street.

Oostduinen is a quiet area that borders Scheveningen's busy centre. Most of it is given over to a nature reserve, which runs along the coast, although there is also a small residential area. The reserve is a great spot for long cycle rides and walks.

While the coastal village of **Duindorp** has been around for 700 years, the sub-district that grew around it in the last century was originally built for the local fishermen.

The area is one of the most picturesque in The Hague, thanks largely to the architecture of its houses, which range from mansions and detached villas in the centre to more modest homes on the fringes.

Duinoord has a bohemian, cosmopolitan feel to it. It is popular with young people and the international community, since it is close to several international organisations. There are a few shopping streets, most notably Reinkinstraat. At the centre of the district is Sweelinck-plein, a public square bordered by wide streets and three-storey brick houses. Other types of residence in Duinoord include portico houses, used as apartments, and so-called 'basement houses', which consist of a basement and ground floor, with an entrance for each.

Like many parts of The Hague's city centre, Duinoord is in the midst of urban renewal.

More than a thousand units have already been demolished and hundreds of new homes built in their place. During this restructuring period, emphasis has also been placed on creating public spaces. One of the forthcoming projects in the district is the creation of a play area for children.

Belgisch Park, one of the most prosperous areas of The Hague, was originally built in the 19th century by a tram company, so that there would be more passengers for the local trams.

Many grand houses were built just before and after the second world war around the district's oldest part, the Belgian Square. These lovely houses took the form of large villas with wide wooden verandas, set among the trees. They were constructed in a wide range of different styles: old Dutch, baroque, gothic, renaissance and art nouveau.

Belgisch Park has been partly renovated in recent years, with a fairly new apartment tower giving the northwestern end a new look

Van Stolkpark is another villa park in Scheveningen, just next to Scheveningen Bosjes. A large pond lies sheltering behind the trees.

The first villas here were built at the turn of the 20th century, although the area changed significantly over the subsequent decades.

Many mansions and villas have been converted into offices and schools. Other villas have been altered into expensive and upmarket apartments. Much of the green space has disappeared. Some park areas have been paved over to create parking lots. A restaurant and inn that once stood near the Van Stolkpark pond is now a sports complex.

Westbroekpark takes its name from the wonderful park that makes up most of it (p162). It is a peaceful area located between Madurodam and the centre of Scheveningen.

It has a similar feel to Belgisch Park, but with fewer residents. There are many green spaces around the area's expensive houses. A large proportion of its residents are elderly Dutch, many of whom come from outside The Hague.

The district is known for the hundreds of varieties of roses in its gardens, from miniature blooms to climbing vines. New specimens are sent to the park every year from all over the world.

Thick with trees, **Zorgvliet** was built in the early 20th century, although it was badly damaged during the second world war.

Today, many of its large houses are used as ambassadors' residences. Some international institutions, such as the International Criminal Tribunal for the former Yugoslavia (ICTY), are also here.

This is where you'll find the Peace Palace (p152), one of The Hague's most distinctive buildings, housing the Permanent Court of Arbitration, the International Court of Justice, and The Hague Academy of International Law.

ESCAMP

This is one of the older areas of The Hague, although it has seen a fair bit of new development in recent years.

Escamp is divided into seven smaller districts, separated from each other by large thoroughfares and green tracts of land: Bouwlust, Leyenburg, Moerwijk, Morgenstond, Rustenburg-Oostbroek, Vrederust, Wateringse Veld.

Most of the houses are pre-war, although the districts of Morgenstond and Bouwlust are newer.

Much of **Bouwlust** was constructed during the 1950s in response to the needs of an increasing population. It is mostly residential with some green spaces.

Leyenburg is a quiet neighbourhood mostly made up of small houses and apartment buildings. The most noticeable building in the area is Leyenburg Hospital. Just next to Leyenburg is Zuiderpark, a sprawling 100-hectare area of parkland (p162). Another green recreational area is the Uithof, which has tennis courts, an ice-skating rink and an indoor ski area.

Moerwijk is located south of Zuiderpark (p162). The district is a melting pot of different ethnic groups, particularly Moroccans, Surinamese, Antilleans and Turks. Moerwijk has its own railway station, designed by the Dutch architect Willem Dudok, with regular trains to The Hague, Rotterdam, Dordrecht and Breda.

Morgenstond is known for its shopping centre. This area was part of Loosduinen until 1923.

Rustenburg-Oostbroek once belonged to the district of Loosduinen. It has a population of nearly

Orientation

20,000, roughly half of whom are foreigners. Housing here consists mainly of small apartments.

Vrederust is a poor neighbourhood, mainly residential.

Wateringse Veld is a newer residential area of The Hague and fairly well-off. The area was formerly used for horticulture.

SEGBROEK

Segbroek has a diverse population and its neighbourhoods vary from prosperous Vogelwijk, with its large and expensive houses, to Regentessekwartier and the Valkenboskwartier, where many residents live in social housing. Segbroek has a higher-than-average population density.

Some of the more popular public areas in Segbroek are its shopping streets Fahrenheitstraat, Thomsonlaan and Thomsonplein.

Valkenboskwartier runs between Weimarstraat, Laan van Meerdervoort and Beeklaan. The district was intended for housing the well-paid worker. There are many beautiful houses and streets in the neighbourhood. The northern part of the district — around Weimarstraat and the upper half of Fahrenheitstraat — has a nice shopping area. The southern part is more downmarket.

Regentessekwartier is considered a pleasant neighbour to live in. It is particularly attractive for young families because of the relatively low cost of housing. Many of the building façades are in neo-renaissance style.

Bomen en Bloemenburrt is a mostly residential area. It remains fairly quiet and has managed to sidestep the disruption brought about by urban redevelopment. Recently, a growing number of businesses have moved into the area,

with residential apartments giving way to office space.

Vogelwijk was created as a garden district. Its name translates as 'bird neighbourhood', and indeed you'll find that many of the streets and public areas are named after different varieties of birds. The district is still very green, with a number of parks lying between the broad avenues.

Vogelwijk has a high number of older residents, and incomes are generally fairly high.

There are many public areas for recreation, sports matches and cultural events such as concerts.

Many of the houses were built in the 1920s, although a number of these were destroyed during the second world war. Today, Vogelwijk has a very active neighbourhood association, and urban renewal has become a priority.

Part of Vogelwijk lies along the North Sea coast. Its beach, the Zuiderstrand, is popular among visitors and locals alike for its white sands and clean water.

LAAK

Laak, the smallest of The Hague's districts, takes its name from a small peat river that runs through the centre. It is divided into just two areas: Laakkwartier and Binckhorst.

Laakkwartier is a fairly green area popular with immigrants and students from the nearby Hague University. The children of parents that have settled in the neighbourhood are starting to move away in search of better opportunities, and so the ethnic mix of the area is gradually changing.

Binckhorst is a predominantly commercial and industrial area. Part of it is given over to office blocks that house large organisations such as telecoms giant KPN and the International Criminal Court. You will find such things as car junkyards in the northern part of the neighbourhood. There is also a small residential district.

LOOSDUINEN

Loosduinen is a former village, now part of The Hague. The current area is much smaller than the village and consists mainly of residential districts. The main attraction of this area is the seaside resort of Kijkduin (p156), with its dunes and pretty seascape. Bloemendaal, a large psychiatric hospital complex, is also situated here.

LEIDSCHENVEEN-YPENBURG

This is a relatively new residential area, built on the site of an old airfield. The airfield became a military airbase after the second world war, but was permanently closed in 1992. Five years later, construction of the new neighbourhood began.

The A12 motorway bisects the district into the quarters of Hoornwijk and Ypenburg in the southwest and Forepark and Leidschenveen in the northeast. Rolling fields, streams and farmland run along the A12.

The neighbourhood is generally quiet. It has an urban section with office buildings and apartment blocks, as well as more rural residences.

The area is predominantly Dutch, although a large number of residents originally came from outside The Hague.

▶ See p192 for more information about Ypenburg.

Orientation

Orientation

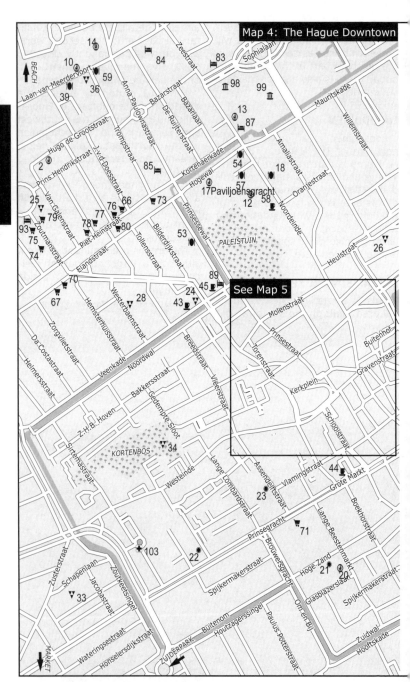

Map 4: The Hague Downtown

See Map 5

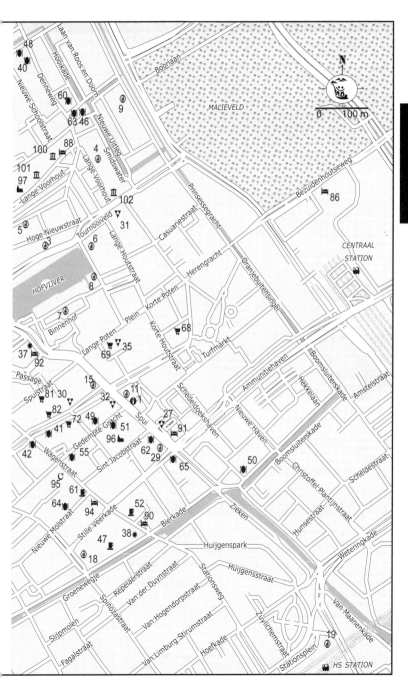

The Hague Downtown

Information ❶
1. Tourist office & library	INFORMATION

What to see ❷
2. Authors' former house	OTHER
3. Bredius Museum	MUSEUM
4. Escher Museum	MUSEUM
5. Hague Sculpture	OTHER
6. Historical Museum	MUSEUM
7. Knights' Hall	BUILDING
8. Mauritshuis	ART
9. Meermanno	MUSEUM
10. Mesdag Museum	MUSEUM
11. New Town Hall	BUILDING
12. Noordeinde Palace	BUILDING
13. Panorama Mesdag	ART
14. Peace Palace	BUILDING
15. Poster Gallery	ART
16. Red Light District	OTHER
17. Royal Stables	BUILDING
18. Spinoza's House	MUSEUM
19. Strijkijzer Hofwijckstraat	BUILDING
20. Van Kleef Distillery	MUSEUM

Hofjes ●
21. Geefhuisjes	HOFJE
22. Geesthof	HOFJE
23. 't Hooftshofje	HOFJE

What to do ✌
24. Aerobicworld	GYM
25. Bikram Yoga	YOGA
26. Diligentia	THEATRE
27. Dr Anton Philips Zaal	CONCERTS
28. Fit 2000	GYM
29. Filmhuis	CINEMA
30. Healthcity	GYM
31. Koninklijke Schouwburg	THEATRE
32. Pathé	CINEMA
33. Stadsboerderij	CITY FARM
34. Table-tennis	SPORT
35. Tango Centro	DANCE
36. Van der Meulen-Wesseling	DANCE

Tours ●
37. ProDemos	RIDDERZAAL
38. The Ooievaart Foundation	BOAT TOUR

Where to eat & drink ⑩ ⚑
39. 3 Stones	AFRICAN
40. Alexander	SEAFOOD
41. Amazing Oriental	CHINESE
42 Australian Homemade	ICE-CREAM
43. Baklust	CAFÉ
44. Boterwaag	BAR
45. Café De Bieb	BAR
46. Casa Caironi	ITALIAN
47. De Paas	CAFÉ
48. De Wankele Tafel	VEGETARIAN
49. Eazie	CHINESE
50. El Barrio	SPANISH
51. Fat Kee	CHINESE

52. Jazz Bodega est est est	BAR
53. Kiraku	JAPANESE
54. Le Gone	FRENCH
55. Little V	VIETNAMESE
56. Maharani	INDIAN
57. Mazie	FRENCH
58. O'casey's	BAR
59. Rhodos	GREEK
60. San Telemo	ARGENTINIAN
61. Scallywags	CAFÉ
62. Spize	THAI
63. Taj Mahal	INDIAN
64. 't Syndicaat	EETCAFÉ
65. Warung Mini	SURINAME

Shopping ☂
66. Alaska	RUSSIAN
67. Albert Heijn XL	SUPERMARKET
68. Alien Brewing Company	BEER
69. American Book Center	BOOKS
70. De Ruijter Kaasmarkt	CHEESE
71. Emmaus	SECOND-HAND
72. Hema	DEPARTMENT STORE
73. Italy	ITALIAN
74. Kelly's	BRITISH
75. Karolinka	POLISH
76. Kringloop	SECOND-HAND
77. Marius	WINE
78. Matroesjka	RUSSIAN
79. Ponto de Encontro	PORTUGUESE
80. Rutten	FRUIT & VEG
81. Selexyz	BOOKSHOP
82. V&D	DEPARTMENT STORE

Where to sleep ⚑
83. Carlton Ambassador	HOTEL
84. Court Garden	HOTEL
85. Delta	HOTEL
86. Hampshire Hotel — Babylon	HOTEL
87. Hilton	HOTEL
88. Hotel des Indes	HOTEL
89. La Ville	HOTEL
90. Maff Appartement	HOTEL
91. Mercure	HOTEL
92. Novotel	HOTEL
93. Sebel	HOTEL
94. Wahdo	HOTEL

Religious ☪ ☧
95. Al-Akasa	MOSQUE
96. Nieuwe Kerk	CHURCH
97. Kloosterkerk	CHURCH

Embassies ⚏
98. Canada	EMBASSY
99. Italian	EMBASSY
100. Spain	EMBASSY
101. United Kingdom	EMBASSY
102. United States	EMBASSY

Hospitals ✚
103. MCH Westeinde	HOSPITAL

Orientation

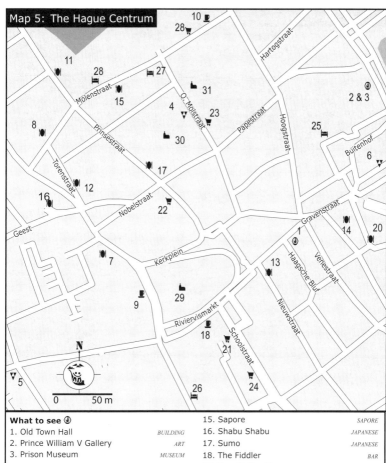

Map 5: The Hague Centrum

Orientation

What to see ⓐ
1. Old Town Hall — *BUILDING*
2. Prince William V Gallery — *ART*
3. Prison Museum — *MUSEUM*

What to do ⓥ
4. Dansschool Universala — *DANCE*
5. LingGan — *YOGA*
6. Pathé — *CINEMA*

Where to eat & drink 🍴🍺
7. Bodega La Riojana — *SPANISH*
8. Catering Per Tutti — *ITALIAN*
9. Cheesecake Company — *CAFÉ*
10. Coffee Company — *CAFÉ*
11. Dayang — *INDONESIAN*
12. Florencia — *ICE-CREAM*
13. Genki Tei — *JAPANESE*
14. Los Argentinos — *ARGENTINIAN*
15. Sapore — *SAPORE*
16. Shabu Shabu — *JAPANESE*
17. Sumo — *JAPANESE*
18. The Fiddler — *BAR*
19. Very Italian Pizza — *ITALIAN*

Shopping 🛒
20. Chez Nicole — *FRENCH FOOD*
21. De Snuffel — *CARNIVAL*
22. En Garde — *KITCHEN TOOLS*
23. Michel — *PÂTISSERIE*
24. Stanley & Livingstone — *BOOKSHOP*

Where to sleep 🛏
21. Corona — *HOTEL*
22. Ibis — *HOTEL*
23. Paleis — *HOTEL*
24. Park — *HOTEL*

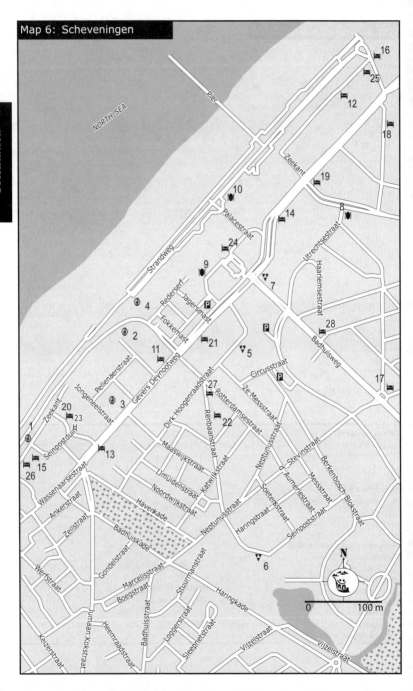

Map 6: Scheveningen

Scheveningen

What to see 👁

1. Fairytale Sculptures by the Sea   *SCULPTURE*
2. Images by the Sea   *MUSEUM*
3. Scheveningen Museum   *MUSEUM*
4. Sea Life   *AQUARIUM*

What to do ⛋

5. AFAS Circustheater   *THEATRE*
6. De Blinkerd   *SWIMMING POOL*
7. Pathé   *CINEMA*

Where to eat & drink 🍴

9. Bombay Palace   *INDIAN*
9. India Palace   *INDIAN*
10. Strandclub Doen   *SEAFOOD*

Where to sleep 🛏

11. Albion   *HOTEL*
12. Aquarius   *HOTEL*
13. Badhotel   *HOTEL*
14. Bella Vista   *HOTEL*
15. Boulevard   *HOTEL*
16. Carlton   *HOTEL*
17. Corel   *HOTEL*
18. Duinzicht   *HOTEL*
19. Europa   *HOTEL*
20. Hage   *HOTEL*
21. Ibis   *HOTEL*
22. Mimosa   *HOTEL*
23. Noordzee   *HOTEL*
24. Steigenberger Kurhaus   *HOTEL*
25. Strandhotel   *HOTEL*
26. Strandzicht   *HOTEL*
27. 't Sonnehuys   *HOTEL*
28. Witte Huys   *HOTEL*

Orientation

OPENING HOURS

Most shops in the centre of The Hague are open from 10am until 6pm Tuesdays to Saturdays. They tend to have a later start on Mondays: from 11am, with some only opening in the afternoon. Shops are open on Sundays. The larger stores may be open in the morning, but most tend to only open at noon.

There is late-night shopping in the city centre every Thursday (until 9pm) and every Friday during the summer months at the Palace Promenade in Scheveningen (until 10pm).

Supermarkets in the Netherlands have very convenient opening times. Most of the bigger ones are open daily from 8am to 8pm. Some are open even later, until 10pm. Hours on Sunday tend to be reduced, with most supermarkets not opening until at least 10am (sometimes later) and closing by 6pm.

Markets are held throughout the week in different locations of The Hague, from 8am to around 4 or 5pm, although the selection of food produce is generally better in the morning.

Banks operate different opening times — typically 9am to 4pm Tuesday to Friday and 1 to 4pm on Mondays. All banks are closed on Saturdays and Sundays.

SUPERMARKETS

Albert Heijn (💻 www.ah.nl) is the largest supermarket chain in the Netherlands. There are 800 stores nationwide, ranging from small convenience-type stores to hypermarkets (known as Albert Heijn XL). Albert Heijn mainly offers food and household cleaning products, and have a reasonable selection of foreign products. Larger stores also sell a selection of stationary, pots, DVD and lingerie. You can get good discounts with their loyalty card (p49). Albert Heijn also offers online shopping.

Jumbo (💻 www. jumbosupermarkten.nl) is the

THE BEST PLACES TO BUY

Dutch supermarkets are well-stocked. However for meat, vegetables, fish and wine, you might want to think about specialist shops.

Meat, in particular, can be very disappointing — tough and lacking in taste. If you are happy to spend a few euros more, you are much better off finding a local butcher (p132).

There is also a limited variety of fresh fish in the supermarket — local markets are the best place for this.

Fruit and vegetables are okay but you will find much more variety at a much lower price if you go to the markets (p133).

The best place for Asian food is the Chinatown district (p132).

Special foreign food products and gourmet products can be found in local food shops (p131).

Wine can also be disappointing at supermarkets — generally unexciting commercial brands. For something more exotic, visit a dedicated wine shop (p134).

ROUGH PRICE GUIDE FOR SUPERMARKET ITEMS

Product	Price
Instant coffee (200 g)	€5.48
Rice (1 kg)	€2.49
Eggs (10)	€1.65
Apples (2.5 kg)	€3.70
Bottle of wine	from €4
Salmon (1 kg)	€22
Loaf of bread	€0.65
Bag of sugar (1 kg)	€1
Chicken breasts (1 kg)	€6.50
Red bell pepper (1)	€0.55
Potatoes (1 kg)	€1.50
Toilet paper (8 rolls)	€2.50

BAGS AND BOTTLES

It is usual for supermarkets to ask for refundable deposits on plastic bottles and on glass bottles from the larger breweries. The deposit is automatically factored into the price — return the bottle and you will get it back.

Bottles are usually returned by inserting them into an automated machine located within the shop, which prints out a receipt redeemable at the cashier.

You can return bottles at any supermarket that sells the same product; it doesn't need to be the one where you bought it.

Shopping bags are not generally free.

Shopping

second-largest chain in the country. It also offers a good selection of foreign products — some foreign products that can't be found in Albert Heijn can be found here. Prices are generally cheaper than Albert Heijn, although the supermarket runs less offers. Meat tends to be better here than in many of the other supermarkets.

C1000 (🖥 www.c1000.nl) was bought in 2011 by Jumbo, although for now retains its old name. It offers a similar range of products to its parent company.

The low-budget **Lidl** (🖥 www.lidl.nl) and **Aldi** (🖥 www.aldi.nl) stores offer the same discounts that you would expect to find in other European countries. The shops are very convenient for cooking oil and staple products. There are weekly offers on non-food items.

Hoogvliet (🖥 www.hoogvliet.com) is a Dutch chain of supermarkets named after a borough in Rotterdam. You'll find branches in The Hague, Rijswijk, Scheveningen and Leyweg. If you plan to shop here regularly, you should get their loyalty card.

There are two **F&S supermarkets** (🖥 www.freshensnack.nl) in The Hague (🏠 Hobbemastraat 173 and 🏠 Stationsweg 16). These stock a good range of multicultural products, especially Turkish. However, other European products tend to be slightly more expensive than elsewhere.

Convenience stores (known as *avondwinkels* or evening shops) are found all over the Netherlands. They are generally open from late afternoon until late at night, and so are useful when the regular supermarkets are closed. However, they tend to have a smaller selection and prices are usually higher.

Ekoplaza (🖥 www.ekoplaza.nl) is the largest chain of organic shops in the Netherlands. You can find a good variety of flowers, seeds and organic yoghurt. You can find plenty of vegetarian options, including fruit and vegetables that may be harder to find elsewhere. The chain is now starting to sell ready-to-eat organic meals.

Natuurwinkel (💻 www.natuurwinkel.nl) is similar to Eko-plaza, although has fewer outlets.

Sligro (💻 www.sligro.nl) is a huge supermarket that mainly supplies companies, such as restaurants. Some inter-governmental organisations and large companies also have an arrangement that allows their staff to obtain a Sligro membership card. You will also be able to shop at Sligro if you have The Hague Guest Card (p48). Prices are not necessarily cheaper, but the selection of meat and fish is impressive.

Marqt (💻 www.marqt.nl; 🏠 Hofweg 11) purports to offer authentic, additive-free food. It runs a 'no cash' policy, meaning that you can only pay with card. The founder likes to compare the supermarket to the slow food movement that originated in the Piemontese hills of northern Italy.

DIY STORES AND GARDENING

Gamma (💻 www.gamma.nl) is the largest chain of DIY stores in the Netherlands. It has a good range of equipment for hire, such as drills, grass-cutters and bigger machines. The store runs regular weekly offers. If you obtain the store's loyalty card (which is free), you will also be entitled to other benefits, such as a free service that cuts wood to the size you require. Gamma offers home delivery for €25. **Praxis** (💻 www.praxis.nl) and **Karwei** (💻 www.karwei.nl) have a similar range of products, although in addition they also sell kitchens and household appliances such as washing machines. Karwei tends to be slightly pricier than its competitors.

Bo-Rent (💻 Bo-rent.nl) specialises in renting all sorts of equipment, from power machines to vehicles.

Most of the DIY stores mentioned above will also have a range of garden equipment. For a store dedicated garden specialist, visit **Tuincentrum Ockenburgh** (🏠 Loosduinse Hoofdstraat 875; ☎ 070 397 1173; 💻 www.tuincentrumockenburgh.nl).

SPORTS SHOPS

Intersport (💻 www.intersport.nl) and **Perry** (💻 www.perrysport.nl) are well-known sports shops in the Netherlands. They sell a wide range of sporting equipment from some of the best-known manufacturers.

Bever (💻 www.bever.nl) is an outdoor activity and travel shop that offers more specialized kit, including camping equipment, trekking clothes and high-quality bike bags.

If you have a car, you might consider visiting **Decathlon** (💻 www.decathalon.nl), a French chain with a branch located not far from the Arena south of Amsterdam. The store is very large with reasonable prices.

Several shops selling water sports and winter sports equipment are located near **the harbour** in The Hague.

ELECTRICAL AND HOUSEHOLD GOODS

Mediamarkt (💻 www.mediamarkt.nl) isn't the cheapest place to buy electronic equipment, but it is well-stocked and has convenient opening times (until 10pm, Monday through to Saturday; on Sunday it closes at 6pm). The store in The Hague also has a computer repair service and a digital-photo printing machine.

Kijkshop (💻 www.kijkshop. nl) is a popular shop selling a bit of everything: household electrical items, heaters, bikes, camping equipment. Simply look at the display windows, write down the item number you want and present this paper, with payment, to the cashier. Alternatively you can order online and pick your purchase up at the store for free — you get a better selection this way.

Xenos (💻 www.xenos.nl) has a bit of everything, from curtains to cooking tools and bathroom items. Quality isn't the best, but prices are attractive.

Blokker (💻 www.blokker.nl) stocks cleaning tools, household appliances and cooking tools. It also has a cheap range of DVDs and toys. There are regular weekly offers.

BEAUTY AND TOILETRIES

Kruidvat (💻 www.kruidvat.nl) has weekly offers on well known brands. **Rituals** (💻 www.rituals. com) is a Dutch chain with it's own high-quality range of beauty products. **Etos** (💻 www.etos.nl) is a large chain offering mostly toiletry products, particularly common in train stations.

DEPARTMENT STORES

V&D (💻 www.vd.nl) sells almost everything, from perfumes to clothes and toys. Most V&Ds also have a good-value café on the ground floor called La Place.

Hema (💻 www.hema.nl) is smaller and mostly sells its own range of products. Prices are attractive and remain fairly consistent

throughout the country, even in airports and stations. In the stores, you can find clothes, make-up, stationary, kitchen utensils and a decent bike department. Hema stores also have their own café, which is very popular with the Dutch though less so among foodies.

Bijenkorf (💻 www.debijenkorf. nl) is more upmarket than the other department stores. It has a huge make-up and beauty department on the ground floor, a good selection of DVDs on the top floor and a Nespresso boutique in between.

SHOPPING MALLS

There are a couple of good-szed ones around the city:

* MegaStores (🏠 Van der Kunstraat 123; 💻 www. megastoresdenhaag.nl).

* In De Bogaard (🏠 Prinses Beatrixlaan 969; 💻 www. indebogaard.nl).

FOREIGN SHOPS

British

Kelly's (🏠 Zoutmanstraat 22a; ☎ 070 346 9753; 💻 www. kellys-expat-shopping.nl) is a friendly shop with helpful staff. Streaky bacon, onion rings, clotted cream, Fray Bentos pies, Quavers — they're all there and if they're not they can usually be ordered in. There is also a branch in Wassenaar (🏠 Luifelbaan 50; ☎ 070 511 8729).

Thomas Greens (🏠 Frederik Hendriklaan 71; ☎ 070 358 7586; 💻 www.thomasgreen.eu) sells British, American and South African products, both fresh and frozen. It also has an online shop.

French

Chez Nicolle (🏠 Molenstraat 5; ☎ 070 326 5042; 🖵 www.cheznicolle.nl) is a French *épicerie fine* that sells foie gras, delicious macaroons, chocolate, wine and all the little things you might be missing from France. The shop also organises French lessons and occasional food-tasting.

Italian

Italy (🖵 Piet Heinstraat 20; ☎ 070 363 9652; 🖵 www.italydenhaag.nl) is a real Italian *salumeria*, selling fresh products such as mozzarella, ravioli and a selection of wines, pasta and Italian specialities.

Portuguese

Try: **Apipa** (🏠 Prinsestraat 62; 🖵 www.apipa.nl) or **Ponto de Encontro** (🏠 Zoutmanstraat 51; ☎ 070 361 5312; 🖵 www.ponto-encontro.nl) for some *vinho verde* or *pastel de natas*.

Oriental

Amazing Oriental (🏠 Grote Marktstraat 113; ☎ 070 363 1552; 🖵 www.amazingoriental.com) is the largest Asian supermarket in The Hague. It has a huge range of Asian ingredients, from packaged and frozen products to fresh. The store also sells a small range of cooking utensils.

Wah Nam Hong (🏠 Gedempte Burgwal 8; ☎ 070 360 1977; 🖵 www.wnh.eu) also has a good selection of Asian products and great range of kitchen tools.

Other Asian shops are dotted throughout **chinatown**.

East European

Matroesjka (🏠 Piet Heinstraat 99; ☎ 06 5084 5529; 🖵 www.matroesjka-denhaag.nl) offers Russian, Balkan, Georgian and Lithuanian products.

Alaska (🏠 Jacob van der Doesstraat 2; ☎ 070 362 0254; 🖵 www.russkidvor.com) is slightly smaller and staff often don't speak English — you need Dutch or Russian to communicate.

Emigrant (🏠 Prins Hendrikstraat 98; ☎ 06 8570 7923) is a well-stocked Polish shop.

BUTCHERS

't Oude Ambecht (🏠 Reinkenstraat 10; ☎ 070 364 4225; 🖵 scharrelslagerij-oudeambacht.nl) sells good-quality meat and gourmet products, like the delectable truffle salami. Staff are extremely friendly and helpful, and there is always a genuinely cheerful buzz in the shop.

P.J. van den Broek (🏠 Obrechtstraat 177; ☎ 070 365 1400; 🖵 www.slagerijvandenbroek.nl) is another good butcher. Staff are happy to help with any cut of meat. If you are looking for something in particular, you can tell them in advance and they will see what they can do.

Slagerij de Jong (🏠 Willemstraat 1; ☎ 070 303 0147; 🖵 www.slagerijdejong.nl) is a butcher in Rijswijk that sells choice cuts.

BAKERIES AND PÂTISSERIES

Michel (🏠 Oude Molstraat 17; ☎ 070 346 8784; 🖵 michelfood.nl) is a French *boulangerie* with some scrummy breakfast options. It is open on Sunday.

Marakesh (🏠 Stationsweg 134 and Vaillantlaan 361; 🖵 www.

marakesh.nl) is a Moroccan bakery selling a good selection of sweet and savoury pastries at reasonable price. It also sells typical Moroccan desserts. The one at Stationsweg has a few places to sit and sells freshly-squeezed orange juice. Its proximity to Hollands Spoor makes it a good option for a quick bite if rushing to catch a train. The branch in Vaillantlaan is smaller and mainly sells sweets.

Pâtisserie Philippe Galerne (🏠 Art van de Goesstraat 24; ☎ 070 338 8662; 🖥 www. philippegalerne.nl) sells delicious cakes and croissants. It is also open on Sunday mornings.

Het Dessert Atelier (🏠 West-vlietweg 66; ☎ 070 365 4155; 🖥 www.dessertwinkel.nl) prepares cakes and high tea. On Sunday, from 8.30am to 12noon, it also offers croissants and other breakfast items.

Pâtisserie Chocolaterie Jarreau (🏠 Van Hoytemastraat 42; ☎ 070 324 8719; 🖥 www.jarreau. nl) offers a touch of chic but no croissants. It is also closed on Sunday.

Klink & Englebert (🏠 Theresi-astraat 73 and Van Arembergelaan 72; ☎ 070 362 7433; 🖥 www. klink-engelbert.nl) is a Dutch bakery with branches near Centraal Station and in Voorburg. The shops sell pastries, cakes and bread. Most come for take away, but there are also some tables at which you can sit.

Maison Kelder (🏠 Arabislaan 56 and Weissenbruchstraat 1 in The Hague, Kerkstraat 71 in Wassenaar) has been around since 1934, as is very well-regarded among locals. Many cafés around The Hague sell their cakes, but you can also go to Maison Kelder and buy them directly there. Maison Kelder is not very central, but you can also order online and get products delivered.

Van Boheemen. (🏠 Laan van Nieuw Oost Indië 225; ☎ 070 385 9447; 🖥 www. banketbakkerijboheemen.nl) is another long-running bakery selling an excellent variety cakes, pastries and chocolates.

CHEESE

Simon de Vogel (🏠 Frederik Hendriklaan 70; ☎ 070 354 4375; 🖥 www.simondevogel.nl) is a gourmet shop that also sells particularly good cheeses.

Other good places to try include **De Kaasspeciaalzaak** (🏠 Fahrenheitstraat 625; ☎ 070 363 1819; 🖥 www.kaasspeciaalzaak.nl), which has a very large variety, and **De Ruijter Kaasmarkt** (🏠 Eland-straat 158; ☎ 070 346 5455), which is centrally-located next to the big Albert Heijn.

Zuivelland (🏠 Theresiastraat 248 and Bankastraat 44; 🖥 www. zuivelland.nl) is a well known cheese franchise with branches throughout the country.

MARKETS

Haagse Markt (🏠 Herman Costerstraat; 🖥 www. dehaagsemarkt.nl) is the main market of The Hague. It has a great range of general items, including plants, bike tools and clothes. The main attractions of the market, however, is the food section — attractive prices and a great variety (550 stalls in total). Choose your vendor well, though, since some are more honest than others. Opening days are Mondays, Wednesdays, Fridays and Saturdays, from 9am until about 5pm. You'll get cheaper

Shopping

Shopping

products later in the day, but the selection won't be as good.

For smaller local markets, try **Leyweg** (🏠 Escamp; ⏰ Tue: 9am to 5pm), **Loosduinse** (🏠 Loosduininen Hoofdplein; ⏰ Wed: 9am to 5pm), **Stevinstraat** (🏠 Scheveningen; ⏰ Thu: 9am to 5pm) and **Steentijdsingel** (🏠 Ypenburg; ⏰ Fri: 9am to 5pm).

An **organic farmer's market** is held every Wednesday — and Thursday during the spring and summer months — on the Hofweg, from 10am to 6pm. They have a good stall selling a huge variety of wild and cultivated mushrooms. Unfortunately, products are rather pricey.

An **antique and book market** is held from mid-May to the end of September on 🏠 Lange Voorhout, open Thursdays and Sundays 10am to 6pm.

Markthof is a small covered market in the centre of The Hague (🏠 Zuidwal), which also has a few eateries. It is open every day apart from Sundays, late-night opening on Thursdays.

Rijswijk has two markets. **Bodgaardplein Market**, held every Thursday from 9am to 5pm, is a medium-sized market just outside the main shopping centre. **Herenstraat Market** is a small and pretty market held on Saturdays, 8am to 4pm, around the old church in the town centre.

FISH

Haagse Markt (🏠 Herman Costerstraat; 🖳 www.dehaagsemarkt.nl) has a very big variety of fish with some of the lowest prices in town, but you should be good at spotting fresh fish and careful not to get ripped off as an unsuspecting tourist. Getting to know the traders can help.

Simonis (🖳 www.simonisvis.nl) has shops in several locations throughout The Hague. The shops offer fresh fish, sushi and fish sandwiches to go. Some of the shops have a fish restaurant attached.

Vishandel Roeleveld (🏠 Dokter Lelykade 158; ☎ 070 354 9626; 🖳 www.vishandelroeleveld.nl) is also a good place to try. It sells fresh and frozen fish, as well as some small morsels to eat.

Scheveningse Vissershaven, (☎ 070 338 5807 or 070 338 5800; 🖳 www.unitedfishauctions.com) has fish auctions on Fridays, from 7am.

WINE AND LIQUOR SHOPS

Gall & Gall (🖳 www.gall.nl) is the biggest chain of wine shops in the Netherlands. They have all the regular stuff, as well as a small selection of more interesting wines — although admittedly the range isn't as exciting as might be.

Better places to try are **Le Bouchon** (🏠 Valeriusstraat 51; ☎ 070 345 7784; 🖳 bouchon.nl) and **Marius** (🏠 Piet Heinstraat 93; ☎ 070 363 3100; 🖳 www.jouwwijnvriend.nl).

Think of yourself as something of a connoisseur of wine? Then perhaps try **Pavie Wines** (🏠 Reinkenstraat 13; 🖳 www.pavie.nl), which specialises in top-end wines.

Van Driel (🏠 Prins Hendrikstraat 43A; ☎ 070 363 7016) has friendly service and a good selection of wine and spirits.

De Gouden Ton (🏠 Denneweg 81; ☎ 070 346 9216; 🖳 www.degoudenton.nl) is a fabulous wine shop, housed in a lovely building with very knowledgeable staff. They have a good range of prices, too.

Van Kleef (🏠 Lange Beestenmarkt 109; ☎ 070 345 2273; 🖳 www.museumvankleef.nl) sells a good range of liquor made by local producers. Good products and an enthusiastic vendor. You can also visit their museum (p146).

PHOTOGRAPHY AND PHOTO PRINTING SERVICES

For passport photos, there are many places that offer this service — look for the 'pasfoto'. There are several places around Chinatown and along Prinsengracht. For specific shops: **FotoProf** (🏠 Frederikstraat 16; 🖥 www.fotoprof.nl) and **Foto Americaine** (🏠 Wagenstraat 41).

The large chains — such as **Hema** (🖥 www.hema.nl), **Mediamarkt** (🖥 www.mediamarkt.nl) and **Kruidvat** (🖥 www.kruidvat.nl) — also offer the use of photo printing machines, convenient if you only want to print a few photos

Camera Compleet (🏠 Thomsonlaan 96 in The Hague and Koningin Julianaplein 10 in Voorburg; 🖥 www.cameracompleet.nl) has a good range of cameras and other photography equipment, even for the most discerning of customers.

FotoHafo (🏠 Wagenstraat 67; 🖥 www.fotohafo.nl) is another specialist camera shop.

HAIRDRESSERS

Booking is essential for most hairdressers, particularly the more upmarket ones. Most hairdressers in The Hague are unisex. They tend to be quite pricey, for both men and women, although there are some cheaper options around.

Popular and well-known hairdressers are located between Molenstraat and Prinsestraat. **Louis Coiffure** (🖥 louis-coiffure.com) and **Gaga Style** (🖥 gaga-style.nl) are rather upmarket. For a cheaper option, try **Kappersakademie** (🏠 Koningin Marialaan 9; 🖀 070 890 0656; 🖥 www.kappersakademie.nl), which is where hairdresser students practice (under supervision!)

Cheap barbers are located in the Haagse Markt area and in Valliantstraat. There are plenty to choose from and reservations are not usually required. Prices from €10.

FRUIT & VEGETABLES

Supermarkets are okay for fairly basic fruit and vegetables, although prices tend to be rather on the high side. Depending on the season, you may find some more exotic offerings, such as mango, persimmon fruit and avocado.

By far the best place to shop for fruit and vegetables is the central Haagse Markt. Here, it is possible to get a big bag of fruit for as little as €1.

If you are looking for something special, try **Rutten** (🏠 Piet Heinstraat 86; 🖀 070 346 2445), which has a wide range of vegetables, including some less well-known ones. It is the place to go if you are desperate for globe artichokes or wild mushrooms.

SECOND-HAND SHOPS

Kringloop (🏠 Piet Heinstraat 69 and Loosduinsekade 156; 🖥 www.kringloopdenhaag.nl) is a chain of charity shops that sells everything from furniture to household appliances, clothes and DVDs. Stores are all over the country. If you are looking for something and you can't find it in a particular outlet, they will often be able to direct you to another one that does have it. Kringloop also collects anything reusable for free. Simply call to fix an appointment (in The Hague: ☎ 070 0335 1155).

Emmaus (🏠 Prinsegracht 36; ☎ 070 363 9273; 🖥 www. emmausdenhaag.nl) is a second-hand shop with rather peculiar opening times (only Thursdays 7 to 9pm and Saturdays 11am to 1pm). You can find everything here, from books to crockery and clothes.

Second Best (🏠 Korte Molenstraat 7; ☎ 070 364 4044; 🖥 www.emmausdenhaag.nl) is a second-hand clothes shop offering good-quality items and well-known brands.

KITCHEN EQUIPMENT

DOK (🏠 Passage 19; ☎ 070 346 9696; 🖥 www.dokcookware.com) is a large store, full of nifty ideas for kitchen paraphernalia.

En Garde (🏠 Prinsestraat 6; ☎ 070 364 7352; 🖥 www.en-garde.nl) is smaller, but the friendly staff can help track down most items that you might be looking for.

LAUNDRY, DRY-CLEANING AND TAILORS

Almost all automatic laundromats have been converted to dry-cleaners (*stomerij*). However, **Veldkamp** (🏠 Frederik Hendriklaan 254; ☎ 070 355 9061; 🖥 www.veldkampwassen.nl) still operates a self-cleaning service, as well as its regular dry-cleaning business.

Some of the larger Albert Heijns also provide dry-cleaning services.

Other reputable dry-cleaners include **Tip Top** (🏠 Spui 242; ☎ 070 364 0602; 🖥 www.tiptop-opmaat. nl), **Stomerij Panda** (🏠 Rijnstraat 14; ☎ 070 335 1712; 🖥 stomerijpanda.nl) and **Twins**

(🏠 Molenstraat 18A; ☎ 070 363 7099; 🖥 twinskledingreparatie.nl).

A lot of dry-cleaners also have a tailor attached. For a shop that is specialised in repairing clothes, try **La Sartoria** (🏠 Piet Heinstraat 55; ☎ 070 345 5263) and **Samy** (🏠 Zoutmanstraat 49; ☎ 070 345 7241).

DVDS

DVD rental is not all that common, and to a large extent has been superseded by pay-for-view download movies (🖥 pathethuis.nl and 🖥 moviemaxonline.eu). Still, the movie chain **Videoland** (🏠 Dierenselaan 184-186; ☎ 070 346 6368; 🖥 www.videoland.nl) offers DVDs for rent.

Alternatively, you can rent DVDs and CDs at libraries (providing you are a member). The main library in Spui has the biggest selection, but smaller branches also have them.

The following shops offer DVDs for sale:

- **Blokker** (🖥 www.blokker.nl)

- **Free Record Shop** (🖥 www. freerecordshop.nl)

- **Bijenkorf** (🖥 www.debijenkorf. nl)

- **Mediamarkt** (🖥 www. mediamarkt.nl).

PHARMACIES

Normal opening hours for pharmacies are from 8.30 to 5.30pm. After that time, **Apotheek Bronovo** (🏠 Bronovolaan 5; ☎ 070 324 6085) is open from 5.30pm to midnight. During normal working hours, some options are:

- **Havinga**: 🏠 Prins Hendrikplein

Shopping

3; ☎ 070 345 6100; 🖳 apoth-eek-havinga.nl

- **Hofstad**: 🏠 Korte Poten 7A; ☎ 070 346 4748; 🖳 www.apotheekhofstad.nl

- **Scheveningen**: 🏠 Badhu-isstraat 163; ☎ 070 352 3223; 🖳 apotheekscheveningen.nl

- **Boots**: 🏠 Westeinde 148; ☎ 070 356 1276; 🖳 denhaag.nl.boots.com

- **Apotheek Jan Hendrikmore**; 🏠 Jan Hendrikstraat 18; ☎ 070 711 2450; 🖳 artsenzorg.nl

BOOKSHOPS

The American Book Center (🏠 Lange Poten 23; 🖳 www.abc.nl 070 364 2742) offers a great selection of English-language best-sellers and magazines.

Stanley & Livingstone (🏠 Schoolstraat 21; 🖳 www.stanley-livingstone.nl; ☎ 070 365 7306) is a well-stocked travel book-shop with a great English selection, as well as a selection of guidebooks in German and French.

Van Stockum (🏠 Herengracht 60; ☎ 070 302 8110; 🖳 www.vanstockum.nl), a short walk from Centraal Station, has a good selec-tion of English books. You can buy second hand books and sell your books online.

Selexyz (🏠 Spuistraat 21; ☎ 070 206 0230; 🖳 www.selexyz.nl) is the Netherlands' biggest book chain, offering a good selection of books in English and other foreign languages. In The Hague, it now shares its premises with second-hand bookshop **De Slegte**.

Booksellers van Hoogstraten (Noordeinde 98, ☎ 070 365 2845; 🖳 www.hoogstraten.nl) is one of the oldest independent bookshop of

The Hague, selling English books of all genres.

Paagman (🏠 Frederik Hen-driklaan 217; ☎ 070 338 3838; 🖳 www.paagman.nl) is a well-stocked bookshop that mostly sells Dutch books, but also has a decent selection of English titles. There is a café inside.

Couvée Boekhandel (🏠 Van Hoytemastraat 66; ☎ 070 324 7930) sells French books.

CARNIVAL AND PARTY CLOTHES

Desnuffel (🏠 Schoolstraat 7; ☎ 070 364 8882; 🖳 www.desnuf-fel.nl) is a unique shop in The Hague, containing all sorts of out-landish costumes for donning dur-ing Carnival, Queen's/King's Day or any other celebration.

Zorg Voor Party (🏠 Laan van Nieuw Oost Indië 104; 🖳 www.zorgvoorparty.nl) is another good

option for those that live nearby.

KEY CUTTERS

Sleuteldirect (🏠 Prinsegracht 120; ☎ 070 389 4955; 🖳 www.sleuteldirect.nl) is a centrally-locat-ed key specialist, which copies all sorts of keys. It also sells door locks and safes.

Another option is **De Halve Zool** (🏠 Torenstraat 89; ☎ 070 365 9261).

CAR BOOT SALES AND FLEA MARKETS

Car boot sales are rare in the Netherlands. The most reputa-ble one is 🖳 www.carbootsale.nl, which is held once a month in the small city of Oss (🏠 Gielekespad 10).

Shopping

On Queen's/King's Day, *vrijmarkten* ('free markets'). take place all over the country. During this day, people are allowed to sell things in the streets without having to pay any tax on their sales. People may set up stalls or simply spread their goods on blankets. It is not just the car boot sales or flea market sales that are exempt from tax — commercial traders benefit from this one day of tax-free sales. Naturally, the amount of sales clocked up on this one day is huge.

Flea markets are frequently arranged in various locations, such as at gyms or in parking lots. There is no fixed time for these — they are generally announced in the free local newspapers or through posters placed around town.

BIKE REPAIR

The majority of shops that sell bikes also carry out repair work. Many of the larger *OV-fiets* bike rental shops, found at train stations, also sell basic tools for bike repair.

Kringloopwinkel Fiets (🏠 Weimarstraat 364) is a charity shop dedicated to the repair and sale of bikes. Repairs are generally of a high standard and slightly cheaper than elsewhere.

Van der Velden Tweewielers (🏠 Vaartdreef 57; ☎ 079 593 7714; 🖥 www.fietszoetermeer.nl) is a good repair shop in Zoetermeer.

Mammoet (🏠 Stationsweg 36; 🖥 www.mammoet.nl) is a very well-stocked shop for bike repair parts and you will find most things that you might need here. Quality is not bad.

CYSE (☎ 06 1419 3284; 🖥 www.cyse.nl) offers a call-out service to repair your bike if you can't take it into the shop.

ONLINE SHOPPING

Buying online is often cheaper, and has more variety, than physically popping into a store. Delivery times are generally quite fast, too.

Here are a few online stores to try:

- For **TV and computer cables** 🖥 www.kabeltje.com

- For **printer and ink cartridges** 🖥 www.123inkt.nl

- For **household appliances and computers** 🖥 www.redcoon.nl and 🖥 www.neck.nl

The Hague

1: The Hague's modern skyrises — VP

2: Binnenhof, home of Parliament since 1446 (p148) — VP

3: The iconic Steigenberger Kurhaus Hotel (p185) — VP

4: Het Plein, one of The Hague's top chillout spots (p148) — VP

Photos: Violetta Polese (VP), Blake Evans-Pritchard (BEP), Laurent Virassamy (LV), David Wilkinson (DW), Giorgio Benassi (GB)

5: Parade outside Parliament — VP

6: Van Kleef distillery (p146) — VP

7: Art deco in Denneweg — VP

8: Grote Markt (p147) with the Grote Kerk (p145)
in the background — VP

9: Beelden-aan-Zee Museum (p156) — VP

10: Gateway to Chinatown
(p145) — VP

11: Stork, symbol of The
Hague, atop signpost — VP

12: Graffiti artwork on Raamstraat — VP

13: Hofje van Nieuwkoop, the most impressive *hofje* in the city (p144) — VP

14: Neo-Renaissance building presently housing the Ministry of Justice — VP

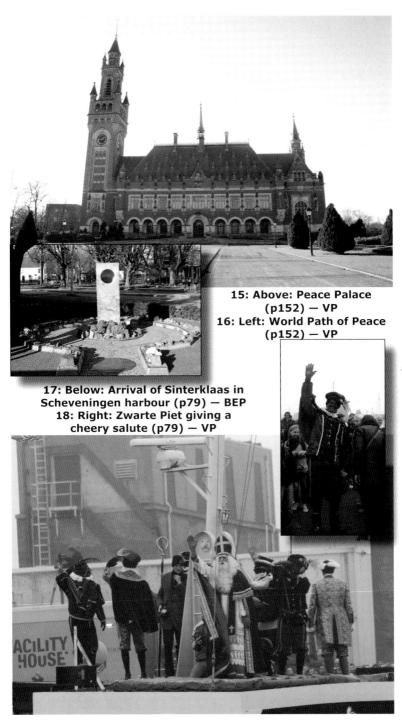

15: Above: Peace Palace
(p152) — VP

16: Left: World Path of Peace
(p152) — VP

17: Below: Arrival of Sinterklaas in
Scheveningen harbour (p79) — BEP
18: Right: Zwarte Piet giving a
cheery salute (p79) — VP

19: Phillips Hall Theatre and Lucente Theatre (p166) — VP

20: Outside the City Museum (p151) — DW

21: Klap-schaats for speed-skating — VP

22: Playing hockey on a frozen lake in Haagse Bos (p162) — VP

23: Hofvijver, just outside the Binnenhof, displaying the 12 flags of the different provinces of the Netherlands (p148) — VP

24: Madurodam (p152) — LW

25: Pillow fight in Grote Markt (p159) — VP

26: Fairytale Sculptures by Tom Otterness (p154) — VP

27: Chillaxing on Scheveningen's beach (p161) — VP

28: Oud Stadhuis (p148) — VP

29: Above: The Snoeptrommel, now a clothes shop (p114) — VP

30: Below: Passage, housing some fancy shops (p148) — VP

32: Noordeinde Palace (p148) and statue of William of Orange— VP

31: Mauritskade, one of the few uncovered canals of The Hague — VP

33: Above: town hall, tourist information and library - VP
34: Right: Public transport - VP
35: Below: Mad New Year's dash into the sea (p87) - GB

www.thecitytrail.com

36: All VP apart from top right, which is DW

HAGUE CENTRE

Mauritshuis

This museum is most famous for holding some of Johannes Vermeer's best-known master pieces, including *View of Delft* (1660-1661), and *Girl with a Pearl Earring* (1665-1667).

The museum also boasts paintings from other Dutch masters from the Golden Age, including Rembrandt, Peter Rubens and Anthony van Dyck.

The museum itself is housed in a beautiful baroque building — a 17th century palace, fitted out with an 18th century interior.

Unfortunately, the museum is closed for renovations until the middle of 2014. The idea is to expand it into an adjacent building. This new building will become the main entrance to the museum, with an underground passageway leading to the other one.

Whilst these renovations are taking place, a number of the masterpieces of the Mauritshuis museum will be on display at the Gemeentemuseum (p151).

🏠 Korte Vijverberg 8

💲 Adults: €13.50; Children under 18: free; Ⓜ

☎ Tue-Sun 11am to 5pm; Closed until mid-2014

🖥 www.mauritshuis.nl

Escher Museum (ESCHER IN HET PALEIS)

If there is just one art museum that you visit whilst in The Hague,

THE MUSEUMKAART

Planning on visiting several museums in The Hague? Then you might want to think about buying the Museumkaart (p49), which gives you free yearly access to most museums in the country.

it really ought to be the Escher Museum.

M.C. Escher is best remembered for his seemingly impossible drawings — the waterfall that flows up as well as down, the never-ending staircase, the man that climbs a ladder into a building only to end up on the outside.

Terrific art — and a terrific museum in which to exhibit such art.

Not only does it contain a marvellous collection of Escher's works, but it also explains some of the thinking behind the great man, as well as explanations for how the paintings were constructed.

Perhaps the most amazing thing that you can learn about Escher is that he did not just sketch his drawings on parchment or canvas. Because he was a business man as well, and wanted to make sure he could earn a living as an artist, he intricately carved his pictures on printing blocks, which could then be used to create multiple prints for sale.

The building itself is magnificent. It used to be a palace and much of the interior dates from the 18th century.

The chandeliers in the rooms are a fairly recent addition to the museum. Local Rotterdam artist Hans van Bentem has used glass to fashion the most bizarre designs, such as a giant skull and bulbous spider.

🏠 Lange Voorhout 74

💲 €8.50

☎ Mon: closed; Tue-Sun 11am to 5pm

🖥 www.escherinhetpaleis.nl

Van Kleef Distillery (DISTILEERDERIJ VAN KLEEF)

It is now possible to visit the oldest distillery of The Hague for a fascinating insight into the time-honoured tradition of manufacturing strong Dutch liquor.

Unfortunately, Dutch rules mean that alcohol is no longer made at this historic distillery. Instead, Van Kleef works with local distilleries around the country to produce the alcohol that is sold at its shop to authentic traditional recipes.

Members of staff and tour guides are passionate about the distillery business, and will provide you with a fascinating explanation of products and history — in Dutch, German, French or English.

The place is both a museum and shop, and you can buy all sorts of interesting spirits and liqueurs. The traditional Dutch drink *jenever* (p104) is available here. You can usually ask to sample the drinks before you make a purchase.

It is free to wander around the shop and museum. With a reservation, you can also book a taste tour, which usually include some small morsels prepared by the Italian chef. Sampling five drinks, for example, will cost €9.95.

🏠 Lange Beestenmarkt 109

💲 Free. Pay separately for tasting.

☎ Mon 1 to 6pm; Tue-Sat 10am to 6pm

🖥 vankleef.org

📷 Photo 6

Public Transport Museum (OPENBAAR VERVOER MUSEUM)

Housed in the old tram depot building, which closed down in 1983, the public transport museum offers a fascinating glimpse into the world of the city bus and tram. A rich collection of trams and buses is on display, and you can even take an historical tram ride through The Hague city. Entrance to the museum is free, but you have to pay a few euros for each tram ride.

🏠 Parallelweg 224

☎ 070 445 1559

💲 Free (only pay for historical rides)

☎ Apr-Oct: Sun: 1 to 5pm

🖥 www.hovm.nl

The Hague Sculpture (DEN HAAG SCULPTUUR)

Regular sculpture exhibitions are shown around The Hague. Locations and opening times vary, so the best thing to do if you want to find out about the latest events is to consult the website (below).

Exhibitions are temporary and regularly change. Recent artists have included Fernando Botero, Damien Hirst and Manolo Valdés.

In the summer, an interesting series of sculptures are displayed in the open in Lange Voorhout, just outside the official office of the organisation.

🏠 Lange Voorhout 15

What to See

🖥 www.denhaagsculptuur.nl

Prison Gate Museum (MUSEUM DE GEVANGENPOORT)

This museum gives an intriguing glimpse into the world of crime and punishment as it was in mediaeval times.

The museum's building is a former prison — it was converted into a museum in 1882 — and, as much as possible, has retained its original character.

It is definitely worth taking a guided tour of the prison complex, included in the admission price. The guides bring colour to any visit, through tales of famous prisoners, valiant escapes and the cruellest of punishments.

Tour guides tend to be extremely knowledgeable and passionate about their work. Unfortunately, though, tours are only available in Dutch — something that we sincerely hope the curators of the museum will rectify soon. You do get a leaflet in English, which is supposedly a translation of what you are told on the tour, but many of the more colourful descriptions are left out.

Many of the tour guides do speak English, though, so if you turn up when things are not too busy they may be willing to translate some of the more important points.

Tours are every hour, starting at 10.45am.

As part of the tour, you will get to see the cramped conditions in which many of the prisoners lived. When the guide turns the light off, you will appreciate how sunless the cells are. Not the best place to come for sufferers of claustrophobia!

You do not have to take a tour to see the museum, but if you don't many of the more interesting rooms will be closed off to you.

The museum can get exceedingly cold during the winter months, so bring warm clothes if visiting then (and spend some time thinking about those inmates that were forced to endure such a winter).

Perhaps the most important inmate of the prison was Cornelis de Witt, the member of a prestigious family and, briefly, an influential part of Dutch politics. In 1672, the House of Orange perceived him to be a threat and had him arrested on false accusations of treason. You can visit the room at the prison where he was held — in relative luxury, compared to his fellow in-mates, since he had the money to pay for better treatment.

He was eventually murdered outside the prison on the day he was due to be released, along with his brother Johann who had turned up to escort him from the prison. As they walked out of the prison gates, a lynch mob was waiting for them; the false accusations of treason had fuelled popular resentment and suspicion.

The museum regularly organises night tours as well. A particularly atmospheric way of experiencing the museum, though slightly more expensive: €17.50 for an hour and a half tour. You must be older than 13.

The museum also offers children's parties, complete with quizzes and games connected to the prison.

🏠 Buitenhof 33

☎ 070 346 0861

💲 Adults: €7.50; Children under 13: €5.50; Museum card: free

🕙 Mon: Closed; Tue-Fri: 10am to 5pm; Sat-Sun: 12 to 5pm

🖥 www.gevangenpoort.nl

What to See

Prince William V Gallery (GALERIJ PRINS WILLEM V)

Adjoining the Prison Gate Museum is a collection of paintings once owned by Price William V. The entrance fee to the Prison Gate Museum also covers entrance to this gallery.

The gallery essentially consists of a single oblong room, with paintings rather crammed together, trying to occupy every space of the rather limited viewing area. This makes viewing somewhat confusing. Moreover, it is very difficult to see exactly who the artist of a particular painting is, without getting extremely close to the picture and looking at the writing on the frame. But, when you do this, you have a good chance of setting off the museum alarm, with all the red-faced embarrassment that is likely to cause. A visit to the Prince William V gallery is almost always accompanied by intermittent soundings of the alarm, as people approach too close to the painting, followed by the duty security guard quickly calling downstairs, to tell everyone that things are okay.

There are around 150 paintings in the gallery, mainly from Dutch and Flemish masters, such as Jan Steen, Paulus Potter, Frans van Mieris, Gerard van Honthorst and Peter Rubens. Paintings tend towards the baroque images associated with the Netherlands' Golden Age (p66).

🏠　Buitenhof 33

💲　€5 Ⓜ

⏰　Mon: closed; Tue-Sun: 12am to 5pm

🖥　gevangenpoort.nl/page/galerij-pwv

Meermanno Museum

This museum is devoted to the history of the art of the book, and is located in the former house of Dutch writer and book collector Baron van Westreenen van Tiellandt. The museum is named after his cousin Johan Meerman, who was also a book collector, as well as a traveller and diarist.

The museum has a collection of books from all periods of Western history, but unfortunately the rooms are confusingly laid out with no clear narrative running through them. This is made even worse by much of the text, as well as the audio on televisions in the museum, being only in Dutch.

Some explanation is available in English, thrust into your hand as you enter, but this is inadequate for really understanding what the museum is about.

For real enthusiasts of book collecting, the highlight of the museum is likely to be a small collection of medieval manuscripts, along with information about their manufacture and restoration.

There is also a small room dedicated to the development of writing and books.

The baron didn't just collect books, though. He gathered other artefacts from around the world and his Egyptian collection is particularly fascinating. He was also one of the first Dutchmen to start collecting Egyptian texts on pieces of papyrus.

The museum is spread over three floors, but is not actually all that big. Temporary exhibitions, usually showcasing the work of a more contemporary artist, can be found on the lower ground floor.

The museum has a lovely outside terrace and garden, where you can take refreshments.

What to See

🏠 Prinsessegracht 30

☎ 070 346 2700

💰 €8; ▭M▭

🕗 Tue-Sun: 12am to 5pm

🖥 www.meermanno.nl

Historical Museum (HISTORISCH MUSEUM)

First impressions of the museum is of a huge art gallery, which uses paintings to tell the story of The Hague, its government and its inhabitants through the ages. Proceeding further into the museum, some historic relics are also exhibited, such as the small collection of dolls houses on the uppermost floor.

The museum is housed in the former building of the old civic guard, which was dissolved in the late 18th century. Since this dissolution, the building was used as a hotel and a courthouse before eventually being turned into a museum in 1986.

Temporary exhibitions with a Hague twist are regularly shown in the museum.

🏠 Korte Vijverberg 7

☎ 070 364 6940

💰 €7.50; ▭M▭

🕗 Tue-Fri: 10am to 5pm; Sat-Sun: 12noon to 5pm

🖥 www. haagshistorischmuseum.nl

Bredius Museum

The Bredius Museum displays the private collection of the art historian Abraham Bredius (1855 to 1946). Over his considerably long life — he lived to be nearly 100 — Bredius amassed a great wealth of important Dutch artwork, with the most notable coming from the Netherlands' Golden Age.

During your tour, you will glimpse work from such masters as Vermeer and Rembrandt. Besides paintings, delftware and furniture are also exhibited.

What makes the museum so interesting is the brochure that is thrust into your hand as you enter, containing excellent descriptions of the paintings in English, French and German. The descriptions really bring the paintings to life, not only explaining the history behind them but also offering some analysis of the world that the artist was trying to capture.

The museum is not particularly big — there are perhaps no more than a couple of dozen main paintings — and so you should need no more than an hour to visit it.

🏠 Lange Vijverberg 14

☎ 070 362 0729

💰 €6

🕗 Mon: Closed; Tue-Sun: 11am to 5pm

🖥 www.museumbredius.nl

Spinoza's House (SPINOZAHUIS)

The Jewish-Dutch philosopher Baruch Spinoza lived here until his death in 1677. Spinoza is probably best known for his participation in the 17th century cultural movement of philosophers — known as the Enlightenment — that began to challenge the established ideas grounded faith and tradition.

There is a reference library that visitors can access by appointment.

There is a statue of the philosopher just outside the museum.

🏠 Paviljoensgracht 72

💲 Free with museumkaart

☎ Tue-Sun 1 to 5pm

🖳 www.spinozahuis.nl

Poster Gallery (GALERIJ DE AFFICHE)

Beneath Spui tram station, you can view a series of posters that hang in illuminated frames. The Poster gallery is open early morning until late evening and admission is free. The selection of posters on display changes every few months.

🏠 Spui

💲 Free

☎ Anytime when the trams are running

Binnenhof

Tucked away in the centre of The Hague is a charming inner courtyard known as the Binnenhof.

It is here that you will find the Dutch Parliament and the splendid Knights' Hall (or Ridderzaal). The architecture is magnificent. Just outside the Binnenhof is a small pond, Hofvijver, which often freezes during the winter months to become a giant ice-skating rink.

It is possible to attend public sessions at the Parliament — you should remember to bring your ID as you won't get in without it. Plenary sessions take place on Tuesdays, Wednesdays and Thursdays. Committee meetings take place on all days of the week apart from Fridays.

Alternatively, you can also arrange a tour, which includes the Ridderzaal. ProDemos, which organises the tours, has an office just outside the Binnenhof, on Hofweg.

It is worth coming to the Binnenhof on the third Tuesday of September. This is when the state opening of parliament takes place and ruling monarch drives to parliament in his or her golden carriage to give the opening address.

🏠 Binnenhof 8a
ProDemos: Hofweg 1

💲 ProDemos tour: €4 to €6

☎ ProDemos: 070 364 6144

🖳 www.prodemos.nl

📷 Photo 2

Hofjes

A 'hofje' is a courtyard, often surrounded by almshouses that were established in order to bestow largesse upon the poor. Sometimes they were used by Catholic women living together in a cloister.

The houses were usually built in a U-shape, with the courtyard in the middle and a gateway as an entrance. More than 100 *hofjes* still exist in The Hague today, most dating from the 18th or 19th century.

These days, many *hofjes* provide quiet and pleasant living areas for the elderly. Most *hofjes* are accessible to the public, but visitors should always respect the privacy of those that live there.

The oldest surviving *hofje* of the city is **Heilig Geesthof** (📷 #13) in Paviljoensgracht 51, founded in 1616. Other *hofjes* include: **Hofje Van Wouw** (🏠 Lange Beestenmarkt), **Hofje van Nieuwkoop** (🏠 Warmoezierstraat), **Geefhuisjes** (🏠 Hoge Zand 2-24) and **'t Hooftshofje** (🏠 Assendelftlaan 53-89). To visit them you can also join a tour (p157).

💲 Free

☎ Daytime

Clandestine churches
(SCHUILKERKEN)

Schuilkerken are churches that were concealed behind other buildings and do not show a public façade to the street.

They owe their origins to the Reformation, an era when the practicing of minority religions was often banned, and sometimes penalised by exile or execution. Only through concealing their buildings of worship were those of faith afforded some modicum of security.

It is possible to see two examples of these hidden churches in The Hague. **Jocobus Augustinus** (🏠 Juffrouw Idastraat 7; 💻 denhaag.okkn.nl) has guided tours every Saturday, meeting at 🏠 Molenstraat 44. It is also possible to attend Sunday services. **The Willibrord Chapel** (🏠 Oude Molstraat 35; 📞 070 356 4385; 💻 www.willibrordushuis.nl) is a particularly beautiful example of a 16th century church. Entrance to the church is normally restricted, but it is possible to attend mass there on Tuesday and Wednesday mornings at 7.30am.

Al-Akasa Mosque (AL-AKASA MOSKEE)

Located in what was previously the Jewish neighbourhood, this neoclassic building was originally used as a synagogue. However, the deportation of Jews during the second world war meant that, by the time the guns stopped firing, the building stood mostly empty. The synagogue eventually closed in 1975.

Past decades have seen a surge in the number of Muslims living in the area and so in 1981 the building was sold to the Turkish Islamic Association (later to become the Netherlands Islamic Foundation)

and converted into a Mosque. The minarets were added in 1987.

🏠　Wagenstraat 101

💲　Free or with a tour (p157)

Saint James' Church
(SINT-JACOBSKERK)

Known by most simply as the Grote Kerk, this 15th century Protestant church is one of the oldest buildings in the city. It was all but destroyed by a fire in 1539. Only two of the original stain glass windows survived — the others were repaired by leading glass artists shortly after the fire.

The Church is not used for service anymore. It is formally owned by the City of The Hague and is managed by the Stichting Grote Kerk Den Haag, which conducts restoration activities and rents it out for events such as concerts. It is generally only possible to visit the interior of the church during such events. Even if you don't have the opportunity to go in, though, you should take a moment to wander round the outside.

🏠　Rond de Grote Kerk 12

💻　www.grotekerkdenhaag.nl

New Church (NIEUWE KERK)

Completed in 1656, Nieuwe Kerk is considered a highlight of early Protestant architecture in the Netherlands. The church became a concert hall in 1969 and is now part of the Dr Anton Philipszaal and Lucent Danstheater.

The church contains the tomb of the 17th century philosopher Baruch Spinoza (p143). The church is one of UNESCO's top 100 Dutch monuments.

🏠　Spui 175

💰 Depends on event

☎ Anytime, from outside only

🖥 www.nieuwekerkdenhaag.nl

💲 Free

☎ Anytime (outside only)

📷 Photo 28

New Town Hall (NIEUWE STADHUIS)

The town hall has changed location a number of times over the years. The current one was designed by American architect Richard Meier and completed in 1995. It is located in the new city centre, and incorporates the council chamber, the main public library, the city's tourist office and a number of cafés. Regular exhibitions take place here. The brilliant white colour of the building earned it the nickname of IJspaleis (Ice Palace).

It is possible to take the elevator up to the 11th floor in order to get a good impression of the building's architecture.

In the atrium of the Nieuwe Stadhuis, there is a permanent film exhibition called 'The Hague Impressions' — very interesting indeed!

🏠 Spuiplein 70

💰 Free

☎ Mon, Tue, Wed and Fri 8am to 2pm; Thu 12noon to 8pm

Old Town Hall (OUDE STADHUIS)

The Old City Hall is a renaissance-style building on the Groenmarkt near the Grote Kerk. It was once the seat of the city's government. These days, it still performs some public duties and is where people come to have their civic wedding ceremonies. It is also where members of the royal family register births (less noble folk do this at the current city hall, on the Kalvermarkt).

🏠 Dagelijkse Groenmarkt

Strijkijzer

The Strijkijzer is a 132-metre tall skyscraper in The Hague, consisting of 41 floors. It was inspired by the Flatiron Building in New York City. In fact the name, '*strijkijzer*', can be translated as 'clothing iron'.

This fancy building contains more than 300 studio flats and around 50 luxury apartments. There is a cocktail bar and restaurant at the very top, with a fantastic panoramic terrace. A dedicated lift whisks patrons up there.

💰 Free

☎ Anytime, best in the afternoon until 6pm

🖥 hetstrijkijzer.nl (restaurant: www.thepenthouse.nl)

🏠 Hofwijckstraat (separate access for restaurant)

Noordeinde Palace (PALEIS NOORDEINDE)

Noordeinde Palace has been the working palace of the Queen since 1984, and will now become the office of the new king Willem-Alexander. You can only see it from the outside; it is not open to the public. Just in front of it there is a statue of Willem I, prince of Orange.

🏠 Noordeinde 68

💰 Free

☎ Anytime (outside only)

What to See

Royal Stables and Palace Garden (KONINKLIJKE STALLEN EN PALEISTUIN)

The Royal Stables, designed by 19th century architect Hugo Pieter Vogel, are located not far from the Noordeinde Paleis. This is where the horses belonging to the royal family are kept, as well as the golden carriage that is used for ceremonial occasions. Unfortunately, you can only see the stables from the outside; they are not open to the public. Behind the stables, you'll find the Palestuin. This small garden is generally open to the public from sunrise to sunset, although it is closed when there are important guests at the palace. Look out for the model lunarscape.

🛈 Free
🕓 Anytime (outside only)

Plein

This is where all the corporate suits and yuppies turn up for a drink after 5pm. It isn't unusual to see ministers and secretaries of state walking around. Even the prime minister likes to frequent this lively square. In winter, the square hosts the antique book market (p134).

The square is also very interesting from an historical and political point-of-view. Here you'll find the Sociëteit de Witte (White Society) debating club, founded in 1851 but still existing today. You'll also find the Logement van Amsterdam and the Logement van Rotterdam here, where visiting dignitaries from these cities would stay when on official business. Today, these buildings are, respectively, used by the Dutch legislature and by the Ministry of Defence.

Rearing up over the Plein, you'll see the more modern sky-rises that house a handful of important Dutch ministries: the Ministry of Education, the Ministry of Internal Affairs and the Ministry of Justice.

In the centre of the square, there is a statue of William of Orange.

🏠 Plein
🛈 Free
🕓 Anytime, best from 5pm
🖥 www.pleindenhaag.nl

Grote Markt

The Grote Markt is where the young and hip hang out in the evenings. Lots of activities take place in the middle of the square, from modern live music to old-school roller discos and skateboarding competitions.

A number of the bars and cafés in the square put on regular live music events.

The Boterwaag is a bar that is steeped in history. It used to be where butter and cheese were brought to be weighed, before going off to market, and in fact you can still see part of the huge scale in the bar, dating from 1682. The building next door used to be the Boterhuis, a wholesaler of daily products.

🏠 Grote Markt
🛈 Free
🕓 Anytime, best from 12noon to 6pm
🖥 www.gmdh.nl

Chinatown

Located in the heart of the city centre, the area that is now Chinatown used to be The Hague's Jewish neighbourhood. Mass deportation of Jews during the second world war left this area largely empty and impoverished. In the 1970s, the municipality decided to renovate the district and, at the same time, a growing number of ethnic Chinese started to settle here.

The distinctive Chinese gates on Wagenstraat (📷 #10) were built in 2009 with material shipped from China. Many of the street signs in the neighbourhood are now also in Chinese.

Behind the gate you'll find a variety of Asian restaurants, supermarkets, acupuncturists and furniture shops.

🏠　Amsterdam Veerkade, Wagenstraat, Gedempte Burgwal

💲　Free

🕾　Anytime, best from 12noon to 6pm

🖥　www.chinatown-denhaag. com

Red Light District (ROSSE BUURT)

Everyone knows about the red light district in Amsterdam (p251), and it is usually on the itinerary of most visitors to the city. The same is not true for the much smaller red light district in The Hague, but it is worth going there just to make a comparison. You'll find far fewer curious tourists here just wandering around and, because of this, the area has a more genuine feel to it. As with Amsterdam, don't take photos if you value your camera.

🏠　Geleenstraat and Hunsestraat

💲　Free

🕾　Anytime, busiest in the evenings

Passage

This kind of covered glass-ceiling shopping mall was popular in major American and European cities during the latter half of the 19th century. The Passage is the only surviving example of this type of architecture in the Netherlands.

The oldest part of the structure — the Spuistraat and Buitenhof wings — dates from 1882, and was built in renaissance style by the architects Herman Wesstra and Jan Christiaan van Wijk.

The more modern Hofweg wing was not added until 1928, and displays a distinctive expressionist influence.

The glass-roofed mall is home to a number of interesting specialist shops.

🏠　Entrances from Venestraat, Hoogstraat, Haagsche Bluf, Grote Marktstraat and Spuistraat

💲　Free

🕾　9am to 6pm

🖥　www.depassage.nl

📷　Photo 30

Haagsche Bluf

Tucked away in a hidden corner of The Hague, where an old cinema used to stand, is Haagsche Bluf. Entering the area, you will be confronted with an intriguing mix of old and new façades. But all is not as it seems. The façades are in actual fact facsimiles of famous buildings around the city, such as the Pagehuis and a striking art nouveau building on the Denneweg (📷 #2), hence the name 'The Hague's Bluff'.

Others suggest the association of its name with the typical Dutch dessert of the same name, which is made with beaten egg whites and sugar.

The square doesn't sell the typical dessert, but has a small shopping area and a couple of nice cafés. Grand Café (🖥 www.

grandcafetwitter.nl) and Kaldi
(🖥 www.kaldi.nl) both have very
nice terraces in the summer. Kaldi
serves good coffee.

🏠 Haagsche Bluf

💲 Free

⏰ Anytime

Markets (MARKTEN)

The city has many interesting
markets such as the huge open air
Haagse Markt, the organic market
and the antique and book market.
You can visit them on your own
(p133), but if you would prefer to
go with a guide City Mondial arranges tours (p133).

PEACE PALACE AREA

Peace Palace (VREDESPALEIS)

Built between 1907 and 1913, the
Peace Palace has become an iconic
symbol of The Hague's self-branded
image as the seat of international
justice.

The Palace was created to provide a home for the Permanent
Court of Arbitration (PCA), which
was established in 1899. The PCA
still resides within the Palace, along
with the International Court of Justice (ICJ) and The Hague Academy
of International Law.

Andrew Carnegie, a
Scottish-American industrialist and
philanthropist, paid for the construction of the Palace out of the
vast fortunes he had amassed in
the steel industry. A bust of him is
contained within the Palace, along
with other notaries that fought for
justice in some way or other, including Nelson Mandela and Ma-
hatma Gandhi.

The Palace is impressive to behold from outside. Inside, the
rooms are filled with countless gifts

from different nations — including
huge Ming vases from China, giant
silk tapestries from Japan and intri-
cate gold finery from Pakistan.

Outside the Palace, before the
entrance gates, you will see an
eternal flame that was erected in
1999 as a symbol of world peace.
Not far from this is a monument
called the World Path of Peace, consisting of 196 stones from as many
countries. Each country contributed
a stone from their soil in order to
symbolise world peace.

The eternal flame and the World
Path of Peace can be seen at any
time of day or night. Tours of the
Peace Palace operate only at the
weekend (when the building is not
being used for other purposes) —
you can book through their website.

The visitor centre, which adjoins
the Peace Palace, offers a fascinating audio tour for free, explaining a
little more about the history of the
building and international justice
more generally. The audio tour also
gives an insight into the work of the
PCA and the ICJ, using entertaining
cartoons and clear language to explain some fairly complex themes.

🏠 Carnegieplein 2

💲 Visitor centre free; tours inside €8.50. No reductions.

⏰ Visitor centre Mon: closed,
Tue-Sun: 10am to 5pm;
Tours: check website

🖥 www.vredespaleis.nl

Panorama Mesdag

The main attraction of this small
art gallery is the quite extraordinary masterpiece painted by Hendrik Willem Mesdag in 1881. Mesdag was assisted in the endeavour
by his wife, Sientje van Houten,
and some young student artists

from The Hague School, of which Mesdag was a member.

Painted in 1881, the Mesdag Panorama — one of the largest panoramas in the world — is breathtaking to behold. Upon first inspection, it seems almost impossible to tell where the artificially-created landscape ends and the painting begins.

The painting is 14 metres high and has a circumference of almost 100 metres, completely encircling the room. You are kept at least 14 metres away from the painting at all times, which helps create the illusion that it isn't a painting at all.

The panoramic painting depicts the North Sea and the dunes around Scheveningen, as it looked more than a century ago. The attention to detail is remarkable. The panorama is lit by natural light, giving it an interesting reflection of the changing conditions outside. This also means, of course, that you'll get a better impression of the panorama if you go on a sunny day.

An audio commentary accompanies the panorama. Somewhat unusually, the commentary doesn't use headphones, but is broadcast across the entire room in whatever language you requested when you entered.

Don't forget that the panorama isn't the only thing to see in the museum. The other pictures of Mesdag — mainly of seascapes and coastal hamlets — may not be as impressive as the central masterpiece, but they're definitely worth viewing. The museum regularly hosts temporary exhibitions of other artists.

🏠 Zeestraat 65

💲 Adults: €7; Children under 12: €3.50; [M]

🕙 Mon-Sat: 10am to 5pm, Sun: 12noon to 5pm

🖥 panorama-mesdag.com

Museon

If your kids are bored with traipsing round The Hague's manifold museums, then a quick visit to the city's very own natural history museum might just set them right.

What makes the museum so different from all the others is that, scattered among the usual dusty relics trapped behind sheets of glass, are countless interactive exhibits, making the educational experience of visiting the museum a great deal of fun. From competitive quizzes to computer simulations of how bees gather nectar, these interactive displays have been brilliantly developed to make the whole museum experience highly recommended. Most of the interactive exhibits are also in English.

The museum is spread over two floors. The ground floor holds temporary exhibitions, whilst the more permanent exhibitions are located upstairs. The top floor is divided into five broad categories: geology, anthropology, biology and the environment, history and archaeology and the natural world.

The museum also runs regular activities for kids — such as learning how plants grow or how to cut precious stones — which are great fun. Check the website for details of these.

🏠 Stadhouderslaan 37

💲 €10

🕙 Mon: Closed; Tue-Sun: 11am to 5pm

📞 070 338 1338

🖥 www.museon.nl

What to See

City Museum (GEMEENTEMUSEUM)

The Hague's City Museum is just next door to the Museon. This isn't the place to come if you want to further your understanding of The Hague's history — the Historical Museum (p143) is for that. Rather, the Gemeentemuseum inventively combines political and historical exhibits with a range of works from Dutch artists stretching back over the past two centuries.

Exhibitions rotate roughly every six months, although the museum does have one semi-permanent exhibition on the works of Dutch artist Piet Mondriaan (1872 to 1944). Staff at the museum say that this exhibition could eventually be replaced, but there is no sign of it happening in the near future and it remains extremely popular.

Mondriaan is perhaps most famous for embracing the De Stijl ('The Style') artistic movement, which began in 1917 and lasted until the early 1930s. The De Stijl movement played a pivotal role in European avant-garde, and has helped to shape both architecture and city design.

De Stijl artists sought to simplify the shapes and colours used in their pictures, thereby creating an abstraction of real-world objects. The idea was to move beyond the traditional function of a painting as an accurate depiction of reality. In this way, the artistic style can be thought of as a precursor to what is now regarded as modern art.

At the moment, the Gemeentemuseum houses many of the more important works of the Mauritshuis (p144), which is currently undergoing renovation.

Other displays at the museum are quite varied, from Dutch impressionists to more modern works. However, the layout of the museum can appear confusing, with no clear idea of what artistic period you are wandering through.

There is also a permanent, though fairly small, exhibition about The Hague School. Heavily influenced by French realists such as Jean-François Millet, the school lasted from 1860 and 1890 and was where Hendrik Mesdag (p149) took most of his inspiration from.

The museum building is a masterpiece in itself, since it was designed by prominent Dutch architect Hendrik Berlage.

🏠　Stadhouderslaan 41

💰　€12.50

🕐　Tue-Sun: 11am to 5pm

☎　070 338 1111

💻　www.gemeentemuseum.nl

Photo Museum (FOTOMUSEUM) and Museum of Contemporary Art (MUSEUM VOOR ACTUELE KUNST)

Officially, these two small galleries are part of the *gemeentemuseum* but they have a separate entrance fee. All exhibitions are temporary and rotate every few months or so.

When your researchers visited, just one relatively small room was given over to photography, showcasing the work of one particular contemporary from France, whilst the rest of the building housed contemporary paintings from two other artists.

The building is a reasonable size, but the work tends to be quite spread out and it shouldn't take you too long to see it.

🏠　Stadhouderslaan 43

☎　070 338 1144

What to See

🛈 Adults: €6; Children under 18: Free; Museum card: Free

🕑 Mon: Closed; Tue-Sun: 12am to 6pm

🖥 www.fotomuseumdenhaag.nl

Mesdag Museum

The former family home of Mesdag and his wife is just around the corner from the panorama gallery. Here you will find the private collection of paintings that Mesdag gathered during his lifetime, including such luminaries as Jean-François Millet, Henri Rousseau, Gustave Courbet and Charles-François Daubigny (although not their most famous work). Mesdag was the benefactor of Italian painter Antonio Mancini for nearly 20 years, and many of his works are on display in the museum.

Some paintings by Mesdag and his wife, Sientje, are also on display.

Besides paintings, you'll find a room dedicated to tapestries and vases, most of which come from the Far East — something that was very fashionable in the late 19th century.

Downstairs, the museum runs regular temporary exhibitions.

If the sun is shining, it is particularly pleasant to wander out into the lovely gardens that are attached to the museum.

🏠 Laan van Meerdervoort 7F

📞 070 362 1434

🛈 Adults: €7.50; Children under 17: Free; Ⓜ

🕑 Mon-Tue: closed, Wed-Sun: 12noon to 5pm

🖥 demesdagcollectie.nl

HAAGSE BOS AREA

Madurodam

Come to the Madurodam to get a taste of what the Netherlands has to offer.

The park is home to hundreds of miniature models of buildings from all over the country. Here you can visit Schiphol airport, the Deltaworks, the Dutch East Indies Company, Kinderdijk, Rotterdam's harbour, the Rijksmuseum and much more besides — all within 18,000 square metres.

All models are 25 times smaller than the real thing. Most of them are developed and maintained by the museum's very own workshops, located not far from the main park (although closed to the public).

The care, attention and inventiveness that has been lavished on this park makes it one of the must-see attractions of The Hague. Extensive renovations took place in the park between November 2011 and April 2012, to make the whole "miniature world" experience that much more interactive.

There are now some great activities, which are particularly popular with kids, such as unloading and loading ships at Rotterdam's harbour or trying to plug a hole in a dyke with your finger, following the legend of Hans Brinker who supposedly did the same in Haarlem.

Video terminals throughout the park explain aspects of Dutch history (the films are in Dutch, but subtitled in one of seven other languages).

A really nice touch is that the park tries to move with the seasons. So in winter time, miniature ice-skaters will appear. And, for the

European football championships in 2012, the park was decked out in orange banners — which no doubt added to the disappointed when the national team failed to live up to expectations.

One small criticism is that, whilst the main models are labelled, some of the less obviously-identifiable ones are not — and this can be a little frustrating. Also, the videos, whilst humorous, do not always go into as much detail as one might like.

Remember that the park is outdoors so, if you choose to go when it's raining, you're going to get wet.

🏠   George Maduroplein 1

💲   €14.50

🕙   9am to 8pm

☎   070 416 2400

💻   www.madurodam.nl

Huis Ten Bosch Palace

This was the official residence of Queen Beatrix from 1981 until 2013. Now that she has abdicated (p61), her eldest son Willem-Alexander will take up residence there.

The palace lies to the north-east of The Hague in the Haagse Bos. It dates from the 17th century and was originally intended as a summer residence for Amalia van Solms-Braunfels, wife of Frederick Henry, Prince of Orange. However, her husband died whilst the palace was still being constructed, so it was hastily turned into a mausoleum.

In 1899 the palace hosted the First World Peace Conference, an initiative of Tsar Nicholas II, Russia's last emperor.

The palace had a lucky escape during the second world war. The Germans, occupying the country at the time, wanted it pulled down, but it was ultimately spared.

After the war, the palace gradually slipped into disrepair until it was saved by a massive restoration effort in 1977. Since 1980, the palace has been home to the royal family once again.

You can only see the palace from outside; it is not open to the public.

🏠   Haagse Bos, near Leidsestraatweg

💲   Free (outside only)

🕙   Daytime

Japanese Garden

Situated in Clingendael Park, to the northeast of the city centre, the immaculately-kept Japanese Garden is definitely worth a visit. Unfortunately, due to the fragile nature of the park, it is only open for a very a short period of time each year. This is usually between late April and mid-June and again for a couple of weeks in October. The park is most impressive during the summer months, when the whole garden is in bloom. You can take a bike into Clingendael Park but not into the Japanese Garden. The garden is not terribly big.

🏠   Within Clingendael Park

💲   Free

🕙   Late April to mid-June: 9am to 8pm

Louwman Museum

Dating back to 1934, this museum houses an amazing collection of cars through the ages, some of which are stunningly unusual. The variety and wealth of cars is staggering. Look out for the original Bond car that Sean Connery drove in Gold Finger.

The whole museum is very well laid-out, with interesting descriptions in both Dutch and English.

What to See

If you want to see the entire museum, you'll probably need to set aside at least two hours.

The museum is situated in a lovely green area, within easy walking distance of Huis-Ten-Bosch Palace (p153) and Haagse Bos (p162). It is a bit outside the city centre. Buses 24, 43 and 90 (all of which you can catch at Centraal Station) stop nearby.

- 🏠　Leidsestraatweg 57
- ☎　070 304 7373
- 💰　€13.50; parking €5
- ☎　Tue-Sun: 10am to 5pm
- 🖥　www.louwmanmuseum.nl

Fishnet stocking viaduct (VIADUCT NETKOUS)

Netkous Viaduct is an impressive open tubular structure that is part of the RandstadRail network in the Bezuidenhout are of The Hague. The viaduct is located along line 3 and 4 at the Beatrixkwartier stop.

- 🏠　Prinses Beatrixlaan
- 💰　Free (or price of a tram ticket if you want to see it from the tram)
- ☎　Anytime, best during the day

SCHEVENINGEN

Images by the Sea Museum (BEELDEN-AAN-ZEE MUSEUM)

This museum of contemporary art hosts three or four exhibitions a year. These are sometimes thematically organised or may be dedicated to a single artist. The museum also has a free outdoor exhibition of 23 sculptures based on fairytale stories (p154).

The building itself is intriguing. Designed by Dutch architect Wim Quist, it uses sand-coloured materials in order to blend in with the undulating dunes of its surroundings. Much of the museum is under the ground, with some outside terraces tucked away behind the dunes.

- 🏠　Harteveltstraat 1
- 💰　€12; Ⓜ
- ☎　Tue-Sun: 11am to 5pm
- 🖥　www.beeldenaanzee.nl

Fairytale Sculptures by the Sea (SPROOKJESBEELDEN AAN ZEE)

On the new promenade that runs alongside Scheveningen's main beach, you will encounter a series of bronze figures inspired by fairytale characters. The sculptures are the creation of American sculptor Tom Otterness. The objects on display include three large and 20 smaller sculptures. The most noticeable sculptures are The Herring Eater and The Crying Giant. Smaller ones include Humpty Dumpty, Gulliver from Gulliver's Travels and Hansel and Gretel.

The sculptures are officially part of the Beelden-aan-Zee Museum (p156), but they are outside and free to look at.

- 🏠　Scheveningen Boulevard
- 💰　Free
- ☎　Anytime
- 🖥　www.beeldenaanzee.nl

Scheveningen Museum (MUZEE SCHEVENINGEN)

This museum offers a glimpse into Scheveningen's history as an important seaport. The museum is fairly small, but includes a small pub / restaurant.

The museum includes displays on deep-sea fishing, the history of the famous Scheveningen beach, a collection of shellfish and reconstructions of traditional fishermen homes. In one room, the inside of a fishing vessel has been rebuilt.

The museum is housed in a former school — in fact, '*gemeenteschool*' is still etched in stone above the entrance. Local volunteers are on hand to answer questions about the history of Scheveningen or Dutch seafaring.

🏠 Neptunusstraat 90-92

💲 €7; 50% discount with Ooievaarspas; ⬛ Ⓜ

🕐 Tue-Sun 1 to 5pm

🖥 www.muzee.nl

Ship Museum (MUSEUMSCHIP MERCUUR)

You'll find the ship museum in a small boat moored alongside a quay in Scheveningen harbour. The H.M. Mercuur was once a minesweeper belonging to the US navy, which served in the second world war. The ship has been renovated to look much as it did when it was in service.

Aboard the vessel, you will be able to experience what it was like to work for the navy on this particular ship. You can visit the museum with or without a guide. Guides are mostly former employees from the Dutch navy, who tell fascinating stories about their own experiences.

🏠 Dr Lelykade

💲 €5,00, children €2,50, 50% discount with Ooievaarspas

🕐 May-Sep: Tue-Sun 10am to 5pm, Oct-April: only weekend

🖥 www. museumschip-mercuur.nl

Pier

Scheveningen's famous peer currently hosts a restaurant, a handful of shops, some exhibition space where artists often showcase their work and a 60-metre bungee jump (🖥 www.bungy.nl). However, in March 2012, the pier was put up for sale and so it's future looks uncertain. No buyer has yet been found.

An assessment of the historic structure has revealed that it is not fire safe, and that it will need a considerable injection of money in order to bring it up to national safety standards.

The 380-metre long pier was built in 1900. During the second world war, the pavilion served as a storage facility for the occupying German forces. The Germans tore down the pier in 1943. It was rebuilt after the war and inaugurated by Prince Bernhard in 1961.

The pier is currently owned by hospitality company Van der Valk, who purchased it in 1991 for a token amount of one guilder.

🏠 Strandweg

💲 Free entrance. Pay separately for activities.

🕐 Anytime (see separate websites for activities time)

🖥 www.pier.nl

Sea Life

The Hague's aquarium is located on the seafront at Scheveningen, and is particularly popular with kids. In parts, the interior is reminiscent of a submarine or ship. Visitors are taken on a fascinating journey through different parts of the world and their species. The aquarium is also involved with breeding programmes for endangered species, such as seahorses. The place is surprisingly small and so can get quite crowded at peak times, such as weekends.

🏠 Strandweg 13

💲 €16, until 11 years €11, discount with online purchase, annual pass €45/35

🕐 10am to 6pm; in July and August until 8pm

🖥 www.visitsealife.com/ Scheveningen

Steigenberger Kurhaus

The Steigenberger Kurhaus is the oldest hotel in The Hague. It was built 1884 and 1885 by the German architects Johann Friedrich Henkenhaf and Friedrich Ebert. It was originally intended as a concert hall plus adjoining hotel. In fact, performances were staged here as recently as the 1960s. The last band to perform at the Kurhaus was the Rolling Stones in 1664. The building fell into disrepair and was closed in 1969. It was saved from demolition when it was listed as an historic building in 1975. It reopened as a hotel in 1979. An iconic symbol of Scheveningen, it is definitely worth a visit. The outside is particularly striking, but don't ignore the fabulous interior.

🏠 Gevers Deynootplein 30

💲 Free

🕐 Anytime

🖥 www.kurhaus.nl

Kijkduin

An alternative to Scheveningen's famous, though often quite crowded, beach is Kijkduin. This slightly more downmarket seaside resort has a similar set-up to Scheveningen: pavilions on the beach offering food and drink, shops along the promenade and plenty of sand. Kijkduin is a place to keep in mind if you're getting a bit fed up with its dandier neighbour.

In 2011, a new peninsula was constructed 10 km off the coast of Kijkduin in 2011. It was named Zandmotor ('Sand Engine') and was built for the purpose of coastal defence and coastal maintenance. The idea is that, over the years, the natural currents will distributed the sand all along the coast, thereby reinforcing existing embankments.

🏠 Deltaplein

OUTSKIRTS

De Vlieger

This is one of the few windmills in that is easily accessible by public transport from The Hague. Built in 1621, the windmill is now owned by the municipality of Leidschendam-Voorburg. It has been completely renovated and is now fully operational.

It is possible to have a tour of the windmill, given by enthusiastic volunteers. The interior looks much as it would have done at the turn of the last century.

🏠 Essepad 3, Voorburg

💲 Free

🕐 April-October on Wed and Sat from 1.30 to 4.30pm

🖥 www.molendevlieger.nl

TOURS

If you prefer to discover The Hague with a tour, there are plenty available to suit all budgets. A lot of them are in Dutch, but most of them also have an English option. Some are available in other languages, too.

Canal cruise	
Ooievaart: Bierkade 18B; ☎ 070 445 1869; 🖥 www.ooievaart.nl	Boat tours in both English and Dutch: €10 for adults and €6 for children under 13. Tours last approximately 90 minutes and take place every Saturday during the summer months (June to September) at 4pm. Additional theme-based tours are run most Sunday mornings, starting at 10.30am. Past themes have included canal-side vegetation, aquatic plants and historic buildings.
Salonboot: ☎ 070 211 6105; 🖥 www.salonbootdenhaag.nl	Wine and beer tasting cruises. Evening or weekend cruises cost €34.95. The company also rents boats for private parties.
Bike tour	
Totzo: 🏛 Noordeinde 91; ☎ 070 326 5790; 🖥 www.totzo.org	Offers different themed tours, such as 'music, art and architecture' or 'sea, dunes and woodlands'. Tours are available in English. A three-hour tour costs €24.50, which includes bike rental, hot drink, a small treat, water and a rain poncho. A shorter hour-long tour costs €19.50.
Walking tour	
Gilde: 🏛 Riviervismarkt 2; ☎ 070 356 1281; 🖥 www.gildedenhaag.nl	Historical walking tour of the city. Tours are every Thursday at 1.30pm, although it is requested that you book at least two days in advance. The tour costs €4 and lasts around one and a half hours.
Greeters: 🏛 Godetiaweg 113; ☎ 06 5182 9693; 🖥 www.denhaaggreeters.nl	Fantastic walking tours given by volunteers who are living in The Hague and have a deep understanding of the city. It is advisable to book a least one week in advance — you can do so online. You will be asked to specify what you are interested in and say what day and time you prefer. Tours are given in Dutch, English, French, Spanish, Italian and German. You can arrange one-to-one tours or as part of a small group.

What to See

VVV (tourist office): ☎ 070 361 8860; 🏠 Spui 68	Art nouveau / Hofje walking tour. The tourist office, in collaboration with Gilde, offer city tours on different themes including art nouveau. Tours run on Tuesdays and Thursdays. They start at 1.30pm and last around two hours, costing €4. The tourist office can also organise other tours. Pop into their office or call them for more details.
Citymondial: 🏠 Wagenstraat 193; ☎ 070 402 3336; www.citymondial.nl	This company arranges tours in slightly less usual areas of The Hague, including Chinatown, Stationsbuurt, Schilderswijk and the markets. Tours last an hour and a half. Prices start from €9.75, depending on the number of people on the tour. They also organise bike and boat tours.
Political tour	
ProDemos: 🏠 Hofweg 1; ☎ 070 364 6144; 🖥 www.prodemos.nl	Organises guided tours to the Ridderzaal (p148) and, Dutch Senate and House of Representatives.

FESTIVALS AND EVENTS

There is a wide range of festivals and events to look out for throughout the year in The Hague. Below, we have listed some of the more popular ones. To find out about festivals taking place over the summer, visit 💻 www.thehaguefestivals.com.

1 January	New Year's Day	Marked in The Hague by a quick dash into the North Sea at mid-day (p87, 📷 #35). Known as *nieuwjaarsduik*.
January	Winternachten	Literary festival showcasing writers from all over the world, held at the Filmhuis. See 💻 www.winternachten.nl
January / February	Dance Festival	The national dance festival features plenty of live performance all over the city. See 💻 denhaagdanst.nl
2014: 31 Jan 2015: 19 Feb 2016: 8 Feb 2017: 28 Jan	Chinese New Year	Worth visiting Chinatown for this, where you will see traditional lion and dragon dances, performers and artists and an Asian market (📷 #10). See 💻 www.chineesnieuwjaarfestival.nl
March	Movies That Matter Festival	A series of movies are screened at the Filmhuis, dedicated to exploring human rights issues. See 💻 www.moviesthatmatter.nl
March	City-Pier-City (CPC) Run	A half-marathon that takes place every year. See 💻 www.cpcloopdenhaag.nl
March	Music Festival	This three-day Hague-based festival features new talent as well as old names. See 💻 www.muziekdriedaagse.nl
April	International Sand Sculpture Festival	Visit Scheveningen to see absolutely stunning creations sculpted out of sand. See 💻 www.sandsculptures.nl
April	International Pillow Fight Day	A festival that takes place all over the world during the first week of April. Grote Markt is usually the venue in The Hague. See 💻 www.pillowfightday.com
29 April	Queen's (or King's) Night	A colourful explosion of street parties and festivals in honour of the reigning monarch.

May	Bevrijdings-festival	A summer music festival. See 🖥 www.bevrijdingsfestivals.nl
Late May or early June	Tong Tong Festival	This Indonesian cultural festival takes place just across from Centraal Station, in the Malieveld. Sample Indonesian cuisine and watch cultural performances. Entrance is around €10 during the week and €13 at weekends. See 🖥 tongtongfestival.nl
Early June	Vlaggetjesdag	Flag Day, as it is known in English, is the celebration of the arrival of the first herring ('*Hollandse Nieuwe*') in The Hague. Hundreds of thousands of people gather in Scheveningen for the festivities, and the fishing boats are decorated especially for the occasion. The first barrel of herring is traditionally sold at an auction on the Thursday preceding the official Vlaggetjesdag and the proceeds go to charity. See 🖥 www.vlaggetjesdag.com
Early June to early September	The Hague Sculpture	A sculpture festival that showcases a new country or theme each year. Location varies each year, but details are available at 🖥 www.denhaagsculptuur.nl
Mid-June	Festival Klassique	A festival spanning several days dedicated to classical music. Performances are centred on the Plein, just next to the Binnenhof.
Last Sunday in June	Parkpop	A hugely popular free summer festival held in Zuiderpark. See 🖥 www.parkpop.nl
August	Jazz in de Gracht	Free jazz performances are staged throughout the city. Simply grab a drink by the side of the canal, sit and watch. See 🖥 www.jazzindegracht.nl
Third week of August	International Fireworks Festival	Every year, fireworks producers from several different countries turn up at the pier in Scheveningen to compete for the Scheveningen Fireworks Trophy. See 🖥 www.vuurwerkscheveningen.nl
September	Prinsjesdag	The State Opening of Parliament, when the ruling monarch arrives in ceremonial golden carriage. You will have a good chance to see the carriage in various locations around the city.

September	Haags UIT	An end-of-summer music festival. See ⬚ www.haagsuitfestival.nl
September	Scheveningen Kite Festival	Visitors can see hundreds of kites of all shapes and sizes soaring over Scheveningen beach. See ⬚ vliegerfeest-scheveningen.nl
October	Shoot Me Film Festival	A film festival in The Hague that promotes independent film-making. See ⬚ www.shoot-me.nl
October	De Betovering	Translated in English as The Enchantment, this international children's art festival takes place during the Autumn school break. Hundreds of performances and workshops take place around the city. See ⬚ www.debetovering.nl
November	Arrival of Sinterklaas	Huge throngs turn out in Scheveningen to see Sinterklaas (Saint Nicholas) arrive by steamboat (p74). See ⬚ www.sinterklaasindenhaag.nl
5 December	Sinterklaas	Saint Nicholas Day, known as Sinterklaas in the Netherlands, is one of the most important days of the year (p79).

BEACHES

Whilst the weather in The Hague may never reach the highs of the Mediterranean, you still shouldn't completely overlook the beaches that the area has to offer.

The Hague has 11 km of beach in total. The most touristic beaches are at Scheveningen and at Kijkduin.

Beaches tend to be sandy and very spacious. Restaurants are strewn along the coastline. Many of these are temporary structures that only appear during the warmer months (from late March to late September). These restaurants are colourful and vibrant places to hang out, with large and comfortable cushions to sprawl upon, open-air barbecues and the occasional DJ pumping out tunes.

Beaches in The Hague are at their busiest during the summer months, but they can also be fun places to come during the winter. Covered with snow, they are the ideal place for a spot of cross-country skiing.

At mid-day on January 1, thousands of people turn up at Scheveningen's beach to dash into the insanely cold waters of the North Sea. This annual tradition, which is known as Nieuwjaarsduik, goes back decades. It was started in 1965 by Dutch swimmer Jan van Scheijndel, who was the first person from the Netherlands to swim the English Channel.

Anyone can participate in the event, for around €3.50, although places are limited. Around 10,000 people participate each year. Once the tickets are sold out, you won't be admitted. Following the swim, hot pea soup (*erwtensoep*) is served. This is included in the price of the ticket.

Observing the event from the sidelines can be great fun, too. A sea of orange sweeps across the beach, as participants don their woolly orange hats for the occasion. Some more daring folk even turn up in their birthday suits.

PARKS AND CITY FARMS

There is no shortage of parks in The Hague, where you can go for an afternoon stroll, a bike ride, a picnic, a barbecue or to let your children have a run-around.

Westduinpark (🏠 Duivelandsestraat) and **Bosjes van Poot** together form a 230-hectare nature reserve, the largest green area of the city. Located west of the old port, the area offers a great location for cycling and walking through the dunes. There are also horse trails. The beach is accessible from a number of points in the park. There is even a nudist beach — but this is well-signposted, so it is unlikely that you will stumble upon it by accident.

It is possible to encounter foxes and rabbits in the area. There are several bunkers built before and during second world war. Most are covered with sand. There is also a small beachcombing museum in the park, known as Uncle John's Shack (🖥 www.jutterskeet.nl). Entrance is free.

You can find out more information about the dunes at the visitor's

centre located in nearby Wassenaar (🏠 Meijendelseweg 40; ☎ 070 511 7276; 🕐 Tue-Fri: 10am to 4pm, Sun: 10am to 5pm).

Scheveningse Bosjes (🏠 Scheveningseweg), located near Madurodam, is a former hunting ground of the royal family and still relatively wooded. It is ideal for cycling and running. It hosts a large playground with a sandpit, next to a skating park and a relatively large pond.

Haagse Bos (🏠 Bezuidenhoutseweg) is just north-east of Centraal Station. During the second world war, it was an important training and military ground for German soldiers. It is a much more pleasant place these days, and is now one of 19 protected cityscapes in The Hague. Regular outdoor concerts are held in the park during the summer months.

There is an enclosure for deer in the park, just in front of Centraal Station. Near the park's lakes, you'll also find an interesting collection of animal sculptures carved from tree trunks, as well as some training equipment used by those participating in boot camp fitness programmes. In the winter, the park's lake becomes an ice-skating rink.

Westbroekpark (🏠 Cremerweg, Scheveningen) is an 18-hectare park located between Madurodam and Scheveningen. It has a relaxed atmosphere and is family-friendly. It hosts some playgrounds and an impressive rose garden that dates from 1961; viewing of the rose garden is best between June and November, when you can admire 20,000 roses in flower. There is also a restaurant at the edge of the park (Rosarium Wok: 🖥 www.westbroekpark.nl), which has a good reputation.

Clingendael (🏠 Clingendael) is a large park, located to the north-east of The Hague. Here you will find a small but well laid-out Japanese garden, which is only open a few months each year (p153).

Speckled with ponds and waterways, **Zuiderpark** (🏠 Moerweg; 🖥 www.zuiderparkdenhaag.nl) lies west of the city centre. Cultural and musical events are regularly put on in the park, of which the Parkpop festival (p160) is probably the best known. It has a skating and hockey rink (which is free to use — providing there is no match taking place), a few kiosks and a couple of cafés. It is possible in the summer months to rent pedalos for €10 per hour (🖥 www.kanoverhuurzuiderpark. nl). Barbecues are allowed in the park, as long you collect all your belongings when you leave, and there is plenty of space for sport and leisure activities.

Oostduinpark (🏠 Duiveland-sestraat) is a dune area of 37 acres. The dunes are relatively high. There are several ponds, and some beautiful nature. It is possible to see deer in the wild and other small animals. No cars are allowed in the park so it is perfect for long cycle rides. At the beginning of the park there is a café and a water tower.

Kortenbos (🏠 Kortenbos) is a small park in the centre of the city. It has a playground for children and a ping-pong table.

Paleistuin (🏠 Prinsessewal) is very centrally-located, not far from Noordeinde Palace. It has a playground for children, a pond and some space to have a picnic. There are several buildings in the park, including the Royal Archives and Royal Stables. Unlike most of the parks, it closes at sunset and for special events.

City farms (*kinderboerderij*) are also very popular. Here, children can look at or touch farmyard animals, such as pigs, rabbits, goats, cows, and horses. Entrance is free. City farms are usually open from 9am to 5pm, closed on Sundays.

Some *kinderboerderij* in The Hague include:

🏠 Tivolistraat, Schilderwijk

🏠 Jacobstraat, Stationsbuurt

🏠 Scheeperstraat, Transvaal

QUIZZES AND GAMES

If being able to answer totally irrelevant trivia is your thing, then you might like to check out one of the pub quizzes that are regularly held around town.

O'Casey's (🏠 Noordeinde 140; 🖥 ocaseys.nl) runs a general-knowledge quiz every Thursday and a music quiz on Fridays, both starting at around 8.30pm. **The Fiddler** (🏠 Riviervis-markt 1; ☎ 070 365 1955; 🖥 www. fiddler.nl) runs general-knowledge quizzes, which take place every other Tuesday.

Both quizzes are relaxed and have a good vibe about them — but remember, like in such games the world over, there are one or two teams that take the quiz so seriously it is very difficult to beat them.

There are a couple of board game clubs that you might like to get involved with. **De Rode Dobbel-steen** (☎ 070 427 4713; 🖥 www. derodedobbelsteen.nl) meets a couple of times per month, on a Tuesday, at 🏠 Dunne Bierkade 21. **SpelgroepPhoenix** (☎ 071 522 6956; 🖥 www.spelgroepphoenix. nl) is a larger board game group, which meets every week on Tuesday in Capelle aan den IJssel (near Rotterdam) and on Wednesday in Leiden.

DANCING

Dansschool Universala — La Bodeguita (🏠 Oude Molstraat 32D; ☎ 070 345 2157 or 06 2304 5862; 🖥 www.universalsa.nl) offers salsa lessons from €80 for an eight-week course. There is also a salsa party that takes place every Thursday and Friday, usually with free entrance. La Bodeguita also offers Zumba Fitness dance lessons — €27.50 for a month's course.

Tango Centro (🏠 Lange Poten 27; ☎ 070 444 4423 or 06 5336 5912; 🖥 www.tangocentro.nl) offers tango lessons for beginners through to advanced. You can attend a free trial lesson, even if you don't have a dance partner. For the actual lessons, though, you will need to find yourself a dance partner.

Van der Meulen-Wesseling, (🏠 Laan van Meerdervoort 50; 🖥 www.dansles-wesseling.nl) offers classical ballroom and Latin American dance lessons.

Regular salsa evenings are held at:

Boterwaag (🏠 Grote Markt 81; 🖥 www.gmdh.nl/de-boterwaag) — every Wednesday and Friday.

Megaplaza Starlight (🏠 Binckhorstlaan 151; 🖥 www.dansschool-megaplaza-starlight.nl) — every third Saturday of the month.

MUSIC LESSONS

For group lessons, the centrally-located Kooorenhuis (p46) has a good reputation. For private lessons, you could try 🖥 www.priveles.com or 🖥 www.muziekles.nl.

LIVE MUSIC

Murphy's Law (🏠 Dr. Kuyperstraat 7; ☎ 070 427 2507; 🖥 www.murphysjazz.nl) is a pub with a good vibe that has jazz evenings most Mondays and Saturdays. It occasionally has Irish-themed sessions, too.

De Paap (🏠 Papestraat 32; ☎ 070 365 2002; 🖥 www.depaap.nl) is a central pub that has regular gigs. Entrance is always free.

De Kikker (🏠 Molenstraat 13 ☎ 070 887 1355) is a good rustic spot that has live music just about every day of the week apart from Mondays. The place isn't terribly big and fills up pretty quickly, so get there early. Free entrance.

Bazart (🏠 Loosduinsekade 725; ☎ 070 323 9652; 🖥 www.bazart.nl) has regular metal bands, but also some more mellow music. The entrance fee varies from €3 to €20 depending on the band.

't Syndicaat (🏠 Nieuwe Molstraat 10; ☎ 070 360 0053; 🖥 www.syndicaat-denhaag.nl) is an *eetcafé* that is also a popular venue for live music and dance (salsa, tango, sevillana) events.

Café De Pater (🏠 Achterom 8; ☎ 070 345 0852; 🖥 www.patermuziek.com) is a great little venue that has been going for a long time. You will hear a range of music in the place — jazz, Latin, funk and experimental — from vibrant young musicians that come from The Hague's music conservatory. The place has a rebellious streak and permits smoking inside, despite an official ban by the government.

Grand Café (🏠 GroteMarkt 1; ☎ 070 365 9686) has live music every day. Upcoming programmes are available on their Facebook page (GrandCafeGM). There is a restaurant on the first floor.

Café de Bieb (🏠 Veenkade 7; ☎ 070 361 7496; 🖥 www.cafedebieb.com) has live music on Thursdays. Music ranges from rock to jazz. It also has a dartboard and serves food thought the day.

Jazz Bodega est est est (🏠 Wagenstraat 144, ☎ 070 785 56 86) has free entrance but drinks are slightly more expensive than you'd find elsewhere. Music 9pm to 1am.

De Libertijn (🏠 Papestraat 30a, ☎ 070 744 9900; ☎ www.delibertijn.com) is a pub that has jamming sessions every Wednesday from 9pm. There is also a pool table and a dartboard.

Societeit Engels (🏠 Koningin Emmakade 4-5 B; ☎ 06 5479 2333; 🖥 societeitengels.nl) is a club where jazz, soul, blues and funk are performed. The weekly jam session takes place on Sunday from 4 to 7pm. Entrance is €8.50.

Supermarkt (🏠 Grote Markt 25; ☎ 070 345 6999; 🖥 www.supermarktdenhaag.nl) has daily events, mainly rock and pop music but also comedy evenings (in Dutch). Entrance is often free, although there may be a small charge (in the region of €3 to €5) depending on the event.

Paard van Troje (🏠 Prinsegracht 12; ☎ 070 750 3434; 🖥 www.paard.nl) has a varied selection of gigs. Sometimes international bands even play here. Entrance is often free, but there may be a cover charge for the bigger names.

At **De Boerderij** (🏠 Amerikaweg 145; ☎ 079 321 1012; 🖥 www.cultuurpodiumboerderij.nl) in Zoetermeer, the line-up is mostly covers of rock greats from yesteryear.

Regular concerts are also organised by **The Hague Conservatory** (🏠 Juliana van Stolberglaan 1; ☎ 070 315 1515; 🖥 www.koncon.nl). The complete agenda is on their website. Some concerts are free but most of them cost around €20.

Concerts and organ recitals are regularly held at the **Kloosterkerk Art Centre** (🏠 Lange Voorhout 4; 🖥 www.kunstcentrum-kloosterkerk.nl).

WINE AND BEER TASTING

Schutter Wijnservice (🏠 Balistraat 81b; ☎ 070 364 8244; 🖥 schutterwijnservice.nl) runs regular wine tasting sessions and courses, as well as food and wine evenings. Check their website for more details.

Alien Brewing Company (🏠 Korte Koediefstraat 5; 🖥 www.abcbeers.nl) runs regular beer tasting — and occasionally beer-brewing — sessions. They also organise some beer-themed events, such as beer tasting combined with river cruise and beer-and-cheese tastings.

ENTERTAINMENT

Cinema

In general, movies are screened in the original language with Dutch subtitling. Dutch movies will be shown without any subtitling.

Pathé (🖥 www.pathe.nl) has three cinemas around The Hague: 🏠 Buitenhof 20 and 🏠 Spui 65 in the centre of town, and 🏠 Karhausweg 2A in Scheveningen. Tickets cost €11 and €8 on Tuesdays — more for 3D movies. Discounts are available (p48). The branch of Pathé in Spui also has an IMAX screen, showing films in greater size and higher resolution (at higher price).

Filmhuis (🏠 Spui 191; ☎ 070 345 9900; 🖥 www.filmhuisdenhaag.nl) shows more arty films from around the world. Entrance is €9.25, less for matinees.

Omniversum (🏠 President Kennedylaan 5; 🖥 www.omniversum.nl) has a giant screen, mostly showing documentaries about science and nature.

Theatre

Most established theatres in the Netherlands have performances mainly in Dutch, although some will also offer occasional English shows. Opera is usually in the original language with Dutch subtitling. For more options in English, consider an evening in Leiden (p215) or Amsterdam (p251).

The English Theatre (🏠 Nassaulaan 17, Wassenaar; ☎ 06 3005 0018; 🖥 www.theenglishtheatre.nl) is a theatre company that regularly produces English-language plays, or promotes performances from other English theatre companies. They are based in Wassenaar and are often on the look-out for people to help with productions. Tickets usually cost between €13 and €25.

The Anglo-American Theatre Group (🖥 aatg.nl) is another theatre company that puts on English-language performances. They run three or four shows a year, including a pantomime at Christmas. They perform in different locations in The Hague and Wassenaar. Typical ticket price is around €15.

World Forum (🏠 Churchillplein 10; ☎ 070 306 6366; 🖥 www.worldforum.nl) has a huge theatre that shows musical and international artists. Performances are often in English.

Laaktheater (🏠 Ferrandweg 4T; ☎ 070 396 6135; 🖥 www.laaktheater.nl), also known as Théâtre Pierrot, is located next to the Moerwijk station and periodically hosts plays in French and in Italian.

Theatre Diligentia (🏠 Lange Voorhout 5; ☎ 070 361 0540; 🖥 www.theater-diligentia.nl) has cabaret shows, stand-up comedy, popular music and family performances. Situated in the beautiful Lange Voorhout area in the centre of The Hague, these theatres also stage various performances in English.

Dr. Anton Philipszaal and Lucent Danstheater (🏠 Spuiplein 150-152; ☎ 070 880 0333; 🖥 www.ldt.nl) offers a large and varied number of dance performances, classical concerts, jazz concerts, operas, family shows and musicals.

Koninklijke Schouwburg (🏠 Korte Voorhout 3; ☎ 070 356 5356; 🖥 www.ks.nl) preserves its original 19th century character podium for international performances. It features plays from playwrights such as Chekhov, Shakespeare and Ibsen.

Theater De Regentes (🏠 Weimarstraat 63; ☎ 070 363 7798; 🖥 www.deregentes.nl) was once the largest indoor swimming pool in Europe, but shut down in the 1980s due to new hygiene laws. In 1995, the decision was taken to dismantle the premises, but the neighbourhood banded together and decided to save the distinctive 1920s building. The building has served as a theatre since 1996. The programming includes drama, youth performances, dance, world music, music theatre and small-scale opera. Several festivals also take place at the theatre, such as the Holland Dance Festival, Day in the Surf, the Cadance Festival and the World Music theatre festival.

Appeltheater (🏠 Duinstraat 6; ☎ 070 352 3344; 🖥 www.toneelgroepdeappel.nl) is a former coach house in Scheveningen, which once housed The Hague's horse-drawn trams. For some plays, the stage is completely re-built to integrate the setting with the play.

AFAS Circustheater (🏠 Circusstraat 4; ☎ 070 416 7600; 🖥 www.afascircustheater.nl), in Scheveningen, hosts international musicals, cabaret, concerts. Big names but mostly in Dutch.

Kooman's Puppet Theatre (🏠 Frankenstraat 66; ☎ 070 355 9305; 🖥 www. koomanspoppentheater.nl) is in an old villa in the Statenkwartier. It is the oldest permanent puppet theatre in the country.

Bowling

Westerpark (🏠 Heuvelweg 4, Zoetermeer; ☎ 079 351 8722; 🖥 bowlingwesterpark.nl), just outside The Hague, has a bowling rink. Booking a lane for an hour costs between €17.50 and €24.50, depending on the time of day.

Bowling Scheveningen (🏠 Gevers Deynootweg 990/2, Scheveningen; ☎ 070 354 3212; 🖥 www.bowlingscheveningen.com) charges between €19.50 and €26 for an hour's lane rental.

There's also a bowling rink at **Ockenburgh Active** (🏠 Wijndaelerduin 25; ☎ 070 368 6639; 🖥 www.ockenburghactive.nl), near Kijkduin.

Go-karting, laser games and other fun stuff

De Uithof (🏠 Jaap Edenweg 10; 🖥 www.deuithof.nl) offers go-karting — €8 for a seven minute heat for kids and €15 for a 12 minute heat for adults. There is a discount for paying for more heats. Opening times vary depending on what day it is.

De Uithof also offers laser games, costing €9.50 per person for eight

minutes and €15 for two games. It is the largest in the Netherlands.

De Uithof also has other unusual games, such as bungee football and laser squash. See their website for more details.

Shooting

Indoor Shooting Noordhaghe (🏠 Kerketuinenweg 29; ☎ 070 402 0506; 🖥 www.noordhaghe.nl) offers indoor shooting, with eight lanes and a range of equipment. There is also a canteen and a pool table. The centre is closed on Sundays — opening times vary on other days.

For clay pigeon shooting, try the **Jacht, Skeet and Trap Club** in Waalsdorp (☎ 070 324 1667; 🖥 www.jst-waalsdorp.nl), just outside The Hague.

SPORTS

Football

Regular football matches take place at **Westvlietweg Sports Park** (🏠 Groene Zoom 2; ☎ 070 386 6595; 🖥 www.vvwilhelmus. nl). Players are mostly expats, although there are a few Dutchies that also turn up. Atmosphere is very friendly. There are also some ladies' teams.

Golf

There are several golf courses in The Hague region, although you will have to obtain a GVB certificate before you are allowed to play on them (see box).

To practice your golf swings — including chipping, putting and driving — you can visit **Swing Away indoor golf centre** (🏠 Binckhorstlaan 174; ☎ 070 315 3040; 🖥 www.swingaway.nl).

GOLF PROFICIENCY

To be able to play on Dutch golf courses, all players are required to pass a golf proficiency test and obtain a *golfvaardigheidsbewijs* (GVB) certificate. The test consists of two parts – a theory test, including questions about golf etiquette, and a practical test. In the practical test, you have to play four holes. The best three scores, when added together, should result in a maximum of 10 over par.

To register for the exam, contact your local golf club. The exam is free for people that are already members of a golf club. The fee for non-members varies from club to club, but is usually around €70.

In addition to passing the GVB test, most clubs will also demand that you produce an official handicap certificate. Handicaps from the European Golf Association (🖳 www.ega-golf.ch) are valid in the Netherlands. Alternatively, you can apply to the local Nederlandse Golf Federatie (🖳 www.ngf.nl) for a handicap.

If you are not a member of a golf club, you will need to pay an additional €20 per year to play golf in the country (such a fee is usually included as part of the annual fee that golf clubs charge).

BurgGolf (🏠 Heuvelweg 3, Zoetermeer; ☎ 079 320 3134; 🖳 www.golfbaan-zoetermeer.nl) is a challenging 18-hole golf course, surrounded by woodland and speckled with *polders* (lakes).

Leeuwenbergh Golf Course (🏠 Elzenlaan 31; ☎ 070 399 1096; 🖳 www.leeuwenbergh.nl) is a flattish 18-hole course with many bunkers and water hazards.

A little way outside The Hague, on the other side of Wassenaar, you will find **Noordwijkse Golfclub** (🏠 Randweg 25; ☎ 025 237 3761; 🖳 www.noordwijksegolfclub.nl), one of the most prestigious clubs in the country and ranked sixth in Continental Europe.

For nine-hole golf courses, try **Golfbaan Duinzicht** (🏠 Theo Mann Bouwmeesterlaan 203; ☎ 070 324 2443; 🖳 www.golfduinzicht. nl), **Golfclub Ockenburgh** (🏠 Wijndaelerweg 125; ☎ 070 325 8904; 🖳 www.golfockenburgh. nl) or **Wassenaarse Groendael Golf Club** (🏠 Groenendaal 3, Wassenaar; ☎ 070 314 4000; 🖳 www. wassenaarsegolf.nl).

Horse riding

There are dozens of equestrian centres in and around The Hague, offering horse riding excursions and lessons. Note that if you want to ride independently outside of a tour, then you will need to apply for a riding licence. For more information on how to do this, consult the website of the Dutch Equestrian Federation (🖳 www.knhs.nl).

Manege Berestein (🏠 Lozerlaan 10; ☎ 070 367 6090; 🖳 www. manegeberestein.nl), just next to De Uithof recreation centre, organises horse and pony riding lessons. Half-hour pony riding lessons are available for children from the age of five.

An alternative, located in nearby Wassenaar, is **Country Stables** (🏠 Nieuweweg 5a, Wassenaar; ☎ 06 2464 4007 or 06 2464 4007; 🖳 www.countrystables.nl). An hour-long private lesson costs €35, whilst participation in a group lesson costs €20. A discount is given if you buy a block of 10 lessons.

BOERENGOLF

Find golf in the Netherlands a tad too snobby and exclusive? Then how about trying a game that is crazily different.

Boerengolf (literally, farmers' golf) is a game played on farm land and born out of the frustration with the costly fees and exclusivity of golf courses in the Netherlands, as well as the need to pass the GVB test before you can play. Since its invention in 1999, it has really taken off and there are now an estimated 70 locations where you can play.

The game is played in much the same way as the official game of golf. The hole is usually made by placing a bucket on the ground, whilst hazards include anything you might find on a farm, such as troughs, rusting machinery and the occasional wandering cow. The ball is larger than a traditional golf ball (14 cm) and made of leather. The club is made by attaching a wooden clog to a length of wood.

To find a place where you can play *boerengolf*, as well as to read the rules (available in both English and Dutch), consult the official *boerengolf* website (⌨ www. boerengolf.nl). To play, contact the relevant farm directly.

Course fees vary from farm to farm, but are generally between €5 and €10, significantly cheaper than an actual golf course.

Boerengolf has now become a registered trademark.

If you're looking for a place where you can play *boerengolf* near The Hague, try Van der Geest (🏠 Wasbeeklaan 31, Warmond; ☎ 025 223 0083 or 06 3496 1848; ⌨ www.boerengolfvandergeest. nl).

Running

Around mid-March every year, The Hague organises a half-marathon called the **City-Pier-City (CPC) Loop** (⌨ www.cpcloopdenhaag. com). Shorter runs (five or 10 km) are also organised. It costs between €14.50 and €23 to participate, depending on the length of run that you do. Early-booking discounts are available.

The Hague hash house harriers (@ HaberDasher@HagueHash. nl; ⌨ www.haguehash.nl) arrange regular running sessions around the city and surroundings. It costs €3.50 per run to participate and the first run is free.

Ice-skating and roller-skating

The best way to experience ice-skating in the Netherlands is without a doubt to strap on a pair of skates during winter and take to the frozen canals and lakes. Popular locations are Zuiderpark, Haagse Bos and Hofvijver (the pond outside the Binnenhof). However, not all spots freeze at the same time. To know where you can skate safely in The Hague, check ⌨ www. denhaagdirect.nl. The website ⌨ www.schaats-en-skate.nl gives you information about the latest trails throughout the entire country, plus other ice-skating tips.

There are a number of indoor options, too.

De Uithof (🏠 Jaap Edenweg 10; ☎ 0900 3384 8463; ⌨ www. deuithof.nl), just south of the city, has a good-sized rink. An adult skating session is €7.50, kids €5.50. Skate hire is extra. Season tickets are available and you get a discount if you buy a block of tickets. You can also arrange skating lessons: 10 for

€135. Opening hours vary throughout the week — it is best to check the website for full details. Evening ice-skating is only available during weekdays. It is also possible to arrange curling lessons here.

SilverDome (🏠 Van der Hagenstraat 20, Zoetermeer; ☎ 079 330 5000; 🖵 www.silverdome.nl) is another option: €6.50 for adults and €5 for children up to 12.

If you want to try speed-skating, the **Hardrij Vereniging Haag Westland** (🏠 Rozentuin 88, Voorburg; ☎ 070 387 3898; 🖵 www.hvhw.nl) can arrange lessons.

Haagsche Ijsclub Houtrust (☎ 06 1294 7566; 🖵 www.hijh.nl) offers lessons in figure skating at De Uithof (🏠 Jaap Edenweg 10).

Or how about some ice dancing? Then you'll probably want to join **Ijsfun** (☎ 070 368 4389; 🖵 www.ijsfun.nl).

Zoetermeer Schaatsschool (🏠 Karperdaal 8, Zoetermeer; ☎ 06 5184 0027; 🖵 www.schaatsschoolzoetermeer.nl) gives ice-staking and roller-skating lessons.

Squash, tennis, and racquetball

Mariahoeve Sports Centre (🏠 Het Kleine Loo 12; ☎ 070 385 7947; 🖵 www.sportcentrummariahoeve.nl) has five squash courts. Courts are open 9am to 11pm during the week and 9am to 6pm at weekends. Squash costs €22 per hour in the evening and €12 in the morning and at weekends. Tennis costs €22 per hour at any time. It also has 10 badminton courts (€27.50 per hour). There is a nice café that sells foods and occasionally organises barbecues. There is a sports shop on the premises.

At **Houtrust Squash & Aerobics** (🏠 Laan van Poot 18; ☎ 070 363 5169 or 070 361 7622; 🖵 www.houtrust.nl), a 45-minute game of squash costs €13 during weekdays and €18 at evenings and weekends. It is slightly cheaper if you buy a prepaid card. There is also a nice café.

Ockenburgh Active has a squash court, too: €13 for non-members or less if you by 10 games at once.

At **Sportcity** (🏠 Verheeskade 105; ☎ 070 330 0400; 🖵 www.sportcity.nl). Squash is included in the monthly fitness package (from €35).

At **Sportcentrum Jack Slagman** (🏠 Theresastraat 145; ☎ 070 382 0203; 🖵 www.jackslagman.nl) squash costs €20 per hour or you can opt for an all-inclusive membership with the fitness club.

Westvliet (🏠 Westvlietweg 55, Voorburg; 🖵 www.westvliet.nl) offers tennis, squash, badminton and racquetball. Rates are €21 for 45 minutes at peak time (evenings and weekends) and €17 at all other times.

Tennispark Houtrust (🏠 Laan van Poot 38; ☎ 070 361 52 03; 🖵 www.tennisparkhoutrust.com) charges €25 per hour for renting a tennis court in the evening and at weekends, €15 at other times.

Tennispark Hanenburg (🏠 Daal en Bergselaan 3; ☎ 070 323 8000; 🖵 www.hanenburg.nl) rents courts for €20 per hour or €30 for two hours.

If you're a regular badminton player, joining a club will be much cheaper. **Drop Shot Badmintonclub** (🖵 www.bcdropshot.nl) trains in Mariahoeve Sports Centre.

Ski and snowboard

Alpine-style skiing is not the first thing that comes to mind when one thinks of the Netherlands.

FINDING A PARTNER

Joining (🖥 www.joining. com) is where you can meet new people to engage in social activities with, such as going to the cinema or doing sports. You can only join if you have a Facebook account.

A similar concept — **Urbeez** (🖥 amsterdam.urbeez.com) is only available in Amsterdam at the moment, but may be rolled out to other cities in due course.

Nonetheless, there are a few indoor slopes available if you fancy brushing up on your technique.

Snowworld (🏠 Buytenparklaan 30; ☎ 079 320 2202; 🖥 www. snowworld.com) in Zoetermeer, just outside The Hague, offers an hour's skiing on artificial snow for €19.95 (€16.95 for kids). Discounts are available if you ski for longer. Renting gear is extra. Ski lessons are available. The centre is open daily from 9am to 11pm.

De Uithof has a similar indoor ski slope with artificial snow. An hour's skiing costs €14.95 (€9.95 for kids), plus equipment hire. Discounts are given in the summer. Lessons are available.

Another place to go, slightly further outside The Hague, is **Bergschenhoek Ski & Skate** (🏠 Rottebandreef 10; ☎ 010 522 0755; 🖥 www.outdoorski.nl). This is an outdoor ski slope offering skiing and snowboarding lessons. A package of three 50-minute lessons costs around €70 for adults and €60 for kids.

Indoorski Discovery (🏠 Waterpas 99, Voorburg; 🖥 www. skidiscovery.nl) is another option.

Table-tennis

For committed players contact the table-tennis association of The Hague (🖥 www.pingwins.nl).

All across the city, you will find concrete table-tennis tables, where you can just turn up and play for free (although you must bring your own bats). Unfortunately, though, these tables are all outside, so the wind can make it somewhat... er... interesting.

The outdoor tables that are close to the centre are in **Kortenbos Park** (p163) and in the children playground in **Schapenlaan** (open from 1 to 6pm).

Table football

There are not many places that have a table football but one of those that does is **Café Triple B** (🏠 Prinsegracht 128A).

EXERCISE

Yoga and aerobics

Yoga is available at **K'dans Studio** (🏠 Merlenstraat 65c; ☎ 070 744 6790; 🖥 www.kdans.nl).

Another option is **LingGan** (🏠 Westeinde 38a; ☎ 070 330 0778; 🖥 www.linggan.nl).

There is also **Sunshine Yoga** (🏠 Witte de Withstraat 11; ☎ 06 5201 5097; 🖥 www.sunshineyoga. nl).

For really sweating it out, try yoga at 42°C with **Bikram Yoga** (🏠 Prins Hendrikplein 2; ☎ 070 365 2202; 🖥 bikramdenhaag. com).

Gyms

Most of the gyms in The Hague require you to subscribe for at least two months. The longer you subscribe for, the lower the monthly tariff. During the week, gyms tend to stay open until 10 or 11pm. On Sundays, it is usual for them to close between 3 and 6pm. Most gyms offer a one-day free trial.

Fit all day (💻 www.fitallday.nl) has several locations around the city: near Hollands Spoor, Uithof, Zoetermeer, Rijswijk. Subscription is from €16.50 per month.

Fit 2000 (🏠 Westerbaenstraat 139; 💻 www.fit2000.nl) is centrally located, costing €47 per month. The gym organises many group lessons. There is also a sauna.

Healthcity (🏠 Grote Marktstraat 157; 💻 www.healthcity.nl) has two sports centres in the same street. One is only for ladies, and the other a premium one with a swimming pool, sauna and steam bath. The all-inclusive subscription starts at €50 per month. Some subscription packages allow you to use any of their sports centres around the Netherlands.

Sport City (🏠 Verheeskade 105; 💻 www.sportcity.nl) has clubs all over the country. Subscription is €35 per month, but there are regular introductory offers. There are many classes, even in the morning.

Aerobicworld (🏠 Veenkade 22; 💻 www.aerobicworld.com), in the heart of The Hague, costs €37 per month. Single entry is possible at €14, with a 10-entrance card.

Healthspa (🏠 De Savornin Lohmanplein 7; 💻 www.healthspa.nl) has subscriptions from €50 per month, more if you want to make use of the swimming pool and spa facilities.

QFitness (🏠 Arnold Spoelplein 75 and Schuytstraat 209; 💻 www.qfitness.nl) costs €32 per month. The location on Arnold Spoelplein also has a swimming pool (€15 extra per month).

Exercise Sportclub (🏠 Bucaillestraat 2a, Voorburg; 💻 www.

exercise.nl) has a different type of subscriptions based on the number of times you use the facilities per month.

Basic-Fit (💻 www.basic-fit.nl) has several locations around the city, including 🏠 Grotemarktstraat 40 (ladies only) and 🏠 De Werf 27. Prices are attractive — from €15 a month.

MARTIAL ARTS

Gyeong Rye (💻 www.taekwondo-denhaag.nl) offers **taekwondo** lessons to suit all abilities. Instruction is of a very high quality, and the atmosphere is friendly. Classes are mainly attended by Dutch people rather than expats. The instructors speak English, but the lessons will be given in Dutch. Location of lessons change according to the day of the week. They take place at 🏠 Diamanthorst 10, 🏠 Carolinalaan 1 and 🏠 Walenburg 25.

Aikido is taught at Seshin-seii (🏠 Helmersstraat 140; 💻 www.aikidodenhaag.nl) and **karate** at Hans van Galen (🏠 Paddepad 8; 💻 www.karatevangalen.nl).

Wu Dea teaches the Chinese martial arts of Wing Chun and Weng Chun (🏠 oosduinsekade 12; 💻 www.wudae.com).

SWIMMING POOLS

Apart from the swimming pools at the sports centres (see previously), the municipality has a number of swimming pools all around the country. Entry is relatively cheap (around €3.50). Pools can become particularly busy at weekends and on Wednesdays, when children finish school early. Many swimming pools also have aqua-gyms and swimming lessons at reasonable prices.

● **Overbosch** (🏠 Vlaskamp 3;

☎ 070 347 4692).

- **Zuiderpark** (🏠 Mr. P. Drooglever Fortuynweg 59; ☎ 070 367 9463).

- **De Blinkerd** (🏠 Seinpoststraat 150; ☎ 070 352 1222).

- **De Waterthor** (🏠 Thorbeckelaan 350; ☎ 070 323 5141).

FISHING

Angling is popular but quite strictly regulated. Before you are able to fish in Dutch waters, you must first obtain a VISpas.

There are two types available. The standard VISpas is only available for those who are members of a fishing club in the Netherlands. The pass entitles you to fish with two rods and all permissible bait. Annual membership of a fishing club, which includes the VISpas, costs between €25 and 45. Fishing clubs are all over the country.

If you don't want to join a fishing club, then you could get the KleineVISpas instead. This permit allows fishing in a limited number of waters with one rod only. It can be ordered online (🖥 www.sportvisserijnederland.nl) or through a local post office. The pass costs €10.50 for a year. There is an additional €2.50 handling fee if you order through the post office.

Further details about the permits, as well as other tips about fishing in the Netherlands, are available from the Sportvisserij (🖥 www.sportvisserijnederland.nl). This website also publishes a list of waters where it is permissible to fish, depending on the type of permit that you have.

People younger than 15 do not need to have a VISpas, as long as they are accompanied by an adult that has one.

Some farms and other places offer fishing on private land, for a fee, which doesn't require a permit.

WATERSPORTS

Canoeing and kayaking

If you fancy renting a kayak or canoe and touring The Hague's many waterways, you have a couple of options.

Kanoverhuur Den Haag (🏠 Groenewegje 144; ☎ 06 8511 8822) and **Kanoverhuur Zuiderpark** (🏠 Johanna Naberweg 5; ☎ 06 2690 4023; 🖥 www.kanoverhuurzuiderpark.nl) both offer canoe hire from €10 an hour. With the latter, you can opt for a traditional kayak or a more romantic swan-shaped boat.

Those who want to canoe on a regular basis might consider joining De Windhappers (🖥 www.windhappers.nl).

Windsurfing

The **Euro Funcenter** (🏠 Vissershavenweg 62; ☎ 070 358 4800; 🖥 www.euro-fun.nl) rents out windsurf equipment (€20 per hour for a full set). The centre also organises windsurfing lessons, for around €85 for three hours.

Funsport Van Vliet (🏠 Het Lange Land 5, Zoetermeer; ☎ 079 342 0046; 🖥 www.funsportvanvliet.nl) can arrange windsurfing lessons: €75 per person for two and a half hours, with a maximum of two people. Group discounts are available.

Kitesurfing

If you want to learn how to kitesurf, which is becoming an increasingly popular pastime in The Netherlands, you could try **Kitesurfschool** (🏠 Verhulstplein 19m; ☎ 0620 234

234; 🖥 www.kitesurfschool.com).
A three day kitesurfing course —
probably the minimum you need to
be able to kitesurf on your own —
costs €350.

White-water rafting

The concept of white-water rafting
in the Netherlands might seem even
more bizarre than skiing, but there
is actually a place where you can do
it. An hour's white-water rafting at
Dutch Water Dreams (🏠 Van der
Hagenstraat 3, Zoetermeer; ☎ 079
330 2500; 🖥 dutchwaterdreams.
com) costs around €29.

Jet-ski

Jet-ski equipment can be rented from **Fun & Fantasy** (🏠 25
Binnenhaven; ☎ 06 2430 9729 or
06 4671 1340; 🖥 www.fun-fantasy.
nl). You do not need to have a special licence in order to rent such an
equipment, although you do have
to follow a pre-marked route and
cannot choose to go wherever you
please. A 15-minute ride costs €40.
Other types of boat are also available, including banana boats (€15
for 10 minutes), fly fish boats (€15
for 10 minutes) and RIB power-
boats (€15 for 15 minutes).

Surfing

Surfles (🏠 Strandweg 1; 🖥 www.
surfles.nl) has surf equipment for
hire, and can also help arrange lessons. A private lesson costs €55,
whilst a group lesson costs €40 per
person.

Where to Eat & Drink

Given that The Hague is such a multicultural city, it seems somewhat surprising that local restaurants don't cater particularly well for the discerning connoisseurs.

The quality of food on offer is starting to improve, but only slowly and the prices for a half-way decent place remain disappointingly high, compared to what you might expect in other major European cities.

The best approach to dining in The Hague is to explore the city's culinary establishments with an open mind, and not be overly fussy about the place that you eventually choose for a meal. After all, The Hague won't be rivalling Paris or London in terms of cuisine any time soon.

AFRICAN

3 Stones (🏠 Laan van Meerdervoort 46a; 📞 070 360 8761; 🖥 www.3stones.info; 💰💰) is a great little Kenyan restaurant. Set on two levels, with the bar downstairs, it is a very convivial place serving decent food. The restaurant is based around the idea of communal eating, and food is usually served on a large African tray for everyone to share. Main courses range from between €10.95 and €16.95. A three course meal, including coffee and aperitif, costs €29.

ARGENTINIAN

San Telmo (🏠 Kazernestraat 116A; 📞 070 310 6266; 🖥 www.santelmo.nl; 💰💰) offers Argentinian-style tapas as well as a selection of main dishes such as paella. Mains cost between €15 and €20, tapas between €3.80 and €8. They also have an eat-all-you-want tapas menu for €19. Nice atmosphere and highly recommended by Argentinian expatriates.

Los Argentinos (🏠 Kettingstraat 14; 📞 070 346 8523; 🖥 www.los-argentinos.nl; 💰💰) is a friendly restaurant that serves excellent stake perfectly cooked to order. Prices are reasonable: a fairly heft sirloin steak (300 gram) costs €16.95. The restaurant also offers eat-as-much-as-you-want spare ribs for €15.95. Accompanying sauces are a slight disappointment, though. Latino atmosphere, generally busy and cosy tables.

BALKAN

Dubrovnik (🏠 Rijswijkseweg 369; 📞 070 399 8705; 💰💰) is a much-overlooked little eatery. The restaurant appears somewhat threadbare at first glance, but worth trying nonetheless because of the friendly atmosphere and opportunity to try something a little bit different. The food is simple and not over-complicated, but tasty. The chef is very accommodating and tries to cater for special requirements.

CHINESE

Chinese restaurants are found all over the city, but the best, both in terms of taste and price, are definitely in Chinatown. Less fancy but more authentic.

Fat Kee (🏠 Gedempte Gracht 675; 📞 070 365 6383; 💰), just on the edge of Chinatown, is great for a cheap eat. Despite low prices — a soup costs €3 and a main €7 — the food is really not bad. Portions are huge — one main course could easily do two people. You also get free Chinese tea. The menu is available in both Dutch and English, although the English one often has out-of-date prices. Good if you want decent food in a hurry, but not a place to come for a slow romantic meal. Service is very much geared towards getting the customer out the door as quickly as possible.

Eazie (🏠 Gedempte Gracht 78; ☎ 070 324 3671; 🖥 www.eazie.nl; 💲) is a regional South Holland chain. Choose from a selection of vegetables or meat and they will fry your meal in a wok whilst you wait. The dish is served with either noodles or rice. You can eat in or take away. Main courses start at €5.95. They also serve wraps from €3.75. Whilst not Chinese, sushi is also available. If you take the food away, make sure you don't let it stand too long in the cardboard boxes as they will absorb all the flavour.

Amazing Oriental (🏠 Grote Marktstraat 113; ☎ 070 363 1552; 💲), an Asian supermarket, has a small kiosk (on your right as you enter) that sells a range of hot food. You can either take the food away or sit on the bench that is next to the counter. The food isn't all that great, but it is incredibly cheap and you can grab a bite for lunch for under €2. Right in the centre of town, that's really not bad.

FRENCH

Mazie (🏠 Maziestraat 10; ☎ 070 302 0286; 🖥 www.restaurantmazie.nl; 💲💲💲) is an elegant little restaurant, located not to far away from the city centre. Service is very friendly and attentive, and prices are not unreasonable. A set menu costs €29.50 or you can order à la carte (mains for €20.50 to €23.50). The chefs do a masterful job of combining flavours without overpowering.

Le Gone (🏠 Noordeinde 200c; ☎ 070 362 5026; 🖥 www.legone.com; 💲💲) is a small bistro owned by a Frenchman from Lyon, who moved to The Hague about 20 years ago. However, it is only worth for a quick a stop to buy fresh French cheese, baguettes to go and foie gras. Lunch unfortunately doesn't match expectations.

FUSION

El Plato (🏠 Frederikstraat 32; ☎ 070 363 6744; 🖥 www.restaurant-plato.nl; 💲💲💲) is a nice fusion restaurant, combining oriental and French cuisine. The website promises "thoughtful and unexpected flavour combinations" and that isn't too far off what you will experience. The restaurant is located in an upper-class area of The Hague. Prices range from €19 to €21.50 for a main.

GREEK

Rhodos (🏠 Laan van Meerdervoort 40b; ☎ 070 365 7050; 🖥 www.rhodosdenhaag.nl; 💲💲) serves decent Greek food at what is for The Hague affordable prices (€16 to 20 for a main course). Portions are huge and all but the hardiest of eaters will struggle to finish them. Many of the dishes are really excellent and have a welcome touch of authenticity. Others, unfortunately, are a little bit hit-and-miss. The Greek yogurt with walnuts is particularly excellent — a lovely light way to finish the meal, especially if you have over-indulged in previous courses.

Periklis Taverne (🏠 Prins Willemstraat; ☎ 070 352 2105; 🖥 Wed-Sun: 5 to 9pm; 💲💲) is a cosy little restaurant serving authentic Greek cuisine not far from the beach. Simple décor but nice service.

INDIAN

There are a handful of decent Indian restaurants scattered throughout the city. However, the range of flavours used in the different dishes can be slightly disappointing, when compared to the tastebud-tingling range that is available on the streets of India or in the UK, almost as though they are limiting themselves in their use of spices.

Maharani (🏠 Noordeinde 93; ☎ 070 365 8874; 🖵 www. restaurantmaharani.nl; 💰💰💰) is reputed to be the best Indian restaurant in town. It is certainly one of the priciest — €22 to 25 for a basic curry, although this is served with rice and two vegetable accompaniments. The food tastes fresh, but disappointingly a lot of the dishes taste very similar. It is sometimes hard to distinguish between a chicken jalfrezi and a balti, for example. Low lights and soft background music make for a romantic setting. The red-and-yellow walls give it a hint of a Maharaja Palace. Service is friendly and they can adapt dishes according to tastes.

Taj Mahal (🏠 Maliestraat 5; ☎ 070 331 0669; 🖵 www. tajmahalrestaurant.nl; 💰💰) is significantly cheaper, where a chicken dish costs between €13 and €16 and a lamb dish between €17 and €20. The food is good and the service very friendly.

Bombay Palace (🏠 Gevers Deynootstraat 16; ☎ 070 354 4382; 🖵 www.bombay-palace.eu; 💰💰), located very close to the beach, has tasty Indian dishes for between €16 and €20. Dishes are authentic and the atmosphere relaxing.

India Palace (🏠 Gevers Deynootplein 223; ☎ 070 354 4457; 🖵 www.indiapalace.nu; 💰💰) is also located next to the beach, but prices are somewhat cheaper (€14 to €17 for a main). The restaurant offers live music and dancing every Friday, along with an eat-as-much-as-you-want buffet for €15.50 per person. The food on the à la carte menu is much better than the buffet, though.

ITALIAN

There are more than a hundred Italian restaurants in The Hague. The following ones are those that endeavour to have a real, authentic Italian flavour.

Very Italian Pizza (🏠 Kettingstraat 13-15; ☎ 070 365 4541; 🖵 www.veryitalianpizza.nl; 💰 to 💰💰) is conveniently located in the centre of town, just around the corner from one of the main cinemas in the city. The restaurant is run by Italians and most of the staff speak Italian. The quality of the wood-fired pizzas is good and prices are very reasonable. A basic margarita costs just €5. The restaurant also serves a range of pasta dishes and other traditional Italian fare, such as bruschetta and carpaccio. The downstairs eating area is huge, although the tables are set uncomfortably close together. There is also an upstairs area, popular for evening drinks (although it is not always open). It is nice to eat out on the terrace in the summer.

That's Amore (🏠 Laan van Meerdervoort 188A; ☎ 070 324 7090; 🖵 www.thatsamore.nl; 🕐 11am to 7pm; 💰) is a family-run delicatessen that serves delicious sandwiches and cold-cuts. It is somewhere between a gourmet shop and a lunchroom: you can buy food to take away or eat at one of the tables there. Try *Il Padrino* (literally, 'The Godfather'), a voluminous sandwich containing pecorino cheese, ham and red pesto. Highly recommended. You can also buy Sicilian *cannoli* and other Italian delicacies.

La Cantina Di Pierino (🏠 Theresiastraat 18A; ☎ 06 2831 4465; 💰) is located next to the station. An unpretentious little number, the restaurant offers good quality food at reasonable prices. The sandwiches are particularly good.

Sapore (🏠 Molenstraat 30; ☎ 070 362 8580; 🖥 www.sapore. nl; 🍴) is more take-away than proper restaurant, although there are a few chairs, both inside and out, where you can sit and eat. It is a popular Italian eatery, largely because of the high-quality Italian products that it uses. The *panini*, made with Italian focaccia, is particularly good. For something more exotic, ask for a *parma tartufo*, which comes with parma ham, truffle sauce and rocket salad. The lasagna and truffle ravioli are also specialities of the house. Delivery and pre-ordering is available via their website.

Pizzeria Taormina (🏠 Stuyvesantstraat 33; ☎ 070 335 1109 or 06 5351 2255; 🖥 www. cateringtaormina.nl; 🍴) is an authentic Sicilian-owned restaurant not far from Laan van Noi station. It is popular among students. The pizzas are good and not that expensive (from €7). Pasta dishes are also available. The décor is simple and unpretentious, and the service is welcoming.

Catering Per Tutti (🏠 Korte Molenstraat 13; ☎ 06 2196 0593; 🖥 www.cateringpertutti.nl; 🍴🍴) is a very small shop selling a range of Italian homemade dishes. It only offers take away. The food is very good but a bit pricey. The owner also runs cookery classes.

Casa Caironi (🏠 Jagerstraat 8; ☎ 070 346 0370; 🖥 www. casacaroni.nl; ⏰ 6 to 11pm; 🍴🍴) is a Tuscan-speciality restaurant close to the Denneweg area in The Hague. It is a small place with a diverse menu (available in both Dutch and English). Dishes start at €14.

JAPANESE

Japanese food is on average much more expensive than in the US or elsewhere in Europe. Eat-all-you-want options have become very popular, with an inevitable reduction in service and quality.

Morikawa (🏠 Balistraat 3; ☎ 070 392 4180; 🖥 www. sushimorikawa.com; 🍴🍴🍴) is an excellent Osaka-style sushi restaurant for those that can afford it. Owned and managed by a Japanese chef, the suggested set menu costs €45. There is also a wider selection of dishes from the à la carte menu. The restaurant offers take-away. An elegant fine dining experience, with all details taken care of.

Kiraku (🏠 Toussaintkade 31; ☎ 070 345 4288; 🖥 www.kiraku. nl; ⏰ Mon-Sun: 6 to 10.30pm; 🍴🍴) is a smallish restaurant, serving very good sushi and sashimi. The typical price for a set (typically two pieces of sushi on a small plate) is between €3.50 and €5.25. Main dishes are available for around €17.75. For something decidedly different, try the Japanese *natto*, fermented soya beans wrapped in seaweed. The Japanese love it, but it is something of an acquired taste. Reservation is recommended.

Sumo (🏠 Prinsestraat 13; ☎ 070 363 2323; 🖥 www.restaurantsumo. com; 🍴🍴) is a great option for those who fancy some sushi but have a limited budget. It is actually a small chain of restaurants and has branches in Scheveningen near the beach (☎ Palacestraat 8; ☎ 070 322 6008), Amsterdam, Rotterdam and Haarlem. The eat-as-much-as-you-want option is very popular, costing €17.50 at lunchtime (12 to 5pm). Monday to Wednesday, the evening cost is €22.50 and on other days it is €24.50. Children from four to 11 can eat for €11.50. A great selection of sushi and reasonable service. The maximum time at the table is two hours and you must finish everything on your plate otherwise you get charged extra. You must also order at least one drink per person. The restaurant gets very busy, particularly for dinner, and so reservation is recommended.

Shabu Shabu (🏠 Torentstraat 138; ☎ 070 362 8679; 🖥 www.shabushabu.nl; 💰💰) is in the same league as Sumo. The price is slightly cheaper, although this is reflected in the quality of the service and in the ambiance. Lunch (12 to 4pm) costs €16.95 for the eat-as-much-as-you-can deal. Dinner costs €21.50 between Monday and Wednesday and €23.80 on other days. Again, you have to pay extra for anything that you do not eat.

Genki Tei (🏠 Schoolstraat 4 ; ☎ 070 363 8839; 🖥 set.com.nl; 💰💰) is an *izakaya*-style restaurant with simple and minimalist interior. It has very reasonable lunch menus from €7.99 to €12 a box. It also has a sushi set to take away.

Mochi (🏠 Mallemolen 12a; ☎ 070 326 0612; 🖥 www.mochirestaurant.com; 💰💰💰) offers Asian and European cuisine combined in a fixed set menu for €40. The menu changes but the homemade fish *frikandel* is the star. Reservation is necessary. Nice décor, but the tables are quite close together and so the restaurant can get noisy when busy. A more relaxing and casual place is the connected *izikaya*, a traditional Japanese bar, where you can go and eat sushi. Pricey but good food.

Sushi Tokyo (🏠 Zoutmanstraat 75; ☎ 070 365 0010; 🖥 www.sushitokyo.nl; 💰💰) is a sushi takeaway outlet that offers good-quality fish at reasonable prices. Home delivery is possible. It was one of the newer additions to The Hague's eating scene.

SEAFOOD

With The Hague being located on the coast, you would expect to find plenty of excellent restaurants serving fish at moderate prices.

Unfortunately, this isn't the case and all fish restaurants in the city are fairly expensive. Moreover, the high prices on the menu don't always translate into good food.

Waterproef (🏠 Lelykade 25-27; ☎ 070 358 8770; 🖥 www.restaurantwaterproef.nl; 💰💰💰) offers a good range of seasonal dishes in elegant surroundings, and an excellent wine selection. The lunch menu costs €29.50 and the dinner menu €39.50.

Alexander (🏠 Denneweg 138; ☎ 070 36 48 175; 🖥 www.restaurant-alexander.nl; 💰💰) serves very good fish, although also has a selection of other dishes on the menu, including meat and chicken. The set daily menu costs €27.50 or you can choose à la carte from €15 to €20 for a main.

Strandclub Doen (🏠 Strandweg 9; ☎ 070 355 7834; 🖥 www.stranclubdoen.nl; 💰💰💰) serves fish courses from €20 to €25 right on the seafront. The catch of the day is worth considering. With its pure white décor the restaurant is going for classy but just falls short of the mark. Not bad but, like other places on the seafront, its clumsy service lets it down.

SPANISH

The tapas experience rarely translates well outside of Spain, and The Hague is no exception. There are a few decent places to go for good Spanish atmosphere and decent food, not to mention copious amounts of *sangria*, but nothing compares to the *crème de la crème* of restaurants that you will find in parts of Spain. The price is much higher, too.

El Barrio (🏠 Uilebomen 2; ☎ 070 392 0359; 🖥 www.el-barrio.nl; 💰💰) is a cosy little restaurant that gets incredibly busy, particularly at the weekends. The tapas is

Where to Eat & Drink

tasty and the service is friendly, but the tables are slightly too close together to be comfortable. Note that you will have to pay an excessive surcharge (€7) if you choose to eat the bread and butter that is brought to you at the beginning of the meal. Individual tapas items cost between €4 and €6. You can also get a menu of assorted tapas, plus a carafe of house wine and a dessert, for €55.

Bodega La Riojana (🏠 Torenstraat 82; ☎ 070 362 9960; 🖥 www. tapasdenhaag.nl; 💲💲) is a friendly and unpretentious place, although it can get a little rowdy and chaotic during busy periods. The place is more like a Spanish bar than a proper sit-down restaurant. It shows most of the major Spanish football matches. Although the restaurant is normally closed on Mondays, if a Spanish match is showing than it will be open. Hot tapas costs between €6 and €8 per item. Other dishes, such as paella and tortilla, are also on offer.

THAI

If you are familiar with authentic Thai cuisine, you may be disappointed by the restaurants on offer in The Hague. True Thai cooking is an explosion of flavours, usually laced with chilli that is guaranteed to bring tears to your eyes. By contrast, the Thai food here is adapted to Western tastes. A few Thai restaurants are really very good, and make a passable attempt at giving you an authentic experience from the country, but... well, you can decide for yourself.

Spize (🏠 Spui 185; ☎ 070 365 2827; 🖥 www.spize.eu; 💲💲) serves exceptionally good Thai food. Centrally located and with very nice décor, definitely a place to consider. The prices are not outrageous, either. The three course meal, which costs €25, is excellent value. The Phad Med Ma Muang

Kai, chicken with cashew nuts, is worth trying. There is also a nice romantic bar where you can have a pre-dinner drink if you want.

De Sissende Sampan (🏠 Laan van Meerdervoort 207c; ☎ 070 362 5435; 💲) is a cheaper option, where a three-course meal costs €15. Okay for the money but don't expect to be wowed.

Warunee (🏠 Laan van Meerdervoort 37a; ☎ 070 42 71 225 or 06 5322 2680; 🖥 www.warunee. nl; 💲💲) offers an informal dining experience, including a rough-and-ready bar with TV. More of an *eet-café* feel to it, but with decent Thai food. Good soup and excellent stir fries. Take away is also possible.

VIETNAMESE

Little V (🏠 Rabbijn Maarsenplein 21; ☎ 070 392 1230; 🖥 www.littlev. nl; 💲💲) is a nice little restaurant on the edge of Chinatown, serving good Vietnamese food. It is located in a small square with outdoor tables where you can eat in the summer. The price is decent — a main course costs between €9 and €14. The menu includes familiar dishes as well as the more exotic. The interior is nicely decorated, with low-hanging lanterns that throw soft illumination across the room. The restaurant gets very packed during the evenings, which means that eating can get a little cramped and you may not have a table to yourself. Advanced booking is definitely recommended.

SURINAME AND INDONESIAN

Over the past centuries, food from these former Dutch colonies has strongly influenced the cuisine of the Netherlands. Distinctively different from traditional Dutch cooking, they are worth trying if you are interested in finding out more about the country's culinary heritage.

Warung Mini (🏠 Amsterdamse veerkade 57A; ☎ 070 365 4628; 🖥 www.warungminidenhaag.com; 💲) is a cheap place to come for some quick Suriname grub. It's not an attractive place to eat — more like a fast-food joint than a proper restaurant — but the quality is excellent and prices are decent (less than €10 for a fairly substantial plate of authentic Suriname fare).

Dayang (🏠 Prinsestraat 65; ☎ 070 364 9979; 💲) is a small Indonesian restaurant that has a good reputation and is always busy in the evening. Unfortunately, taste is sometimes a little bit bland and the food isn't always prepared to order. It is a friendly family-run business, centrally located near the main shopping area and pedestrian zone. The eating area is very small to the point of being uncomfortable, particularly if there is a normal take-away line, but the food is well worth it. Ask for a *bami goreng* or the typical Indonesian dessert *cendol*. Prices used to be low but they have recently been increased by quite a bit.

TURKISH

Maxima (🏠 Prins Hendrikstraat 78; 💲) has the best kebabs in town — good meat, huge portions and durum wraps made on the spot. The eatery also has a small Turkish bakery attached to it, where you can buy excellent *baklava* and Turkish bread. A doner durum wrap costs €3.50.

VEGETARIAN

De Wankele Tafel (🏠 Mauritskade 79; ☎ 070 364 3267; 🖥 www.wankeletafel.nl.nu; 💲) is a charming family-run restaurant, offering some really good and light vegetarian dishes. Prices are extremely reasonable — around €12 for a main course. Décor is simple, with a rustic café feel to it all. The

MONDRIAAN

For a rather different dining experience, try **Mondriaan** (☎ 088 666 3313; @ horeca. reserveringen@rocmondriaan.nl; 🖥 www.rocmondriaan.nl). This chain of restaurants belongs to the biggest hospitality and catering school in The Hague. Students at the school work in the restaurant as part of their course. Food is very good and exceedingly cheap, but service can be slightly slow and of varying quality, as students learn the ins and outs of the catering industry on the job. The restaurants are scattered throughout the city and only open during term-time.

restaurant is fairly small and tends to get quite busy. Unfortunately, you can only reserve in advance if you are at least three people.

Water en Brood (🏠 Hellingweg 127; ☎ 070 399 7455; 💲) is a vegan restaurant located in Scheveningen's harbour. Good for a great price — three courses for €10. Exceptional value. You can only pay with cash and reservation is required.

ICE-CREAM PARLOURS

There are a couple of decent options for ice-cream in the centre of town.

Florencia (🏠 Torenstraat 55; ☎ 070 363 0214) is not the best, but it is really well-known and has been around for a long time. It is fairly cheap.

Australian Homemade (🏠 Voldersgracht 42; 🖥 www. australianhomemade.com) is a Dutch chain near Chinatown. It serves particularly good frappés.

If you are going to Rijswijk, it's worth paying a visit to **Talamini** (🏠 Willemstraat 12; ☎ 070 415 0517; 🖥 www. talaminirijswijk.nl), which offers Italian homemade ice-cream.

Where to Eat & Drink

Where to Eat & Drink

CAFÉS

Cheesecake Company (🏠 Torentstraat 32; ☎ 070 887 8158; 🖥 www.cheesecakecompany.nl; ☎ Tue-Sat: 11am to 6pm, Sun: 12 to 4pm) serves a really delicious selection of homemade cheesecakes and other baked goods. They also serve hot and cold drinks, including freshly-squeezed lemon juice. The main problem with the place is that it has slightly inconvenient opening hours for a bakery-stroke-café. It doesn't open until 11am — which is almost the Dutch lunchtime — and closes early, making it difficult to go for a snack after work. Even enjoying a leisurely breakfast on Sunday mornings is out.

Scallywags (🏠 Wagenstraat 117; ☎ 070 363 3448; 🖥 www.scally-wags.nl; ☎ 8.30 am to 7pm) is a small English-style tea room, serving many British favourites such as English tea (with milk!), chai latte, and Horlicks. It's also a popular place to come for fresh scones with jam and cream. The place is fairly small, so it can be difficult to find a spot to sit, especially during afternoon tea time. The place is something of a shrine to the late Princess Diana — photographs and paintings of her adorn the walls. Lunch is also available. Scallywags has another location a little further down the street (🏠 Wagenstraat 144; ☎ 070 445 1600; 🖥 www.scallywagsrestaurants.com), which is a proper restaurant rather than tea room.

Baklust (🏠 Veenkade 19; ☎ 070 753 2274; 🖥 www.baklust.nl; ☎ Tue-Sun: 10 to 6pm) is actually a vegetarian eetcafé, but it is probably better coming for the cakes and coffee than the lunch.

Juni Lekkernijen (🏠 Molenstraat 63; ☎ 070 360 8106; 🖥 www.junilekkernijen.nl) is a good place to come for breakfast or afternoon tea. Food is fresh and tasty and staff are friendly. There is a good selection of cakes.

Coffee Company (🏠 Noordeinde 54 and 🏠 Korte Poten 21; 🖥 www.coffeecompany.nl; ☎ Mon-Fri: 7.30am to 7pm, Sat-Sun: 9am to 7pm) is a Dutch speciality coffee chain, interesting mainly for its central location and free wi-fi.

Hooistraat (🏠 Hooistraat 5; ☎ 070 345 7878; 🖥 www.hooistraat.nl) is a wonderful little café with scrummy cakes and a nice atmosphere in a lovely location just next to a canal.

BARS

De Paas (🏠 Dunne Bierkade 16; ☎ 070 360 0019; 🖥 www.depaas.nl; ☎ Sun-Thu: 3pm to 1am; Fri & Sat: 3pm to 1.30am) is good for speciality beers.

Café De Bieb (🏠 Veenkade 7-9; ☎ 070 361 7496; 🖥 www.cafedebieb.com; ☎ Sun-Wed: 11am to 1am, Thu-Sat: 11am to 2am) is a friendly local pub where you can play darts, whilst enjoying a drink or Dutch borrel (p76). They also now serve pub grub for lunch and dinner., including the excellent MF burger — ask the bar staff what 'MF' stands for.

A couple of good Irish pubs are **O'Casey's** (🏠 Noordeinde 140; ☎ 070 363 0698; 🖥 www.ocaseys.nl) and **The Fiddler** (🏠 Riviervismarkt 1; ☎ 070 365 1955; 🖥 www.fiddler.nl). Both serve Irish beer and decent food, and regularly screen major sporting events. Both places also regularly hold pub quizzes — every Thursday at O'Casey's and every second Tuesday at The Fiddler. Live music regularly plays at O'Casey's.

Savanna (🏠 Prins Hendrikplein 10; ☎ 070 345 4362; 🖥 www.savanna.nu; ☎ Mon-Tue: 11am to 12am, Wed-Thu: 11am to 1am, Fri: 11am to 1.30am, Sat: 12noon to 1.30am, Sun: 12noon to 12am), a little way from the town centre, is a nice spot for sitting outside during sunny days.

Where to Sleep

Accommodation is listed fist according to area and then according to the price. Often you'll find the best price by booking through an online accommodation website such as 🖥 booking.com.

For cheaper accommodation, you might want to consider 🖥 www.airbnb.com, which allows you to stay in a private room within someone's house. You can also find short-term rental accommodation for entire apartments.

CENTRE

5-Star Hotels

Hotel des Indes (🏠 Lange Voorhout 54-56; ☎ 070 361 2345; 🖥 www.desindes.nl), designed by architect Jacques Garcia, is an upmarket hotel just next to the Escher Museum, with fitness and spa centre and indoor swimming pool. Double rooms start at €190 per night. A delight for those that can afford it.

Hilton (🏠 Zeestraat 35; ☎ 070 710 7000; 🖥 thehague.hilton.com) has all of the plush grandeur that you might expect from a member of this chain of hotels. Service is extremely friendly, rooms and facilities are spotless and the location is quiet yet central. Rooms are airy and generously-proportioned, and come with good-sized 37-inch TVs. Guests have free access to a well-equipped and modern gym. Wireless internet access is not free, however — a somewhat exorbitant €25 per day. Parking is available, but extra: €3 per hour or €25 for 24 hours. Prices change regularly, depending on the season, but expect around €169 for a standard room, €194 for a deluxe, €219 for an executive and €319 for a studio.

4-Star Hotels

Carlton Ambassador (🏠 Sophialaan 2; ☎ 070 363 0363; 🖥 www.carlton.nl/ambassador) certainly lives up to its four stars. It is a comfortable and attractive hotel, located in a quiet part of The Hague but with easy access to the centre. Service is friendly and the building — a 19th century mansion — has a lot of character. The adjoining bistro bar, which has an outdoor area, is a pleasant place to relax and boasts a staggering 230 types of whisky. Your researchers didn't have the chance to taste them all. Free wi-fi is provided throughout the hotel. A laundry service is available, but this isn't free (usually a few euros per garment). Room rates start at €95 for a standard, €129 for an executive. €209 for a deluxe and €629 for a suite.

Paleis Hotel (🏠 Molenstraat 26; ☎ 070 362 4621; 🖥 www.paleishotel.nl) is a nice boutique hotel located between Noordeinde Palace and the Binnenhof. Conveniently close to the centre, the hotel has atmospheric charm and that touch of history.

Hampshire Hotel (🏠 Bezuidenhoutseweg 53; ☎ 070 381 4901; 🖥 www.hampshire-hotels.com) is just next to the central train station and a stone's throw from the city centre. There are numerous government and parliament buildings in the hotel's direct surroundings. The lovely Haagse Bos park is only a few minutes' walk away. The hotel is equipped to meet the demands of both business and leisure travellers.

Parkhotel (🏠 Molenstraat 53; ☎ 070 362 4371; 🖥 www. parkhoteldenhaag.nl) is a 4-star hotel in the city centre. The hotel lives up to the regal character of its surroundings. Besides comfortable rooms, the hotel offers a bar and lounge and versatile conference rooms.

NH Den Haag (🏠 Prinses Margrietplantsoen 100; ☎ 070 381 2345; 🖥 www.nh-hotels.nl) is located just in front of Laan van NOI railway station, and not far from Centraal. It is a primarily a business hotel, offering lower prices at weekends and a Sunday check-out of 5pm. Free wi-fi is available in the lobby. Prices start at €62 per night (breakfast excluded), but consider yourself lucky if you get this price!

Mercure Hotel (🏠 Spui 180; ☎ 070 203 9002; 🖥 www.mercure. com) is conveniently located in the centre of The Hague, with comfortable and stylish rooms and not outrageous prices. Like Mercures the world over, the place is very business-oriented. Service is polite and efficient. Wi-fi is free for guests, but parking is extra (a somewhat excessive €20 for 24 hours). Room rates start at €85.

Corona (🏠 Buitenhof 39-42; ☎ 070 363 7930; 🖥 www.corona. nl) is situated on the Buitenhof, with some rooms overlooking it. The Mauritshuis Museum is only a few doors away. Service is friendly and rooms are comfortable.

Novotel (🏠 Hofweg 5-7; ☎ 070 203 9003; 🖥 www.novotel.com) is a stylish 4-star hotel. Location is convenient though not the quietest. Staff are extremely accommodating. Rooms are not the largest, though comfortable and clean.

3-Star Hotels

Ibis Hotel (🏠 Jan Hendrikstraat 10; ☎ 070 203 9001; 🖥 www. ibishotel.com) offers a comfortable place to stay in The Hague's lively centre. The hotel is easy to reach by both car and public transport.

Court Garden (🏠 Laan van Meerdervoort 96; ☎ 070 311 4000; 🖥 www.hotelcourtgarden.nl) claims to be the first eco-designed hotel in The Hague. It has an official 'green declaration'. Sustainable materials and low-energy systems are used throughout the hotel. Free fair-trade coffee and tea are available in the lounge.

Hotel Sebel (🏠 Prins Hendrikplein 20; ☎ 070 345 9200; 🖥 www. hotelsebel.nl) is a three-star hotel located on the edge of the city centre, not far from the Peace Palace. Rooms are clean and comfortable, though fairly small. Parts of the hotel could do with sprucing up a bit — some of the furniture and facilities look decidedly tatty. Also, not all rooms can be reached by elevator, which is a slight inconvenience when trying to navigate the typically Dutch narrow stairs with suitcase in tow. The hotel has free wi-fi for guests. A room for two people costs around €89. Breakfast is €9 extra.

Hotel Wahdo (🏠 Wagenstraat 127-12; ☎ 070 362 6011; 🖥 www. wahdohotel.nl) is the first Chinese hotel established in The Hague's Chinatown. The entire hotel is decorated in traditional Chinese fashion. The city centre and central train station are within easy walking distance. Hotel Wahdo offers its guests a comfortable stay in a lovely ambiance.

2-Star Hotels

Hotel La Ville (🏠 Veenkade 5-6; ☎ 070 346 3657; 🖥 www. hotellaville.nl) lies near the seat of

Where to Sleep

government in The Hague, within walking distance of the Noordeinde Palace. Rooms are comfortable, tastefully decorated and well-appointed. The historical building has a surprisingly homely feel.

Apartments

Maff Appartement (🏠 Wagenstraat 186; ☎ 070 389 2525 or 06 2631 4680; 🖥 www.maff.nl/appartement-denhaag) offers stylish and trendy self-catering apartments in the centre of The Hague. This is definitely a good choice for weekend or business stays. Free wi-fi and parking are available.

Hostels

Stayokay (🏠 Scheepmakersstraat 27; ☎ 070 315 7888; 🖥 www.stayokay.com) is a relatively quiet, clean and safe hostel for those on a budget. It is conveniently located a short walk from Hollands Spoor train station and near the centre of town.

SCHEVENINGEN

5-Star Hotels

Steigenberger Kurhaus (🏠 Gevers Deynootplein 30; ☎ 070 416 2636; 🖥 www.kurhaus.nl) is more than just a hotel: it is a national landmark of The Hague. This 5-star hotel with its characteristic façade combines modern comfort with an atmospheric, historic ambience. Both tourists and participants in conferences or meetings will appreciate the Kurhaus' style and comfort.

4-Star Hotels

NH Atlantic (🏠 Deltaplein 200; ☎ 070 448 2482; 🖥 www.nh-hotels.nl) is nestled in the dunes, just next to Westduin Park and overlooking the long expanse of Scheveningen beach. Service is a little officious and in light of the price could be better. Room rates start at €66. Rooms are fairly spacious and clean, though the swimming pool is unfortunately quite small. Facilities include an indoor pool, a beauty centre and meeting rooms.

Carlton Beach Hotel (🏠 Gevers Deynootweg 201; ☎ 070 354 1414; 🖥 www.carlton.nl/beach) is beautifully located at the end of the boulevard, overlooking Scheveningen's beach. The hotel offers a fitness room, sauna, solarium and a swimming pool. With public transport, you can easily reach the centre of The Hague.

Bilderberg Europa (🏠 Zwolsestraat 2; ☎ 070 416 9595; 🖥 www.bilderberg.nl) is situated near the Oostduinpark and within walking distance of the beach. In the vicinity you will find a casino and various restaurants, cafés and entertainment venues. Comfortable and friendly.

3-Star Hotels

Hotel Maurits (🏠 Van Aerssenstraat 65; ☎ 070 352 23 41; 🖥 www.hotelmaurits.nl) is located on a quiet street within walking distance of Scheveningen harbour and beach. Staff at the hotel are very friendly, and the rooms are clean. The buffet breakfast (included in the price) is voluminous and free wi-fi is provided for guests. A single room costs €79, single occupancy double room €89, double room for two people €99 and a triple room €122.

Hotel Plato (🏠 Nieuwe Parklaan 125; ☎ 070 338 5222; 🖥 www.hotelplato.nl) offers apartment-style rooms for both long and short stay.

Where to Sleep

It is particularly popular with business visitors on extended trips. Staff are friendly and service is attentive. A regular apartment costs €94-149 and a business apartment €135-€189. Prices are dependent on length of stay and number of people staying. A stay of at least four weeks in a business apartment costs between €71 and €139. Breakfast, parking and wireless internet are all extra.

Badhotel (🏠 Gevers Deynootweg 15; ☎ 070 351 2221; 💻 www.badhotelscheveningen.nl), despite how its name sounds in English, is really quite a good place to stay. (*Bad* actually means 'bath' in Dutch). The hotel is located near the boulevard and the beach. The hotel offers modern rooms with amenities such as air-conditioning and coffee- and tea-making facilities.

Bor (🏠 Haagsestraat 53; ☎ 070 354 5803; 💻 www.hotelbor.nl) is a family-friendly hotel that is close to the beach and promenade of Scheveningen. The hotel also has a number of apartments that are even closer to the beach.

Boulevard (🏠 Seinpostduin 2; ☎ 070 354 0067; 💻 www.boulevard-hotel.nl) has a fantastic location. It lies on the beach, just 200 metres from Scheveningen pier. A comfortable hotel with some stunning views over the North Sea.

Duinzicht (🏠 Alkmaarsestraat 6a; ☎ 070 350 6999; 💻 www.hotelduinzicht.com) is beautifully-located on the foot of the dunes of Scheveningen and offers free parking. The centre and the beach are within close proximity. This cosy family-run hotel has a lot of different room types and apartments, so they can accommodate almost every party.

Strandhotel (🏠 Zeekant 111; ☎ 070 354 0193; 💻 www.strandhotel-scheveningen.nl) is a fairly small family-owned hotel, with a warm and pleasant atmosphere. Affordable prices and comfortable rooms. The hotel has a nice dining room overlooking the beach.

Corel (🏠 Badhuisweg 54-56; ☎ 070 355 9939; 💻 www.hotelcorel.nl) is situated in an historic building just five minutes on foot from the beach. Free wi-fi is available in all areas. Parking is possible nearby but costs €9 per day. The hotel has a nice terrace.

Hage (🏠 Seinpostduin 23) is an unpretentious hotel in the vibrant heart of Scheveningen. Tatty in parts, but comfortable and a wallet-friendly option for staying close to the sea.

2-Star Hotels

Witte Huys (🏠 Bosschestraat 2; ☎ 070 355 3712; 💻 www.wittehuys.nl) is a small and homely family-run hotel, just 150 metres from the beach. Don't expect anything fancy, but accommodation is adequate. Rooms are relatively small but clean and comfortable.

Apartments

Strandzicht Appartementen (🏠 Zeekant 57; ☎ 070 351 5758; 💻 www.strandzicht.nl) offers seven comfortable apartments, some of which have sea views.

Hostels

Jorplace (🏠 Keizerstraat 296; ☎ 070 338 3270; 💻 jorplace.nl) is the only hostel in Scheveningen. It is close to the harbour and the beach. The hostel has 23 rooms with 92 comfortable beds. Not the smartest of places, but it has a great and lively atmosphere and friendly staff. It is conveniently located near shops and restaurants, and only a few minutes from the beach. The price of a bed in a dormitory starts at €19 per night. The hostel arranges activities such as kitesurfing.

PEACE PALACE AREA

5-Star Hotels

Crowne Plaza (🏠 Van Stolkweg 1, ☎ 070 352 5161) is for those that like luxury and don't mind spending more for those little extras (such as the Internet, additional TV channels and the health club/spa). Free wi-fi is available, but only in the lobby. Parking is slightly cheaper than many other city hotels (€15 per day). The hotel is located 300 metres away from the World Forum Convention Centre, and the beach is easy to reach by public transport.

4-Star Hotels

Haagsche Suites (🏠 Laan van der Meerdervoort 155; ☎ 070 364 7879; 🖥 www.haagschesuites.nl) has three luxurious suites to offer, situated in a stately mansion from the 19th century.

Bel Air (🏠 Johan de Wittlaan 30; ☎ 070 352 5354; 🖥 www.belairhotel.nl) is situated mid-way between Scheveningen and The Hague, not far from the World Forum Convention Centre and the Gemeentemuseum. Particularly suited for business travellers, it has excellent conference facilities. Good public transport connections whisk you to Scheveningen in one direction and The Hague in the other. Rooms are modern, clean and comfortable.

Novotel (🏠 Johan de Wittlaan 42-44; ☎ 070 203 9004; 🖥 www.novotel.com) is in the same building as the World Forum Convention Center and a 10-minute tram ride to the city centre. The comfortable 4-star hotel has facilities such as a

fitness centre and a sauna. Popular with business travellers.

3-Star Hotels

Mozaic (🏠 Laan Copes van Cattenburch 38-40; ☎ 070 35 22 335; 🖥 www.mozaic.nl) is a small boutique hotel housed in two renovated historic buildings from 1880. The hotel combines excellent service with a modern design. Your stay includes free coffee and tea, and free wireless internet.

Best Western Petit (🏠 Groot Hertoginnelaan 42; ☎ 070 346 5500; 🖥 www.hotelpetit.nl) is a wonderful small non-smoking hotel in The Hague. It is located in the stylish Ambassadewijk, the embassy area between the city centre and Scheveningen. Business travellers will appreciate the close proximity of the World Forum Convention Center, which is within walking distance. Tourists can easily visit the area's numerous attractions.

Excelsior (🏠 Statenlaan 45; ☎ 070 354 1234; 🖥 www.hotelexcelsior.nl) is housed in a charming early 20th century building. It has a terrific atmosphere and friendly staff. The hotel has free wi-fi as well as free off-street parking. It is in a residential area of Statenkwartier, 15 minutes walk from the harbour and the sea. Convenient public transport runs regularly to the city centre.

2-Star Hotels

Delta (🏠 Anna Paulownastraat 8; ☎ 070 362 4999; 🖥 www.deltahotel.info) is situated in a wealthy part of the city close to plenty of bars and shops. It is within walking distance of the Peace Palace and 15 minutes from the city centre. The hotel is fairly old and doesn't have an elevator. However, the location and comparatively lower rates make it an attractive option.

WASSENAAR

4-Star Hotels

Kasteel de Wittenburg (🏠 Bloemcamplaan 55; ☎ 070 515 1500; 🖥 www.wittenburg.nl) lies in lovely wooded surroundings. It has a beautiful terrace and garden. The elegant rooms are provided with all modern comforts.

Van der Valk (🏠 Zijdeweg 54, Wassenaar; ☎ 070 511 9344; 🖥 www.hoteldenhaagwassenaar. nl) offers modern accommodation with luxurious rooms, a restaurant, a spacious lounge, a bar and good conference facilities. Free parking is available.

3-Star Hotels

Buitengoed Hagenhorst (🏠 Oud Clingendael 7; ☎ 070 512 1200; 🖥 www.hagenhorst.nl) is located in beautiful and peaceful surroundings in the heart of Wassenaar woodland, only a few kilometres from the beach.

VOORBURG

4-Star Hotels

Mövenpick (🏠 Stationsplein 8; ☎ 070 337 3737; 🖥 www. moevenpick-hotels.com) is situated just opposite Voorburg railway station. It is a popular place for those visiting the ICC. It has wi-fi, but only the first four hours are free. After that, it costs €15 per 24

hours. Bicycle rental and a garage are also available.

Hotel Savelberg (🏠 Oosteinde 14; ☎ 070 387 2081; 🖥 www. restauranthotelsavelberg.nl) is located in an 18th century mansion in wonderful surroundings: a beautifully green park, full of ancient trees, which exudes peace and tranquillity. The hotel has a restaurant and an outside terrace.

RIJSWIJK

5-Star Hotels

Hotel & Spa Savarin (🏠 Laan van Hoornwijck 29; ☎ 070 307 2050; 🖥 www.savarin.nl) is a comfortable hotel in attractive surroundings. Its main attraction is a health and spa centre, which offers a sauna, swimming pool, jacuzzi and Turkish steam bath.

4-Star Hotels

Worldhotel Grand Winston (🏠 Generaal Eisenhowerplein 1; ☎ 070 414 1500; 🖥 www. worldhotelgrandwinston.com) is a friendly hotel, although some of the rooms can be a bit noisy. Amenities include a gym, bar and lounge.

3-Star Hotels

Bastion Deluxe Hotel (🏠 Polakweg 12; ☎ 070 307 0169; 🖥 www.bastionhotels.nl) offers good accommodation and facilities at attractive rates. Guests can park their car for free at the hotel. For some relaxation, there is a good restaurant, a bar and even a library.

Surrounding towns

Rijswijk, Voorburg, Zoetermeer, Ypenburg, Wassenaar, Monster

Wassenaar, Rijswijk, Voorburg, Zoetermeer, Ypenburg and Monster all lie in close proximity to The Hague. Many people who work in The Hague choose to live in one of these areas. This is partly because of the greener and more suburban lifestyle that they offer, but also because of lower rental costs.

For details of temporary accommodation in any of these places, see the relevant section in Where To Sleep (p183).

VOORBURG

The centre of Voorburg is wealthy, consisting of pretty houses, small and cute shops and nice patches of green. On Saturdays, you will find a small local grocery market here (🏠 Oosteinde; ⏰9am to 4pm); produce is not as cheap as in the central market of The Hague (p133) but it is prettier.

Voorburg begins at Laan Van NOI station, which is only a 10-minute cycle ride away from The Hague's Centraal Station. Located at the edge of the countryside, Voorburg is a good starting point for cycle trips.

Eurojust and the International Criminal Court (ICC) share a building in Voorburg. The ICC is expected to relocate to new premises in 2015.

Just the other side of Voorburg, you'll find Sligro (p128), a huge supermarket that is mostly dedicated to serving companies.

The webpage of the municipality is 🖥 www.leidschendamvoorburg. nl.

What to do

The **city museum** (🏠 Herenstraat 101; 🖥 www. stadsmuseum-leidschendam-voorburg.nl) will reopen in April 2013, having been closed for a year.

The **Huygensmuseum** (🏠 Westeinde 2a, Voorburg; 🖥 www. hofwijck.nl/huygensmuseum.html) will also reopen at the end of April 2013. This museum showcases the life and works of Constantine Huygens (1596 to 1687), described by the municipality as 'a fascinating man with many talents'. Numbered among these talents are: artist, scientist, musician, poet and linguist. Not to mention secretary to the House of Orange.

There is a **pitch & putt** course just on the edge of Voorburg (🖥 www.pitch-putt.nl).

Voorburg puts on a **culinary and cultural festival** every year in September, together with neighbouring Leidschendam (🖥 www. vlietdagen.nl).

The Voorburg library is located at 🏠 Koningin Julianalaan 257; 🖥 www.bibliotheekaandevliet.nl.

Where to eat

Le Barquichon (🏠 Kerkstraat 6; ☎ 070 387 1181; 🖥 www. lebarquichon.nl) offers classic French cooking in intimate surroundings. Definitely the classier end of Voorburg's dining experience, with prices to match.

Thai Fresh (🏠 Koningin Julianalaan 230; 🖥 www.thai-fresh.nl; ☎ 070 386 3838) is not the cheapest place to go for dinner, but worth paying that extra for good food, pleasant surroundings and friendly service.

Savelberg (🏠 Oosteinde 14; ☎ 070 387 2081; 🖥 www.restauranthotelsavelberg.nl) is pricey but great for a treat. It used to have a Michelin star, but unfortunately lost it in 2012. Style of cooking is French-themed.

WASSENAAR

Wassenaar is a wealthy town some 10 km away from The Hague. Despite being a relatively small town, Wassenaar is well known in the Netherlands as a result of its conspicuous wealth. Areas of the town are amongst the most affluent in the country, which has earned residents something of a reputation for being posh (or, to use the Dutch term, *bekakt*).

Unlike other neighbouring towns, rental prices in Wassenaar aren't cheaper than in The Hague.

There is a fairly large expatriate community of diplomats and business people in the town, largely due to its proximity to both the international organisations and embassies in The Hague and to several international schools. Several ambassadorial residences are also located in Wassenaar, including those of Canada and South Korea. The American Embassy is expected to relocate here in the coming years.

The Netherlands Institute for Advanced Study (NIAS), which provides support for foreign and Dutch scholars, is located here too.

Wassenaar's town centre sports a number of high end shops, delicatessens and bakeries, as well as cafés, bars and restaurants. There's a branch of the British supermarket Kelly's here (☎ Luifelbaan 50; ☎ 070 511 8729).

There is a branch of the well-known pâtisserie Maison Kelder (p133) in Wassenaar, too.

A weekly market is held along Berheistraat every Tuesday between 9am and 4pm.

The website for the municipality is 🖥 www.wassenaar.nl.

What to do

In the centre of Wassenaar, there is a **flour mill** dating from 1668 (🏠 Molenplein; ☎ 070 511 8207). It was in use until 1962 when it was sold to the Wassenaar municipality, which paid for its restoration. You can visit the mill Saturday afternoons, from 12noon to 3pm.

Wassenaar is also where Duinrell amusement park (🏠 Duinrell 1; ☎ 070 515 5255; 🖥 www.duinrell.com) can be found.

There is a well-stocked **library** (🏠 Langstraat 40; 🖥 www.obvw.nl). In the library, you'll also find a branch of the Filmhuis **cinema** (☎ 070 511 3379). The programme is available on the website of the library, and it is possible to book online too.

Wassenaar is also home to **The English Theatre** (🏠 Nassaulaan 17; ☎ 06 3005 0018; 🖥 www.theenglishtheatre.nl) — see p166.

For children the local **petting zoo** (🏠 Kinderboerderij Rodenburglaan 80) may be of interest.

Wassenaar doesn't have a **tourist office**, but the local library can provide you with some regional information. The nearest tourist offices are in Katwijk (🏠 Lighthouse Plein 11; ☎ 071 407 5444) and Noordwijk (🏠 De Grent 8; ☎ 071 361 9321).

Where to eat

La Scala (🏠 Plein 13; ☎ 070 514 1064; 🖥 www.ristorantepizzerialascala.nl) serves classic Italian dishes in a relaxed setting. Food tasty, prices reasonable and service friendly.

Eleni   (🏠 Oostdorperweg
47; ☎ 070 511 3599; 💻 www.
eleniwassenaar.nl) is a nice and
cosy restaurant serving mountains
of Greek food at not unreasonable
prices.

RIJSWIJK

Greener and quieter than The
Hague, not to mention cheaper, Rijswijk is a pleasant town with just
under 50,000 inhabitants.

Here you'll find the headquarters
of the European Patent Office and
Shell and one of the main buildings
of Dutch petrochemical giant Shell.

The town is very well-connected
by public transport to The Hague. It
has its own mainline station (🏠 Sir
Winston Churchilllaan), with trains
running to Den Haag Centraal every
15 to 25 minutes. The last one is at
12.30am. The train journey takes
11 minutes. There are also regular bus connections. You can cycle
quite easily between The Hague
and Rijswijk, which are only a few
kilometres apart

The outskirts of Rijswijk may not
be the prettiest, but the small town
centre has a very different feeling
altogether and is quite pleasant to
stroll around in.

The town is divided into two parts
— the old town (Oud Rijswijk), with
a pedestrian precinct and several
pretty shops, and the area around
the church (Kerkstraat), where on
Saturday there is a weekly market
(p134).

In the centre of Oud Rijswijk,
there is a shopping area (💻 www.
winkelcentrumoudrijswijk.nl) and
an old windmill called Schaapwei-
molen. The station area is much
more modern and hosts a huge
shopping centre called Bogaard
(💻 www.indebogaard.nl), with
several restaurants and cafés.
The town council can be found at:

🏠 Bogaardplein 15; ☎ 14 070;
💻 www.rijswijk.nl in.

What to do

The town's **city museum**
(🏠 Herenstraat 67; 💻 www.
museumrijswijk.nl; 💰 €6), is
housed in an imposing 18th century mansion in the heart of Oud
Rijswijk. The museum exhibits
mainly works of art, with a keen
focus on The Hague School, which
was an artistic club that operated in
the latter half of the 18th century.
Exhibitions rotate every couple of
months.

There is a **theatre** in the centre
of Rijswijk: De Rijswijkse Schouwburg   (🏠 Generaal   Spoorlaan
10; ☎ 070 336 0077; 💻 www.
rijswijkseschouwburg.nl).

Rijswijk has a **golf course**
(🏠 Delftweg   59;   💻 www.
rijswijksegolf.nl) and numerous
parks, including the large and
well-maintained Wilhelminapark.
The Von Fisenne Park has a **petting zoo**.

You'll find a few **sports centres** around the town. De Schilp
(🏠 Schaapweg 4; ☎ 070 336
4700) has an indoor swimming
pool. First Class (💻 firstclass.nl)
has squash courts. There is also
Sport City (💻 www.sportcity.nl), a
well-equipped fitness centre.

Where to eat

China   (🏠 Herenstraat   39;
☎ 070 390 4493) offers decent
Asian cooking using fresh ingredients. The restaurant brands itself
as Chinese-Indonesian, but sadly
the Indonesian side of the menu
lacks the authentic flavours you
find elsewhere.

Anders en Meer (🏠 Willemstraat 15; ☎ 070 737 0425;
💻 www.andersenmeer.nl) is a good
and inexpensive place to come for

Surrounding towns

lunch or afternoon tea. Service is very friendly and attentive.

Paul van Waarden (🏠 Tollensstraat 10; ☎ 070 414 0812; 🖥 www.paulvanwaarden.nl) is an Indonesian place that does good take-away.

Gran Sasso (🏠 Herenstraat 79; ☎ 070 399 4120; 🖥 www.gransasso.nl) is a good Italian restaurant run by Italians. The cheaper menu at lunch consists of salads, soups, sandwiches and pizza. Cooking is fancier at dinnertime, with freshly-made pasta, fish and meat dishes.

Moving to Rijswijk

O&V Makelaars (🖥 www.ovmak.nl) specialises in property in Rijswijk.

A good source of information about the latest goings-on in the town is 🖥 www.rijswijk.nl, but it's only in Dutch.

ZOETERMEER

Zoetermeer is located mid-way between Delft and The Hague, 15 km from both. Its name comes from the Dutch for 'sweet lake', referring to a freshwater lake that once lay to the north of the town (it was reclaimed in 1614). The town has a relatively high population: more than 120,000 people. It is divided into 10 areas, each having a tram stop.

Zoetermeer is well connected to The Hague by RandstadRail trams (p91). However, there is no railway station in the town. This means that, if you rely on a rail discount card, Zoetermeer is a more expensive place to reach from The Hague than some towns that are further away, such as Leiden and Delft.

In the centre of the town, you'll find numerous shops, cafés, restaurants and the town hall. If you walk a short distance out of town,

you'll quickly come across some nice parks and residential areas.

Note that there are some areas of Zoetermeer that have a slightly seedy, unsafe feeling to them.

If you are living in the area, you might consider sending your children to **Alfrink College** (🖥 alfrink.nl) in Zoetermeer runs courses in both English and Dutch.

Zoetermeer's **library** can be found at: 🏠 Stadhuisplein 2; 🖥 www.bibliotheek-zoetermeer.nl, Zoetermeer. The *gemeente* is just next-door: 🏠 Stadhuisplein 1; 🖥 www.zoetermeer.nl.

What to do

There is a **golf course** in Zoetermeer: Burg Golf (🏠 Heuvelweg 3; 🖥 burggolf.nl).

Dutch Water Dreams (🏠 Van der Hagenstraat 3; ☎ 079 330 2500; 🖥 www.dutchwaterdreams.com) is a fabulous water park.

You also have an ice-skating rink at **Silver Dome** (🏠 Van der Hagenstraat 20; ☎ 079 330 5000; 🖥 www.silverdome.nl).

Where to eat

Bo & Ro (🏠 Dorpsstraat 58e; ☎ 079 331 0175; 🖥 www.broodleuk.nl) is a good lunch option.

YPENBURG

Ypenburg became part of the municipality of The Hague in 2002. There are now around 30,000 people living in the town.

The area is accessible by tram number 15 from the centre of The Hague, and tram 19 from Leidschendam and Delft. The district also has its own train station (🏠 Ypenburgse Stationsweg), located right next to the A12 motorway.

There is a small local market every Friday along Steentijdsingel in the centre of Ypenburg, from 9am to 5pm.

Ypenburg's library can be found at 🏠 Schrabber 8; ☎ 070 353 8611.

Although Ypenburg belongs to the municipality of The Hague, it has its own town hall (*stadhuis*) just next to the railway station: 🏠 Brigantijnlaan 303.

Ypenburg is a very green town. Many young families choose to live here because it has a more countrified feeling to it, whilst still retaining good transport connections with The Hague. Apartments are also more affordable.

If you are looking to rent accommodation, even in the short-term, you may want to have a look at 🖥 www.ypenburgcentrum.nl and 🖥 www.wonenmvm-denhaag.nl.

Sport Accent (🏠 Kiekendiefstraat 35; 🖥 www.sportaccent.nl) is a large sports complex that also has a swimming pool.

MONSTER

About 10 km south-west of The Hague you'll find Monster, a pleasant coastal town of some 15,000 inhabitants. Monster was a separate municipality until 2004, but is now part of The Hague.

Exactly where the name 'Monster' came from is unclear. One popular belief is that it is a derivation of the Latin word *monasterium*, meaning 'monastery'. Another explanation is that Monster comes from the old-Dutch word 'monster', which meant 'big church'. This theory is supported by the fact that Monster once had one of the largest churches in the area.

Hervormde Kerk (🖥 www.hervormdegemeentemonster.nl), the church in question, was built between the 14th and 15th centuries, but burnt down in 1901 following a massive fire. The church was subsequently rebuilt and now stands proud in the centre of the town.

Not far from the centre of Monster, you'll find De Vier Winden (🖥 Haagweg 2), a **windmill** that was built in 1882.

Just outside Monster, in Naaldwijk, regular **flower auctions** take place. These auctions are organised by Flora Holland (🖥 www.floraholland.com), which is a co-operative of horticultural producers. The auctions are always amazingly lively, colourful and fun. You can watch the auction from a special gallery reserved for visitors.

There is also a nice **beach** in Monster.

Surrounding towns

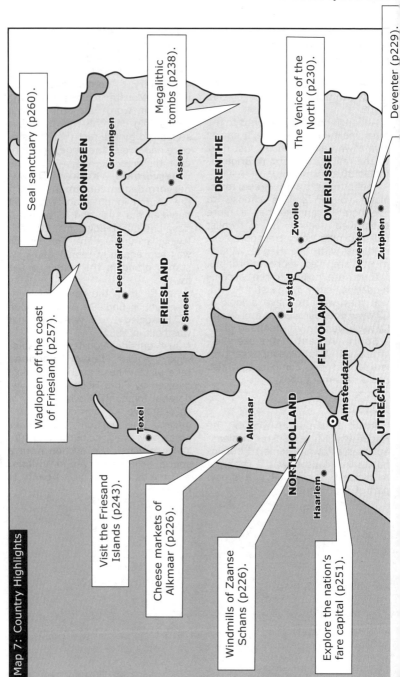

Map 7: Country Highlights

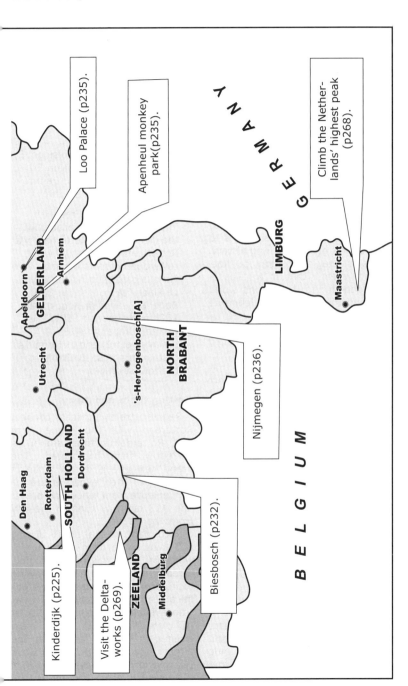

Loo Palace (p235).

Apenheul monkey park(p235).

Climb the Netherlands' highest peak (p268).

GERMANY

LIMBURG

Maastricht

GELDERLAND

Apeldoorn

Arnhem

's-Hertogenbosch[A]

NORTH BRABANT

Nijmegen (p236).

Utrecht

Den Haag

Rotterdam

SOUTH HOLLAND

Dordrecht

BELGIUM

Kinderdijk (p225).

Visit the Delta-works (p269).

ZEELAND

Middelburg

Biesbosch (p232).

ROTTERDAM

Rotterdam, the Netherlands' second-largest city, is located at the mouth of two of Europe's greatest rivers: the Rhine flowing in from Germany and the Meuse (or Maas in Dutch) flowing in from France.

Rotterdam's port — the busiest in Europe (some have claimed the world, but this isn't true: Shanghai takes pole position in this regard) — is world-famous, and attests to the nation's great seafaring history.

The strategic position of Rotterdam meant that it was badly damaged during the second world war, and this has helped define its present-day character.

Gone are the old 18th and early 19th century buildings, replaced with a flurry of post-war architectural modernism. It seems that every well-known Dutch architect has descended on the city over the last 20 years, to add their particular twirl or flourish to Rotterdam's eclectic vibrancy. The tourist office can arrange architectural walking tours for you to appreciate this.

As one might expect of the country's second-largest city, Rotterdam has a pulsating nightlife rivalled in the country only by Amsterdam. It also has a wealth of culture to soak up in the form of art galleries and museums.

It is in Rotterdam where you will find many of the country's largest companies, featuring such household names as Unilever and ArcelorMittal.

Rotterdam may be big (at least by Dutch standards), but you'll still be able to find pockets of romantic tranquillity if you spend some time in the city. Delfshaven (p201), for example, is dotted with picturesque little outdoor cafés and restaurants.

Information

- **Tourist office:** 🏠 Coolsingel 5; ☎ 015 271 0128; ⏰ Mon-Fri: 9am to 6pm, Sat-Sun: 9am to 5pm; 🖥 en.rotterdam.info

- **Internet access:** Free wi-fi internet access is available in the city centre of Rotterdam via Rotterdam Hotspots (🖥 www.rotterdamhotspots.nl) and various cafés around the city: La Place (🏠 Hoogstraat 185), Bagel & Beans (🏠 Hoogstraat 129b and Lijnbaan 150), The Coffee Company (🏠 Eendrachtsplein 2) and McDonald's restaurants. Also available in the tourist office.

Getting there and away

Regular train services connect Rotterdam with The Hague. Note that Rotterdam's train station is currently being renovated. The brand new one is due to open in 2013. Until then expect some inconvenience from fenced-off areas. The A13 highway runs to the city from The Hague.

Rotterdam has a small airport (🖥 www.rotterdam-airport.nl), which in 2010 was renamed 'Rotterdam The Hague Airport', owing to its proximity to the nation's political capital. Transavia (🖥 www.transavia.com) and CityJet (🖥 www.cityjet.com) are the main airlines that fly to and from the airport. Recently, British Airways (🖥 www.britishairways.com), KLM (🖥 www.klm.com) and Air France

FESTIVALS

Here are some Rotterdam-based festivals to look out for:

- **International Film Festival** (🖳 www.filmfestivalrotterdam.dom; 🕓 Jan to Feb) shows a diverse range of independent and experimental films.

- **De Parade** (🖳 www.deparade.nl; 🕓 Jun) is a theatre festival that travels across the Netherlands.

- **North Sea Jazz Festival** (🖳 www.northseajazz.nl; 🕓 Jul), the largest in Europe.

- **Zomer Carnaval** (🖳 www.zomercarnaval.nl; 🕓 Jul) — come for the parades, music and parties. A spectacular procession of tropical colour and pizazz.

- **Wereld Havendagen** (🖳 www.wereldhavendagen.nl; 🕓 Sep) celebrates the prestige of Rotterdam's harbour, with firework displays and ship tours.

- **City Race** (🖳 www.cityracing.nl; 🕓 Aug) a Formula One race inside the city centre.

(🖳 www.airfrance.com) have also started to offer a limited service to and from here.

There is no train station at the airport, but you can easily take a bus. Bus 33 shuttles regularly between the airport and Rotterdam railway station, where you can catch a train to The Hague. If you are coming from The Hague, another way to get to the airport is to take a train from The Hague's Centraal Station to Meijersplein. Note that this train service is not part of Dutch national rail — it is actually operated by the Rotterdam metro network RET. Therefore, in order to find details of the train, you should consult the RET website (🖳 www.ret.nl) and not Dutch national rail. Furthermore, the screens at the central station will not display details of the train. From Meijersplein, take bus 50 to the airport (an *OV-chipkaart* is necessary for this journey). The airport is easily-reached by taxi. From The Hague, you can book online a journey from €36 (p92).

What to see

Railz Miniworld (🏠 Weena 745; ☎ 010 240 0501; 🕓 Weds to Thu: 12noon to 5pm, Fri to Sun: 10am to 5pm; 💲 €9.25; 🖳 www.railzminiworld.com) is an enchanting miniature world dedicated to showcasing the locomotive. Started in 2006 by a single rail enthusiast, this attraction has grown to be the largest indoor model railway in the Netherlands.

The attention to detail is astonishing. Everything is hand-crafted in an on-site workshop, which you can visit if you pay for one of the tours.

The place attempts to simulate night and day, by dimming the lights for four minutes every 20 (therefore making things 60 times faster than in the real world). The computers initially got the data for day and night off the Internet, until people complained it was dark for too long!

The rail enthusiasts that run the model railway are highly knowledgeable and happy to answer any questions that you might care to ask them.

There is something for everyone — and kids can have great

South Holland

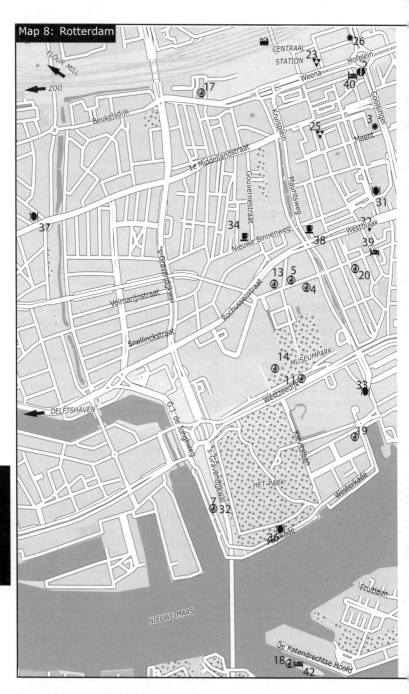

Map 8: Rotterdam

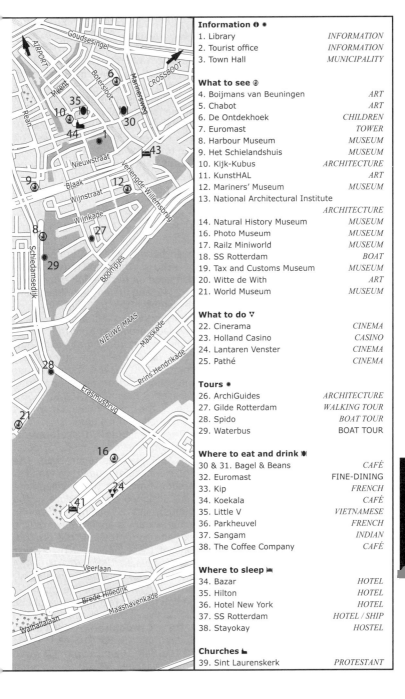

Information ❶ ⁕
1. Library	*INFORMATION*
2. Tourist office	*INFORMATION*
3. Town Hall	*MUNICIPALITY*

What to see ②
4. Boijmans van Beuningen	*ART*
5. Chabot	*ART*
6. De Ontdekhoek	*CHILDREN*
7. Euromast	*TOWER*
8. Harbour Museum	*MUSEUM*
9. Het Schielandshuis	*MUSEUM*
10. Kijk-Kubus	*ARCHITECTURE*
11. KunstHAL	*ART*
12. Mariners' Museum	*MUSEUM*
13. National Architectural Institute	
	ARCHITECTURE
14. Natural History Museum	*MUSEUM*
16. Photo Museum	*MUSEUM*
17. Railz Miniworld	*MUSEUM*
18. SS Rotterdam	*BOAT*
19. Tax and Customs Museum	*MUSEUM*
20. Witte de With	*ART*
21. World Museum	*MUSEUM*

What to do ⅴ
22. Cinerama	*CINEMA*
23. Holland Casino	*CASINO*
24. Lantaren Venster	*CINEMA*
25. Pathé	*CINEMA*

Tours ⁕
26. ArchiGuides	*ARCHITECTURE*
27. Gilde Rotterdam	*WALKING TOUR*
28. Spido	*BOAT TOUR*
29. Waterbus	BOAT TOUR

Where to eat and drink ⅷ
30 & 31. Bagel & Beans	*CAFÉ*
32. Euromast	FINE-DINING
33. Kip	*FRENCH*
34. Koekala	*CAFÉ*
35. Little V	*VIETNAMESE*
36. Parkheuvel	*FRENCH*
37. Sangam	*INDIAN*
38. The Coffee Company	*CAFÉ*

Where to sleep ⊨
34. Bazar	*HOTEL*
35. Hilton	*HOTEL*
36. Hotel New York	*HOTEL*
37. SS Rotterdam	*HOTEL / SHIP*
38. Stayokay	*HOSTEL*

Churches ⌐
39. Sint Laurenskerk	*PROTESTANT*

South Holland

fun playing with the train in the workshop.

SS Rotterdam (🏠 3e Katendrechtse Hoofd 25; ☎ 010 288 6624; 🕓 Mar: 10am to 5pm, Apr to Oct: 9am to 7.30pm; Nov to Dec: 9am to 4pm; 💲 free to enter, tours €12.50; 🖵 www.derotterdam.com) offers a first-hand example of the prowess of Dutch shipbuilding.

The SS Rotterdam, known as 'The Grande Dame', was launched in 1958 by Queen Juliana. She sailed for more than 40 years before she was finally decommissioned in 2000.

Her maiden voyage saw her cruise the 3600 miles from Rotterdam, not far from where she is moored now, to New York. The site of her launching is now marked by the New York Hotel. With the growing popularity of air travel, the SS Rotterdam was permanently retired from transatlantic service in 1969 and began a new life as a cruise ship.

The ship has now been converted into a hotel. Looking upon the ship, you can't help but wonder how on Earth it can stay afloat. It is vast. Viewing the ship is free and you can even go inside for free — after all, it is a hotel — but a tour will cost extra.

The **Netherlands Architectural Institute Museum** (🏠 Museum Park 25; ☎ 010 440 1200; 🕓 Tue-Sat: 10am to 5pm; Sun: 11am to 5pm; 💲 €10.00; 🅼) has one of the world's largest architectural collections on display. It is fascinating to get an insight into the minds of some of the people that rebuilt Rotterdam after the war. The entrance fee for the museum also includes a visit to the Sonneveld House Museum, built in the 1930s, and one of the best preserved examples of a Dutch modernist style known as Nieuwe Bouwen.

The 185-metre **Euromast** (🏠 Parkhaven 20; 🕓 9.30am to 11pm; 💲 €9.25; 🖵 www. euromast.nl; ☎ 010 436 4811) is the tallest building in Rotterdam, offering unrivalled views over the city. There is a rotating restaurant at the top, and also a luxury accommodation suite (☎ 010 241 1788). You can even arrange to abseil off the tower for €49.50.

Sint Laurenskerk (🏠 Grotekerkplein 3; ☎ 010 413 1494; 🖵 www. laurenskerkrotterdam.nl; 💲 €1) is the oldest surviving building in Rotterdam. Built between 1449 and 1525, it is the final remnant of the city's medieval era, which has now been buried beneath the onslaught of history. The church was badly damaged during the Rotterdam Blitz of 1940, and there were initially calls to demolish the building. However, sanity prevailed and architect Jacobus Oud proposed how the church could be restored. An adjoining museum (💲 €5) tells the story of the church. Outside the church stands the nation's oldest statue, honouring Desiderius Erasmus (1469 to 1536), one of the most influential writers and scholars of his time.

The **Overblaak Development** is one of those architectural oddities that just has to be seen. The style of cuboid house that features predominantly in the development was designed by Piet Blom in the 1980s, and is distinct in having some windows angled towards the sky and some towards the ground. One of these houses, **Kijk-Kubus** (🏠 Overblaak 70; ☎ 010 414 2285; 🖵 www.kubuswoning.nl; 💲 €2.50), is open to the public — so you too can feel what it would be like to live in a tilted cube.

De Ontdekhoek (🏠 Pannekoekstraat 55; ☎ 010 414 3103; 🕓 Tue-Sat: 10am to 5pm; 🖵 www. ontdekhoek.nl; 💲 €8) is a great

DELFSHAVEN

No trip to Rotterdam would be complete without a visit to the quarter of Delfshaven. It is here where you will find the city's historical museum (p202), but there are plenty of other reasons that might draw you here too.

Although Delfshaven is a borough of Rotterdam, it was formally a separate municipality until 1886, when it was integrated into the city.

Delfshaven was originally the port for the city of Delft. Although Delft is not located on a major river, it was an important trading hub for many centuries. The harbour of Delfshaven was created to allow the town to receive seafaring vessels and avoid the tolls levied by neighbouring Rotterdam.

These days, Delfshaven is a very picturesque part of the city, with a charmingly relaxed feel to it. There are some very nice historical buildings and cafés (p204), as well as a large number of boutiques and craft shops to stroll around.

place for children — from the age of four until 14 — to come to discover the techniques that go into various trades, such as developing photos in a darkroom, stopping a fast-flowing flood with heavy stones and making crisps from potatoes.

Rotterdam Zoo (🏠 Blijdorplaan 8; ☎ 0900 1857; ⏰ summer: 9am to 5pm, winter: 9am to 6pm; 🖥 www.rotterdamzoo.nl; 💰 €21) is a well-maintained zoo in the centre of the city, popular with families. Friendly staff are on hand to answer questions about the animals. Workshops for children are frequently organised at weekends.

Rotterdam has a very nice and well-maintained **botanical garden** (🏠 Honingerdijk 86; ☎ 010 233 0166; 🖥 www.trompenburg.nl; 💰 €6). Tours are available on Sundays for €2 per person.

There's an old **flour mill** (🏠 Overschiese Kleiweg 775; ☎ 010 467 7299; ⏰ Tue-Sat: 10am to 4pm) in the north-east of the town that is open to the public.

Football fans might like to visit the **Home of History** (🏠 Van Zandvlietplein 1; ☎ 010 492 9444; ⏰ Wed-Thu: 1 to 5pm, Sat: 9am to 5pm), for a look at the Feyenood football club. The 75-minute tour includes a visit to the stadium, the VIP stands, the dressing rooms and the player's tunnel. Guided tours cost €13.50 for adults and €9.50 for children under 13. They can be arranged at 🖥 www.cityguiderotterdam.com. The museum on its own is €5, €2.50 for kids.

Art galleries

Museum Boijmans van Beuningen (🏠 Museumpark 18; ☎ 010 441 9400; ⏰ Tues to Sun: 11am to 5pm; 💰 €12.50; 🖥 www.boijmans.nl; M) is Rotterdam's largest art gallery and thus a crucial element on the itinerary of any art enthusiast.

Spanning two vast floors, the permanent exhibition features such eminent luminaries as Rembrandt, Pablo Picasso, Claude Monet, Vincent van Gogh, René Magritte and Salvador Dalí.

Such names indicate a huge diversity within the museum — both in the era of the artwork and the styles. Particular focus is given in the museum to Dutch painters, many of whom flocked to Rotterdam after the second world war had destroyed the city.

South Holland

The art gallery also has an extensive library, containing more than 120,000 books in a variety of languages. The public are free to search and request books, but may not take them away. There is also an area where you can order prints of your favourite paintings.

The ground floor is dedicated to temporary exhibitions, which change every few months.

Witte de With (🏠 Witte de Withstraat 50; ☎ 010 411 0144; ⏰ Tues to Sun: 11am to 6pm; 💰 €5; 🖥 www.wdw.nl) is the place to come if you want to try something a bit more new-age than the established classic art galleries in the city.

As you approach the art gallery, passing down a narrow street of coffee shops and hippy stalls, you get an idea of what the place is going to be like.

Consider a dozen or so underpants, died pink, and strung up like an upside down cross. Or half a dozen typewriters, with paper scattered all over the floor. Or a plastic monstrosity made to look like a pile of vomit.

The displays in the gallery change every few months, during which time part of the museum will be closed for about a week. If you want to go, check the website beforehand to see which elements will be open.

Chabot (🏠 Museumpark 11; ☎ 010 436 3713; ⏰ Tue-Fri: 11am to 4.30pm, Sat: 11am to 5pm, Sun: 12noon to 5pm; 💰 €6.50; 🚇 M) is dedicated to the Dutch expressionist painter and sculptor Hendrik Chabot. The art gallery is housed in a stark-white modernist villa, which was designed in the 1930s and enlarged in the 1990s. The gallery is not terribly big.

The **KunstHAL** (☎ 010 440 0301; 🏠 Westzeedijk 341;

⏰ Tue-Sat: 10am to 5pm, Sun: 11am to 5pm; 💰 €11) is a large art centre with a dozen or so rotating exhibitions each year.

Museums

Museum het Schielandshuis (🏠 Korte Hoogstraat 31; ☎ 0104 761 533; ⏰ Tues to Sun: 11am to 5pm; 💰 €5; 🖥 www.hmr.rotterdam.nl/museum/schielandshuis) is Rotterdam's city museum — previously called the historical museum, but the word 'historical' was dropped at the start of 2011.

Housed in one of Rotterdam's few remaining 17th century buildings, the exhibition charts the development of some of the city's most prominent streets — such as Coolsingel. The museum also gives some history about what happened during the war. Besides the permanent exhibition, there are also temporary exhibitions that change every so often.

Museum de Dubbelde Palmboom (🏠 Voorhaven 12; ☎ 010 476 1533; ⏰ Tues to Sun: 11am to 5pm; 💰 €5; 🖥 www.hmr.rotterdam.nl/museum/dubbeldepalmboom) is a newer cousin to the main city museum, and is especially geared towards helping children understand their city and environment. With this aim in mind, typical temporary exhibitions have included information about recycling of rubbish. As this guidebook was being researched, plans were afoot to completely revamp the museum. Plans were still sketchy, but it looks as though the whole museum will be dedicated to Delfshaven. The basic four-floor layout will remain the same. The fourth floor tends to house temporary exhibitions, whilst the third floor is more permanent. The first and second floors are semi-permanent, tending to change every five years or so.

Mariniers Museum (🏠 Wijnhaven 7-13; ☎ 010 412 9600; ☻ Tues to Fri: 10am to 5pm, Sat & Sun: 11am to 5pm; 💲€6; 🖥 www.marinemuseum.nl) is the place to come to get a sense of what life on the open waves is like for the Netherlands' naval force. As the museum points out, a marine's work spans the border between the sea and the land.

Owned by the Dutch Ministry of Defence, the museum spans three floors, chronicling the evolution of the marines from 1665 right up until the present day.

Wereldmuseum (🏠 Willemskade 25; ☎ 010 270 7172; ☻ Tues to Sun: 10am to 8pm; 💲free, €12 for the special exhibition; 🖥 www.wereldmuseum.nl) offers a glimpse of the world beyond the Netherlands.

The Wereldmuseum boasts an outstanding ethnographic collection of more than 2,000 artefacts from Asia, Oceania, America and Africa. On display are mummies, pottery, royal textiles, silver and gold. There is a particularly good exhibition about Buddhism around the world.

Every year, in addition to its permanent collection, the museum presents two high-quality themed exhibitions. These exhibitions, comprising masterpieces from museums and private collectors all over the world, are displayed across two floors.

Whilst entrance to the main collection is free, you have to pay to see the themed exhibitions.

The Natural History Museum (🏠 Westzeedijk 345; ☎ 010 436 4222; 🖥 www.nmr.nl; ☻ Tue-Sat: 10am to 5pm; 💲€6; ⌨M) is not terribly big. Stuffed specimens of the Netherlands' fauna permeate. The star attraction is probably the skeleton of the giant sperm whale suspended from the ceiling, which visitors are confronted with as soon as they walk into the atrium.

The open-air **Harbour Museum** (☎ 010 404 8072; 🖥 www.havenmuseum.nl; 💲free) shows a fine collection of ships throughout the ages, many of which are still in good condition, as well as machinery used in the operation of the port. It is very much a 'working' museum — it has its own engineering and wood working facilities to maintain and restore the ships.

The Tax and Customs Museum (🏠 Parklaan 14-16; 💲€5.50; ☻ Tue-Sun: 11am to 5pm; ⌨M; ☎ 088 151 4900; 🖥 www.bdmuseum.nl) might be tackling a subject that is anathema to most people, but it is actually a well-constructed and deeply-interesting museum of how the unpopular service of tax collection has evolved over the ages. Rotterdam has a special place in the history of tax collection. Its status as a major hub of import and export — and as a centre for smuggling — attracted the keen attention of tax collectors. There are countless thousands of artefacts on display, including uniforms, medals, paintings and smuggling paraphernalia. If you're taking the kids, the highlight for the museum will doubtless be the multimedia smuggling exhibition.

Rotterdam's Photo Museum (🏠 Wilhelminakade 332; ☎ 010 203 0405; 🖥 www.nederlandsfotomuseum.nl; 💲€7) offers diverse collections of the work of both amateur and professional photographers, which rotate every few months or so. The museum also has a more permanent exhibition about the history of photography in the Netherlands.

South Holland

Excursions

Whilst a stroll along the harbour front in Rotterdam can be thoroughly pleasant, a somewhat different way of experiencing the iconic area is to take to the water. **Spido** (🏠 Willemsplein 85; ☎ 010 275 9988; 🖥 www.spido.nl; 💲 €10.50) offers daily tours of the harbour lasting 75 minutes (longer trips are possible in the summer).

If you want to see Rotterdam by canal, **De Croosboot** (🏠 Crooswijkestraat 126; ☎ 010 414 9751) offers rides to Delfshaven and Rottemeren, whilst **Waterbus** (🏠 Leuvehaven; ☎ 010 404 8072; 🖥 www.waterbus.nl) includes the Oude Haven and the city's inland waterways — and even goes as far as Dordrecht.

Gilde Rotterdam (🏠 Glashaven 42-50; ☎ 010 436 2844; 🖥 www.gilderotterdam.nl) is an organisation of volunteers that offers truly fascinating guided tours of the city. Most of the volunteers are history enthusiasts or pensioners looking to give something back to the community.

ArchiGuides (🏠 Schiekade 205; ☎ 010 465 2228; 🕙 Mon-Fri: 10am to 6pm; 🖥 www.rotterdam-archiguides.nl) offers regular tours, in both English and Dutch, around Rotterdam's fabulous wealth of architecture.

Guided **bicycle tours** are organised by the same people (🖥 www.rotterdambycycle.nl).

Markets

Rotterdam has 14 markets spread throughout the city. The main ones are: **Binnenrotte** (🕙 Tue, Fri-Sun: 8.30am to 5.30pm, Sun only in summer), **Afrikaanderplein** (🕙 Wed & Sat: 8.30am to 5.30pm) and **Grote Visserijplein** (🕙 Thu & Sat: 8.30am to 5.30pm).

What to do

Skydiving: The Flying Dutchman (🏠 Zaventembaan 5; ☎ 010 415 9450; 🖥 www.skydiverotterdam.com)

Cinema: Pathé (🏠 Schouwburgplein 101; ☎ 0900 1458; 🖥 www.pathe.nl); Cinerama (🏠 Westblaak 18; ☎ 010 411 5300; 🖥 www.cinerama.nl); Lantaren Venster (🏠 Otto Reuchlinweg 996; ☎ 010 277 2277; 🖥 www.lantarenvenster.nl)

Casino: Holland Casino (🏠 Weena 624; ☎ 010 206 8206; 🕙 12noon to 3am)

Where to eat and drink

Koekala (🏠 Nieuwe Binnenweg 79a; ☎ 010 436 47 74; 🖥 www.koekela.nl) is a friendly café with excellent tarts and cakes, such as brownies, cheesecakes and scones. Eat them there or take them away. Good quality at a good price.

Sangam (🏠 Vierambachtstraat 9B; ☎ 010 476 2955; 🖥 www.sangam-tandoori.nl) offers decent Indian food. Not the place you'd come for the décor, but you'll eat well there. Take-away is available.

't Ouwe Bruggetje (🏠 Voorhaven 6a; ☎ 010 477 3499; 🖥 www.historisch-delfshaven.nl) is a little gem of a restaurant and wine bar that is really worth discovering. Definitely the place to come if you like good wine. The restaurant has a dedicated wine steward — or *sommelier* — who will guide you through the selection of wines, and make some recommendations based on your palette or what food you are ordering. Great as a restaurant, but you're quite welcome to just come for a drink. The place has a lovely little terrace overlooking the old canal around Delfshaven. The restaurant gets quite busy, particularly at weekends, so it is worth booking ahead. They also sell imported wine by the bottle, at a much lower price than you'll find in the restaurant.

Little V (🏠 Grotekerkplein 109; ☎ 010 413 1191; 🖥 www.littlev. nl) is a charming little Vietnamese restaurant in the centre of town. Intimate setting, decent food. It is cousin to the restaurant in The Hague of the same name (p180).

Parkheuvel (🏠 Heuvellaan 21; ☎ 010 436 0530/766; 🖥 www. parkheuvel.nl) used to be a three-Michelin-star restaurant, between 2002-2006. It has since lost one of those stars, although the food is still of top quality and the setting provides an elegant dining experience. Menu is French-inspired, offering such temptations as organic goose liver and pan-fried lobster.

Euromast (🏠 Parkhaven 20; ☎ 010 241 1788; 🖥 www.euromast. nl) — for the experience of eating nearly 100 metres in the air. The place is smart, elegant and of course offers fantastic views across the city. Come for the views, though, and modify your expectations about the food. It's okay but nothing to write home about. Prices are perhaps a little on the high side but not outrageously so — €20 to 25 for a main.

Kip (🏠 Van Vollenhovenstraat 25; ☎ 010 436 9923; 🖥 www. kip-rotterdam.nl) offers very good food served in a pleasant atmosphere, with exceedingly friendly service. The restaurant serves a three-course 'surprise' menu, which changes regularly according to what is in season. Style of cooking is French-Mediterranean

De Pelgrim (🏠 Aelbrechtskolk 12; ☎ 010 477 1189; 🖥 www. pelgrimbier.nl), Rotterdam's only brewery, offers meat and fish dishes to mop up those *dubbel* and *tripel* beers. A nice touch is the recommendation of what beer goes with what dish. You probably want to stick to the robust meat dishes if you're going to be quaffing copious amounts of ale. Especially the ale that this place brews.

Where to sleep

Hilton (🏠 Weena 10; ☎ 010 710 8000; 🖥 rotterdam.hilton.com) doesn't look like much from the outside — an architecturally uninspiring grey concrete block plonked unceremoniously in downtown Rotterdam — but the inside tells a different story. Spacious, comfortable rooms, combined with friendly, attentive service. There's wireless Internet throughout the hotel and parking is available for €30 a day. The hotel has a business centre and small fitness area. Room rates vary widely throughout the year — the lowest for a single is about €100.

Hotel New York (🏠 Koninginnenhoofd 1; ☎ 010 439 0500; 🖥 www.hotelnewyork.nl) is located within the former head office of the America Holland Line, which was founded in the late 19th century in order to ferry passengers to New York. Consequently, the hotel is something of a nostalgic look back in time — high ceilings, old wrought-iron staircases, wide corridors. But renovated with a modern touch, to make it feel authentic rather than drab. The lowest room rate is about €100 per night, more if you want a room overlooking the water. Free wi-fi is available.

SS Rotterdam (🏠 3e Katendrechtsehoofd 25; ☎ 010 297 3090; 🖥 www.ssrotterdam.com) is a moored cruise ship that has been retired from service and now serves as one of the city's plusher accommodation options. The 254-room hotel is vast and easy to get lost in. Lovely location to stay in, too, on the water's edge, away from all the hustle-and-bustle of the city centre (but still close enough to pop out

South Holland

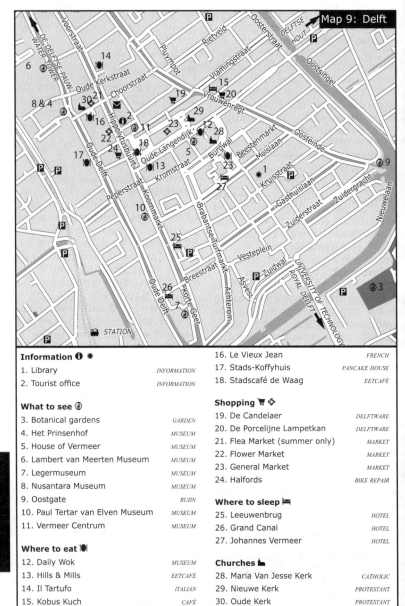

Map 9: Delft

South Holland

Information ❶ ◉	
1. Library	INFORMATION
2. Tourist office	INFORMATION

What to see ◉	
3. Botanical gardens	GARDEN
4. Het Prinsenhof	MUSEUM
5. House of Vermeer	MUSEUM
6. Lambert van Meerten Museum	MUSEUM
7. Legermuseum	MUSEUM
8. Nusantara Museum	MUSEUM
9. Oostgate	RUIIN
10. Paul Tertar van Elven Museum	MUSEUM
11. Vermeer Centrum	MUSEUM

Where to eat ◉	
12. Daily Wok	MUSEUM
13. Hills & Mills	EETCAFÉ
14. Il Tartufo	ITALIAN
15. Kobus Kuch	CAFÉ

16. Le Vieux Jean	FRENCH
17. Stads-Koffyhuis	PANCAKE HOUSE
18. Stadscafé de Waag	EETCAFÉ

Shopping 🛒 🛍	
19. De Candelaer	DELFTWARE
20. De Porcelijne Lampetkan	DELFTWARE
21. Flea Market (summer only)	MARKET
22. Flower Market	MARKET
23. General Market	MARKET
24. Halfords	BIKE REPAIR

Where to sleep 🛏	
25. Leeuwenbrug	HOTEL
26. Grand Canal	HOTEL
27. Johannes Vermeer	HOTEL

Churches ⛪	
28. Maria Van Jesse Kerk	CATHOLIC
29. Nieuwe Kerk	PROTESTANT
30. Oude Kerk	PROTESTANT

in the evening). Rooms are clean, spacious and comfortable. Prices are accordingly high, however.

Hotel Bazar (🏠 Witte de With-straat 16; ☎ 010 206 5151; 🖥 www.bazarrotterdam.com) is a friendly, atmospheric place in the centre of town. It's got an energy and buzz about it that will appeal to younger crowds — lots of shops, cafés, bars and restaurants nearby. Perhaps not the place to come if you are planning a quiet get-away, though. You can stay in an African, Middle Eastern or South American themed room. Décor is original, but slightly faded and worn out in places — could do with a touch-up.

Stay Okay Hostel (🏠 Overblaak 85-87; ☎ 010 436 5763; 🖥 www.stayokay.com) is a clean and safe option for those on a bit more of a budget. It's actually located in one of the bizarre cuboid houses designed in the 1980s by architect Piet Blom (p200) — so you too can feel what it's like to live in a cube. Rooms have a fairly regimented 'samey' kind of feel to them, but location is handy, staff are friendly and beds are comfy.

DELFT

A stone's throw from The Hague lies the somewhat smaller and certainly more laid-back city of Delft. The city, founded around 1074, takes its name from the medieval Dutch word for ditch (*delf*), which refers to the central canal – Oude Delft – around which the city was built.

Compared to its neighbours – Rotterdam and The Hague – Delft is a compact city that is easy to stroll around. Walks through much of the city are made all the more enjoyable by the fact that, for the most part, cars are banned from the city's centre.

In fact, many people who work in The Hague or Rotterdam like the tranquillity of Delft so much that they end up living here and commuting in each day.

Although Delft is by-and-large a charmingly relaxed place to visit, things can get slightly more hectic during the summer months, as droves of tourists descend upon the city.

These days, Delft is probably best known for two things: its distinctive blue-and-white pottery called delftware and the 17th century artist Johannes Vermeer (see box on p210), who became renowned for the way he used colour to depict light and shadow in his paintings.

Delft also has close links with the Dutch royal family, since this is where, in 1572, Prince William of Orange sought sanctuary from the Spanish, with whom he was at war. Ultimately, though, the Spanish caught up with him in 1584 and shot him within the city walls of Delft, just outside the present location of the Het Prinsenhof Museum.

Information

- **Tourist office:** 🏠 Hippoly-tusbuurt 4; ☎ 015 215 4051; 🕐 Sun-Mon: 10am to 4pm, Tue-Fri: 9am to 6pm: Sat 10am to 5pm, reduced hours in winter.

- **Bike rental**: Delftse Hout (🏠 Korftlaan 5; ☎ 015 213 0040; 🖥 www.delftsehout.nl; 💲 €9.50 per day.

Orientation

Delft is a small enough place to comfortably negotiate on foot. The picturesque canals in town are very pleasant to walk along. For a bit more greenery, head south out of the town centre, towards

LOOK FOR THE LOGO

If you want to be certain that the Delftware you are buying is the genuine article, look for the logo imprinted on the bottom. Whilst second-rate Delftware suppliers are able to use the name "Delft" within the confines of the law, these trademarks are protected by trademark law and so they shouldn't be using them.

KONINKLIJKE PORCELEYNE FLES
ANNO 1653
ROYAL DELFT

the campus and grounds of Delft's University of Technology.

Getting there and away

Delft is well-served by trains from The Hague and Rotterdam. A somewhat slower way to get to the city is to take the tram or bus. Take tram 1 from The Hague and bus 129 from Rotterdam. The journey from either destination takes around 30 minutes.

If you are coming by road, the A13 runs south from The Hague and north from Rotterdam. The A4 links Delft with Amsterdam.

Since much of Delft's historic centre is pedestrianised, car parking is limited. There are a few central carparks, costing €2.50 an hour. More car parking space is available on the outskirts of the city, at the lower rate of €2 an hour. Just follow the 'P-route' signs. Of course, if you live in the city you will be entitled to a parking permit.

Markets

The general market on Marktplein and the flower market along the canal by Hippolytutsbuurt take place every Thursday, from 9am to 5pm. Fruit, vegetable and flower markets at Brabantse Turfmarkt and Burgwal are held on Saturdays. During the summer months, you'll also find a Saturday flea market on the Heilige Geestkerkhof.

Delftware

As soon as you arrive in Delft, you are bound to notice the ubiquitous blue-and-white glazed pottery in the shop windows. This is what is known as Delftware.

Delftware, though, does not have to be blue-and-white. You will also see elaborate coloured designs on many plates and vases.

The reason that the blue-and-white design became so popular is because of the emergence of mass production of Delftware a few hundred years ago. Manufacturers quickly found that it was far cheaper to print a single colour on the pottery rather than try to include many different ones.

Interestingly, in the manufacture of true blue-and-white delftware, black (rather than blue) ink is used. The black ink contains copper and cobalt oxides, which, when heated to a very high temperature (in excess of 1000°C), undergo a chemical transformation that turns them blue.

Delftware has its origins in the 17th century, when Dutch explorers — through the Dutch East India Company — brought the style of pottery, and the techniques involved, back from China.

DELFT COMBO TICKET

If you are in a museum mood, you can by a single ticket that allows you into Lambert van Meerten Museum, Het Prinsenhof Museum and Nusantara Museum. This combo ticket, available at all these museums, costs €10 for adults and €6 for children. It is free for children younger than 12.

Somewhat ironically, much of the Delftware that you are likely to find in shops or in the market in Delft is now mass-produced in China. Although they may claim to be hand-painted, this usually means that a very small part of it has been painted by hand and the rest of the design is machine-printed. If the price of the Delftware seems too low to be true, it probably is.

To check if the Delftware is authentic, look for the logo on the bottom (see box). You should also get a certificate of authentication from the supplier.

In fact, there are only three factories that still produce hand-painted Delftware.

Only two of these — **De Delftse Pauw** (🏠 Delftweg 133; ☎ 015 212 4920; 🖥 www.delftsepauw. com) and **De Koninklijke Porceleyne Fles**, otherwise known as Royal Delft (🏠 Rotterdamseweg 196; ☎ 015 251 2030; 🖥 www. royaldelft.com) — produce Delftware according to traditional methods, by using black paint that, when fired, turns blue. De Delftse Pauw only sells its merchandise at its factory, whilst Royal Delft has a number of outlets throughout the city.

De Candelaer (🏠 Kerkstraat 13a; ☎ 015 213 1848; 🖥 www. candelaer.nl) is a somewhat smaller workshop in the centre of town and is therefore more convenient to visit. However, it won't really give you the best sense of authentic Delftware production techniques. It uses blue paint directly on the pottery's surface, since this is cheaper and means that the pottery only has to be fired once.

It is possible to visit all Delftware production sites. De Delftse Pauw and Royal Delft will give you a fascinating tour of the production techniques. However, whilst the tour at De Delftse Pauw is free, Royal Delft charges a somewhat excessive €6.50. De Candelaer is interesting to visit, too, and most days you'll be able to chat with the artists who are hand-painting the designs.

De Porcelijne Lampetkan (🏠 Vrouwenregt 5; ☎ 015 212 1086; 🖥 www.antiquesdelft.com) is a small shop that sells a range of both old and new delftware. Staff are friendly and knowledgeable, and the shop is a reliable place to come if you are in search of authentic products.

What to see

Johanes Vermeer's former family house is located on the corner of Jozefstraat and Oude Langendijk. Although you cannot visit the house, you can have a virtual 3D tour online at 🖥 kalden.home. xs4all.nl.

A distinctive **water tower** (🏠 Kalverbos 22; ☎ 015 213 6999; 🖥 www.dewatertoren.eu) lies at one end of the town. Designed by architect M.A.C. Hartman in 1895 in neo-renaissance style, it strongly resembles a turret of a medieval castle. It is possible to visit the water tower, but usually only by appointment. A shop on the ground floor — again open only by appointment — sells water from around the world.

South Holland

If you want to see one of the old gates of the city, you should track down the twin turrets of the **East Gate** (🏠 Oostpoort 1).

A short 15 minute walk from the centre of town, there is a rather nice **botanical garden** (🏠 Poortlandplein 6; 💻 www.tnw.tudelft.nl; 🕐 Mon-Fri: 8.30am to 5pm, Sat: 10am to 4pm, May-Sep: Sun: 12noon to 4pm). Here you can find a colourful array of tropical and sub-tropical plants, a herb garden and a collection of ornamental plants.

Not far from the station, you'll find a small **reptile zoo** (☎ 015 212 2184; 💻 www.serpo.nl).

Churches

In the centre of town is the distinctive **Oude Kerk** (🏠 Heilige Geestkerkhof 25; ☎ 015 212 3015; 💻 www.oudekerk-delft.nl; 🕐 Mon-Sat: 9am to 6pm, reduced hours during winter; 💰 €3.50), built around 1246. The massive bell tower, 75 metres in height, is actually leaning by about two metres from the vertical axis. Experts suggest that this may be because the church was built on a filled-in waterway. There are two bells in the tower. The largest, the Bourdon Bell, weighs nearly nine tonnes and is only rung on special occasions, for fear that the vibrations could damage the tower. Johannes Vermeer is presumed to be buried here,

JOHANNES VERMEER

For such a well-known artist, it is surprising that so little is known about the illustrious Johannes Vermeer. He was born in Delft in 1632, and lived his entire life there, dying in 1675. He fathered 11 children with his wife Catharina, and died penniless, leaving his family his not inconsiderable debts.

Vermeer might be well-known these days, but appears to have kept quite a low profile during his life. In fact, many of the pictures that he is now credited with painting were initially attributed to other artists.

Vermeer doesn't appear to have painted all that many pictures, which may explain why he was never very wealthy. So far, 35 have been attributed to him. The latest to be confirmed as authentic, *Young Woman Seated at the Virginals*, was presumed to be a forgery until 2004.

Vermeer is particularly well-known for his use of strong, vibrant colours and his mastery of light within his pictures.

The Vermeer Centrum (p211) gives you an insight into the life of this great Dutch artist.

However, if you are looking to see the works of Vermeer, then you should look elsewhere: tragically none remain in his home town.

Arguably his most famous work — *Girl With a Pearl Earring* — is kept by the Mauritshuis gallery in The Hague, and currently on display in the Gemeentemuseum (p151). *View of Delft*, which clearly shows the mastery of light in his paintings, is also kept here.

A few other Vermeers — including *The Milkmaid* — are located in Amsterdam's Rijksmuseum (p255).

Vermeer gained fresh prominence in 2003, when the film *Girl With a Pearl Earring* was released, based on a novel by Tracy Cevalier.

South Holland

although no one knows for certain — there is a plaque erected in his honour. Other famous people buried in the church include naval heroes Piet Heyn (1577 to 1629) and Maarten Tromp (1598 to 1653). It is worth visiting the church just for the pulpit, which dates from 1548 and is widely considered to be one of the most beautiful in the country.

The **Nieuwe Kerk** (🏠 Markt 80; ☎ 015 212 3025; 🖵 www. nieuwekerk-delft.nl; Mon-Sat: 9am to 6pm, reduced hours during winter; 💲€3.50) is new only in relation to the Oude Kerk, since there has been a church on this site since the 14th century. The new church is just as impressive as the old one, with its gargantuan tower looming large over the city. A statue of the famous jurist Hugo de Groot (p211) stands outside the church. William of Orange is buried here — look for the black-and-white marble sarcophagus. More than 40 other members of the House of Orange are buried in the vaults of the church (not open to the public). Climbing the tower of the Nieuwe Kerk, which gives you magnificent views over the town, is an extra €3.50.

Note: the €3.50 ticket price quoted above gives you access to both churches.

Not far from Nieuwe Kerk is **Maria van Jesse Kerk** (🏠 Burgwal 20). The front of the church is flanked by two towers. Both towers have tall spires, but the tops, just below the towers, are quite distinctive. One has an octagonal top story with dormers. The other has a four-sided top story with small turrets. The interior of the church has been richly restored and can be visited.

Museums

Vermeer Centrum (🏠 Voldersgracht 2; ☎ 015 213 8588; 🖵 www.vermeerdelft.nl; 🕙 10am to 5pm; 💲€7) offers a glimpse of the life and work of Johannes Vermeer, one of the most famous artists from the Dutch Golden Age (see box on p210). The centre is housed in the former guildhall of painters — Saint Lucas Guild — where Vermeer was dean for many years.

The **Nusantara museum** (🏠 Sint Agathaplein 4; ☎ 015 260 2358; 🕙 Tue-Sun: 11am to 5pm ;

HUGO GROTIUS

Another of Delft's famous former residents — though perhaps less well-known than Vermeer — is Hugo Grotius (also known as Hugo de Groot), born 1583.

Those outside of the Netherlands who have heard of Grotius have probably learnt his name in conjunction with the contribution that he made to the evolution of international justice.

His most enduring work *De iure belli ac pacis* ('On the law of war and peace'), written in Latin, was published in 1625 and set out the fundamental principles of international law.

Grotius lived at a time when the Netherlands was at war against Spain, and used his writing to urge restraint in conflict.

A power struggle within the Netherlands landed him in gaol in 1619, although he was able to escape two years later, by hiding in a book chest that was used to bring him books to read.

He fled to Paris. Since Grotius refused to ask for a pardon — since this would have implied guilt — he was never repatriated. He died in 1645.

South Holland

€3.50) takes you on a journey through the cultural and religious heritage of Indonesia. The museum consists of a fascinating collection of masks, carvings and other historical relics from the archipelago. The unique collection of musical instruments from the region are especially intriguing. The museum also presents the visitor with a glimpse of the relationship between the Netherlands and Indonesia — a relationship that began more than 400 years ago, when the Dutch set up a key trading post there.

The museum of **Lambert van Meerten** (Oude Delft 199; www.lambertvanmeerten-delft.nl; Tue-Sun: 11am to 5pm) was unfortunately closed, as we were going to press, due to structural problems with the house, and it was uncertain when it might reopen. The museum brings together a rich collection of artefacts that were once owned by the industrialist and art collector Lambert van Meerten, including pottery from the Far East.

The **Legermuseum** (Korte Geer 1; 015 215 0500; www.armymuseum.nl; €7.50) is housed in the former arms depot of the states of Holland and West Friesland, which was built in the 17th century, during the Eighty Year War against Spain (p65). This is one of the best military museums that you are likely to visit in the country. The museum combines a range of inventive and interactive exhibits, primarily targeted at kids, with the more traditional display cases of military paraphernalia typically associated with such a museum. When your researchers visited, the museum was mostly just in Dutch, but was slowly being converted over to English as well. The section on Roman military history is particularly interesting. At weekends and during Wednesday afternoons, the museum often has demonstrations featuring mock Roman soldiers, where you can learn about how they lived and behaved in battle. Films are shown throughout the museum, but mainly just in Dutch. A library attached to the museum contains the largest collection of military history books in the Netherlands.

The **Paul Tetar van Elven museum** (Koornmarkt 67; 015 212 4206; www.museumpaultetarvanelven.nl; €4) is an art gallery dedicated to a renowned teacher of art and copier of master paintings. Visiting his former house, you will see copies of many familiar paintings, as well as a few originals that he painted himself. Besides the work of van Elven, the museum also regularly runs temporary exhibitions that feature the work of other artists.

Het Prinsenhof (Sint Agathaplein 1; 015 260 2358; www.prinsenhof-delft.nl; Tue-Sun: 11am to 5pm; €7.50; M) tells the story of William of Orange, who was assassinated on the very spot where the museum now stands. You can still see evidence of his assassination — two bullet holes near the foot of the staircase where he fell. William of Orange, who lived in the house from 1572 until his death in 1584, led the Dutch revolt against the Spanish during the Eighty Year War (p65). He was assassinated by Balthasar Gérard, a devout Catholic who saw a threat to his religion.

Tours

If you are not too sure what to see in Delft, Combination Delft (015 213 6403; www.uitindelft.nl) runs a series of **historical and cultural tours** for exploring the city. See their website for details of latest programmes.

South Holland

Between April and October, Rondvaart Delft (☎ 015 212 6385; 💻 rondvaartdelft.nl) offers **canal tours** that depart from the Koornmarkt on the corner of Wijnhaven. Tours last 45 minutes and cost €6.75 for adults and €3 for kids between four and 12. Younger kids go free.

An alternative way of exploring Delft's picturesque waterways is to **rent a canoe** from Delflandhoeve (🏠 Schieweg 166; 💻 www.delflandhoeve.nl; ☎ 015 212 9003). Renting a canoe or kayak is €4 per hour or €15 for the whole day. They also rent bikes (€8 per day). They are located in beautiful countryside, not far from the university. You can also camp there.

Horse-drawn carriage tours (☎ 015 256 1828) depart regularly during the summer months from Markt.

What to do

- **Recreation centre**: Delftse Hout (🏠 Korftlaan 5; ☎ 015 213 0040; 💻 www.delftsehout.nl)

- **Squash Delft**: 🏠 Sportring 3; ☎ 015 214 6983; 💻 www.squash-delft.nl

- **Swimming and Squash Centre**: 🏠 Clara van Sparwoudestraat 2; ☎ 015 214 1874; 💻 www.sfd.nl

- **Tennis Delft**: 🏠 Laantje van Levenslust 2; ☎ 015 257 0416; 💻 www.tennisdelft.nl

Where to eat

Stadscafé de Waag (🏠 Markt 11; ☎ 015 213 0393; 💻 www.de-waag.nl) is housed in the former weighhouse of the city, and the scales that used to be used to weigh goods coming into the city are still there. The historical connection of the café is the main reason for going to the place. Atmosphere is nice and the view from the terrace, looking out on the town's looming clock tower, is worth coming for. Food is Dutch-themed, mainly fish- or meat-based. The place also tends to serve food a little later than some other places in the city.

Stads-Koffyhuis (🏠 Oude Delft 133; ☎ 015 212 4625; 💻 www.stads-koffyhuis.nl) offers some of the best pancakes you're likely to try in the Netherlands. There is a huge variety to choose from, featuring such exotic extravagances as beef and mushroom, and Brie and leek. The restaurant is in a lovely location, right on the Oude Delft canal, with a nice outside terrace. Considering the voluminous size of the dishes, prices (around €12 for a pancake) are not unreasonable.

Le Vieux Jean (🏠 Heilige Geestkerkhof 3; ☎ 015 213 0433; 💻 www.levieuxjean.nl) is a small and somewhat old-fashioned boutique restaurant in classical French style. The food is decent, though portions are slightly on the small side. There is also a very good selection of wine (mostly French).

Kobus Kuch (🏠 Beestenmarkt 1; ☎ 015 212 4280; 💻 www.kobuskuch.nl) has top-notch homemade apple pie. A beautiful setting, too, overlooking the old centre of Delft.

Daily Wok (🏠 Oude Langendijk 23d; 💻 www.dailywok.nl) is an Asian restaurant chain in the Netherlands, offering decent food for those on a budget.

Hills & Mills (🏠 Oude Langendijk 6; 💻 www.hillsmills.nl) is a family-run restaurant with bakery attached. Offers great organic lunches — the salads and soups are excellent.

South Holland

Il Tartufo (🏠 Minderbroer-straat 2; 💻 www.iltartufo.nl) is an Italian-owned restaurant, great for late lunches or early dinners.

Where to sleep

Delft can get very busy in the summer, during the height of the tourist season, so it really pays to book ahead. Moreover, Delft is a hive of Dutch industries, meaning that, throughout the year, it can be difficult to find a room during the weekdays, as they are taken over by Dutch businessmen and women.

If you're planning on staying in Delft for some time, you might like to check out the tips on finding accommodation in our Living & Working section (p31). You can also take a look at the listings on 💻 www.kamersdelft.nl.

Delftse Hout (🏠 Korftlaan 5; ☎ 015 213 0040; 💻 www.delftsehout.nl) is a lovely place to pitch your tent, if that is your choice of accommodation. The campsite is calm and friendly, with an outdoor heated swimming pool and an on-site farm for children. The campsite is located a short 15 minutes walk outside the city centre. Prices aren't cheap, though, and can be up to €28 per day in peak season for a camping spot. It is also possible to rent chalets, usually on a weekly basis.

Hotel de Emauspoort (🏠 Vrouwenregt 9-11; ☎ 015 219 0219; 💻 www.emauspoort.nl; 26 rooms) is a charming and friendly little place — set in peaceful surroundings along the banks of the canal, but still central enough to be convenient. Rooms are good-sized and clean, and staff are very helpful. If you're looking for something a little bit different, try staying in one of the gypsy caravans which are clustered around the inner courtyard — comfortable lodgings with a rustic feel. Prices for standard rooms range between €88 and €95 (for one person) and €99 and €100 (for two people). Gypsy caravans cost €85 for one person and €95 for two. The hotel has also designed a deluxe Vermeer Room, with authentic furniture from the period when he lived and a magnificent view over the lake. Prices for this room cost €150. All prices include breakfast, but exclude the tourist tax of €2 a night.

Hotel Grand Canal (🏠 Breestraat 1; ☎ 06 5103 1923; 💻 www.grandcanal.nl; 17 rooms) is also in picturesque surroundings, overlooking Oude Canal. It is fairly small and tends to be quite busy throughout the year — in summer catering to tourists and at other times to businessmen and women. The hotel's restaurant is perpetually busy. Single rooms are €60 and €70 per person.

Leeuwenbrug (🏠 Koornmarkt 16; ☎ 015 2147 741; 💻 www.leeuwenbrug.nl; 36 rooms) is located right in the centre of town. Service is friendly and the rooms are comfortable, but the interior is badly in need of refurbishment and the décor looks as though it is trapped in the 1970s. Still, prices are reasonable. Single rooms start at €69 and go up to €105, with doubles ranging between €99 and €115. All rooms come with a shower and TV. You can pay more to get a bath and a view of the canal.

Hotel Johannes Vermeer (🏠 Molslaan 18; ☎ 015 212 6466; 💻 www.hotelvermeer.nl) is centrally-located on a fairly quiet pedestrianised street. It's determination to get the most out of its namesake is slightly off-putting. Everything — even the furniture — reminds you of Vermeer. There are prints of his paintings hanging throughout the rooms of the hotel. This connection to the great painter, albeit only in name, doubtless explains the higher-than-average price tag for the rooms. Singles start at €112 and doubles at €125.

Jorplace (🏠 Voldersgracht 16–18; ☎ 015 887 5088; 🖵 jorplace. nl/delft) is the only hostel in Delft. With dorm beds starting at €19 (including breakfast), it is definitely suitable for those on a budget. Rooms are clean and comfortable, though pretty basic. Centrally located (just off Markt), the hostel is a handy place to stay whilst exploring the city. Free wi-fi is available, and long stays are possible at a discount.

Delflandhoeve (🏠 Schieweg 166; 🖵 www.delflandhoeve.nl; ☎ 015 212 9003) is a nice, friendly campsite open between April and September. Good value for money: camping costs €4.60 per person. They also rent bikes for €8 per day.

LEIDEN

Besides being the birthplace of Rembrandt, the city's other major claim to fame is having the oldest university in the country — an honour that was bequeathed upon it by William the Silent. Following the city's steadfast refusal to surrender when it was under siege from the Spanish in 1574, William the Silent granted Leiden permission to establish the University of Leiden, which remains a prominent centre for medical and legal study in Europe.

The town may not have the greatest museums in the country — it is, for example, disappointingly short of Rembrandt paintings, despite the great painter being born here (the bigger and more bullying Amsterdam seems to have taken the lion's share of these) — but there are other reasons you might want to give Leiden a brief moment of your attention.

Located on the Old Rhine, Leiden is a very picturesque city with many canals, bars, cafés and cultural activities. The city also has a lively studenty buzz about it.

The prevalence of students means there is a deluge of cheap restaurants, bars and entertainment during the night.

On Saturdays and Wednesday afternoons, there is a great open market along the canal between the Nieuwe Rijn and Vismarktstraat. The market sells delicious tapenades, cheese, vegetables, fruits, fish, flowers, and bread. There is also a clothes market.

Getting there and away

There are frequent trains between Leiden and The Hague, with the journey taking 15 minutes. If you are coming by car, the A4 and A44 encircle Leiden — although note that parking can be difficult in the city centre and, moreover, the city's one-way system can be rather confusing.

What to see

The **National Museum of Antiquities** (🏠 Rapenburg 28; ☎ 071 5163 163; 🖵 www.rmo.nl; 🕐 Tue-Sun: 10am to 5pm; 💰 €9; Ⓜ) contains some interesting ancient treasures from around the world — mostly from ancient Rome and ancient Egypt. There is a surprisingly large collection of mummies. One of the star attractions of the museum — the Temple of Taffeh — was actually given to the Netherlands in 1979, as a token of thanks after the country used its engineering skills to preserve some of Egypt's antiquities from flooding, when the Aswan Dam, in the south of the country, was constructed. There is also quite a bit about archaeology closer to home. Exhibits could be labelled better in English, though.

Stedelijk Museum de Lakenhal (🏠 Oude Singel 28-32; ☎ 071 516 5360; ☾ Tue-Fri: 10am to 5pm, Sat-Sun: 12noon to 5pm; 💲€7.50; ☐M) honours Leiden's contribution to art in the country, with displays of works by the likes of Lucas Van Leyden, Jan Steen, Van Goyen and of course the illustrious Rembrandt (although, of this latter, there are not as many of his works as one might have expected). The museum also includes a fascinating display about the history of the textile industry in the city — the building in which the museum is now housed used to be at the centre of this trade.

Just behind Leiden University, you'll find the city's **botanical gardens** (🏠 Rapenburg 73; ☾ summer: daily 10am to 6pm, winter: Tue-Sun 10am to 4pm; ☐ www.hortusleiden.nl; 💲€6) which were created in the late 16th century as part of the university's research programme. The gardens continue to be used for research by students, but they are also open to the public to stroll around in. A large variety of Asian plants are kept in tropical greenhouses so that they can withstand the harsh Dutch winter conditions.

Just next to the entrance to the gardens is the **University History Museum** (🏠 Rapenburg 73; ☾ Wed-Fri: 1 to 5pm), which briefly tells the story of the university.

Pieterskerk (🏠 Pieterskerk; ☎ 071 512 4319; ☐ www.pieterskerk.com) is no longer a church; these days it is used as a community centre. But it retains a special place within the city's history — this is the church where the Pilgrim Fathers used to worship before setting sail for America and the New World, in order to escape persecution back home. John Robinson, the pastor of the Pilgrim Fathers, is buried beneath the former church.

At the point where the two tributaries of the Rhine meet, you will find a medieval fortification from the 11th century known as the **Burcht** (🏠 Burgsteeg 14; ☎ 071 514 2389; ☐ www.deburchtleiden. nl; 💲free). The circular style of this kind of fortification, known as a 'shell keep', became popular because it was easier to construct and less liable to collapse. The grounds of the Burcht are now a public park.

If you want to visit a windmill whilst in town, **De Valk** (🏠 2e Binnenvestgracht 1; ☎ 071 516 5353; ☾ Tue-Sat: 10am to 5pm, Sun: 1 to 5pm; 💲€3; ☐ molendevalk. leiden.nl) houses a good museum about the history of the windmill in the country. A particularly neat feature of the museum is the intact miller's residence on the ground floor, showing how and where the miller used to live — the only such one in the Netherlands.

The **American Pilgrim Museum** (🏠 Beschuitsteeg 9; ☎ 071 5122 413; ☾ Wed-Sat: 1 to 5pm; ☐ www. leidenamericanpilgrimmuseum.org; €3) is a fairly small museum located in a beautifully-preserved house from the 14th century. It tells the story of the founders of New England in America — the pilgrims who briefly settled in Leiden during the early 1700s in order to escape persecution back home. Here you'll get an idea of how they lived during that time.

The **National Ethnography Museum** (🏠 Steenstraat 1; ☎ 071 516 880; ☐ www.rmv. nl; ☾ Tue-Sun: 10am to 5pm; 💲€7.50; ☐M) offers an eclectic collection of displays about cultures from all over the world. Some of the displays are temporary and change every few months, others are more permanent. The museum itself has an interesting history — it was founded in 1837 by the first king of the Netherlands, William I, who had a deep interest in propagating learning throughout his kingdom. This museum may therefore be one of the oldest ethnographic museums in the world.

The **Boerhaave Museum** (🏠 Lange St. Agnietenstraat 10; ☎ 071 521 4224; 🖥 www.museumboerhaave.nl; 🕐 Tue-Sat: 10am to 5pm, Sun: 12noon to 5pm; 💰 €7.50) takes you on a fascinating tour of the history of medicine and dentistry in the Netherlands, starting from the 16th century and moving rapidly forwards to the present day. The museum is named after Herman Boerhaave, a pioneering physician and surgeon who is widely regarded as one of the founders of clinic teaching.

Naturalis (🏠 Darwinweg 2; ☎ 071 568 7600; 🕐 10am to 5pm; 🖥 www.naturalis.nl; 💰 €11; Ⓜ) is the country's national museum of natural history. On display are an array of fossils and dinosaur bones, a large number of stuffed animals and countless numbers of mineral samples. Well laid-out and informative. The museum also regularly hosts temporary exhibitions, which are changed every few months. Check their website for details.

There are a number of picturesque **courtyards**, known as *hofjes* (p149), scattered around Leiden that you might like to visit. Popular *hofjes* include 🏠 Jeruzalemhof, 🏠 Groot Sionshof, 🏠 Sint Stevenshof, 🏠 Sint Anna Aalmoeshuis, and 🏠 Sint Annahof of Joostenpoort. A walking tour of the city's *hofjes* starts every Sunday at 2pm. It leaves from the Burcht and costs €2.25 per person.

Tours

If you want to see some of Leiden's waterways, Rederij Rembrandt (🏠 Blauwpoorthaven 5; ☎ 071 513 4938; 🖥 www.rederijrembrandt.nl) offers hour-long boat trips, for €10.

Alternatively, you could rent a rowing boat or kayak from Botenberhuur 't Galgewater (🏠 Galgewater 44a; ☎ 071 514 9790; 🖥 www.galgewater.nl), for around €6 per hour.

Entertainment

Leiden has a large selection of cinemas. See 🖥 bioscopenleiden.nl for more details.

Where to eat and drink

Being a student town, Leiden has a number of cheap eateries nestled alongside the posher places.

Bistro Bord'o (🏠 Apothekersdijk 2; ☎ 071 513 0131; 🖥 www.bistrobordo.nl) offers terrific bistro cuisine-style food with French influence, accompanied by an impressive selection of wines. One of the newer places in town showing definite promise. Not the cheapest, though, at €35 for three courses.

Oudt Leyden 't Pannekoenhuisje (🏠 Steenstraat 51; ☎ 071 513 3144; 🖥 www.oudtleyden.nl) offers impressively voluminous pancakes well-suited to both a student's appetite and budget. The place has a welcome Dutch feel to it, though the ubiquitous blue-and-white Delftware is perhaps a tad over-the-top.

Sushi Bento (🏠 Haarlemmerstraat 191; ☎ 071 566 1136; 🖥 www.sushi.eu) is not a particularly large restaurant — and can get quite noisy at peak times — but definitely the place to come for decent sushi.

Annie's (🏠 Hoogstraat 1a; ☎ 071 512 5737; 🖥 www.annies.nu) is in a top location, looking out over the Oude Rijn. The restaurant is actually under a bridge, giving it a slightly unusual feeling inside, with a platform bobbing up and down on the water, where you can eat if the weather allows it. Very popular among students, so can get quite rowdy, particularly on Fridays and Saturdays. Food is tasty, though not overly-exciting — Dutch themed, with occasional Asian influence. The soups are worth sampling.

Lebkov (🏠 Bargelaan 8; 🖥 www.lebkov.com) is good for a quick bite near the station. Salads are particularly recommended.

Portopino (🏠 Haven 40; ☎ 071 521 9505; 🖥 www.porto-pino.nl) is a nice little restaurant serving very good and authentic Italian food. There is a fixed menu for €35, which includes a large number of courses.

The Frisian bakery **Friese Brood en Banket Bakkerij Us Bertus** (🏠 Groenhazengracht 10) does excellent pastries and freshly-baked bread.

Where to sleep

De Beukenhof (🏠 Terweeweg 2-4; ☎ 071 517 3188; 🖥 www.debeukenhof.nl) is set in a very attractive old-style building, located in a quiet suburb of Leiden some distance from the city centre. A definite bed-and-breakfast feel to the place, making a refreshing change from the stuffiness of other fancy hotels in town. Not cheap, though — singles start at €125.

Van der Valk (🏠 Haagse Schouwweg 14; ☎ 071 573 1731; 🖥 www.hotelleiden.nl) is one of Leiden's more upmarket places, eminently suited for business travellers. Very friendly and attentive service, though some may find it a little overly-formal. The cheapest standard room for one person is around €83.50.

Stochemhoeve (🏠 Cronesteyn 3; ☎ 071 572 1141; 🖥 www.stochemhoeve.nl) is a picturesque camping site on the southern fringes of Leiden. Rates are reasonable — €11.30 for two people in a small tent. There are also some log cabins available for rent.

Nieuwe Minerva (🏠 Boommarkt 23; ☎ 071 512 6358; 🖥 www.nieuwminerva.nl) is housed in an 18th century canal house in the centre of Leiden — a convenient location for soaking up the city's vibrant atmosphere, although you need to be prepared to put up with sometimes high levels of noise from the street, especially during weekends. Rooms are fairly basic, though some enjoy terrific views over the canal. Some of the 'themed' rooms have intriguing décor. Singles from €75.

KEUKENHOF

About 15 kilometres north of Leiden is one of the most visited attractions of the Netherlands — the **Keukenhof gardens** (☎ 0252 465 555; 🖥 www.keukenhof.com; 💲€15). More than seven million tulips, daffodils and hyacinths across 32 hectares of land.

The garden is only open a few months each year — from late March until mid-May. It is best to come at the beginning of the season, when the flowers are in full bloom and you will be surrounded by an astonishingly variety of tulips of all sizes and colours.

The park is closed to the public for the rest of the year, although in October, a Flower Bulb Weekend is held, when you can buy your own bulbs to take home with you. Check the website for exact dates.

Allow at least half a day to wander around the park and its temporary exhibitions.

There is no direct train connection to the park, so the best way to get there is with your own vehicle. The nearest train station is at Hillegom, five kilometres to the north.

Whilst the Keukenhof might be the most famous place to see tulips in the Netherlands, you can also experience this most Dutch of flowers outside of the park. If you cycle around Lisse and the outskirts of Leiden during tulip season, you will encounter an explosion of colourful fields being cultivated. But don't arrive too late in the season — this scenery is not just to please the tourists, and the heads get lopped off early for sale in the shops.

NOORDWIJK

In nearby Noordwijk, there is a fascinating museum about space exploration: **Space Expo** (🏠 Keplerlaan 3; 🖥 www.spaceexpo.nl). The museum is housed in the visitor's centre of the European Space Agency's main technology development and test centre. You can admire models of actual spacecraft and engage in interactive learning activities. Noordwijk is also a popular Dutch summer destination, so during warm days you can combine a visit to the Space Expo with a trip to the beach.

KAAG LAKES

The Kaag Lakes — Kagerplassen — is a small and picturesque lake system located 6 km north of Leiden. The lakes are popular for boating, watersports, fishing, camping and walking. Rederij van Hulst (🏠 www.rederijvanhulst.nl) offers **boat trips** on the lakes. Boats depart from the harbour of Warmond every day at 2.30pm, returning around 4.30pm. The trip includes a 45-minute stop in a small village, where you can visit a local

cheese farm or have a drink in a café with a great view of the water. The family-run farm Van der Geest (🏠 www.boerengolfvandergeest.nl) rents out **kayaks** for €10 per hour. This is also where you come to play the typically Dutch game of **boerengolf** (p169). There is a sports centre in Warmond (🏠 Veerpolder 14; 🖥 www.dekkerwarmond.nl) where you can play both squash and tennis. The sports centre also rents out boats.

You can easily cycle to Warmond from Leiden. Alternatively, bus number 50 runs there from just outside Leiden train station. Note that Van der Geest is not accessible by public transport.

DORDRECHT

📷 | Photo 46

Ah — serene and amicable Dordrecht, seemingly a world apart from Rotterdam, just down river. This is a place to get away from everything for a bit, with low-key restaurants and little in the way of nightlife.

Three rivers encircle Dordrecht. The Maas (Meuse in French) sweeps in from France, whilst the Merwede and Noord (both branches of the Rhine) flow in from Germany.

The town's history has been shaped by its position on these important European rivers, not least in its involvement in the wine trade. Wine shipped from France to Germany would pass through Dordrecht (where it would be taxed). You can still see some of the old wine warehouses along the Wijnhaven and in other parts of the city.

The rivers have also influenced the city's history in somewhat less cheery ways. Until Dutch engineers won the battle against water in the country, floods were a recurring problem for Dordrecht. During the second world war, the city also attracted the attention of the Germans, as they parachuted in to secure the waterways.

Dordrecht was one of the first cities to rise up against the Hapsburgs. It was here, in 1572, that a secret meeting known as the Union of Dordrecht (*Unie van Dordrecht*) took place, in which William of Orange was recognised as the official leader of the revolt.

Dordrecht was not so heavily bombed during the war, and therefore many of the 17th and 18th century buildings, which were razed in Rotterdam, still remain in Dordrecht.

Dordrecht marks the start of the Biesbosch (p232) and is a good place to base yourself if you want to explore the national park.

Information

- **Tourist office:** 🏠 Spuiboulevard 99; ☎ 0900 463 6888; 🖥 www.vvvdordrecht.nl.

- **Internet access:** The tourist office has free wi-fi, the central library (🏠 Groenmarkt 153) charges one euro-cent a minute.

Getting there and away

There are two direct **trains** an hour from The Hague to Dordrecht, with the journey taking around two hours. The train station lies to the north of the city centre.

Hourly **buses** run from just outside Dordrecht's train station to Rotterdam and Utrecht.

By road, Dordrecht can be reached via the A16 from the north and the south, and the A15 from the east. The E19, running south to Belgium, passes nearby.

If you want to travel **by boat**, Fast Ferry, Waterbus (☎ 0800 023 2545; 🖥 www.waterbus.nl) operates services to and from Rotterdam.

What to do

If you want to cycling in the Biesbosch national reserve, you can rent a bike from the station or from one of the campsites.

You can also rent kayaks and canoes at one of the nearby campsites (p223).

What to see

Kyck op Den Dyck (🏠 Noordendijk 144; ☎ 078 631 0001; ⏰ Sat: 10am to 4pm; 🖥 www.molen-dordrecht.nl) is a popular mill to visit in town, with its own café and shop selling locally produced products, which is open on Saturdays. The mill was originally built in 1612 as a wooden corn mill, but subsequently replaced with a sturdier stone structure a century later. In 1932, electric turbines replaced the mill, which slowly fell into a state of disrepair. The mill was restored in 1997.

Dordrecht's Museum (🏠 Museumstraat 40; ☎ 078 770 8708; ⏰ 11am to 5pm; 💰 €10; 🖥 www.dordrechtsmuseum.nl) is a small local art gallery housed in beautifully-restored mid-19th century building. Most of the artists on display were either born in Dordrecht or lived much of their life here. Other established artists — such as Rembrandt — occasionally make guest appearances. The museum tries to rotate displays regularly. The museum is an interesting mix between classical paintings and more modern 20th century art.

The building that now houses the tourist office was once a bank, and you can still visit the old **bank vault** that lies beneath it (🏠 Spuiboulevard 99). It's free. Simply turn right once you walk in the door, and head downstairs. You can see the old bank safe, though it is doubtful that it still contains any money.

Grote Kerk (🏠 Lange Geldersekade 2; ☎ 078 614 4660; 🕐 Tue-Sat: 10.30am to 4.30pm, Sun: 10am to 4pm; 🖥 www.grotekerk-dordrecht.nl; 💰€1) is one of the most important gothic churches in the Netherlands. It is the only one built in true Brabantine style rather than one of the local variants. The distinctive tower, designed by Antoon Keldermans, was originally intended to be twice as tall, but these plans were scaled back after it emerged that the tower was starting to lean; it now visibly leans by more than 2.5 metres. The church dates back to the 11th century, the tower to the 15th century.

The **Augustine Kerk**, (Kuipershaven 139; 🖥 www.augustijnenkerk.nl) built around 1293, is currently owned by the Dutch Reformed Church. Just behind it is the Augustinian monastery **Het Hof**. It was here that the First Assembly of Free States gathered in 1572, to launch a rebellion against Spanish rule.

Dordrecht may not have suffered the devastation inflicted upon nearby Rotterdam during the second world war; nevertheless its strategic position at the intersection of three rivers meant it had a pivotal role in the fighting and was occupied early on by Germany. It is this historic tale that **Museum 1940-1945** (🏠 Nieuwe Haven 27-28; ☎ 078 613 0172; Tue-Wed & Fri-Sat: 10am to 5pm, Sun: 1 to 5pm; 💰€2; 🖥 www.museum19401945.nl) attempts to tell. The museum has a wealth of artefacts from the war, as well as some good audiovisual material charting the rise of Nazi occupation in the country.

The **Huis Van Gijn**(🏠 Nieuwe Haven 29-30; ☎ 078 639 8200; 🕐 Tue-Sun 11am to 5pm; 💰€7; 🖥 huisvangijn.nl) offers a glimpse of what life in Dordrecht was like more than one a century ago. Simon van Gijn was a prominent banker who lived between 1836 and 1922. His house dates from 1729. During his generous life-span, he collected a number of objects from around the world, including porcelain ceramics, prints, antique furniture and toys. Many of these are now on display at his former house.

There are **two city gates** still standing in Dordrecht. Groothoofdspoort, lying to the north of the city, dates from around 1618. Blauwpoort (otherwise known as Catherijnepoort) lies more to the west and is slightly newer, from around 1652. Both offer great views over the river Maas. Look out for a house next to the Blauwpoort, which is decorated with a number of sculpted figurines, including that of a beaver and a sheep, which give the house its name: *Beverschaep* House.

If you want to see Dordrecht by water, the local restaurant De Stroper organises regular **boat trips** (🏠 Wijnbrug 1; ☎ 078 613 0094; 🖥 www.destroper.com). An hour-long ride costs €6.50 for adults. There is a slight reduction for children.

Where to eat

Dordrecht's culinary arsenal is somewhat limited, but the following places can be recommended.

Yama Yama (🏠 Wijnstraat 70; ☎ 078 631 1338; 🖥 www.yama-yama.nl) offers good and fairly inexpensive Japanese cooking, with a dinner-time eat-as-much-as-you-want deal for €17.95 (lunch is slightly cheaper and weekends are more expensive). The food is tasty and service is unhurried. The waiters do not lean over you, expecting you to order your next dish; you can eat at your own pace.

Piccola Italia (🏠 Voorstraat 259; ☎ 078 614 4950; 🖥 www. piccola-italia.nl) is a great little restaurant with an authentic Italian atmosphere. Relaxing vibe, soothing music, good food — the pizzas are particularly delectable (€14.50 to 19.50). Unfortunately, the selection of wines is not so great.

Bellevue Groothoofd (🏠 Boomstraat 37; ☎ 078 633 25 00; 🖥 www.bellevuegroothoofd.nl) offers a fine-dining experience in a very pleasant location, overlooking the Oude Maas. The menu is fairly sparse — choose from a couple of fish, a couple of meat and a couple of veggie dishes — but the quality is there, as one might expect for the price (around €25 for a main). Dining is in pristine white surroundings. The hotel also has a slightly cheaper brasserie, although the views offered here are not quite as picturesque.

Miro (🏠 Voorstraat 256b; 🏠 078 620 0017; 🖥 www.tapasmiro.nl) is a nice place to come for some tapas and a beer. €4-5 per tapas portion, though the portions are fairly small. Centrally-located, it's a good resting point from all your sightseeing.

De Stroper (🏠 Wijnbrug 1; ☎ 078 613 0094; 🖥 www.destroper.com) is one of the better fish restaurants in town. Service is friendly — though perhaps overly-formal at times — and the food is well-balanced. An extensive selection of wine compliments the experience well. A main costs €21-24.

Where to sleep

Aan De Haven (🏠 Achterhakkers 71; ☎ 078 648 3332;

🖥 www.bedbreakfastdordrecht. com) is a beautifully-located B&B in the harbour, a five-minute walk from the centre and a little further to the central station. A double including breakfast is €65.

Het Tuin House (🏠 Dubbeldamseweg Zuid 362; ☎ 078 614 9924; 🖥 www. bedandbreakfasthettuinhuis.nl) is located in a quiet area, a 15-minute walk from the central train station. The charming rooms are in a cottage behind the house. Doubles are from €80 per night.

't Hofhuysje (🏠 Vriesepoortshof 23; ☎ 078 613 1283; 🖥 www. dordrechtbedandbreakfast.nl) is close to the town centre and in a restored building. Doubles from €63.

The **Bellevue Groothoofd Hotel** (🏠 Boomstraat 37; ☎ 078 633 2500) is one of the city's finest accommodation offerings. The hotel is located in a beautiful historic building, set in lovely surroundings overlooking the Oude Maas. The rooms are comfortable, although slightly on the small side. Many of them enjoy splendid views. Staff are friendly and the atmosphere is serene. Singles start at €125 a night.

Dordrecht Hotel (🏠 Achterhakkers 72; 🖥 www. hoteldordrecht.nl; ☎ 078 613 6011) is a friendly enough place, though has a slightly dated feel about it. Rooms and bathrooms are fairly basic, with many signs of poor maintenance. The central location is a plus, though. Single rooms start at €90 and doubles at €110. You can pay extra for a double room with a whirlpool.

Inner City Hotel (0Johan De Wittstraat 35-37; 1078 611 9933; 2www.innercityhotel.nl) is a slightly cheaper option, with singles starting at €79 and doubles at €89. Rooms are comfortable and clean, although fairly basic and not overly-large. Breakfast is un-inspiring, as you might expect for the price. Just up from the station, you won't have far to carry your luggage.

For nature lovers there are two quiet **campsites** that also of-fer kayak and canoe rental: Het Loze Vissertje (🏠 Loswalweg 3; 🖥 www.campinghetvissertje.nl) and De Kleine Rug (🏠 Loswalweg 1; 🖥 www.dekleinerug.nl).

They are very close to one another, just on the edge of the Biesbosch. Both are reachable by train — get off at Dordrecht Stadspolders and the campsites are a 10-minute walk away. Alternatively, you can take bus 3 from the central station in Dordrecht.

GOUDA

Gouda markets itself well as a destination for cheese-lovers — indeed, the region accounts for roughly 60% of all cheese pro-duced in the country — but there are a host of other reasons that you might think of visiting the town.

Situated on the banks of the Gou-we, Gouda's history can be traced back to the 11th century when the Van der Goude family built a castle on the river. At the time, the area was mostly marsh, and became an important source for peat-harvesting over the next two centuries.

In 1272, a canal was built in order to connect Gouda to the Old Rhine. Thus the town started to develop as an important regional trading centre along the Amsterdam / Rot-terdam shipping route. This promi-nence is reflected in the size of the town — the largest in Europe.

These days, Gouda is a pretty town. It has some lovely canals to stroll along, some beautiful build-ings and a very good art gallery. The central church is very impressive.

Information

- **Tourist office:** 🏠 Markt 27; ☎ 0900 4683 2888; 🖥 www.vvvgouda.nl

Events

The most celebrated event that takes place in Gouda's is the **cheese and crafts market**, held every Thursday in Markt during the sum-mer months (mid-June to the end of August). The market starts at around 10am and lasts until 2.30pm. Traditionally, hundreds of local farm-ers would bring their cheeses to the central square in order to be weighed and tested. They would be graded according to how much moisture they contained, what they smelt like and their taste. The price that the cheese was sold for would depend on the grade it received from the official testing committee.

These days, the cheese market is a slightly more showy affair, with locals in traditional dress hawking their cheeses and other wares to Gouda's seemingly endless stream of tourists. The cheese market is a fun thing to experience, but more a slice of Disney than an honest re-flection on what is a very important part of the town's history.

Gouda's **pre-Christmas festivi-ties**, held in mid-December, have become hugely popular with Dutch and foreigners alike. Here you'll find Christmas markets, music events and an ice-skating rink on the main square. Worth going to — if you don't mind the crowds.

In the summer months, open air concerts in the town Check 🖥 goudseconcerten.nl for the cur-rent programme.

What to see

Gouda isn't terribly big so you probably won't have to spend too long in the town before you encounter the **central market** square (Markt), which is the largest in the Netherlands. A market is held here twice a week — on Thursdays and Saturdays, between 8.30am and 5pm.

Here you'll find the 15th century **Stadhuis**, adorned with shutters in the painted red-and-white colours of the municipality. Look for a charming little clock that depicts the granting of the town's charter in 1272. Donated by a local business man, it chimes twice an hour at two minutes past.

Just next to the town hall, you will find the local **weigh house**, where cheese used to be weighed. The building, built in 1668, was designed by Dutch architect Pieter Prost.

The weigh house is now home to the local **cheese museum** (📍 Markt 35-36; ☎ 018 252 9996; 🖥 www.goudsewaag.nl), which features exhibitions on the development of the dairy industry, the history of Gouda cheese and the nutritional value of cheese. You can also find out all about the art of cheese-making.

Just east of Markt is **St Janskerk** (📍 Achter de Kerk 16; ☎ 018 251 4119; 🖥 www.sintjan.com), the longest church in the Netherlands, measuring 123 metres. The most impressive thing about the church is its stunning array of stain glass windows — 70 of them in all. Given the precarious history of the church, it is remarkable that so many have survived. The church was originally Catholic, but with the arrival of the Reformation became Calvinist in 1573. The stain-glassed windows were spared the destruction that was often meted out on Catholic relics — which is very fortunate for visitors to the building, who can glimpse something of the shift from Catholicism to Calvinism. The pre-Reformation windows (1555

to 1573) depict traditional biblical themes, whilst the post-Reformation windows are more allegorical.

The **Catharina Gasthuis Museum** (📍 Oosthaven 9; ☎ 0182 331 000; 🖥 www.museumgouda. nl) is housed in a lovely little building, with a charming ornamental gateway set over the small canal that runs behind St Janskerk. The building, which dates back to 1542, actually used to be a hospital — and part of it once held the town's leper colony. The museum offers a glimpse into Gouda's history. It has a selection of paintings, a collection of dolls and some antique toys. The gruesome 'torture room' feels oddly out of place.

Verzetsmuseum Zuid Holland (📍 Turfmarkt 30; ☎ 0182 520 385; 🖥 www.verzetsmuseum-zh.nl; Ⓜ) provides an interesting insight into the resistance movement of South Holland. Not to be confused with the Verzetsmuseum in Amsterdam.

An old **flour mill** (📍 Vest 67; ☎ 0182 522 041; 🖥 www. flourpower.nl) lies on the southern outskirts of the town centre — open to the public, and with a small shop selling flour and other products. The windmill dates back to 1727.

The **Harbour Museum** (🖥 www. museumhavengouda.nl) is described in the literature not so much as a 'museum' but as a harbour for historical vessels. There are berths for a total of 18 ships, though not all of them are always in use. Historic ships can be moored there for a fee. Visitors can wander along the harbour side, looking at the ships. However, since many of the ships are occupied, it is not possible to venture inside them.

Eating and drinking

Buiten Eten + Drinken (📍 Oosthaven 23a; ☎ 018 252 4884; 🖥 w w w . b u i t e n e t e n e n d r i n k e n .

nl) is a friendly place with intimate atmosphere. Food is French/Mediterranean-inspired. Setting is great, overlooking the canal, and food is decent. Prices not unreasonable.

Jean Marie (🏠 Oudebrugweg 4; ☎ 0182 516 262; 🖥 www.jean-marie.nl) is certainly one of the pricier options in town, but thankfully the food lives up to this. If you're going to treat yourself to a fancy restaurant meal whilst in Gouda, this is probably one of your better options — French-themed, great food, beautiful location.

Lange Groendal is a charming pedestrian street with independent shops and some cafés.

Try, for example, **Van den Berg** (🏠 Lange Groenendaal 32; 🖥 www.vd-berg.nl), traditional bakery with tea room attached — the place to come in town for sampling the delectable *stroopwafel*.

Or a grab a sandwich or a small treat at **Adriatika** (🏠 Lange Groenendaal 42; 🖥 Adriatika.nl). It serves food from those countries bordering the Adriatic sea.

Sleeping

Keizerskroon (🏠 Keizerstraat 11-13; ☎ 018 252 8096; 🖥 www.hotelkeizerskroon.nl) is a friendly little hotel located on a fairly quiet street not far from the centre of town. Clean rooms and reasonable prices, though some of the décor could perhaps do with a quick sprucing up. The typically steep staircase, made for Dutch legs, may prove awkward if you have lots of luggage. Free wi-fi is provided. The standard price for a single is €50 and for a double €85.

Utrechtsche Dom (🏠 Geuzenstraat 6; ☎ 0182 528 833; 🖥 www.hotelgouda.nl) is an affordable option with friendly service and a nice setting — taking breakfast on the small outside patio, when the sun is shining, is pleasant. Staff are attentive to needs. Rooms are comfortable, though some are quite small.

How to get there

Direct trains run between Den Haag Centraal and Dordrecht, taking between 20 and 25 minutes. There are no direct trains from Hollands Spoor — you will have to change at Centraal.

KINDERDIJK

🖥 | www.kinderdijk.com

There is a reason why thousands of tourists come here every year. Even in the land of the ubiquitous windmill, it is still not all that common to find 19 beautiful windmills all one after the other in such a picturesque setting.

You can walk or cycle between the them. Two of the windmills, as well as a pumping station, are open to the public. Visits are possible daily from April through to the end of October. Out of season, visits take place only at weekends (11am to 4pm for the windmills and 10.30am to 4pm for the pumping station).

Tickets to visit the windmills and pumping station are €6 for adults and €4 for children.

A nice way of seeing the windmills is by riverboat. A 30-minute cruise costs €4.50 for adults and €3 for children. Cruises are only available between April and October.

There is a small café where you can buy something to eat and drink plus some souvenirs and postcards. Because the windmills are so close together there is only a thin stretch of land on which people can walk. Therefore, whilst a picnic in the area might sound a nice idea, it's not really practical.

Many people arrive in the area by group tourist buses. If you're not part of a tourist group, it's best to have your own transport. There are no buses that go to Kinderdijk, but there is a boat that you can take from Rotterdam (🖥 www.rebus-info.nl).

North Holland

ZAANSE SCHANS

🏠	Schansend
📷	Photo 14
🖥	www.zaanseschans.nl
👍	The best place to come for windmills

Zaanse Schans is a picturesque reconstruction of a traditional 17th century Dutch village, located not far from Amsterdam along the banks of the river Zaan.

There are dozens of working **windmills** in the area, six of which are open to the public. You can also visit a **cheese factory** (featuring a demonstration on how to make cheese and a shop where you can sample the produce), a **bakery museum**, the site of the first **Albert Heijn** grocery store and a **clock museum**. From April to October, you can also enjoy a picturesque 45-minute **cruise** along the Zaan.

Zaanse Schans is a short 20-minute **train** journey from Amsterdam. Take the *stoptrein* in the direction of Alkmaar for four stops. Get off at Koog-Zaandijk and walk for about 15 minutes until you reach the village. You'll know you are walking in the right direction when you catch the pungent whiff of cocoa in the air, emanating from a nearby **chocolate factory**. On the way, you will also pass a **good cake shop** and a **windmill**.

If you want to get there by **bus**, number 391 operates twice-daily from Amsterdam Centraal train station, stopping at Sint Michael College just next to the Zaans Museum.

Coming from The Hague, it may be quicker to change at Amsterdam Sloterdijk.

ALKMAAR

🏠	Van Ostadelaan
📷	Photo 38
🖥	www.kaasmarkt.nl
👍	Best spot for finding out about traditional Dutch cheese markets

Records show that as far back as the 14th century farmers from all over the country would bring their cheese to Alkmaar to be officially weighed. They would receive a certificate indicating the weight and quality of the cheese, which could then be used in the region where they chose to sell their wares.

Today, the tradition lives on in the form of a **cheese market**, () held on the first Friday of April and then every subsequent Friday until the

	Adults	Group	Children	CJP/65+	Museum card	Student
Zaans Museum	€9	€7.50	€5	€7.50	Free	
Windmills	€3	€2.50	€1.50			
Bakery Museum	€1		€0.50	€0.50	Free	
Clock Museum	€8		€4 to 6		Free	€6
Albert Heijn Museum	Free	Free	Free	Free	Free	Free
Boat trip	€6		€3			

first one of September. The market takes place between 10am and 12.30pm, although it is best to arrive early since things can get quite busy. The location for the market is on the Waagplein, just next to the tourist office.

The event isn't what you might expect from a typical cheese market. In fact, you will not even be able to buy cheese there! But it is a remarkable spectacle of how things would have worked in years-gone-by.

You will be able to participate in the weighing of the cheese on traditional scales, and chat with the experts who carefully examine the quality, colour and texture of the cheese. Jolly cheese porters mill around, dressed in period costume.

The whole charade may be too touristy for some, but it is actually taken very seriously by the cheese producers. Right in front of your eyes, you will see cheese producers starting to negotiate with cheese buyers, and slapping each others' hands in traditional fashion when concluding an agreement.

Besides the cheese market, Alkmaar is a pretty Dutch town to stroll through. Much of the original medieval layout of streets has been preserved.

If you take a **train** from The Hague, you will have to change in Haarlem; the journey takes 1hr20.

EDAM

 | www.edam.com

👍 | Discover traditional cheese-making

There is no longer a real cheese market at Edam, but during the tourist season **markets** are organised to show the traditional way of trading cheese. Markets typically take place on Wednesday mornings (10am to 12.30pm) and Saturday evenings (9 to 11pm), but check exact timings with the local tourist office (💻 www.vvv-edam.nl).

The name 'Edam' has found worldwide fame through the successful marketing of the characteristic red-and-yellow ball of cheese that bears the town's name. But it wasn't cheese that brought prosperity to the town; it was **shipbuilding**. Edam once had more than 30 shipyards. Many of these have since closed down, but some still continue to this day.

There are no train connections to the town, but regular **buses** run to the city from just outside Centraal Station in Amsterdam: 310, 312, 314, 316, 317 and 318. The journey time is around 45 minutes.

VOLENDAM AND MARKEN

👍 | Traditional wooden houses on stilts

Volendam is a traditional Dutch **fishing village**, popular with tourists because of the distinctive traditional clothing that is still worn by some villagers (mainly on Sundays).

The village is also famous for the **Dutch wooden clog**, and there are some factories on the outskirts where you can see them being made.

The **harbour** is a lovely place to explore, full of shops and restaurants, although you may find them to be a little touristy. The back streets are more authentic, with some extremely pretty houses.

From May to June, **a weekday fish auction** is held in the harbour (volendamvisafslag.com). It costs €2.50 to enter (€1.50 for children).

From Volendam you can take a **ferry to Marken** (⌨ www.markenexpress.nl), a former island that nowadays is connected to the mainland with a causeway. The ferry ride takes around 30 minutes and costs €8 return.

Despite its close proximity to Amsterdam, Marken's status as an island means that it has retained some sense of its traditional heritage and culture although, sadly, this is slowly disappearing.

Distinctive features of the island are the old wooden houses that have been built on stilts, as a defence against regular incursions of the sea.

These days the island has become tragically touristy, although some insight into the old Dutch way of life is still possible. There is a museum on the island (⌨ www.markermuseum.nl) that offers a glimpse of what a traditional Marken home is like. There is also a factory where traditional wooden clogs are still made by hand.

Direct **buses** leave from CS IJsei in Amsterdam (a few minutes walk from Centraal Station) to both Volendam (bus 110 and 311) and Marken (bus 311). The journey takes around 40 minutes. Once in Volendam, you can take a **ferry** over to Marken, as described above.

TEXEL

See separate section on the islands (p243).

DEVENTER

📷 | Photos 37 and 42

👍 | Consider timing your visit to coincide with one of the town's many festivals

Deventer is a wonderful example of a medieval town. It is pleasant to visit in its own right, but it also host a number of hugely popular festivals (see box), so you could time your visit to coincide with one of those.

To this long list, one might also be tempted to add that the town is the most — or at the very least one of the most — enchanting places in the country.

The basic layout of the town has been unchanged for centuries — ever since an extension was tacked on in the 13th century — and this adds to the location's quiet serenity. Winding streets lead you past charming shops, bakeries and cafés. You really don't need a map to explore this place. Simply aimlessly wandering through the cobbled streets is enough to appreciate it.

As is often the case, such quiet serenity belies a troubled past.

In 882, Vikings from the north laid siege to the town, raping, pillaging and looting at will. Much of the village was burnt and destroyed. The Deventines, a hardy bunch, responded by working diligently to rebuild the town, and erected an **earthen wall to keep future Viking attacks out**. Part of this wall has since been excavated.

The town also became embroiled in the struggle for supremacy between the Calvinists and the Catholics. Evidence of this is given by **the Lebuïnskerk** (🏠 Klein Poot 7), in

---

FESTIVALS OF DEVENTER

Although Deventer is a great place to visit at any period of the year, consider timing your visit to coincide with one of the festivals held in the town.

The **Dickens Festival** (🖥 www.dickensfestijn.nl) takes place every year in December, in celebration of the works of 19th century British author Charles Dickens. Streets in the centre of town are transformed to resemble those of Victorian England, whilst participants don the attire of characters from Dickens' stories. The central street of the festival, Walstraat, can get incredibly busy.

Deventer Op Stelten (🖥 www.deventeropstelten.nl), which takes place during the first weekend of July, is an international street theatre event, where most actors and artists give their performances on stilts.

Deventer's book fair, the largest book market in Europe, takes place in August.

The town's **Comedy Festival** — *humorfestival* — takes place at the end of December each year, featuring stand-up acts, cabaret, theatre and musical performances.

---

the centre of town. Although now a church, it was in fact a Catholic cathedral between 1559 and 1579.

The church measures 100 metres in length (in the inside), making it one of the longest in the country, bested only by the one in Gouda (p223).

Deventer also lays claim to the **oldest stone house**

(🏠 Sandrasteeg 8; 💻 www. buveburcht.nl) in the Netherlands, which you can visit by making an appointment with the tourist office (🏠 Brink 56; ☎ 0900 353 5355; 💻 www.vvvdeventer.nl).

Whilst in Deventer, you might also like to visit the **Etty Hillesum Centre** (🏠 Roggestraat 3; ☎ 0570 641 003; 💻 www.ettyhillesumcentrum. nl), dedicated to a young Jewish woman who kept a diary during the second world war, in similar vein to Amsterdam's more famous Anne Frank (p254).

If you want to stop for afternoon tea, **Bussink** (🏠 Brink 84; 💻 www.deventerkoekwinkel.nl) is a great little place. It is often referred to simply as the Koekhuis and is particularly well-known for the famous *koek* honeycake (see box). The tea room has a delightfully homely feel to it.

Another good place to eat is **7e Hemel** (🏠 Grote Kerkehof 28; ☎ 057 064 4597). This quaint little *eetcafé* has some of the most reasonably-priced food in Deventer. Not only is it cheap and substantial, it's actually quite good too. Avoid the *pannenkoeken* (pancakes). which are not made here, and go for the typically Dutch *uitsmijter* (fried egg and ham).

If you're after some Indian cooking, then you could do worse than **The Famous Kohinoor of India** (🏠 Zandpoort 15; ☎ 0570 649 965 or 0570 642 261; 💻 www. kohinoorofindia.nl). The food isn't as fresh as it might be and some of the fried dishes, such as the onion bhajis, have clearly been microwaved. But the price isn't bad and the quantities are substantial. Taste is fairly authentic — closer to Delhi than Birmingham. On Thursdays, from 4pm, you can enjoy an eat as much-as-you-want buffet for €14.99.

DEVENTER HONEYCAKE

The Deventer *koek* is a type of spiced bread, made with honey, which makes the texture quite sticky. The cake is often sold in loaves, like common bread, or in boxes of smaller bite-sized squares. There are many different varieties of the cake sold in Deventer and it can be flavoured with all sorts of different spices. Some of the most common ones include ginger, cinnamon and orange. The *koek* has a history going back at least 500 years. The cake was originally developed as a way of preserving rations for sailors on their long journeys across the ocean.

Deventer is on the main east-west **train** line from The Hague. The journey takes a little over an hour and a half.

GIETHOORN

👍 | Some lovely waterways to explore

The charming and idyllic town of Giethoorn was founded around 1230 by a group of fugitives fleeing persecution in southern Europe. The original founders obviously didn't think too carefully about where they were choosing to settle, because Giethoorn was actually founded on a strip of marshy and infertile land.

These days, the town is a lovely place to explore. Cars are still banned from the old city centre, although there is now a bicycle path.

The town earned its nickname — the Venice of the Netherlands — from the network of canals that weave their way through the streets. These waterways were dug out over the centuries for the transportation of peat. Many areas where extensive mining of peat took place became lakes.

The picturesque thatched houses that you'll see in the town date back to the 18th century.

Water taxis leave from pretty much everywhere, costing around €6 for an hour-long trip. There are also countless places where you can rent motorboats, canoes and dinghies.

If you don't have your own transportation, it can unfortunately be quite a challenge to get to Giethoorn. First make your way to Zwolle; from The Hague you can take a **train** there, but you will need to change at Gouda or Utrecht (journey time just under two hours). **Bus** 71 will then take you to Zwartsluis, and bus 70 the rest of the way. Total journey time from Zwolle is about an hour and a half.

BOEKELO

    www.ontdekboekelo.nl

👍   Classic car show in November

Every November, car enthusiasts from all over the Netherlands — and indeed from other European countries — descend on the pretty Dutch town of Boekelo to show off their **classic automobiles**. You can also visit an **old-fashioned steam train**. More details about both of these attractions, including timings, are available on the town's website (above). Even if you're not interested in cars, Boekelo is a very picturesque town to visit.

Overijssel

North Brabant

DE BIESBOSCH

🖥 | www.biesbosch.org

👍 | One of the country's top national reserves

The Biesbosch is one of the Netherlands' largest natural reserves, a meandering expanse of wetland that is teaming with wildlife. Whilst it is partially in South Holland, most of the park lies across the provincial border, in North Brabant.

The park is one of the last remaining freshwater tidal areas in Europe, although the tidal influence was significantly reduced when the Haringvliet Dam was competed in 1970.

The origin of the Biesbosch as a wetland can be traced back to 1421, when a severe flood transformed the area into an inland sea. The topography changed almost overnight. The tides were no longer restrained by banks, and the agricultural farmland rapidly gave way to willow woods and grasslands, which exist to this day.

Cars are allowed in the Biesbosch, but by far the best way to experience the nature reserve is on bike. The only problem with this is that many of the paths are exceedingly poorly signposted; it appears that visitors to the park rather fancy these signs as take-home souvenirs.

Ferries offer passage across the park's many bodies of water. Most of these are little more than floating rafts. A few take cars, but many are just for people and bikes. If you are on foot or just have a bike, you should pay no more than a euro or two to cross. You'll have to pay more for a car. Simply hand the money to the ferryman when he asks.

Whilst in the park, you might want to visit the **Biesbosch Museum** (🏠 Hilweg 2; ☎ 0183 504 009), which provides some information about the history of the area and the animals that used to live here, before the Haringvliet Dam changed their natural habitat forever.

You can also explore much of the Biesbosch by **water**. Zijlmans Watersport (☎ 0162 682 385; 🖥 www.diepstraten-botenverhuur.nl) or Drima (☎ 0162 682 400; 🖥 www.drima.nl), both in Drimmelen on the edge of the reserve, have various types of boat for rental.

Horse-riding is a popular pastime in the reserve. Selevia Hoeve (🏠 Galeiweg 1, Werkendam; ☎ 0183 504 190; 🖥 www.selevia.nl) can arrange this. They also have a small campsite.

Many visitors to the Biesbosch use neighbouring Dordrecht (p219) as a base for exploring the area. Direct trains run from The Hague to Dordrecht, taking around 40 minutes.

'S HERTOGENBOSCH

🏠 | Torenstraat 16; 's Hertogenbosch

🖥 | www.sint-jan.nl

👍 | One of the most beautiful cathedrals in the country

Sint-Janskathedraal (Torenstraat 16) dates back to the 14th century and is widely considered to be the most beautiful such cathedral in the Netherlands.

The interior boasts 150 pillars and there are numerous fine features to see, such as the baptismal font, the grotesque statuettes inspired by the artwork of Hieronymous Bosch and the chapel of Zoete Lieve Vrouwe. You can also climb to the top of the cathedral's tower.

There is no direct **train** from The Hague to 's Hertogenbosch — you will need to change in Utrecht. The total journey, including change, will take around an hour and a half.

TILBURG

👍 | The home of Trappist beer in the Netherlands

The university city of Tilburg is worth a visit simply for the lively student buzz that pervades its streets. But there are also a couple of things in particular that might draw you to the place.

In July, Tilburg plays host to the **largest funfair** in the country. People from all over Europe flock to the 10-day event. The Monday during the funfair is called 'Roze Maandag' ('Pink Monday'), and is primarily gay-oriented although everyone is welcome.

You might also like to visit the Koningshoeven Abbey (🏠 Eindhovenseweg 3, Berkel-Enschot; ☎ 013 540 8508; 🖳 www.koningshoeven. nl), just on the outskirts of Tilburg, which is the only place in the Netherlands still to brew what is purported to be authentic **Trappist beer**.

Trappist beer was originally brewed by the monks of the Cistercian monastery of La Trappe in France, who were doing so at least from 1685. Monastery breweries swiftly spread to other regions of Europe. There are eight recognised Trappist breweries. Six are in Bel-

gium, one in Austria and the other in the Netherlands.

It is possible to have a tour of the brewery (☎ 013 535 8147; 🖳 www.latrappetrappist.com) — €10 for the basic tour and €17.50 with beer tasting afterwards.

It is also possible to stay at **the abbey's guest house** for €40 a day. However, this should be considered a retreat: silence must be observed during meals and after 9pm.

It takes just over an hour to get to Tilburg by **train** from The Hague. If you want to visit the abbey, **bus** 141 will whisk you up there from the centre of town.

EFTELING

🖳 | www.efteling.com

🏠 | Europalaan 1, Kaatsheuvel

👍 | A magical fairytale land

Efteling, located in the picturesque Dutch village of Kaatsheuvel, is one of the largest and most-visited theme parks in the Netherlands.

It was designed by children's illustrator Anton Pieck as a way of bringing fairytales to life, introducing life-size models of characters into an atmospheric wood.

Since first opening in 1952, the park has expanded beyond simply being a home for ingeniously-designed models to a fully-fledged theme park, with all sorts of inventive rides.

Efteling spans 160 acres in total. It's a good choice for a family day out, with elements of the park appealing to both young and old. It is possible to arrange to stay overnight in the park, too.

The basic entrance fee, for both adults and children over four, is €32.

It's easiest to get to the park if you have a **car**, but you can also take **bus** 137 from Tilburg (journey time 20 minutes).

HILVARENBEEK

 www.safaripark.nl

'Big Five' safari park

Just outside Tilburg, you'll find the largest safari wildlife park in the country (🏠 Beekse Bergen 1). Visitors can explore the park in their own car, without any barriers between animals and vehicles. There is also a boat that visitors can take through the park, and it is possible to walk through some parts.

If you don't have your own car, you can take the safari park's bus instead. Bergen is a huge safari park with a great variety of wildlife — it can easily absorb the entire day.

It is also the only safari park in the Benelux countries where you can see the big five game animals of lion, elephant, buffalo, leopard and rhinoceros.

Basic ticket price is €21.50 per person, cheaper in winter.

Best to visit if you have your own **car** (just off the E312/A58), but also reachable by public transport. Take a **train** from The Hague to Tilburg, and then bus 143 to the park.

North Brabant

The Netherlands

37: Deventer's 'Festival on Stilts' (p229) — VP

38: Alkmaar's cheese market (p226) — VP

*Photos: Violetta Polese (VP), Blake Evans-Pritchard (BEP),
Giorgio Benassi (GB), Laurent Virassamy (LV), David Wilkinson (DW)*

39: The crest of Nijmegen in flower form (p236) — VP

40: The windmills of Zaanse Schans — BEP

41: Hiking along mudflats in the Wadden Sea (p257) — VP

42: Artwork from the Dickins festival in Deventer (p229) — BEP

43: Chlling on a boat along the canals of Leiden (p215) — VP

44: The old canal houses of Amsterdam (p251) — VP

45: Scales used to weigh suspected witches, Oudewater (p265) — VP

46: Aerial view of Dordrecht (p219) — GB

47: Boating on the canals of Utrecht (265) — VP

48: Erasmusbrug in Rotterdam (p196) — GB

49: Fun on Texel beaches (p243) -VP

50: The Keukenhof garden, famous for the tulips (p218) — VP

51: Typical Dutch houseboat — VP

52: The delights of Maastricht (p266) — VP

53: Kinderdijk (p225) — VP

54: Above: Heineken brewery (p255) — VP

55: Left: De Poepende Man, Lelystad (p261) — LW

56: Traditional clogs (p76) — VP

57: Hoefje (p144) — VP

58: Carnaval in Rotterdam (p196) — BEP

59: Kitted out in orange, Dutch football fans support their national team in the 2010 World Cup — VP

60: Catamaran sailing in Texel (p247) — VP

61: Veere, picturesque village in Zeeland (p270) — VP

62: The mysterious megalithic tombs of Drenthe (p238) — BEP

63: The monkeys of Apenheul (p235) — VP

64: The grounds of the fabulous Loo Palace (p235) — GB

65: View of the old Maastricht — VP

66: Queen's Day (soon to become King's Day) in Utrecht (p264) — VP

67: Modern architecture of Rotterdam (p196) — VP

68: Kibbeling — VP

69: Kroketten — VP

70: How to eat a herring — VP

71: Pannekoek — VP

72: *'Uit de muur eten'* vending machines — VP

73: Oliebollen vendor and (in-set) *stroopwafels* — VP

74: Bitterballen — VP

Gelderland

APELDOORN

🖥 | www.paleishetloo.nl

👍 | Good on a rainy day if you don't mind skipping the garden

One of the main reasons for visiting the overly-bustling municipality of Apeldoorn is to pay a trip to the fabulous palace (🏠 Koninkijk Park 1) located there.

Het Loo Paleis ('The Woods Palace') was built between 1684 and 1686 in classic Dutch baroque style. Initially built for William III and his wife Mary II of England, it served as a residence of the House of Orange until 1962. Following the death of Queen Wilhelmina, the palace passed to the Dutch state.

The palace is vast and countless hours can be whiled away navigating the endless corridors and hallways. The most impressive part of the palace is the **expansive garden**. There's also a nice collection of **classic cars** in the stables.

Worth a visit, even on a rainy day, the standard entrance fee for the museum is €10, although it is free with a museum card. Parking is an additional €3.

Apeldoorn is on the main east-west **railway** line from The Hague (1hr30). The palace lies north of the centre, a 45-minute trek from the central station. **Bus** 102 goes there from outside the station (20 minutes).

APENHEUL PRIMATE PARK

🖥 | www.apenheul.com

🏠 | J.C. Wilslaan 21

👍 | A walking safari through the world of the monkey

This is not your typical monkey enclosure. The moment that you walk into the park, you will find yourself surrounded by literally hundreds of monkeys, most of which seem hell-bent on stealing anything that you have on your person and have not previously squirrelled away. You will be provided with a monkey-secure bag upon entrance to the park for just this reason.

It is indeed a thrilling experience to walk freely among the monkeys, chirruping and squabbling around you, and to feel that you are not in a zoo but on a real safari.

The idea for such a woodland park was conceived by nature photographer Wim Mager in the 1960s. At that time, it was legal to own monkeys as private pets in the Netherlands.

The park officially opened in 1971, containing only a few species — it now has more than 30, as well as a selection of birds.

The spider monkeys are particularly fun and will not hesitate in trying to scramble up your clothes, particularly if you are wearing colourful garments.

Since its inception, the park has grown from half an acre to 12 acres, though further expansion will be difficult.

Definitely an experience not to be missed, even if the prices are a little on the high side (€19.50 for adults, €17.50 for children).

Apenheul Primate Park is just outside Apeldoorn (direct **trains** run to the town from The Hague). It takes just under an hour to walk there from the train station, or you can take **bus** 2, which runs every

20 minutes and takes 16 minutes to get there.

NIJMEGEN

| 🖵 | Photo 39 |
| 👍 | The oldest city in the Netherlands |

Nijmegen is a city steeped in history. It is considered to be the oldest city in the country and was founded more than 2000 years ago by the Romans. It's name comes from the Latin name Noviomagus, meaning 'new market'.

Unfortunately, Nijmegen was heavily bombed during the second world war, which destroyed many of the ancient buildings. Many of those that survived the intense bombing suffered during the large-scale post-war urban redevelopment in the town.

Despite such upheaval, Nijmegen is still a very pleasant place to visit, particularly around the harbour.

The Valkhof Museum (🏠 Kelfkensbos 59; 🖵 www.museumhetvalkhof.nl; ☐M) has a permanent display about the history of Nijmegen.

The Waalbrug is an arch bridge over the Waal River in Nijmegen. In 2001 it was designated a national monument. When Queen Wilhelmina opened it in 1936, the bridge's arch was the largest in Europe, being 244 metres in length and 65 metres high.

The **Belvedere restaurant** (🏠 Kelfkensbos 60; 🖵 www.restaurantbelvedere.nl).is worth visiting for its lovely 15th century architecture. From the observation turret, you can enjoy a great view of the Nijmegen Waal Road Bridge.

The Netherlands' largest bicycle museum — Velorama (🖵 www.velorama.nl) — is also to be found here.

Apart from its history, Nijmegen has two big events that really draws people to the city.

In the last weekend of August, a magnificent **medieval festival** takes place in the city (🖵 www.gebroedersvanlimburgfestival.nl), with a big parade, arts and crafts markets and theatre shows.

The other big event is **The International Four Day March** (🖵 www.4daagse.nl), which begins on the third Tuesday of July. During the march, participants can choose whether to walk 30, 40 or 50 km a day, depending on their age and general level of fitness. The march takes participants through wonderful Dutch countryside and pretty little towns. Each day of the event is named after the town that it passes through. Due to the event's popularity, you should register well in advance, which you can do so on the website.

Bakkers Café (🏠 Castellastraat 29; 🖵 www.bakkerscafé.nl) is a nice place to come for lunch. They bake their own bread, and also serve a great range of coffees, teas and fresh juices. The lunchroom also has a social purpose, providing work for people with disabilities.

For a fine-dining experience, try **De Nieuwe Winkel** (🏠 Hertogstraat 71; 🖵 www.denieuwewinkel.com) — dinner only.

There is no direct **train** from The Hague to Nijmegen; you must change at Utrecht. Total journey time is around 1hr50.

ZUTPHEN

| 👍 | Lovely cycle-ride from Deventer |

Twenty kilometres upriver from Deventer (p229) is the somewhat smaller, though eminently charming, town of Zutphen. On a fine day, the canal path between the two makes for a wonderful cycle ride. A little outside Zutphen is **Fort Bronsbergen** (☎ 0575 538 438; 🖳 www.bronsbergen.nl), which offers a great place to dine overlooking the lake and has chalet-style accommodation.

There is also a **health spa and sushi restaurant** nearby (🖳 www.ryokan.nl).

If you're coming to Zutphen from The Hague, the easiest way to reach the town is to take a **train** to Apeldoorn and change there. Alternatively, regular trains run from Deventer.

The eastern province of Drenthe is a woefully under-appreciated region of the Netherlands — not only by the Dutch but by those who come to visit.

Those from the more prosperous west of the country tend to regard the region as a quaint but sadly impoverished agricultural backwater.

Foreigners often skip over a visit to Drenthe in favour of the better-known regions of the Netherlands.

This is a real shame, since Drenthe is a very pleasant part of the country in which to travel around.

It is the most sparsely-populated province of the whole country. Agriculture has been of vital importance to the region for centuries, and this continues today.

Drenthe has its own regional dialect, which is quite distinct from the Dutch spoken in other parts of the country. Even if you speak good Dutch, you may not be able to understand the dialect.

Drenthe is also a place of huge archaeological interest. It is here that you will find the greatest abundance of ancient megalithic tombs (*hunebedden*) in the country. It also hosts the biggest zoo of the Country.

MEGALITHIC TOMBS

📷 | Photo 62

👍 | Most of the tombs can be visited and at any time — but best if you have your own transport

The ancient people who lived in the region over 5,000 years ago made these giant tombs, known as *hunebedden*, by rolling together giant boulders beneath which they could bury their dead.

> ### SKIK
>
> The Dutch band Skik comes from Drenthe. One of their biggest hits, *Op Fietse* ('On Bike'), describes a bicycle ride through the southeast part of Drenthe, where lead singer Daniel Lohues was born. The VVV tourism board of Drenthe used the song for promoting a bicycle route, known as the Skik-route, through the province.

Only two *hunebedden* in the Netherlands survive outside the region of Drenthe — one in Friesland and the other in Groningen.

There is a map of *hunebedden* in the region on p240, along with a short explanation of why they are important.

The **Hunebed Centre** (🏠 Bronnegerstraat 12; ☎ 0599 236 374; 🖥 www.hunebedcentrum.eu) is found in Borger. Staff are extremely helpful, friendly and knowledgeable. The largest *hunebed* in the whole of the Netherlands — The Great Hunebed — is just next to the museum, so if you don't have the time or means to visit too many *hunebedden*, you should at least check this one out. You can get to the centre even if you don't have your own transportation. Take a **train** from The Hague to Assen and then **bus** number 24 to the centre of Borger. The Hunebed Centrum is a pretty 15-minute walk away.

EMMEN

 | One of the best zoos in the country, complete with reconstructed African savannah

One of the Netherlands' **best-known zoos** (⌨ www.dierenparkemmen.nl) is located only a 10-minute walk away from Emmen station. The zoo is particularly noted for its reconstruction of an authentic African savannah, which you can experience from the safety of a viewing verandah. The park is divided in to two parts and is fairly well spread-out. Seeing it all may be a challenge for less able-bodied people, since there is no transportation that connects the different areas. The zoo has a big indoor playground area for children.

There are no direct trains from The Hague to Emmen: you will have to change at Emmen. The total train journey takes just under three hours.

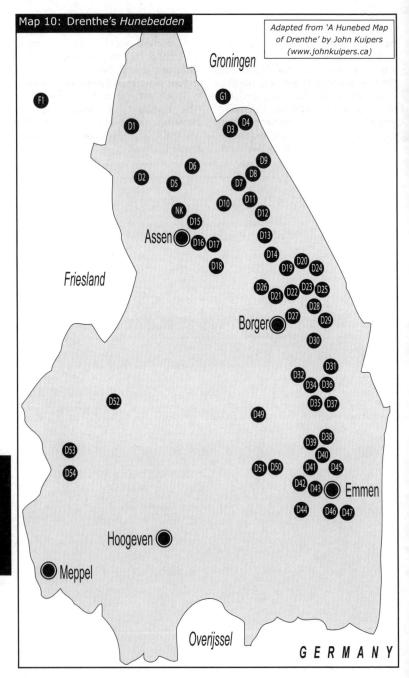

Map 10: Drenthe's *Hunebedden*

Adapted from 'A Hunebed Map of Drenthe' by John Kuipers (www.johnkuipers.ca)

Groningen

Friesland

Assen

Borger

Emmen

Hoogeven

Meppel

Overijssel

GERMANY

Drenthe

F1 Rijs sits in the bush of an oak and birch forest. It originally had four large capstones, with an entrance on the long southern side, but the stones were all carried off for road-building after its discovery in 1849.

G1 Noordlaren is at the edge of a bush overlooking some fields. Simple but impressive for the size of its large capstones.

NK Norg Kerk is not officially recognized or listed as a *hunebed*. Information is scarce about this grave. Two capstones and several supporting stones protrude from the ground. It may be that an old church was built on the site.

D1 Steenbergen is perched halfway up a dune overlooking a large sandy hollow. Fairly large and complete, with distinctive portal.

D2 Westervelde is a small *hunebed* with a portal close to the ancient bush of Norgerholt, Overlooks fields on the east side of the village of Westervelde.

D3 and D4 Midlaren nestle beside a picturesque ruined farmhouse on the edge of the village of Midlaren. They are in a rather rough state, but recent restorations have led to discoveries of Funnelbeaker pottery on the terrain.

D5 Zeijen is a small *hunebed* that sits in a hollow. The remains of the barrow that once covered it are visible all around — the result of half-finished excavations in the 19th century.

D6 Tynaarlo is one of the best-preserved *hunebedden* in the country. Elegant and compact, it was a favourite of 19th century painters. Excavations here turned up a treasure trove of flint axes, arrowheads, potsherds and beadwork.

D7 Anloo sits on a rise at the edge of the bush. There are numerous burial mounds in the vicinity, as well as remains of settlements. It is along an ancient system of trackways.

D8 Schipborg is a fairly large *hunebed* in heavy bush. There are numerous burial mounds in the vicinity, as well as remains of settlements.

D9 Noordlo is incomplete, with marker stones filling in for the many missing boulders. It has its own bus stop, so is easy to get to.

D10 Gasteren sits on the edge of a vast dune area. Treasure hunters in the 19th century left the monument largely ruined, but its location amid pine forest, dunes and heath give it a certain ambience.

D11 Anloo is well-hidden deep in the woods just south of the village of Anloo, this medium-sized *hunebed* has remained largely undisturbed since first investigated. One capstone and one portal stone are missing.

D12 is small but rather picturesque in its bucolic setting. Tucked away in a small clump of trees in the middle of expansive fields around the little village of Eext.

D13 Eext is nicknamed the Voice Mount ('*Stemberg*' in Dutch) because of sounds that were reputedly heard by a hunter when he knocked on the burial mound that houses it in 1730. When it was subsequently excavated it revealed a unique form, with four stone steps leading down into the chamber. It remains in its original mound surrounded by trees.

D14 Eexterhalte is a large and impressive *hunebed* lying in a grove of trees. It bears the scars of the frequent destruction of *hunebedden* for church, road and dyke construction. Bore holes are still visible, where attempts where made to split apart some of the great boulders. Folk legend describes a stone-tossing match between the giants of Gieten and Rolde; each couldn't throw quite far enough to reach the other village, and so the *hunebedden* (D14 here, and D17 and 18 in Rolde) ended up just outside each settlement.

D15 is one of the more complete *hunebedden*, with a mostly intact ring and entrance portal, overlooking the small village of Loon. Archaeological finds indicate that the site was in use for a long time. The well-formed oval ring is made up of relatively large stones, and it still had most of its earthen covering in 1870 when it was excavated.

D16 Balloo has lost a number of capstones since 1872, but remains sizeable and impressive.

D17 & D18 Rolde are in a small grove of trees. D17 is larger and more sprawling, straddled by an old oak tree.

D19 & D20 Drouwen sit in a large field at the edge of the bush. D19 is the smaller of the two. Many important finds have been unearthed here, shedding light on the culture of the *hunebed* builders. In fact, the site gives its name to a key pottery style in the archaeological record: Drouwenware.

D21 & D22 Bronneger are not large, but are notable for the rich finds that have been unearthed beneath them — Funnelbeaker pottery, tools and remains of hundreds of burials. D21 hugs an old birch tree, whilst D22 is tucked away behind an old tree trunk, with only two stones visible.

D23, D24 & D25 Bronneger form a triangle of burial sites that were probably part of a larger complex, most of it now lost. The three *hunebedden* are in a fairly ruinous state. D23 is the smallest and D25 the largest.

D26 Drouwenerveld is fairly complete and includes a stone ring. An offering pit was found at the entrance portal, and many pots were found when the site was excavated. It sits, fairly hidden and obscure, in a small clearing in the bush at the edge of fields outside Drouwen.

D27 Borger, known as The Great Hunebed, is the largest single *hunebed* in the Netherlands. The Groningen poetess Titia Brongersma conducted the first serious *hunebed* excavation here in 1685, finding a wealth of pottery, tools and other artefacts. Less intrusive scanning is now being used to investigate this important site further. This is where you will also find the Hunebedden Museum.

D28 & D29 Buinen In a large wooded grove just off the road from Borger to Buinen. In spite of nearby traffic, it is surprisingly peaceful and atmospheric. D29 is distinguished by a partially-collapsed capstone that resembles a broken heart.

D30 Exloo lies in a clearing in the bush north-west of Exloo. When excavated in the early 20th century, it still had most of its covering mound in place. Three original capstones remain, with a fourth added during restoration.

D31 Exloo occupies a hilly slope surrounded by dense bush, bordering the fields between Exloo and Valthe. Only one of five original capstones remains, but its fairly dramatic setting more than makes up for its dilapidated state.

D32 Odoorn lies at the end of a sand road in a small wooded peninsula jutting into fields between Odoorn and Borger. While its capstones are sunken, its location amid tall trees gives it considerable atmosphere.

D34 Valthe is on wooded land at the edge of the fields between Valthe and Odoorn. Its ruined, wild state doesn't undermine its authority in the landscape. It had a near-twin until 1955, when the stones of D33 — now completely vanished — were carried off for the restoration of D49.

D35 Valthe sits in a wooded area bordering the heathland between Kilijndijk and Valthe. Only two of the original four capstones.

D36 & D37 Valthe are in a peaceful location in a grove of trees. D36 has only one of its five original capstones. D37 is more crooked and scattered but still has three of its capstones.

D38, D39 & D40 Emmen are set in a heather field surrounded by forest. D38 is fairly skeletal, with only two capstones remaining. D39 is in an even worse state, having just a solitary capstone. D40 is the largest monument in the triangle — it is reasonably compact but has two enormous capstones.

D41 Emmen stands alone in an open field between a trailer camp and apartment blocks at a busy intersection on the western edge of Emmen. It is fairly intact and its ambience belies its anachronistic surroundings.

D42 Westenes lies just outside Emmen at the edge of a bush overlooking fields near the village of Westenes. Straddled by a large oak tree, it is unique for the three pairs of stones that make up the entrance portal (most have two pairs or less).

D43 Emmen is unique in the Netherlands — a large kerbstone enclosure containing two passage graves inside. It was built in two separate phases as the stone ring was gradually expanded, along with an 'offering pit' added in a third phase. Two more of the pits were found just outside, and the monument was still used in the Bronze Age. Although the two *hunebedden* are in a ruined state, it offers a good impression of the original monument, protected by a grove of trees that open on to the surrounding fields.

D44 Emmen-Westenes consists of a few orthostats and a lone capstone, making it hard to discern its original form. It is the only *hunebed* in the Netherlands that still sits on private property, along the road in the front yard of a farm in the village of Westenes.

D45 Emmen spans a rolling dune hill in the pine forest on the edge of Emmen.

D46 Emmen-Angelslo is obscurely located in a park in the Emmen neighbourhood of Angelslo.

D47 Emmen-Angelslo is remarkably intact and surprisingly atmospheric among the trees, despite being surrounded by apartment blocks of the Emmen neighbourhood of Angelslo.

D49 Schoonoord, commonly called the Papeloze Kerk (popeless church), has been reconstructed to partially show the mound that would have originally covered the *hunebedden*. Its name supposedly refers to its role in the 16th century as a place where Protestants could worship away from the Catholic authorities — but may also hark back to its importance as a pre-Christian place of worship.

D50 & D51 Noord-Sleen stretch along a rise overlooking the fields around the village of Noord-Sleen. D50 offers an impressive glimpse of the structure of an intact *hunebed*, whilst the much more dilapidated *hunebed* D51 has its own shy charm.

D52 Diever was restored by archaeologist A.E. van Giffen in 1953. When it was first reported 100 years earlier, it was fairly intact, and one of the capstones displayed a large carving of a human hand. By 1918, it was in a completely ruined state and could be reconstructed only with difficulty.

D53 & D54 Havelte sit on a hilly expanse of heathland. D54 was dismantled during the second world war in order not to draw Allied attention to the German airfield that had been built on the sandy terrain. It was restored by 1950.

The Frisian Islands

👍 A popular summer destination, pretty bleak in winter with many attractions closed

The Frisian Islands, also known as the Wadden Islands, stretch along the coast of North Holland, into Germany and then on up to Denmark.

The islands lie between the mudflat regions of the Wadden Sea and the wider North Sea.

Many of these islands are protected nature reserves, popular with birdwatchers.

The Netherlands lays claim to five islands — Texel, Vlieland, Terschelling, Ameland and Schiermonnikoog — as well as a handful of uninhabited sandbanks, which are perfect breeding grounds for birds.

The islands can be reached either from Friesland or from North Holland. In the summer, boats link up all the islands and it is possible to hop from one to another. But, out of season, travel is restricted and you will have to choose whether to depart from Friesland or North Holland, depending on whether you want to see the southern or the northern islands. Many tourist and accommodation facilities are closed in the winter.

The islands can become very busy during summer school holidays, so it is worth booking accommodation in advance.

With the German border only three hours' drive away, it should come as no surprise to learn that the vast majority of visitors to the islands are German holidaymakers. Consequently, many people there speak better German than English, and many of the tourist leaflets will only be available in German or Dutch.

TEXEL

👍 The largest of the islands with the greatest number of things to do

Texel (pronounced 'Tessel') is the largest and most populated of all the Wadden Islands. It is the only island to be part of the province of North Holland rather than Friesland.

Don't think of Texel as just a single destination to explore, but as a series of intriguing little towns, each with their own set of characteristics, knitted together by a series of picturesque little routes and paths that criss-cross the island.

The island is an idyllic place to get away from it all, with some truly splendid beaches and countryside to explore. In the summer, the main towns offer a surprisingly vibrant nightlife, and there are many activities to occupy your time here, such as go-karting, golf and a wide range of watersports.

Texel is also home to the **Royal Netherlands Institute for Sea Research** (www.nioz.nl), which promotes sustainable use of the seas and oceans through scientific research and education.

Den Burg

This town is the capital of the island and is where you'll find the tourist information office (🏠 Emmalaan 66; ☎ 0222 314 741).

The town itself is quite charming, with a well-preserved historical city centre and a church from the Reformation (built around 1400 AD). There is also a smaller Roman

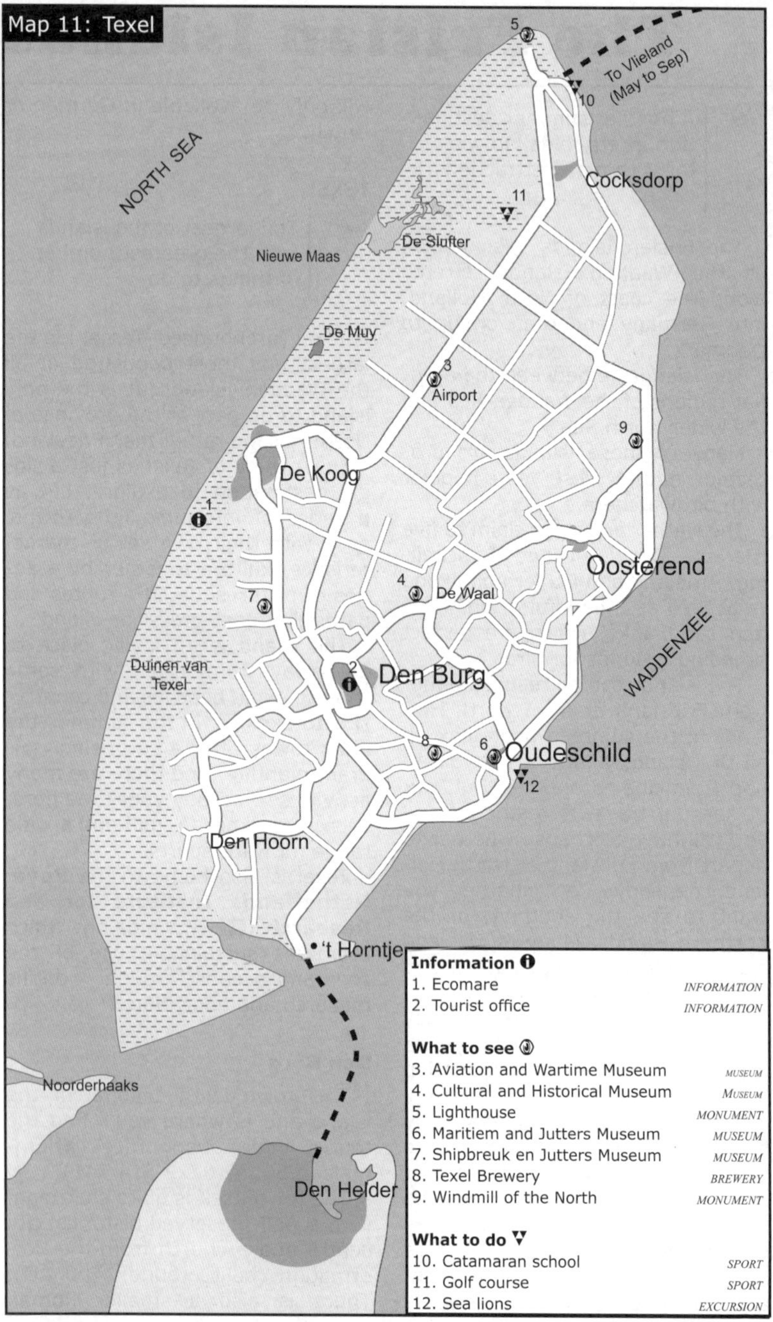
Map 11: Texel
NORTH SEA
To Vlieland (May to Sep)
Cocksdorp
De Slufter
Nieuwe Maas
De Muy
Airport
De Koog
Oosterend
De Waal
Duinen van Texel
Den Burg
WADDENZEE
Oudeschild
Den Hoorn
't Horntje
Noorderhaaks
Den Helder

Information

1. Ecomare — *INFORMATION*
2. Tourist office — *INFORMATION*

What to see

3. Aviation and Wartime Museum — *MUSEUM*
4. Cultural and Historical Museum — *MUSEUM*
5. Lighthouse — *MONUMENT*
6. Maritiem and Jutters Museum — *MUSEUM*
7. Shipbreuk en Jutters Museum — *MUSEUM*
8. Texel Brewery — *BREWERY*
9. Windmill of the North — *MONUMENT*

What to do

10. Catamaran school — *SPORT*
11. Golf course — *SPORT*
12. Sea lions — *EXCURSION*

Catholic church, built in 1863. A market takes place in the centre of town every Monday morning. In the summer, a separate folkloric market takes place on Wednesdays.

The town has a **cinema** (☎ Gravenstraat 33; ☎ 0222 312 027; 🖥 www.cinematexel.nl) and a go-karting rink (☎ Akenbuurt 14; ☎ 0222 313 921; 🖥 www. kartingtexel.nl).

On the road to Oudeschild, you will find the local **Texel Brewery** (☎ Schilderweg 214b; ☎ 0222 313 229; 🖥 speciaalbier.com), which runs regular guided tours.

Halfway between Den Burg and De Koog is the **Shipbreuk en Juttersmuseum** Flora (🖥 www. juttersflora.nl), a massive collection of junk that has been washed up by the sea and found by one of Texel's many assiduous beachcombers.

There are a handful of pretty decent **restaurants** in the centre of Den Burg.

If you want a good eating experience, try the bruin café De 12 Balcken (☎ Weverstraat 20; ☎ 0222 312 681; 🖥 www.12balcken. nl) or De Kern (☎ Gravenstraat 16; ☎ 0222 320 043; 🖥 www. restaurantdekern.com).

There are a number of options for **staying in the town**. Stay Okay (☎ Haffelderweg 29; ☎ 0222 315 441; 🖥 www.stayokay.com), 700 metres from the centre of town, is part of a Dutch chain of hostels. A smarter, more upmarket place is De Smulpot (☎ Binnenburg 5; ☎ 0222 312 756; 🖥 www.desmulpot.nl). If you want to camp in the area, the pick of the bunch is Camping De Bremakker (☎ Tempelierweg 40; ☎ 0222 312 863).

Den Hoorn

This is a picturesque little village about four kilometres from the ferry

TEXEL: WHERE TO GO?

There are numerous reasons to come to Texel, and where you base yourself depends on what you are looking for. Here are a few of the things on offer.

Beaches: De Koog
Birdwatching: Cocksdorp
Brewery: Den Burg
Catamaran: Cocksdorp
Cinema: Den Burg
Crazy golf: Cocksdorp
Golf: Cocksdorp
Go-karting: Den Burg, De Koog
Lighthouse: Cocksdorp
Nightlife: De Koog
Prawn fishing: Oudeschild
Sea lions: Oudeschild
Skydiving: Cocksdorp
Ten-pin bowling: De Koog
Theatre: Den Hoorn
Wadlopen: Cocksdorp

port. The town centre includes a couple of restaurants, a post office, a butcher and a Spar supermarket.

Bike rental is available at Vermeulen (☎ Herenstraat 69; ☎ 0222 319 213; 🖥 www.vermeulenbikes. nl).

The town has the only **theatre** on the island: Klif 12 (☎ 0222 319 633; 🖥 www.klif12.nl), which often hosts unique dinner-cabaret evenings.

A good option for **eating** in the town is Inn De Knip (☎ De Naal 2; ☎ 0222 31 99 46; 🖥 www. inndeknip.nl), offering lovely rustic fare and particularly sumptuous soups. Het Kompas (☎ Herenstraat 7; ☎ 0222 319 360; 🖥 www. whiskybarplaza.nl) uniquely combines a great eating experience with an incredible selection of whiskies: almost 1700 different types in fact.

For those that fancy **staying** in the town, there is a good range of accommodation options. At the higher end of the market, you have Bij Jef (🏠 Herenstraat 34; ☎ 0222 319 623; 🖵 www.bijjef.nl). If your budget is more modest, but you still want that touch of luxury, try the B&B at Klif 1 (🏠 Klif 1; ☎ 0222 888 950; 🖵 klif1.nl). There is a wide range of campsites in and around the town. Try Texelcamping Loodsmansduin (🏠 Rommelpot 19; ☎ 0222 317 208; 🖵 www.texelcampings.nl) or Hoeve Vrij en Blij (🏠 Westerweg 80; ☎ 0222 319 263; 🖵 www.hoevevrijenblij.nl).

De Koog

Located on the west coast of the island, with long sandy beaches and a lively town centre, De Koog tends to be a favourite base from which to explore the rest of Texel. From here, it is very easy to reach — by bike or on foot — the island's main national parks. Ecomare, Texel's nature museum and visitor centre, is also only a short ride away.

The town's main thoroughfare, where most of the bars and cafés are located, is Dorpsstraat. The centre has a somewhat twee American-theme-park feel to it.

If you want to **rent bikes** in De Koog, a couple of options are Fiets Inn Texel (🏠 Nikadel 75; ☎ 0222 317 841; 🖵 www.fietsinn-texel.nl) and Bruining Nikadel (🏠 Nikadel 60; ☎ 0222 317 333; 🖵 www.bruiningtexel.nl).

Between May and September, a **tourist bus** (called the Borrelbus) runs from De Koog to the main tourist destinations on the island (🖵 www.texeltours.nl).

You are unlikely to be bored in De Koog. Besides a good range of nightlife and restaurants, the town also has an indoor **go-karting centre** (🏠 Stappeland 2; ☎ 0222 327 000; 🖵 www.

kartingdekoog.nl) and a **ten-pin bowling rink** (🏠 Dorpsstraat 127; ☎ 0222 317 672; 🖵 www.bowlingvereniging-texel.nl/bwlk-oogel.html).

For places to **eat**, Vogelhuis Oranjerie (🏠 Dorpsstraat 204-206; ☎ 0222 317 279; 🖵 www.vogelhuis.com) is an excellent choice, serving freshly-caught fish accompanied by mountains of seasonal vegetables. De Taveerne (🏠 Nikadel 44; ☎ 0222 31 75 85; 🖵 www.taveernetexel.nl) also uses seasonal local produce to produce excellent dishes.

There are numerous **campsites** around the town. One of the best-located ones is Texel Campings Kogerstrand (🏠 Badweg 37; ☎ 0222 317 208; 🖵 www.texelcampings.nl), just metres from the beach and a short walk from the town centre.

Another option is to stay in a pension such as Duin Blick (🏠 Ruijslaan 19; ☎ 0222 317 466).

Cocksdorp

Cocksdorp is the best place on the island to come for **birdwatching**. Vogelinformatiecentrum (🏠 Kikkerstraat 42; ☎ 0222 316 249; 🖵 www.vogelinformatiecentrum.nl) offers all sorts of handy tips and information about the pastime, including a daily update about what birds have been seen where.

Bike rental in the town is available at Van der Linde (🏠 Kikkertstraat 3; ☎ 0222 316 432; 🖵 www.fietshurenoptexel.nl).

A few kilometres away from the town centre, surrounded by a vast dune area called Eierlandse Duinen, stands a **lighthouse** (🏠 0222 317 741; 🖵 www.vuurtorentexel.nl), built in 1864.

The only **golf course** on the island is located here, too: De Texelse

(🏠 Roggeslootweg 3; 🏠 0222 31 6539; 🖥 www.texelse.nl).

If you fancy a game of **crazy golf**, check out Midgetgolfbaan (🏠 Kikkertstraat 30-32; ☎ 0222 31 64 85) in the centre of town.

The town is also popular for watersports. **Catamaran sailing lessons** are available at De Eilander (🏠 De Volharding 6; ☎ 06 20 63 44 13; 🖥 www.deeilander.nl).

There are a couple of **long beaches** near the town. A particularly popular one is just next to the lighthouse. Another one is slightly closer to the centre of town.

Skydiving trips can be arranged at Paracentrum (🏠 Postweg 128; ☎ 0222 311 464; 🖥 www.paracentrumtexel.nl). Next to the airfield is an aviation and wartime museum (🏠 Postweg 126; 🖥 www.lomt.nl).

If you want to experience walking on the mudflats, Rederij de Vriendschap (🏠 Vuurtorenweg 100; ☎ 0222 316 451; 🖥 www.waddenveer.nl) can organise **wadlopen** tours.

If you want to **camp** in and around Cocksdorp, try Camping De Krim (🏠 Roggeslootweg 6; ☎ 0222 390 112) and De Hoek (🏠 Vuurtorenweg 86).

De Waal

De Waal is a tiny village in the centre of the island, enchanting passers-by with its idyllic surroundings and low-set cottages. There's not a great deal to do or see in the town, but you might like to pop along to the **Cultural and Historical Museum** (🏠 Hogereind 6; 🖥 www.cultuurmuseumtexel.nl).

Oudeschild

On the east of the island is Oudeschild, the old fishing port of Texel. The harbour, tucked away behind a dyke, is a pleasant place to relax with a drink in one of the town's many cafés and bars. But the main draw of the town is as a launching point for boat trips to see **sea lions** or learn about catching — and shelling — **sea prawns**. The tour operators Garnalalen Vissen (☎ 06 51 49 86 14; 🖥 www.garnalenvissen.nl) and TX35 Zeester (☎ 06 51 52 81 74; 🖥 www.zeestertx35.nl) runs tours that combine the two activities. Zeehondentochten (☎ 06 20 92 05 94; 🖥 www.zeehondentexel.nl) only runs tours to see sea lions.

All these tour operators, plus some that have not been mentioned, are huddled together along the quayside. Simply stroll between the boats and pick the one that suits you best.

If you prefer dry land, then the local museum, the **Maritiem & Jutters Museum** (🏠 Barentsztraat 21; ☎ 0222 314 956; 🖥 www.texelsmaritiem.nl) takes you on a fascinating journey through Texel's maritime heritage.

If you like fish, by far the best place to eat in town is De Oude Vismarkt (🏠 Vlamkast 53; ☎ 0222 310 783; 🖥 www.deoudevismarkt.nl).

In terms of **where to stay**, Haven Hotel (🏠 Haven 2; ☎ 0222 310 234; 🖥 www.havenhoteltexel.nl) is a clean and spacious hotel overlooking the Wadden Sea. A little further along the quay is Havenzicht Hotel (🏠 Haven 6; ☎ 0222 312 602; 🖥 www.havenzichttexel.nl).

Oosterend

Oosterend is a sleepy little hamlet on the east of the island. More residential and less touristy than Oudeschild, it is where many of the island's local fishermen live, even though the village is some kilometres from the coast.

The village is built around a church called Maartenskerk, which is the oldest church on the island. The western wing of the church dates back to the 11th century. The tower was added on to the church in the 15th century. It once had a spire, but it is thought that a lightening strike, followed by a fire, destroyed it in the 1700s.

Slightly outside the town centre, on the corner of Oranjestraat and Achtertune, stands a distinctive statue of a sheep with two lambs: a tribute to the island's ovine heritage.

On the other side of Oosterend, you will find a small botanical garden maintained by volunteers. Here, wild plants are gathered, cultivated and preserved.

Heading north-east from Oostend, towards the coast, you will find the Molen Het Noorden, or the **Windmill of the North**. The mill — a grand, octagonal structure — is one of the largest that still exists in North Holland. It was built in 1878 to drain the *polder* and reclaim the land from the sea.

VLIELAND

👍 | Virtually car-free

For those travellers that want a quieter getaway than Texel offers, its smaller neighbour Vlieland is a good option.

The island is mostly car free. The only vehicles there are those owned by residents, a handful of taxis and the occasional bus.

The island consists of a single town — Oost-Vlieland — and wide expanses of natural beauty. There used to be a second village on the island — West-Vlieland — but that was lost to the sea during severe floods around 1736.

A scattering of houses and hotels lie outside the main town, mostly in the north of the island.

Like the other Wadden Islands, much of Vlieland's landscape is made up of sandy dunes. However, there are some areas of woodland as well — the trees were planted to stop the sand from blowing away.

On the west of the island lies the Vliehors, a large open sandy plain that is a great breeding ground for **birds**. It is also a good area in which to spot **seals**.

The Dutch air force have a base here, where they conduct military exercises, and so it is not always possible to visit this area. The area is usually only accessible at weekends or with an organised tour.

In August, look out for the "Into the Great Wide Open" **festival** (🖥 greatwideopen.nl) — a family-friendly event devoted to film, visual arts, music and nature. Most of the bands that turn up are from the Netherlands, Germany and Belgium.

In the centre of Oost-Vlieland is the oldest building on the island. It used to house the post office, but now contains the **Tromp's Huys Museum** (🏠 Dorpsstraat 99; 🖥 www.trompshuys.nl).

If you want to do a **tour of the island**, there are a few options. The Vliehors Express (🏠 Dorpsstraat 125; ☎ 0562 451 971; 🖥 www.vliehorsexpres.nl) runs excursions in big yellow trucks, which take you over the dunes to the sandy plains of Vliehors on the west of the island. Taxi Langeloo (🏠 Betzy Akerslootglop 3; ☎ 06 5271 1722) offers more private tours to Vliehors. During the breeding season, the Forestry Commission offers organised excursions to the *polders* — ask at the tourist office.

The easiest way of **getting to Vlieland** is from the West Friesian town of Harlingen. Rederij Doeksen (💻 www.rederij-doeksen.nl) operates the ferries. Because you cannot take your car over to the island, a car park is available just in front of the ferry terminal on the mainland.

Between May to September, a ferry service also runs from Texel to Vlieland. It is operated by Rederij De Vriendschap (💻 www. waddenveer.nl).

TERSCHELLING

 | Small farms selling local produce

Terschelling is the second-largest Wadden Island after Texel. As with the other islands, most of the land is taken up with national park and wonderful cycling trails. Terschelling also has the **longest beach** of all the islands, stretching 30 kilometres along the northern coast. Most of the urban settlements are along the southern coast of the island, where a single main road weaves its way through picturesque villages and towns. The mainstay of the island is tourism, but there are also a **number of farms** on the island where you can buy a great range of local agricultural produce.

For a rather impressive collection of jetsam gathered from the sea, visit **Wrackenmuseum** (💻 wrakkenmuseum.nl). The museum is privately owned by a diving enthusiast and you're certain to get a warm welcome there.

Rederij Doeksen (💻 www. rederij-doeksen.nl) operates regular **ferries** to the island from the West Frisian town of Harlingen. You can take your own car over to the island but, should you wisely choose to leave it behind, there are plenty of bike hire places and buses to get you around.

AMELAND

 | A fairly compact island, but still with plenty of things going on in the summer

For such a small island, Ameland can get insanely busy during the summer months, particularly at weekends.

Most of the island is made up of sand dunes. There are four villages on the island. Nes is the second-largest and most touristy. It is where the ferry from Holwerd on the mainland will deposit you. Hollum, located on the west coast, is the largest village and home to the island's **lighthouse**. Ballum is the smallest village, and houses the island's **airfield**. The eastern-most village of the island is Buren, where there is a particularly nice, though windswept, **beach**.

The island is not terribly big and the nicest way to see it is to jump on a bike and go where the country lanes might take you.

There are a number of **hotels** on the island. For example: Nobel (🏠 Gerrit Kosterweg 16; ☎ 0519 554 157; 💻 www.nobelhotel.nl) in Ballum and Ameland (🏠 Strandweg 48; ☎ 0519 542 150; 💻 www.hoteldolores.nl) in Nes.

SCHIERMONNIKOOG

 | Something of the Dutch wilderness

Measuring just 16 km long and 4 km wide, Schiermonnikoog is the smallest of all inhabitable Wadden islands. Just under 1000 people live on the island.

The island is virtually car free. You are not allowed to take your own vehicle, and only a small number of residents have applied for a permit to own a car on the island.

This is probably one of the best places to come to experience something of the Dutch wilderness.

The best way to get around the island is to walk or cycle. There is a single bus line, but buses are not particularly frequent.

There are a handful of hotels and bed-and-breakfasts offering accommodation on the island, although the great majority of visitors are day-trippers.

The only public transport to Schiermonnikoog is a ferry from the harbour complex of Lauwersoog in northern Friesland.

The Hague may be the seat of government, but it is not the legal capital of the Netherlands. That privilege, according to the country's constitution, falls to the somewhat larger and more vivacious city of Amsterdam.

Settled as a small fishing village in the late 12th century, Amsterdam became one of the most important ports in the world during the Dutch Golden Age (p66).

The city has a more tolerant attitude towards sex and drugs than many other regions of the country, largely because the city's tourist industry is so dependent on this. Despite a recent down-sizing, Amsterdam's red light district remains the largest in the country, and you will find far more coffee shops and smartshops (which sell various psychoactive substances) than anywhere else.

There is so much more to the great city than sex and drugs, though. Look a little way beyond this and you will find that Amsterdam has a rich cultural heritage, a colourful history and a vibrant artistic pulse that still exists to this day.

FESTIVALS

As one of Europe's leading cultural centres, it should come as no surprise that Amsterdam is a hotbed of frantic festival activity for much of the year. Whenever you're visiting the city — be it in summer or winter — you'll be certain to find some cultural event that you can attend.

Details of upcoming festivals can be found at ⌨ www.iamsterdam. com. Below we mention a few of the larger ones that are really worth experiencing.

In January or February (depending on the year) Amsterdam puts on a spectacular celebration in honour of the **Chinese New Year**: lively street performances, a special cultural programme put on by the Buddhist Temple and delicious Asian food.

No one does **Queen's Day** (April 30) — soon to become King's Day — quite like Amsterdam. If you've seen one too many Queen's Days in The Hague, then check out Amsterdam's interpretation of this important Dutch festival. Crazy, frantic and buzzing. When people make a special effort to attend Queen's Day in the Netherlands, it will usually be Amsterdam where they head.

In July or August, Amsterdam hosts its **Gay Pride** celebration (⌨ www.amsterdamgaypride.nl), replete with street parties, lively clubbing events and the famous parade along the canal. One of Amsterdam's busiest weekends.

Amsterdam's **festival of lights** (⌨ www.amsterdamlightfestival. com) takes place between early January and mid-December. During this festival, you'll see light sculptures created by leading artists and buildings illuminated in all manner of inventive ways.

WHAT TO SEE

Amsterdam's world famous **red light district** makes it on to the itineraries of most visitors to the city. Although prostitution is legal in many European cities, nowhere has it become such a major tourist attraction as in Amsterdam.

All sorts of people visit the area — not just those looking for sex, but also those drawn there out of curiosity. This means that the area

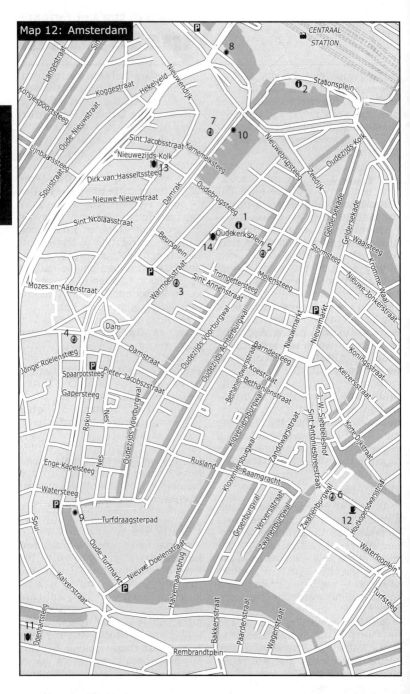

Amsterdam

Amsterdam

Information ❶

1. Tourist office	*INFORMATION*
2. Prostitution Information Centre	*INFORMATION*

What to see ⓙ

3. Condomerie	*SHOP*
4. Madame Tussauds	*WAXWORKS*
5. Red light district	*AREA*
6. Rembrandt House	*MUSEUM*
7. Sex Museum	*MUSEUM*

Tours ●

8. Holland International	*BOAT CRUISE*
9. Rederij Kooij	*BOAT CRUISE*
10. Rederij Plas	*BOAT CRUISE*

Where to eat ❙●❙

11. Sichuan Food	*CHINESE*
12. The Coffee Gallery	*CAFÉ*
13 & 14. Wok to Walk	*ASIAN*

has much less of a seedy feel than some of the other red light districts find in the country, including the one in The Hague (p148).

Despite Amsterdam's acclaimed reputation for tolerance, the red light district has been down-sized recently in a bid to smarten up the city's image. This has resulted in a number of prostitutes having to seek work elsewhere, often in sex clubs or through private escort agencies.

The red light district is not difficult to find, being a short 10-minute walk south of the main railway station. Simply make for the Oudezijds Voorburgwal and you will find yourself there. You'll know you're in the right place because of the soft red lights emanating from doorways, and the scantily-clad women flirtatiously beckoning men inside.

The area is open for business around the clock. However, you'll find it most atmospheric in the evening or after nightfall.

You should not take photos whilst in the district. You will almost certainly be stopped and your camera may be confiscated or even destroyed.

More information about the red light district and prostitution in the Netherlands is available at the **Prostitution Information Centre** (🏠 Enge Kerksteeg 3; 🖥 www. pic-amsterdam.com). The office is identified simply by the letters 'PIC'. You're more likely to find it open in the afternoon or early evening. The centre can help arrange walking tours of the red light district, often led by former sex workers. For €65, women are able to participate in a workshop that gives a feel for what it is like to work as a prostitute and have men gawping at you all day long. The workshop explains how to look at potential passers-by and how to refuse customers if necessary. You'll also get the chance to stand behind a window, dressed as sexily or provocatively as you wish (although men will not come in!)

Not far from the red light district, you'll find **a condomerie** (🏠 Warmoesstraat 141; ☎ 020 627 4174; 🖥 condomerie.com), selling all manner of strange and unusual condoms.

To complete your tour of Amsterdam's sex industry, consider a trip to the **sex museum** (🏠 Damrak 18; ☎ 020 622 8376; 🖥 www. sexmuseumamsterdam.nl), just down the road from Centraal Station. It provides a fascinating insight into Dutch attitudes towards sex, and how these have evolved over the ages. It also has an exhibition on sexual practices from around the world.

One of the most compelling stories of the second world war is the account of a young 13-year old Jewish girl forced to go into hiding to avoid persecution by the Nazis. That girl was **Anne Frank** (p70), and it is in Amsterdam that you can visit her house (☎ Prinsengracht 263-267; ☎ 020 556 7100; 🖥 www.annefrank.org).

The Anne Frank House is powerful in its simplicity, and one really gets transported back to that terrible period of the 20th century. The fear, the terror and the humiliation that the Frank family must have faced is palpable.

The house, for the most part, has been left as it would have been during the war. The focus of the museum is, of course, the secret annex of the house where the Franks lived until they were anonymously betrayed. Standing in the dark and cramped quarters, trying to imagine how Anne Frank and her family must have felt, is a deeply moving experience.

For more insight into Jewish culture and heritage, you can also visit the **Jewish Historical Museum** (🖥 Nieuwe Amstelstraat 1; ☎ 020 531 0310).

Amsterdam is home to the oldest zoo in the Netherlands, **Artis Zoo** (☎ Plantage Kerklaan 38-40; ☎ 0900 278 4796; 🖥 www.artis. nl). According to the Dutch tourist board, the zoo pulls in around 1.2 million people each year and is the second-most visited attraction in the city, after the Van Gogh Museum. Its success owes much to its place in Dutch history, the diversity of species and the creative attempts to make the zoo enclosures as natural as possible. The zoo includes a botanical garden, aquarium and a butterfly house. Not cheap at €18.95, though. Parking is €7 extra.

The **Rembrandt House** (☎ Jodenbreestraat 4; ☎ 020 520 0400; 🖥 www.rembrandthuis. nl) is the former residence of the world-renowned Dutch artist from the country's Golden Age, Rembrandt Harmenszoon van Rijn. He lived there from 1639 until he went bankrupt 20 years later and his belongings were auctioned off. It is now a museum dedicated to his life's work, showcasing those items that he would have owned at the time. Some of Rembrandt's paintings — as well as those of other artists — are on display, although many of his more famous works have been distributed between museums and private collections around the world.

The museum is centrally-located, a 30-minute walk south from Centraal Station. You can take the metro to Waterlooplein Station. Trams 9 and 14 also run there.

The **Van Gogh Museum** (☎ Paulus Potterstraat 7; ☎ 020 570 5200; 🖥 www.vangoghmuseum. nl) is Amsterdam's top tourist attraction. Vincent van Gogh was a Dutch post-impressionist painter that lived in the latter half of the 19th century. As we were going to press, the Van Gogh Museum was still undergoing renovations, with most of the artwork being on display at the Hermitage (☎ Amstel 51; 🖥 www.hermitage.nl). Renovation is expected to be complete by April 2013.

The museum has the largest collection of Van Gogh works in the world. Many visitors come for what is arguably one of his most famous paintings, *Sunflowers*, but there are plenty of others to look out for, including: *The Potato Eaters*, *Yellow House*, *The Painter of Sunflowers* and *Wheat Field with a Lark*.

A wonderful way of experiencing Amsterdam is by **riverboat**. There are a large number of tour companies that offer canal cruises from different departure points throughout the city and in a multitude of different languages. A few of the better-known operators include Holland International (☎ Prins

Hendrikkade 33A; ☎ 020 625 3035; 💻 www.hir.nl), Canal Company (☎ 020 623 9886; 💻 www.canal.nl), Blue Boat (🏠 Stadhouderskade 30; 🏠 020 679 1370; 💻 www.blueboat.nl), Rederij Kooij (🏠 Rokin 125; ☎ 020 623 3810; 💻 www.rederijkooij.nl) and Rederij Plas (🏠 Damrak 3; ☎ 020 624 54 06; 💻 www.rederijplas.nl).

Some tour operators also offer dinner cruises — check their website for details. Pannenkoekenboot (💻 www.pannenkoekenboot.nl) serves pancakes during boat trips.

If you'd like to break up your canal cruise with a spot of sightseeing, the 'hop-on hop-off' service offered by Canal Bus (💻 www.canal.nl — details as above) is an excellent way to do so.

Many visitors to Amsterdam may view **Madame Tussauds** (🏠 Dam 20; ☎ 020 522 1010; 💻 www.madametussauds.com) as touristy tackiness to be avoided at all costs. After all, there's a very famous Madame Tussauds in London, so why travel all the way to Amsterdam to visit the one here? But it remains an incredibly popular tourist attraction, drawing hundreds of thousands of visitors each year.

The Madame Tussauds phenomenon is world-famous. Established by the French wax sculptor Marie Tussaud, the museum displays intricately sculpted wax models of famous celebrities. The Madame Tussauds in Amsterdam includes important figures from Dutch history, culture and politics, as well as more internationally-recognisable celebrities.

The **Rijksmuseum** (🏠 Jan Luijkenstraat 1; ☎ 020 674 7000; 💻 www.rijksmuseum.nl) has been closed for renovation for the past 10 years. It was supposed to reopen in 2008, but a number of set-backs meant refurbishment took longer than expected. It is now due to reopen in April 2013. The museum uses art to tell the story of the Netherlands from the Middle Ages to the present day. There is a particularly large collection of paintings from the Dutch Golden Age, as well as a sizeable number of Asian artworks. *The Night Watch* by Rembrandt remains the most famous painting on display. The museum also has some historical artefacts, such as the stern of the British battleship HMS Royal Charles, which was captured by the Dutch in 1667 during an incursion into British waterways.

The **Heineken Experience** (🏠 Stadhouderskade 78; ☎ 020 523 9222; 💻 www.heinekenexperience.com) is a monument to the Netherlands' most universally-recognisable brand of beer. During an hour-long tour, you will be guided through the Heineken brewing process, learning how the beer is made and put into bottles. At the end of the tour, you will get two free beers (as long as you are over the age of 18), which can be quaffed in a really neat Heineken bar, made from strips of beer cans and glass bottles. Well, it's neat only as long as you don't have an aversion to the colour green.

WHERE TO EAT AND DRINK

Wok to Walk (💻 www.woktowalk.com) is a very good chain of noodle restaurants that you'll find throughout Amsterdam. Order noodles with whatever meat or vegetables that you fancy, plus accompanying sauce, and it will be cooked right in front of you. Great for those on a budget. Some of the more central locations can get very busy, and you may have to wait a little while before you are served.

Opera Prima (🏠 Kinkerstraat 228; ☎ 020 683 2383) is a great

Amsterdam

place to come for lunch or afternoon tea. It serves excellent sandwiches and other delicacies, such as duck-and-date pastry wraps. But the biggest reason for coming to the place is for the sumptuous cakes and pastries that are on offer. The place is more like a coffee lounge than restaurant, with the result that some of the tables are too low for comfortable eating. That aside, though, this is a great choice. The area is pretty, too, and nice for a post-lunch stroll.

Paloma Blanca (🏠 Jan Pieter Heijestraat 145; 🖥 www.palomablanca.nl) is a delightful Moroccan restaurant, with welcoming service and great food. The décor adds to the enchanting ambiance. Great couscous and more inventive dishes, such as catfish with zucchini.

Mangiancora (🏠 Ferdinand Bolstraat 170; 📞 020 471 4311; 🖥 www.mangiancora.com) is a Neapolitan pizzeria that also sells good quality Italian products such as olive oil. The décor is nothing special, but the pizzas are excellent and authentic, cooked in traditional wood-fired ovens.

If you are looking for classy Chinese fare, you might like to try **Sichuan Food** (🏠 Reguliersdwarsstraat 35; 📞 020 626 9327; 🖥 www.sichuanfood.nl). In 1993, it became the first Chinese restaurant in Europe to be awarded a Michelin star. It has since lost this accolade, but the quality of the food remains high. Unfortunately, so do the prices.

The Coffee Gallery (🏠 Jodenbreestraat 94; 🖥 www.thecoffeegallery.nl) serves real Italian coffee. The owner is a Neapolitan chap with a true passion about his country and culture. The place is unique, decorated with coffee makers and other typically Italian paraphernalia. Unfortunately, the café is quite small and can get fairly crowded, so customers often feel uncomfortable if they stay for too long.

Cafezinho (🏠 Tweede Laurierdwarsstraat 50; 🖥 www.cafezinho.moonfruit.com) serves good, strong coffee with a friendly atmosphere and free wi-fi. It is located in a pretty neighbourhood of Amsterdam. The café serves sandwiches and fresh juices. Try the traditional Brazilian *pão de queijo* (cheese bun) and the pure *açaí* juice, which comes from a particular type of palm tree that is native to Latin America.

HOW TO GET THERE

Regular trains run between Amsterdam and The Hague, taking around 50 minutes. Throughout the day, there are six trains per hour, two of them direct and the others with a change in Leiden. At night, there is one train per hour between Den Haag Hollands Spoor and Amsterdam Centraal.

Friesland & Groningen

WADLOPEN

👍 | Hiking along the mudflats of the Wadden Sea

📷 | Photo 40

Wadlopen is one of the more unusual pastimes that you can participate in during your stay in the Netherlands. The activity involves hiking over mudflats in the Wadden Sea, sometimes trudging for kilometres across open plains of sludge that can come up to your knees or even your waist.

Wadlopen is only possible during spring and summer, usually from April or May to the middle of September. The route that you walk depends on the whims of the sea; some places will be inaccessible at high tide.

You should not attempt Wadlopen without a licensed guide, since taking the wrong route across the mudflats can be treacherous.

Shorter Wadlopen tours last no more than a few hours. But, for the really fit and adventurous, there are walks that lead all the way to the islands of Ameland and Schermonnikoog.

Make sure you take the right clothing and equipment before you embark on any tour. A pair of shoes or boots that you don't mind getting dirty, or can easily wash, are essential (waterproof diving boots work well). Wellington boots are not recommended since they can become very heavy with the mud and thus exceedingly difficult to walk in.

Waterproof garments and a waterproof backpack are a good idea. However much you try not to fall over, you are going to get grubby — so don't wear your best attire. Bring a dry set of clothes to change in to after the tour, plus a towel. A sturdy walking stick is an optional extra.

It's possible to do Wadlopen all the way along the northern coast of Friesland, and different tour companies will set off from different spots. Some of the better-known companies are: Wadloopcentrum Fryslan (☎ 0519 242 100; 🖥 www. wadlopen.net), Wadloop Centrum Pieterburen (☎ 0595 528 300; 🖥 www.wadlopen.com), Dijkstra's Wadlooptochten (☎ 0595 528 345; 🖥 www.wadloop-dijkstra.nl), Uitsluitend (🖥 www.wadlopen.nl) and De Vrije Wadlopens (🖥 www. vrijewadlopers.nl).

Wadlopen tours tend to start from places slightly outside town centres, so it is best if you have your own vehicle to reach them. Alternatively, some tour companies offer a pick-up service.

LEEUWARDEN

👍 | Discovering Frisian history

If you are interested in Frisian history and cultural ancestry, what better place to start than the province's capital?

Leeuwarden isn't, to be honest, the kind of place that everyone immediately warms to. First impressions are of a clumsy fusion of the old and the new. But one shouldn't overlook the historic appeal of the city.

Leeuwarden's compact **medieval city centre** is certainly worth a wander around. Then there is, of course, the **Friesmuseum** (🏠 Wilhelminaplein 92; ☎ 058 255 5500;

www.friesmuseum.nl), dedicated to the history of the province. It is closed for renovations until September 2013, but when it reopens it will be the best place to go to get a sense of what it means to be Frisian. The museum gives an excellent insight into the historical culture and people that have made the region what it is today. The museum also delves into the lives of notable figures from Frisian history, such as Mata Hari, a dancer who was executed as a spy during the second world war, and Grutte Pier, a freedom fighter who launched a rebellion against Habsburg rule in the 14th century.

Direct **trains** run between The Hague and Leeuwarden (journey time three hours).

ELFSTEDENTOCHT

 | Ice-skating race across 11 cities

 | Starts at Leeuwarden

The Elfstedentocht is a 200 km ice-skating event that takes place between the 11 major cities that make up Friesland. There are two principal events. One is a speed-skating match with around 200 professional contestants. The other is a leisure-skating tour that anyone can join in, subject to availability.

However, the event is only held when the ice between the participating cities is thick enough. It has to be at least 15 cm across the entire course, and this means that the event is a very rare occurrence. It was last held in 1997 and before that in 1986. The ice was almost thick enough for the race to be held in 2012, but it was called off at the last minute, to widespread disappointment.

Radio Netherlands Worldwide (www.rnw.nl) will publish details about whether the tour is to take place.

The tour starts from Leeuwarden, easily reachable from The Hague by **train**. When the tour starts, though, expect trains to be pretty full. In fact, since the temperature will inevitably be cold, they may not be running at all — or only running with severe delays.

SNEEK

👍 | Come for one of Europe's largest sailing events

If you like doing things on or under the water, consider a trip to Sneek, which is just on the banks of one of the largest freshwater lakes in the country: the Sneekermeer.

JFT Watersport (www. jft-watersport.nl) can offer advice on what activities are available, and during which season they can be done. **Sailing**, **windsurfing**, **water-skiing** and **diving** are all popular on the lake. JFT Watersport rents out equipment and boats, including **yachts**, **dingies** and **speedboats**.

Sneekweek (www. sneekweek.nl), the largest sailing event on European inland waterways, takes place in August. It starts on the Friday evening before the first Saturday of the month, with a colourful boat parade and fireworks. During the week, there is music along the canals, street festivities and various regattas. Sailing enthusiasts travel from all over the world for the event.

You can come as a spectator for free. You won't see much of the race, which takes place at sea, but the boat parades and other side events are fun.

Friesland & Groningen

There are no direct **trains** from The Hague to Sneek. You will have to change at Leeuwarden. Total journey time: 3hr15.

GRONINGEN

👍 | Laid-back yet lively

Groningen has a lively student buzz to it and many out-of-towners descend on it when they want to let their hair down and kick up their heels. In fact, official statistics suggest that as many as a third of Groningen's 200,000 inhabitants are students.

Regular night buses run to destinations outside of the city, such as Emmen in Drenthe, making it a popular destination for those looking for livelier nightlife than they can find in their home town.

Groningen used to be a port, but a flood in 1953 prompted city planners to reinforce defences and push the sea back to where it now lies.

There used to be a high-speed train connection between Groningen and Amsterdam, but this was cancelled not along ago, making the city feel even more detached from the economic hub of the Netherlands'.

How to get there

Direct **trains** run to Groningen from The Hague, taking a little under three hours.

What to see

In the winter, you can see a large number of **old ships** moored along the canals, enjoying a well-earned break from their summer job of ferrying tourists around the Wadden Sea.

There are a couple of museums that are really worth seeing. One is the **StripMuseum** (🏠 Westerhaven 71; 🖥 www.stripmuseum.nl), an impressively-large museum dedicated to children's comic books. The labelling of the works is all in Dutch, but since much of it is visual this doesn't matter too much. Great fun for kids and interesting for adults. The other museum worth visiting is the architecturally-intriguing **Groninger Museum** (🏠 Museumeiland 1; 🖥 www.groningermuseum.nl), easily recognisable just outside the station for its odd shape and vibrant colours.

The building was actually designed by three different architects, which accounts for its somewhat unusual and disjointed appearance. Philippe Starck, from France, designed the silver cylindrical building; Italy's Alessandro Mendini designed the yellow tower; and the Austrian construction firm Coop Himmelb(l)au provided the pale blue deconstructivist space.

You don't need to go into the museum to appreciate the architecture, but there's usually some interesting photography and design exhibitions within.

You'll also find one of Europe's largest **baroque organs** in Groningen. Housed in the Martinikerk (🖥 www.martinikerk.nl), it consists of a staggering 5000 pipes and measures 97 metres in height.

Groningen's **train station**, just south of the city centre, is also very interesting. The former first and second-class waiting rooms, which now house a café, have been left as they would have been a hundred years ago. There is a large 1896 map of the train tracks pinned to the wall. The supermarket Albert Heijn is in the old third-class waiting room.

Where to eat

Muller (🏠 Grote Kromme Elleboorg 13; ☎ 050 318 3208;

 www.restaurantmuller.nl) is a quality restaurant in the town that has one Michelin star, though of course it is pricey. Nice atmosphere, great food and French-themed.

The best Italian restaurant in town is by far **Osteria da Vinci** (Turfsingel 33-1; 050 312 4044; www.osteriadavinci.nl) — lovely relaxing atmosphere with a courtyard to sit out in the summer, great authentic food and an excellent selection of wine.

PIETERBUREN

 | Visit a seal sanctuary

The small village of **Pieterburen** is situated in the northern part of the province of Groningen. It's a pleasant enough place, but the reason many people stop by is because of the seal sanctuary that is to be found there.

The sanctuary (Hoofdstraat 94a; www.zeehondencreche.nl) rescues seals from all over the region, and seeks to educate people about the dangers that seals face. Workers from the Seal Rehabilitation and Research Centre (SRRC) are at the centre every day throughout the year to answer questions about the seal programme, and you can see seals being taken care of. A highly educational experience. A day ticket to visit the sanctuary costs €8 — children under the age of three are free.

It is also possible to arrange wadlopen tours from Pieterburen (Hoofdstraat 84; 0595 528 558; www.wadlopen-pieterburen.nl).

If you don't have your own transport, the easiest way to get to Pieterburen is with **bus** 68 from Winsum, which is a short train ride from Groningen city.

Friesland & Groningen

Flevoland

A hundred years ago, much of Flevoland lay beneath the Zuiderzee, an unpredictable waterway stretching from the Wadden Sea well into the Netherlands. Only the former islands of Schokland and Urk, which are now part of Flevoland, have a longer history.

In 1913, Dutch Queen Wilhelmina announced a daring proposal to reclaim the land. The idea had already been talked about for some time, but it wasn't until she gave it her royal seal of approval that it started to become a reality.

The 30-kilometre long dyke from Wieringen to Friesland — Afsluitdijk — was completed in 1932, thus turning the Zuiderzee into a lake (the IJsselmeer). Five years later, reclamation of the northeastern part of the region was initiated. In 1957 Eastern Flevoland fell dry, and in 1968 Southern Flevoland also became land.

All this means that, if you choose to visit Flevoland, you are really stepping into the heartland of the Dutch battle against the sea.

LELYSTAD

🏠 | Lelystad

Lelystad, the capital of the province, is not a particularly endearing city in itself. However, there are a couple of reasons that you may choose to visit it.

For an intriguing insight into the history of Flevoland, and the extraordinary battle of the Dutch against the sea, take a wander down to the **Nieuwe Land Poldermuseum** (🏠 Oostvaardersdijk 113; ☎ 0320 225 900; 🖥 www. nieuwlanderfgoed.nl). A large part of the museum is dedicated to the construction of the dykes, the

draining of the new *polders* (reclaimed land) and the occupants that came to settle here.

Discover the Netherlands' rich history of shipbuilding with a visit to the Batavia Shipyard (🏠 Batavia Stad; ☎ 0320 261 409; 🖥 www. bataviawerf.nl), named after a famous ship that sunk off the coast of Australia in 1629 during its maiden voyage.

The shipyard rebuilt the Batavia over a 10-year period (between 1985 and 1995). It's latest project is to reconstruct De 7 Provinciën, a 17th century battleship. Similarly grand projects are promised in the future.

The shipyard also gives workshops on the skills used to create 17th century ships, such as woodcarving, metalworking and rigging.

The shipyard is a not-for-profit organisation. It is run by volunteers and also provides work for the long-term unemployed.

There's also a rather distinctive giant iron sculpture that you might want to take a look at (📷 #55). Named '*Exposure*' by its creator Antony Gormley, but known by most as '*De Poepende Man*' (translation probably unnecessary), the sculpture is the fruit of nearly six years' work that was beset by a catalogue of setbacks, including funding withdrawals and technical difficulties. The crouching man weighs 60 tonnes and if he stood up would be over 100 metres tall. If you stand next to the statue, you may just be able to peek over his feet. **Bus** 10 from Lelystad's main train station will take you to Batavia Stad bus stop, a 10-minute walk away from the sculpture.

URK AND SCHOKLAND

👍 | Back to Flevoland's routes

Before the Zuiderzee was drained, the islands of Urk and Schokland were really all that existed of the land that was to become Flevoland. Thus a visit to either of these places, which still exist as villages, is a step back through the corridors of history.

Urk used to be a small fishing island with a history going back at least 700 years. These days, it is very pleasant to stroll through the picturesque streets, past the neat and tidy fisherman's cottages of old. On Sundays, you can sometimes see a few of the older residents wearing the **traditional dress** of the town as they skitter off to church. The whole town gets dressed up in traditional costume for Ukerdag, usually held in May to commemorate the town's heritage. There is a **lighthouse** in the town (🏠 Vuurtorenstraat 80; ☎ 0527 681 582; 🖵 www.urk.nl), which can be visited during guided tours, and an interesting **museum** (🏠 Wijk 2; ☎ 0527 683 262) that tells the story of a culture that has mostly been lost.

Schokland was originally a medieval settlement, but under constant threat of flooding it was abandoned in the latter half of the 19th century. According to Dutch national statistics, just five people are registered as living in the area. Today Schokland is an important **archeological site** and host to the Schokland Museum (🏠 Middelbuurt 3; ☎ 0527 251 396; 🖵 www.schokland.nl).

It is easiest to visit Urk and Schokland with your own **car**. But, if you don't, you can reach both by public transport from Kampen, which is a short **train** ride away both from Zwolle and Lelystad. **Bus** 141 will take you to Urk and bus 681 to Schokland.

AFSLUITDIJK

👍 | Take a drive over the country's longest dyke

The Afsluitdijk is the reason that Flevoland exists in the state that it does. Without this extraordinary construction, most of the province would be underwater and the sea would come and go as it pleased.

The dyke was constructed between 1927 and 1933, connecting the former island of Wieringen to Friesland (Wieringen had been joined to the mainland of North Holland by a similar causeway only a few years earlier, in 1924).

What better way to experience and understand the great prowess of Dutch engineering than by taking a drive over the dyke between North Holland and Friesland? You'll see the IJsselmeer on one side and the Wadden Sea on the other.

The German army attempted to take control of the Afsluitdijk in May 1940, but was unsuccessful. However, this setback ultimately turned out to be insignificant and they were able to overrun the country anyway.

OOSTVAARDERSLAND

🏠 | Flevoland's natural beauty

Flevoland's natural reserve, considered to be one of the finest in the country, is definitely worth visiting.

The 56-square-kilometre park is in a *polder* that was created in 1968, and rapidly developed into a lush wetland.

A large number of birds can be spotted in the area, as well as a variety of herbivores, including the Polish Konik pony and red deer. Park rangers deliberately introduced these herbivores to the park in order to replicate the type of ecosystem that would have existed in such an area before human disturbance.

Unfortunately, the confined nature of the reserve and lack of shelter means that a large number of animals die each year. If the ecosystem was truly the work of Mother Nature, then the herbivores would be able to migrate away from the over-grazed areas in the winter, to find shelter and forage elsewhere. But, since the reserve has been fenced off, their ability to seek shelter as they would in a natural environment is limited, and this is why so many of them die.

To deal with this problem, plans are afoot to link Oostvaardersland with other national reserves in the country through a series of corridors. This would allow animals to move freely with the changing of the seasons. Such a scheme could also be extended to link up with reserves in other countries, such as Germany.

A new nature activity centre is expected to open in the park in 2013. Check 🖵 www.flevoland.nl for latest details.

The Oostvaardersplassen visitor centre can be found at 🏠 Kitsweg 1, Lelystad.

The easiest way to visit Oostvaardersland is with your **own transport**. The small town of Almere is on the outskirts of the park and reachable with a direct **train** from The Hague (journey time one hour). You might want to consider taking your bike to Almere and cycling from there.

Flevoland

UTRECHT

👍 | A pretty city rich in history

Canals, cobbled streets, old well-preserved houses and its beautiful cathedral make Utrecht a lovely place to spend a few days.

Utrecht is a good alternative to Amsterdam as a place to spend **Queen's Day**, which from 2014 will be King's Day, since it is far less crowded but still very picturesque.

Utrecht is home to one of the oldest and most prestigious **universities** in the country.

The main canal running through Utrecht, **Oudegrecht**, is particularly striking in that a large part of it is some distance below street level. This is because of high walls that were put in place to prevent flooding. Unfortunately, these walls made it impossible to load or unload canal boats at street level. The solution was to build wharves as a second street at water level. Some of the wharves are still in use for loading and unloading ships, but most of them have been turned into terraces for the many restaurants and cafés that run alongside the canal.

Utrecht is easy to reach from The Hague. **Trains** run there every 10 to 15 minutes throughout the day, either direct or with a short change in Gouda. The journey takes around 40 minutes.

Canal cruises and tours

A lovely way of exploring Utrecht is along the waterways. Two companies that offer **river cruises** are Schuttevaer (💻 www.schuttevaer. com) and Rederij De Ster (💻 www. rederijdester.nl). Tours last around an hour. Alternatively, you could rent a pedalo from Canal Company (💻 www.canal.nl) or a canoe from Kanoverhuur Utrecht (💻 kanoverhuurutrecht.nl). For something really different, you can arrange to be ferried on an Italian-style gondolier through the waterways of Utrecht. Prices are high though: €100 for an hour, plus extra for wine and snacks. De Rijnstroom (💻 www. rijnstroom.nl) offers day trips outside of Utrecht, to the castles of Amelisweerd, Ridderhofstad Rhijnauwen and Beverweerd.

City walks are organised every Sunday at 2pm from 🏠 Domplein 9 by Gilde Utrecht (💻 www. gildeutrecht.nl). The walks last around one hour and cost €5. You don't need to book in advance and can just turn up.

What to see

The cathedral is an impressive structure with a looming tower that seems to follow you around, wherever you go in Utrecht. The cathedral has some magnificent stained glass windows, but only in places: many of the windows are plain and nondescript. You can climb the tour for €8; buy tickets at the tourist office nearby (🏠 Domplein 9-12; 💻 www.domtoren.nl)

For children, there is the Juliana Park, which includes a petting farm, open in the afternoons on Wednesday, Saturday and Sunday.

On the outskirts of Utrecht (12 km from the centre) there is one of the most stunning castles of the Netherlands: De Haar castle (🏠 Kasteellaan 1; 💻 www.kasteeldehaar.nl). It's not easy to get to the castle by public transport. Take bus 127 from Vleuten station in the direction of

Kockengen and get off at the Kasteel Haarzuilens stop. From there, the castle is a 15 minute walk.

OUDEWATER

 Prove that you're not a witch

Located 25 km from Utrecht, Oudewater has a fascinating history. Hundreds of years ago, it was the only place in the Low Countries that was officially allowed to issue certificates that could save people from being convicted of witchcraft.

People from all over Europe — at least, those that could afford it — would descend on the town, desperate to avoid being burnt at the stake by proving that they were not engaged in witchcraft.

To prove that people were not a witch, the authorities of Oudewater would weigh them. As everyone knows, a true witch has no soul and therefore weighs significantly less than a non-witch. If a witch was too heavy, she would also not be able to fly on her broomstick.

A small museum (🏠 Leeuweringerstraat 2; ☎ 0348 563 400; 🖥 www.heksenwaag.nl) houses the original pair of scales that was used to weigh witches, dating from 1482. A visit to the museum includes an audiovisual presentation and exhibition about witch-hunting, in both English and Dutch. Afterwards, visitors can weigh themselves on the official scales to prove that they are not witches. You'll receive a certificate attesting to this.

Apart from the museum, the town is a pleasant place in which to have a stroll. You'll notice extremely tiny houses and old well-preserved architecture. There are a few nice cafés that have a lovely local atmosphere (at least, outside of tourist season), some local shops and good places to eat.

There is no **train** station in the town, but it is reachable by **bus**. From Gouda take bus 180 and get off at Molenwal stop in Oudewater (20 minutes). From Utrecht, take bus 180 (40 minutes).

Utrecht

The southernmost province of the Netherlands has a distinctive character, particularly affected by shifting Dutch, French and German influences. It even has its own language, Limburgish, which is still in active use in the province.

You'll notice the scenery change in Limburg, too. Gone is the drab flatness of the other parts of the country, to be replaced by hills. It is here that you'll find Vaalserberg (p268), the highest point in the European part of the Netherlands, rising to a rather modest 322.7 metres.

MAASTRICHT

👍 A wonderful city for gastronomy

The capital of the region is a city steeped in history, culture and local folklore. Picturesque squares, romantic streets, historical buildings and good cuisine make this a great place for spending a long weekend.

Maastricht is a popular university city with a growing international student population.

The city is where, in 1992, European leaders signed the Maastricht Treaty, which ultimately led to the creation of the euro.

Maastricht is situated on both sides of the Meuse river. The centre is compact and easy to explore on foot. Much of it has been pedestrianised and tourist attractions are relatively close to one another.

The old St. Servaas bridge links the old town with more modern neighbourhoods and with the central train station.

Maastricht is a mere two and a half hour train ride away from The Hague, with direct trains running throughout the day.

Tours

The tourist office (🏠 Kleine Straat 1) organises **city walking tours** in Dutch, English and German. A fortress city walking tour is also available. Prices start at €6.

Rederij Stiphout (🖥 www.stiphout.nl) organises **boat tours** from Maaspromenade 58, costing between €7.50 and €12.75. The same company also organises guided tours of Maastricht in old yellow school buses.

Events

Many agree that Maastricht is the best place to come to see Carnival (🖥 www.carnavalinmaastricht.nl), held in February just before Lent. People dress up, paint their faces and create floats for the parades. Thousands of people descend on the city. There is now even a 'Carnival Maastricht' app that you can download for your smartphone.

Maastricht is the hometown of world-famous violinist and conductor Andre' Rieu. He often puts on **concerts** in the city, usually in July. Check his website — 🖥 www.andrerieu.com — for the latest agenda and for purchasing tickets

The largest **gastronomy festival** in the Netherlands is held in Maastricht during the last week of August. The festival, known as Preuvenemint (🖥 www.preuvenemint.n) is held in the central Vrijthof square, where visitors get the chance to taste all sorts of produce, both local and exotic, and enjoy a variety of live music.

Maastricht aan Tafel (⌨ www. maastrichtaantafel) is another gastronomic event held in the city. The name comes from what the Dutch will exclaim when calling people for dinner.

What to see

Maastricht is best explored by throwing your map away and ambling through the streets in your own time. Here are some tips on what to look out for.

The city still has many old fortifications, including the **oldest city gate in the Netherlands** (🏠 Sint Bernardusstraat 1), built in 1229. The name of the gate, Helpoort, means 'Hell's Gate'.

A large part of Maastricht's cultural heritage is actually **underground**. Tickets to this hidden part of the city cost €5.25 and are available from ⌨ www. maastrichtunderground.nl

Book-lovers will appreciate the amazing Selexyz shop in the town, which is housed in a fabulous **13th century Dominican church** (🏠 Dominikanerkerkstraat 1).

Maastricht boasts a few lovely town squares.

Vrijthof is home to Sint-Servaas Church and Sint-Jan's Cathedral, and has many bars, cafés and restaurants. The city's main theatre, with a neoclassical façade is also here.

Markt is home to the 17th century town hall and, on Wednesday and Friday mornings, a small market.

Onze Lieve Vrouweplein is a pleasant and picturesque tree-lined square with an abundance of pavement cafés. The 11th century church Basilica of Our Lady is also to be found here.

Where to eat

Beaumont (🏠 Wycker Brugstraat 2; ☎ 043 325 4433; ⌨ www.beaumontrestaurant.nl) offers classy French-style fine dining, conveniently close to the station. Despite the large size of the dining hall, the place gets very busy in the evenings and you must book in advance.

Pêt Thai (🏠 Boschstraat 93; ☎ 043 326 1026; ⌨ www.petthai. nl) is a wonderful Thai restaurant in the heart of the city, offering sumptuous dishes and great service. Décor is nothing special and the place isn't terribly big, so you really should book ahead. The spiciness of the food is indicated with a number of chillies on the menu, but when they say hot they really do mean it!

Teazone (🏠 Koestraat 9; ☎ 043 311 3246; ⌨ www.teazone.nl) is a splendid treasure trove of exotic paraphernalia. Sitting at the low tables, you feel very much as though you are in an enchanting attic that hasn't been explored for decades rather than a tea room. You can browse through the stuff if you wish, since much of it is for sale, but prices are rather on the high side. A tremendous variety of tea is on offer. Perhaps best to avoid the more expensive special teas, since they aren't really that special and the others are much more interesting. The vegetarian dishes are particularly recommended.

Spice of India (🏠 Achter het Vleeshuis 27; ☎ 043 321 6375; ⌨ www.spiceofindia.nl) is a fairly small restaurant but with delicious Indian cooking.

AROUND ROERMOND

👍 | Limburg's natural beauty

Limburg has an abundance of nature spots for hiking and cycling.

In the east of the province, just the other side of the city of Roermond, you'll find the **Meinweg National Park** (💻 www.np-demeinweg.nl). The park is a popular spot for cyclists, although there are more ups-and-downs here than you will find in other regions of the country. Bicycles can be rented from Roermond train station (☎ 047 535 0085) and Piet Daemen in Vlodrop (🏠 Tussen de Bruggen 10; ☎ 0475 401 727).

On the west of Roermond, you'll find **Maasplasen**, the largest area for water sports in the Netherlands. The lakes were artificially created in the 20th century.

VAALSERBERG

 | The highest point in the Netherlands.

Vaalserberg is the highest point in the Netherlands, or at least that part of the country that is within Europe. Parts of the Dutch Antilles, an archipelago in the Caribbean, are higher.

The 322.7 metre hill can be found on the border between the Netherlands, Belgium and Germany. The countryside is very pretty and the views rewarding.

The nearest town to Vaalserberg is Vaals. Vaals doesn't have a train station but **bus** 50 runs there from Maastricht (journey time 40 minutes).

NEDERWEERT

 | Pretty town — great ice-cream.

Limburg is well-known for ice-cream parlours, and there are several rather good ones dotted throughout the province. But by far the best one that your researchers were able to discover was the **Florence Ijssalon** in Nederweert (🏠 Brugstraat 23; ☎ 0495 626 178; 💻 www.ijssalonflorence.nl). It offers a terrific variety of elaborate desserts and it is worth going out of your way just to sample one of them. The town is lovely to visit, too.

The easiest way to get to Nederweert is with your **own transportation**, but you can also take **bus** 82 from Roermond (journey time 40 minutes) or bus 61 from nearby Weert (journey time 15 minutes). **Trains** run from The Hague to both Roermond and Weert, with a change in Utrecht.

Zeeland

Zeeland, the western-most province of the Netherlands, consists of a number of islands that are now inter-linked by a network of bridges and tunnels.

Much of the province lies below sea level and has been reclaimed by inhabitants over the years.

THE DELTAWORKS

👍 | An important part of the Netherlands' struggle against the water.

For centuries, Zeeland was prone to serious flooding, which washed away farmland and destroyed livelihoods. Then came along the Deltaworks (💻 www.deltawerken.com), a massive construction project that was started shortly after the devastating North Sea flood of 1953. There hasn't been any serious flooding since.

A number of the Delta works are open for the public to visit: the Haringvlietdam, the Maeslantkering, the Western Scheldte Tunnel and the Oosterscheldekering. You can cycle or walk around the area, or drive over the dams and dykes by car.

MIDDELBURG

👍 | Great base for exploring the southern peninsula of Zeeland. Great cycling country.

Modern Middelburg has preserved much of its historic and picturesque character. There are lavish 17th and 18th century merchant houses and storehouses standing alongside pretty canals.

The town is fairly low-key and on Sundays can feel a bit deserted.

Middelburg doesn't have a tourist office but they do have a website: 💻 www.visitmiddelburg.nl.

Middelburg's **Abbey** (💻 Abdij 9), from 1127, is worth seeing. It was severely bombed during the second world war, but has now been restored to its original form. There are three **churches** nearby: the Nieuwe Kerk, the Koorkerk and the Lange Jan. All have their own distinctive character. The Lange Jan has a tower that you can climb up (💻 www.langejanmiddelburg.nl).

There is a weekly **market** on Thursdays in the main square.

Direct trains run from The Hague to Middelburg, taking two hours.

There are a number of options for **eating** in the town.

De Geere (🏠 Langeviele 51; ☎ 0118 613 083; 💻 www.cafedegeere.nl) is a small *eetcafé*, serving delectable sandwiches, Spanish gaspacho and Italian pasta dishes. Atmosphere friendly and food very good.

De Gouden Bock (🏠 Damplein 17; ☎ 011 861 7484; 💻 www.degoudenbock.nl) serves fish dishes and salads.

Het Hof (🏠 Vlasmarkt 20; ☎ 011 861 7972; 💻 www.kaffeethof.nl) is a pub that serves bar snacks as well as proper meals.

Di-vers (🏠 Vlasmarkt 13; 💻 basdi-vers.weebly.com) is to be noted for employing people with mental disabilities, but the good is also rather good. Choose between a two-course meal for €15 or a three-course meal for €19. The cuisine is Mediteranean-themed.

For **sleeping**, Hotel aan de Dam (🏠 Dam 3; 🖵 www.hotelaandedam.nl) is centrally located in an historical building, providing free wi-fi and a garden terrace. Guesthouse 1560 (🏠 Kinderdijk 20; 🖵 www.guesthouse1560.com) is in a 16th century townhouse, with a lovely courtyard, beautiful for taking breakfast during sunny summer days.

VEERE

🖵 | Photo 61

👍 | A simply charming Dutch village to get away from it all. Best if you have your own transport.

This delightful historical village is built on the edge of an inland lagoon, Veerse Meer. Its cobbled streets and lovely old buildings are definitely worth a wander round. On one side of the village there is a boat filled canal that links the Veerse Meer to the Netherlands' network of canals.

Veere obtained city rights in 1353. It was once a fishing town, but the small marina now mostly provides mooring for yachts.

The waterfront has retained its old dyke, which is still lined with old cannons that once provided defences for the town.

The town is a very popular tourist destination for the French and Belgians, and you'll find most menus have a French translation.

The **sea resort** of Dombourg, 14 km along the coast from Veere, is popular for its beaches, picturesque villages and lively shopping streets.

The **tourist office** can be found at: 🏠 Oudestraat 28; 🖵 www.vvvzeeland.nl.

For restaurants,

De Peperboom (🏠 Kapellestraat 11; ☎ 011 850 1307; 🖵 www.peperboom.nl) is a very good **restaurant** with reasonable price. It is conveniently located near the town centre.

For **sleeping**, De Campveerse Toren (🏠 Kaai 2; 🖵 www.campveersetoren.nl) is a more upmarket place, located in a beautiful area with a great panorama (make sure you ask to be seated in the tower). This is actually where William of Orange and Charlotte of Bourbon were wed in 1575. A three-course meal costs €45. The food is not always up to expectations but generally good.

The town is very popular for camping during the summer months. Minicamping De Veerse Pot (🏠 Polredijk 2) is small but conveniently-located. It is on the edge of the estuary and just 2 km from the centre of Veere. Prices start at €4.

There are also some B&B options. For example: **Bed en Brood** (🏠 Kerkstraat 7; 🖵 www.bed-en-brood.nl).

Veere is located 7 km north of Middelburg. There are no **trains** to get there, but there is an easy well-signposted cycle route from Middelburg. **Bus** 54 also goes there, but the buses are not very frequent. They pass every hour during peak time, and every two hours off-peak.

VLISSINGEN

👍 | Popular seaside resort — busy in summer

The pleasant seaside town of Vlissingen can trace its origin back to 620, when it was then a small fishing community on the edge of the North Sea. It was granted city rights in 1315.

The name Vlissingen actually means 'Flushing' in English, although the exact origin of the name is unclear. One possibility is that it is derived from the Dutch word for tides, *vles*. Another story holds that the town's name is based on the corruption of the Dutch word for bottle, *flesse*, fishermen invariably being the drinkers that they are.

These days, Vlissingen is a fairly laid-back port town — deceptively so, given that it is in actual fact the third-largest port in the country, after Rotterdam and Amsterdam.

In the summer, Vlissingen really comes into its own and is a popular destination for Dutch sun-seekers. With some nice beeches and small-town charm, it unsurprisingly can become quite busy in the summertime.

But in the winter you may find it eerily quiet. Due to its location and exposure, it can get quite cold too!

In the 17th century Vlissingen was a main harbour for ships of the Dutch East India Company (VOC).

Vlissingen has produced an illustrious band of seamen, foremost among whom is the great Michiel De Ruyter, who commanded navy battles against the British and the French in the 17th century. A statue of him stands near the harbour.

There is an **amusement arcade** on the waterfront: Carousel Casino (🖵 www.carrousel-amusement.nl). They have a range of arcade machines plus a number of air hockey tables. The prizes you win are in the forms of tokens, redeemable for merchandise within the casino.

If you want to **eat** in the town, there is a good Chinese restaurant, try Da Xin (🏠 Beursplein 5; ☎ 011 841 4766; 🖵 www.da-xin.nl). You can either opt for the a-la-carte menu (expect to pay around €13 per dish) or the buffet (€18 for eating as much as you want). With the buffet, you not only get pre-prepared dishes. You can also order dishes that are stir fried in front of you. Simply choose your vegetables, as well as what meat or fish you want, and the Chinese chef will do the rest. In the evenings the restaurant also does take-away. Service can be slow, though.

Bed By The Sea (🏠 Spuistraat 59; ☎ 0118 411 611; 🖵 www.hotelbedbythesea.com) is a small and homely **place to stay** not far from the sea. There is free wi-fi throughout the hotel and all rooms have a private bathroom. Some rooms also have a balcony. Due to the size of the hotel, it is best to book ahead if you want to stay here.

Direct **trains** run twice an hour from The Hague, taking a little over two hours.

Language

With English so widely-spoken in the Netherlands, you may consider attempting to learn Dutch to be an unnecessary endeavour. But there are some advantages to being able to speak the language.

It allows you to become truly immersed in Dutch culture, to travel around remoter areas and crucially, to understand official documents such as tax returns and housing contracts.

The locals love to say that learning their language is difficult, but in fact it is no harder to learn than any other European language. The only thing that makes it so challenging is that everyone appears determined to speak English, even if you attempt to communicate in Dutch. The Dutch are just trying to be helpful, but if you are learning the language and really want to practise, their accommodating gesture can be immensely frustrating. You just need to persevere and your efforts will eventually be rewarded. The Dutch may speak good English, but they still appreciate it when their language is acknowledged.

This chapter gives you a foundation in Dutch, using phrases and scenarios that might be immediately useful to you when you arrive in the country. Audio files to accompany this chapter can be downloaded at 🖥 www.thecitytrail.com/audiofile. You might also consider taking a course in Dutch whilst in the country (p45).

DUTCH AROUND THE WORLD

If you tell Dutch friends that you are learning their native language, you will probably be confronted at first by bewilderment and then appreciation. The truth is that Dutch isn't spoken by all that many people around the world, and few people choose to learn it as a foreign language.

The majority of Dutch speakers come from the Netherlands and northern Belgium (Flanders), where the language is called Flemish. In total, there are approximately 23 million people in the two countries who speak the language, which makes Dutch the seventh language of the European Union.

You will find Flemish (and some regional dialects in the south of the Netherlands) to be smoother and less guttural than the different language types spoken in The Hague and further north.

Dutch is still the official language of Suriname, despite the fact that 40% of the country do not speaking it as their mother tongue.

Afrikaans, spoken in South Africa, is a derivative of Dutch and sounds very similar to how the language would have been spoken hundreds of years ago.

SPELLING AND PRONUNCIATION

Dutch spelling is quite easy compared to many other languages because it is based on some fairly fundamental principles that don't tend to vary all that much. The same goes for the conjugation of Dutch regular verbs.

Once you know the conjugation rules, you can conjugate any Dutch verb. Irregular verbs, however, must be learned by heart.

For some, mastering Dutch pronunciation can be something of a challenge, whilst others may find it relatively easy. This often depends on where you come from. The guttural 'g' is easier for Spanish or Arabic speakers than for English or Japanese speakers. The double vocals 'ui', 'eu' and 'uu' are quite difficult.

GRAMMAR

Personal pronouns (persoonlijke voornaamwoorden)

ik	I
jij	you
u	you (formal)
hij	he
zij	she
wij	we
jullie	you
zij	they

Possessive pronouns (bezittelijke voornaamwoorden)

mijn	mine	*Waar is mijn boek?*	Where is my book?
jouw	your	*Is dat jouw boek?*	Is that your book?
uw	your (formal)	*Is dat uw boek?*	Is that your book?
zijn	his	*Waar is zijn hoed?*	Where is his hat?
haar	her	*Waar is haar tas?*	Where is her bag?
ons/ onze (het)/ (de)	our	*Waar is ons huis?* *Waar is onze hond?*	Where is our house? Where is our dog?
jullie	your	*Meneer en Mevrouw, Roberts, is dat jullie auto?*	Mr and Mrs Roberts, is this your car?
hun	their	*Waar is hun huis?*	Where is their house?

THE GREEN BOOKLET

The Green Booklet (*Het Groene Boekje*) is the official list of words that exist in the Dutch language, including the article that accompanies these words (which is not always published in other dictionaries). The Green Booklet is maintained by the Dutch Language Union (*Nederlandse Taalunie*). The Green Booklet is published in the Netherlands by Sdu (🖳 www.sdu.nl) and in Flanders by Lannoo (🖳 www.lannoo.be). It is available as a paper edition and on CD Rom. There is also a free Internet version of the list (🖳 woordenlijst.org).

Articles (lidwoorden)

There are three articles to learn: the indefinite article 'een' (a) and the definite articles 'de' and 'het' (the). The 'de' article is also used for the plural of both forms.

	de-nouns	*het*-nouns
	de	het
singular	de man	het huis
	(the man)	(the house)
	de	de
plural	de mannen	de huizen
	(the men)	(the houses)

Unfortunately, there is no way of knowing which article the noun has; you simply have to learn this. If in doubt, consult the Green Booklet (see box).

In composite words the article used depends on the second word. For example:

> *badkamer -> de kamer -> de badkamer* (the bathroom)
> *tekstboek -> het boek -> het tekstboek* (the textbook)

Demonstratives (aanwijzende voornaamwoorden)

The Dutch demonstrative pronouns are: '*dit*' (this), '*deze*' (this, these), '*dat*' (that), and '*die*' (that, those). In order to know which to use, you must know which article the word has.

For example:

Het-nouns -> *dit / dat*
| *dit huis (deze huizen)* | this house (these houses) |
| *dat huis (die huizen)* | that house (those houses) |

De-nouns -> *deze / die*
| *Deze hond (deze honden)* | this dog (these dogs) |
| *Die hond (die honden)* | that dog (those dogs) |

Colours (de kleuren)

zwart	black	*rood*	red
blauw	blue	*wit*	white
bruin	brown	*roze*	pink
groen	green	*geel*	yellow
oranje	orange	*paars*	purple

Comparative and superlative (trappen van vergelijking)

In English a few adjectives form comparatives and superlatives by adding '-er' and '-(e)st'. Dutch follows the same pattern.

klein — kleiner — kleinst	small — smaller — smallest
groot — groter — grootst	big — bigger- biggest
lief — liever — liefst	sweet — sweeter — sweetest

Adjectives that end in '-r' require a 'd' before the comparative suffix:

duur — duurder — duurst	expensive — more expensive — the most expensive
raar — raarder — raarst	strange — stranger — the strangest

As in English a few adjectives have irregular forms:

goed — beter — best	good — better — best
weinig — minder — minst	few — fewer — fewest
veel — meer — meest	many — more — most

The present

The **present** is formed by adding an appropriate ending to the stem, depending on the subject. No ending is required in the first-person. For the second- or third-person singular, you should add a 't'. In the plural, you generally add 'en' (although there are exceptions if the stem ends in a vowel).

The stem of a verb is found by dropping the 'en' or 'n' at the end of the infinitive. For example, the stem of '*werken*' (to work) is '*werk*'.

Ik	werk
Jij/hij/u/zij	werk**t**
Wij/jullie/zij	werk**en**

The stem can never end with two of the same consonants, so the extra consonant should always be removed. For example, the stem of '*rennen*' (to run) would be '*ren*' and not '*renn*'.

Language

A stem can never end with either a 'v' or a 'z'. The 'v' turns into an 'f' and the 'z' turns into an 's'. For example, the stem of '*verven*' (to paint) is '*verf*', whilst the stem of '*reizen*' (to travel) is '*reis*'. However, note that the 'v' or 'z' returns in the plural. So it would be '*wij verven*' (we paint) and not '*wij verfen*'.

The present continuous

The present continuous is used to indicate an action that is still taking place. For example, in English, one might say 'I am singing'.

The typical way to form the present continuous in Dutch is simply to use the present. So, '*Ik zing*' can mean 'I am singing', 'I sing' or 'I do sing', depending on the context.

You can also use a verb to indicate state — such as '*liggen*' (to lie), '*lopen*' (to walk), '*staan*' (to stand) or '*zitten*' (to sit) — plus 'te' followed by the infinitive of the verb that you want to use.

The present form of '*zijn*' (to be) can also be used to indicate the present continuous, as in the following examples:

Ik ben aan het fietsen	I'm riding the bike
U bent aan het eten	You are eating
Hij is aan het dansen	He is dancing
Wij zijn aan het praten	We are talking
Jullie zijn aan het drinken	You are drinking
Zij zijn aan het zwemmen	They are swimming

The simple past

The easiest way to form the past tense is simply to add the appropriate suffix to the stem of the word: '*te*' or '*de*' for all the persons in the singular and '*ten*' or '*den*' for the plural.

The precise ending depends on the exact consonant that the stem ends with. One trick is to consider the consonants contained in the phrase 'soft ketchup'. If the word has one of these consonants in, use the 'te/ten' ending, otherwise use 'de/den'. For example:

Ik praatte	I talked
Ik deelde	I shared

Unfortunately, there are many irregular verbs that must simply be learnt by heart.

The present perfect

Another way to talk about something in the past is to use the present tense of the verb 'to have' (*hebben*) or 'to be' (*zijn*), followed by a past participle. This works the same as in English — for example, 'I have heard' — and is used to express a past event that has present consequences.

In Dutch, the past participle is generally formed by adding the stem of the verb to the 'ge' prefix and then appending either a 't' or a 'd', according to the 'soft ketchup' rule (see previously). So, in the previous example, 'I have heard' would be '*Ik heb gehoord*'.

However, some verbs have an 'en' ending instead. For example, 'I have read' would be '*Ik heb gelezen*'.

Ik heb gehoord	I have heard
Ik heb gelezen	I have read

Future

Both English and Dutch form the future in the same way.

In Dutch, the English 'shall' or 'will' plus the infinitive becomes the present tense '*zullen*' plus infinitive. For example:

Wij zullen met de auto gaan   We will go by car

To be (zijn)

The verb 'to be' (*zijn*) is used in a similar fashion to how it is used in English.

It is used mostly as an auxiliary verb — i.e., to add additional meaning to another verb, as in the expression 'I am working today' — but it can also be used as a notional verb meaning 'to exist'.

The key forms of the verb are as follows:

Ik ben	I am
Jij bent / ben jij(*)	You are (informal, singular)
Hij, zij is	He, she is
U bent	You are (polite, singular or plural)
Wij zijn	We are
Jullie zijn	You are (informal, plural)
Zij zijn	They are

(*) In inverted sentences, such as questions, where the personal pronoun follows the verb, 'ben' (instead of 'bent') is used with 'jij'. For example, 'Jij bent een student' ('You are a student'), but 'Ben jij een student?' ('Are you a student?')

Word order in Dutch (woordvolgorde in het Nederlands)

A standard sentence in Dutch follows this basic structure:

Subject	Finite verb	Time	Manner	Place	Other verbs
Ik	*ga*	*vandaag*	*op de fiets*	*naar Amsterdam*	*rijden*

Language

In questions, and for any sentence that doesn't start with a subject, you will need to invert the order of the subject and the verb.

Regular	*Je gaat vandaag naar Amsterdam*	You go today to Amsterdam
Inverted	*Vandaag ga je naar Amsterdam*	Today you go to Amsterdam
Question	*Ga je vandaag naar Amsterdam?*	Do you go today to Amsterdam?

Subordinating conjunctions (onderschikkende bijzinnen)

Subordinating conjunctions are words that link sentences together. Here are some of the most common ones:

omdat	because	*voordat*	before
als	if	*nadat*	after
hoewel	although	*zodra*	as soon as
terwijl	while	*toen**	when

* Only if you are talking about the past.

The most important thing you have to remember is that the verb always comes at the end. For example:

Ik eet brood <u>omdat</u> ik honger heb	I eat bread because I'm hungry
Hij praat <u>terwijl</u> hij eet	He talks while eating
Zij gaat naar het feest <u>hoewel</u> ze erg moe is	She goes to the party although she is very tired

VOCABULARY

Basic phrases (basiszinnen)

Goededag	Good day
Goedemorgen	Good morning
Goedemiddag	Good afternoon
Goedenavond	Good evening
Goedenacht	Good night
Hoi	Hi
Hallo	Hello

Language

Dag / Doei	Bye
Tot ziens	Goodbye
Tot straks	See you later
Tot snel	See you soon
Dank je wel	Thank you
Graag gedaan	You're welcome
Ja	Yes
Nee	No
Hoe gaat het met je / u?	How are you?
Hoe oud ben je / bent u?	How old are you?
Ik ben … jaar oud	I am … years old
Wat zei je /u ?	What did you say?
Goed / heel goed	Good / very well
Hoe heet je?	What is your name?
Ik heet...	My name is…
Aangenaam	Nice to meet you
Waar komt u / kom je vandaan?	Where are you from?
Ik kom uit Engeland / Schotland / Frankrijk / Italië	I'm from England / Scotland / France / Italy
Waar woon je?	Where do you live?
Ik woon in Den Haag	I live in The Hague
Spreek je Engels?	Do you speak English?
Sorry, ik begrijp het niet	Sorry, I don't understand
Ik spreek niet zo goed Nederlands	I don't speak Dutch very well
Veel plezier!	Have fun!
Veel succes!	Good luck!
Wees voorzichtig!	Be careful!

Language

Numbers (getallen)

1	*één*	25	*vijfentwintig*
2	*twee*	30	*dertig*
3	*drie*	40	*veertig*
4	*vier*	50	*vijftig*
5	*vijf*	60	*zestig*
6	*zes*	70	*zeventig*
7	*zeven*	80	*tachtig*
8	*acht*	90	*negentig*
9	*negen*	100	*honderd*
10	*tien*	150	*honderdvijftig*
11	*elf*	200	*tweehonderd*
12	*twaalf*	300	*driehonderd*
13	*dertien*	400	*vierhonderd*
14	*veertien*	500	*vijfhonderd*
15	*vijftien*	600	*zeshonderd*
16	*zestien*	700	*zevenhonderd*
17	*zeventien*	800	*achthonderd*
18	*achttien*	900	*negenhonderd*
19	*negentien*	1000	*duizend*
20	*twintig*	2000	*twee duizend*

Expressing time (het uitdrukken van tijd)

een dag	a day
een week	a week
een maand	a month
een jaar	a year
de tijd	the time
vandaag	today
nu	now

later, straks	later
morgen	tomorrow
gisteren	yesterday
een maand geleden	a month ago
over een maand	in a month
overmorgen	the day after tomorrow
eergisteren	the day before yesterday

Days of the week (dagen van de week)

maandag	Monday
dinsdag	Tuesday
woensdag	Wednesday
donderdag	Thursday
vrijdag	Friday
zaterdag	Saturday
zondag	Sunday

Months (maanden)

januari	January
februari	February
maart	March
april	April
mei	May
juni	June
juli	July
augustus	August
september	September
oktober	October
november	November
december	December

Language

Questions (vraagwoorden)

Hoe?	How?
Waar?	Where?
Wie?	Who?
Wanneer?	When?
Wat?	What?
Waarom?	Why?
Hoeveel?	How much / how many?
Waar naartoe?	To where?
Van waar?	From where?
Hoeveel kost het?	How much does it cost?
Heb je Spa rood*?	Do you have sparkling water?
Ja, dat hebben we	Yes, we do.
Nee, dat hebben we niet	No, I'm afraid we don't.
Wat is dat?	What is that?
Hoe kom ik bij het station?	How do you get to the station?

Prepositions (voorzetsels)

in	in	*na*	after
uit	out	*voor*	before
aan	on	*voor, tegenover*	in front of
boven / op	above	*met*	with
onder	under	*links*	left
naast	next	*rechts*	right
dichtbij	near	*tussen*	between
ver	far	*tegenover*	across

Professions (beroepen)

directeur	director
manager	manager
dokter / arts	doctor
docent / leraar	teacher
verpleegster	nurse

vertaler	translator
vrijwilliger	volunteer
politieagent	police officer
advocaat	lawyer
rechter	judge
medewerker	employee
collega	colleague

Places (plaatsen, plekken)

café / bar / kroeg	café
bedrijf	company
ambassade	embassy
ziekenhuis	hospital
hotel	hotel
gemeentehuis	town hall
kantoor	office
politiebureau	police station
postkantoor	post office
supermarkt	supermarket
winkel	shop
restaurant	restaurant

Language

Feelings (gevoelens)

Ik heb honger	I am hungry
Ik heb dorst	I am thirsty
Ik zit vol / ik heb ge-noeg gegeten	I am full
Ik ben boos op jou	I am angry with you
Ik ben blij	I am happy
Ik ben verdrietig	I am sad
Ik heb geluk	I am lucky
Ik ben moe	I am tired
Ik ben misselijk	I feel sick
Ik ben ziek	I am ill
Ik ben slaperig	I am sleepy

Around the house (spullen in huis)

Keuken	Kitchen	Badkamer	Bathroom
koelkast	fridge	borstel	brush
vriezer	freezer	tandenborstel	toothbrush
schaal	bowl	tandpasta	toothpaste
lepel	spoon	deodorant	deodorant
mes	knife	scheerapparaat	electric razor
vork	fork	parfum	perfume
glas	glass	shampoo	shampoo
bord	plate	zeep	soap
eten	food	handdoek	towel
magnetron	microwave	wassen	to wash
oven	oven	drogen	to dry
gootsteen	sink	kam	comb

Eten en drinken	Food and drink	Meubels	Furniture
brood	bread	bed	bed
boter	butter	stoel	chair
sap	juice	bureau	desk
melk	milk	deur	door
koffie	coffee	bank	couch / sofa
thee	tea	spiegel	mirror
koekje	cookie	kussen	pillow
eieren	eggs	deken	blanket
uien	onions	laken	sheet
knoflook	garlic	tafel	table
aardappelen	potatoes	kast	closet
groenten	vegetables	lade	drawer
vlees	meat	televisie	television
kip	chicken	lamp	lamp
vis	fish	stapelbed	bunk bed
varkensvlees	pork	matras	mattress
rundvlees	beef	wasmachine	washing machine

Language

kaas	cheese	*afwasmachine*	dishwasher
zout	salt	*kledingkast*	wardrobe
peper	pepper	*wekker*	alarm
water	water	*stofzuiger*	vacuum cleaner
olie	oil		

SITUATION DIALOGUES

In de winkel	**In the shop**
Wie is er aan de beurt?	Who is next?
Ik.	I am.
Zegt u het maar.*	How can I help?
Ik wil graag 200 gram Goudse kaas, in plakken gesneden.	I would like 200 grams of Gouda, sliced.
Anders nog iets?	Is there anything else?
Ja, ik wil graag een fles volle melk en een heel brood.	Yes, I would like a bottle of whole milk and a loaf of bread.
Is dat alles?	Is that all?
Ja, dank u.	Yes, thank you.
Hoeveel is het bij elkaar?	How much is the total?
Dat is dan 10 euro.	That will be 10 euros.
Kan ik met een creditcard betalen?	Can I pay with credit card?
Ik ben bang van niet. Hier kunt u alleen pinnen**.	I am afraid not. We only accept debit cards.
Alstublieft***.	Here you are.
Bedankt. Wilt u een bon?	Thank you. Would you like a receipt?
Nee, dank u.	No, thank you.
Hier is uw wisselgeld.	Here is your change.
Bedankt. Dag.	Thank you. Goodbye.

Language

(*) In a clothes shop they would say '*Kan ik u helpen*'?

(**) Paying by debit card is a very common method of payment when you are out shopping, and there is even a verb ('*pinnen*') to indicate this in Dutch.

(***) '*Alstublieft*' literally means 'please', but it is often used when something is given to you, be that change in a shop or a product that you have just brought.

In het restaurant	**In the restaurant**
Goedenavond.	Good evening.
Ik heb gereserveerd voor twee.	I have a reservation for two.
Onder welke naam?	Under what name?
Meneer Roberts.	Mr Roberts
Loopt u met mij mee. Hier is uw tafel.	Please follow me. Here is your table.
Mag ik de menukaart?	May I see the menu, please?
Alstublieft.	Here it is.
Het staat allemaal in het Neder- lands. Heeft u de kaart ook in het Engels?	It is all in Dutch. Do you have a menu in English?
Nee, sorry. Die hebben we niet.	No, sorry. I'm afraid we don't.
Kunt u mij vertellen wat u heeft?	Could you please tell me what you have?
We hebben erwtensoep en hete kippenvleugeltjes of stamppot.	We have pea soup, hot chicken wings or *stamppot**.
Heeft u ook vis?	Do you have any fish?
Nee, sorry, dat is op.	No, sorry, it is finished.
Oké. Ik wil graag de soep en de stamppot.	Okay. I would like the soup and the *stamppot*.
Voor mij hetzelfde graag.	I'll have the same.
Om te drinken, willen we graag een fles rode wijn en een grote fles water.	For drinks, we'll have a bottle of red wine and a big bottle of water.
Alstublieft. Eet smakelijk.	Here you are. Have a nice meal.
Bedankt.	Thank you.
Na de maaltijd...	**After the meal...**
Mag ik de rekening, alstublieft?	May I have the bill, please?
Dat is dan vijfendertig euro.	It is 35 euros.
Dank u.	Thank you.
Tot ziens.	Goodbye.

(*) When asking for water in a restaurant, the Dutch very often refer to the popular brand Spa. Sparkling water is 'spa rood' and still is 'spa blauw'. The colour refers to the colour of the bottle sold by Spa. That doesn't actually means that the brand of water you are going to be served is Spa. A less common way to ask is: 'met bubbeltjes' ('with bubbles') and 'zonder bubbeltjes' ('without bubbles').

(**) Stamppot is a typical Dutch dish similar to the English bubble-and-squeak. See p105.

Telefonisch bestellen	Ordering by phone
Goedenavond. Pizzeria Da Gino. Met Andrea*.	Good evening, Pizzeria Da Gino. This is Andrea.
Goedenavond. Ik wil graag twee pizzas bestellen.	Good evening. I would like to order two pizzas.
Dat Kan. Welke pizza's wilt u?	No problem. Which pizzas would you like?
Een Hawaï en één Margherita met extra kaas.	One Hawaiian and one Margherita with extra cheese.
Wat is uw adres en telefoonnummer?	What's your address and telephone number?
Mijn adres is Prinsestraat 68 en mijn telefoonnummer is 06 0438 4923. Hoe lang duurt het?	My address is Prinsestraat 68 and my phone number is 06 0438 4923. How long will they be?
Ze worden binnen 30 minuten bezorgd.	They will be delivered in about 30 minutes.
Oké bedankt, dag.	Okay thank you, goodbye.

(*) When answering by phone, the Dutch start with the name of the company, followed by the name of the person answering the phone.

Een taxi nemen	Taking a taxi
Ik moet naar de Euromast in Rotterdam.	I need to get to the Euromast in Rotterdam.
Oké, stap maar in.	Please get in.
Hoeveel gaat het kosten?	How much does it cost?
Dat hangt van de meter af, maar het zal rond de 15 euro worden.	It depends on the metre, but it should be around 15 euros.
Hoe lang duurt de rit?	How long will the journey take?
Ongeveer 15 minuten.	About 15 minutes.
Oké, dan kom ik op tijd.	Great, then I will arrive on time.

Als de taxi er eenmaal is...	Once the taxi arrives...
Sorry, ik heb geen wisselgeld. Heeft u het gepast?	Sorry I don't have any change. Do you have the exact amount?
Alstublieft.	Here it is.
Bedankt. Dag.	Thank you. Goodbye.

Language

Naar de weg vragen

Meneer, mag ik u iets vragen?*

Natuurlijk / Jazeker.

Kunt u mij vertellen hoe ik naar het Centraal Station kom?

Volg deze weg en neem de eerste rechts. Sla bij de derde stoplichten af naar links en dan sta je voor het station.

Is het ver?

Het is ongeveer 15 minuten lopen. Je kan ook vier haltes met tram 17 gaan.

Perfect. Bedankt!

Asking directions

Excuse me, sir

Yes?

Could you tell me how to get to Centraal Station?

Continue along this road and take the first right. Turn left at the third set of traffic lights and the station will be in front of you.

Is it far?

It is about a 15-minute walk. You can also take tram 17 for four stops.

Perfect. Thank you!

(*) When stopping a stranger to ask something, you always ask permission to ask the question first.

Bij de huisarts

Goedemorgen. Ik heb een arts nodig.

Waarom? Wat is er aan de hand?

Ik heb koorts en een vreselijke hoofdpijn.

Oké, neemt u plaats. Als de dokter klaar is dan wordt u geroepen.

Dank u wel.

At the doctor's

Good morning. I need to see a doctor.

Why? What is the matter?

I have a fever and a terrible headache.

Okay, please have a seat. We will call you when the doctor is free.

Thank you.

Na een paar minuten...

Neemt u de tweede kamer links. Er wacht een dokter op u.

Zei u de tweede rechts?

Nee, de tweede links.

Oké bedankt.

After some minutes...

Please enter the second room on the left. A doctor is waiting for you.

Did you say the second on the right?

No, the second on the left.

Okay thanks.

In gesprek met de dokter...

Goedemorgen. Ik hoor dat u zich niet goed voelt.

Ja, dat klopt.

Speaking with the doctor...

Good morning. I was told you don't feel well.

Yes, that's right.

Sinds wanneer heeft u koorts?   How long have you had a fever for?

Sinds zaterdag, toen begon de hoofdpijn.   Since Saturday. That's when the headache started.

Oké, het lijkt op een normale griep. Ik raad u aan om te rusten en wat aspirientjes te nemen. Dan zult u zich na een tijdje zeker beter voelen.   Okay, it seems to be an ordinary case of flu. I suggest you get some rest and take some aspirins. You will feel better soon.

Oké, dat zal ik doen, bedankt.   Okay, I will, thank you.

VERB CONJUGATION

In this overview you will find the conjugation of the irregular verbs in the present, past tense, and present perfect tenses.

To work (werken)

Present	Present perfect	Past
Ik werk	ik heb gewerkt	Ik werkte
jij werkt	jij hebt gewerkt	Jij werkte
hij werkt	hij heeft gewerkt	Hij werkte
wij werken	wij hebben gewerkt	wij werkten
jullie werken	jullie hebben gewerkt	jullie werkten
zij werken	Zij hebben gewerkt	zij werkten

To be (zijn)

Present	Present perfect	Past
ik ben	*ik ben geweest*	*ik was*
jij bent	*jij bent geweest*	*jij was*
hij is	*hij is geweest*	*hij was*
wij zijn	*wij zijn geweest*	*wij waren*
jullie zijn	*jullie zijn geweest*	*jullie waren*
Zij zijn	*zij zijn geweest*	*zij waren*

To have (hebben)

Present	Present perfect	Past
ik heb	ik heb gehad	ik had
jij hebt	jij hebt gehad	jij had
hij heeft	hij heeft gehad	hij had
wij hebben	wij hebben gehad	wij hadden
jullie hebben	jullie hebben gehad	jullie hadden
zij hebben	zij hebben gehad	zij hadden

To go (gaan)

Present	Present perfect	Past
ik ga	ik ben gegaan	ik ging
jij gaat	jij bent gegaan	jij ging
hij gaat	hij is gegaan	hij ging
wij gaan	wij zijn gegaan	wij gingen
jullie gaan	jullie zijn gegaan	jullie gingen
zij gaan	zij zijn gegaan	zij gingen

To be allowed to (mogen)

Present	Present perfect	Past
ik mag	ik heb gemogen	ik mocht
jij mag	jij hebt gemogen	jij mocht
hij mag	hij heeft gemogen	hij mocht
wij mogen	wij hebben gemogen	wij mochten
jullie mogen	jullie hebben gemogen	jullie mochten
zij mogen	zij hebben gemogen	zij mochten

To be able to (kunnen)

Present	Present perfect	Past
ik kan	ik heb gekund	ik kon
jij kunt	jij hebt gekund	jij kon
hij kan	hij heeft gekund	hij kon
wij kunnen	wij hebben gekund	wij konden
jullie kunnen	jullie hebben gekund	jullie konden
zij kunnen	zij hebben gekund	zij konden

To become (worden)

Present	Present perfect	Past
ik word	ik ben geworden	ik werd
jij wordt	jij bent geworden	jij werd
hij wordt	hij is geworden	hij werd
wij worden	wij zijn geworden	wij werden
jullie worden	jullie zijn geworden	jullie werden
zij worden	zij zijn geworden	zij werden

Shall (zullen)

Present	Past
ik zal	ik zou
jij zult	jij zou
hij zal	hij zou
wij zullen	wij zouden
jullie zullen	jullie zouden
zij zullen	zij zouden

To do (doen)

Present	Present perfect	Past
ik doe	ik heb gedaan	ik deed
jij doet	jij hebt gedaan	jij deed
hij doet	hij heeft gedaan	hij deed
wij doen	wij hebben gedaan	wij deden
jullie doen	jullie hebben gedaan	jullie deden
zij doen	zij hebben gedaan	zij deden

To hit (slaan)

Present	Present perfect	Past
ik sla	ik heb geslagen	ik sloeg
jij slaat	jij hebt geslagen	jij sloeg
hij slaat	hij heeft geslagen	hij sloeg
wij slaan	wij hebben geslagen	wij sloegen
jullie slaan	jullie hebben geslagen	jullie sloegen
zij slaan	zij hebben geslagen	zij sloegen

To come (komen)

Present	Present perfect	Past
ik kom	ik ben gekomen	ik kwam
jij komt	jij bent gekomen	jij kwam
hij komt	hij is gekomen	hij kwam
wij komen	wij zijn gekomen	wij kwamen
jullie komen	jullie zijn gekomen	jullie kwamen
zij komen	zij zijn gekomen	zij kwamen

To see (zien)

Present	Present perfect	Past
ik zie	ik heb gezien	ik zag
jij ziet	jij hebt gezien	jij zag
hij ziet	hij heeft gezien	hij zag
wij zien	wij hebben gezien	wij zagen
jullie zien	jullie hebben gezien	jullie zagen
zij zien	zij hebben gezien	zij zagen

To stand (staan)

Present	Present perfect	Past
ik sta	ik heb gestaan	ik stond
jij staat	jij hebt gestaan	jij stond
hij staat	hij heeft gestaan	hij stond
wij staan	wij hebben gestaan	wij stonden
jullie staan	jullie hebben gestaan	jullie stonden
zij staan	zij hebben gestaan	zij stonden

Language

References

CULTURE

Undutchables by Colin White and Laurie Bouckie, 2010
An astonishingly popular book about Dutch culture and stereotypes. Whilst the book is on the ball in many areas, the writing and jibing appears a little callous at times. Still, it is a bestseller now in the sixth edition, and is widely read by the Dutch as well as foreigners, proving that the Dutch can laugh at themselves after all.

FICTION

Girl with a Pearl Earring by Tracy Chevalier, Harper, 1999
Acclaimed bestseller, now a motion picture, that fictionionalises the painting of *Girl With a Pearl Earring* by Dutch artist Johanne Vermeer's The story is one of an artist's desire for beauty.

FILM

Oorlogswinter
One of the most successful Dutch films of recent years, about a young Dutch boy that tries to help the resistence during the second world war.

INTERNATIONAL JUSTICE

Madame Prosecutor: Confrontations with Humanity's Worst Criminals and the Culture of Impunity by Carla Del Ponte and Chuck Sudetic, Other Press, 2009
Carla Del Ponte, former prosecutor of the International Criminal Tribunal for Yugoslavia, tells about her time prosecuting the very worst of humanity.
An introduction to the International Criminal Court by William Schabas, Cambridge University Press, 2011
If you want to get some idea of what this International Criminal Court

(ICC) is, then this book, written by an eminent law professor, provides a good foundation.
From Nuremberg to The Hague by Philippe Sands, Cambridge University Press, 2003
A collection of essays about the evolution of international justice.

TRAVEL

The Best Campsites in the Netherlands, Belgium and Luxembourg by Alan Rogers, Alan Rogers Guides Ltd., 2013
Camping is a wonderful way to explore the Benelux countries, and this book provides a comprehensive overview of the campsites that you can stay at.
Bicycle Touring Holland by Katherine Widing, Van Der Plas Publications, 2012
Books about bicycle touring in the Netherlands are a dime-a-dozen. This is not a bad one to try.
Inland Waterways of the Netherlands by Louise Busby and David Broad, Imray, Laurie, Norie & Wilson Ltd, 2008
For those planning a water-based tour of the country.

THE HAGUE

Architectural Guide to The Hague by Gonda Buursma, Uitgeverij, 2008
A book really only for those that are seriously into their architecture. A knowledgeable and comprehensive overview.

HISTORY

The Diary of a Young Girl by Anne Frank, Puffin, 2007
First published in 1947, this iconic masterpiece of Nazi oppression is a must-read for anyone interested in this dark episode of Europe's history.

The diary was published from writings
that Anne Frank made herself whilst
hiding with her family from the Nazis.

**The Embarrassment of Riches,
Harper Perennial, 2004**

A riveting account of the Dutch
Golden Age and how such an eclectic mix of cultures and communities
transformed themselves into one of
Europe's most formidable economic
powerhouses.

POLITICS

**Murder in Amsterdam: The Death
of Theo van Gogh and the Limits of
Tolerance by Ian Buruma, 2007**

A gripping read, delving into the murder of controversial film maker Theo
Van Gogh and what his death meant
for the rest of Dutch society.

Listings

EMBASSIES AND CONSULATES

Argentina
🏠 Javastraat 20; ☎ 070 311 84 11;
🖥 www.epbaj.mrecic.gov.ar

Australia
🏠 Carnegielaan 4; ☎ 070 310 8200;
🖥 www.netherlands.embassy.gov.au

Belgium
🏠 Alexanderveld 97; ☎ 070 312
34 56; 🖥 diplomatie.belgium.be/
netherlands

Bulgaria
🏠 Duinroosweg 9 ; ☎ 070 350 3051;
🖥 www.mfa.bg

Canada
🏠 Sophialaan 7 ; ☎ 070 311 1600;
🖥 www.canada.nl

Croatia
🏠 Amaliastraat 16; ☎ 070 363 2942;
🖥 nl.mfa.hr

Czech Republic
🏠 Paleisstraat 4; ☎ 070 313 0011;
🖥 www.mzv.cz/hague

Denmark
🏠 Koninginnegracht 30; ☎ 070 302
5959; 🖥 nederlandene.um.dk;

Finland
🏠 Groot Hertoginnelaan 16; ☎ 070
346 9754; 🖥 www.finlande.nl,

France
🖥 www.ambafrance-nl.org

Germany
🏠 Groot Hertoginnelaan 18-20;
☎ 070 342 0600; 🖥 www.den-haag.
diplo.de

Greece
🏠 Amaliastraat 1; ☎ 070 365 2343;
🖥 www.greekembassy.nl

Hungary
🏠 Hogeweg 14; ☎ 070 350 0404;
🖥 www.hungarianembassy.nl

Indonesia
🏠 Tobias Asserlaan 8; ☎ 070 346
9771; 🖥 www.indonesia.nl

Ireland
🏠 Scheveningseweg 112; ☎ 070 363
0993; 🖥 www.embassyofireland.nl

Israel
🏠 Buitenhof 47; ☎ 070 376 0500;
🖥 www.israel.nl

Italy
🏠 Alexanderstraat 12; ☎ 070 302
1030; 🖥 www.ambaja.esteri.it

Japan
🏠 Tobias Asserlaan 2; ☎ 070 346
9544; 🖥 www.nl.emb-japan.go.jp

Kenya:
🏠 Nieuwe Parklaan 21; ☎ 070 350
4215; 🖥 www.kenyanembassy-nl.
com

Latvia
🏠 Balistraat 88; ☎ 070 306 5000;
🖥 www.am.gov.lv/lv/netherlands

Luxemburg
🏠 Nassaulaan 8; ☎ 070 360 7516;
🖥 lahaye.mae.lu

New Zeeland
🏠 Eisenhowerlaan 77N; ☎ 070 346
9324; 🖥 www.nzembassy.com/
netherlands

Poland
🏠 Alexanderstraat 25; 🖥 haga.msz.
gov.pl; ☎ 070 7990100

Portugal
🏠 Zeestraat 74 (Consular: Ba-
zarstraat 1); ☎ 070 363 0217

Romania
🏠 Catsheuvel 55; ☎ 070 3223 613;
haga.mae.ro

Russia
🏠 Andries Bickerweg 2; ☎ 070 346
8888; 🖥 www.rusembassy.nl

South Africa
🏠 Wassenaarweg 40; ☎ 070 392
4501; 🖥 www.zuidafrika.nl

Spain
🏠 Lange Voorhout 50; ☎ 070 302
4999; 🖥 www.maec.es/embajadas/
lahaya

Sweden:
🏠 Jan Willem Frisolaan 3; ☎ 070 412
0200; 🖥 www.swedenabroad.com/
en-GB/Embassies/The-Hague

Switzerland
🏠 Lange Voorthout 42; ☎ 070 364
2831; 🖥 www.eda.admin.ch/denhaag

United Kingdom
🏠 Lange Voorhout 10; ☎ 070 427
0427; 🖥 ukinnl.fco.gov.uk

United States
🏠 Lange Voorhout 102;
☎ 0703102209; 🖥 thehague.usembassy.gov

EMERGENCY

Police, Ambulance, Fire brigade (emergency)
☎ 112
Police (non-emergency)
☎ 0900 8844
International Card Services
☎ 020 660 0611
Gas & Electricity
☎ 0800 9009
Sea Rescue / Coast Guard
☎ 0900 0111
Tourist Medical Service
☎ 020 592 3355
Breakdown Service (ANWB)
☎ 088 2692 888
Animal Ambulance
☎ 034 352 1751

HOSPITALS (DELFT)

Reinier de Graaf Groep
☎ 015 260 3060; 🖥 www.rdgg.nl

HOSPITALS (LEIDEN)

Leids Universitair Medisch Centrum
☎ 071 526 9111; 🖥 www.lumc.nl

HOSPITALS (THE HAGUE)

MCH Westeinde
☎ 070 330 2000; 🖥 www.mchaaglanden.nl
HagaZiekenhuis
☎ 070 210 0000; 🖥 www.hagaziekenhuis.nl
Ziekenhuis Bronovo
☎ 070 312 4141; 🖥 www.bronovo.nl
KLM Travel Clinic
🖥 www.klmtravelclinic.nl; ☎ 0900 109 1096; 🖥 www.klmtravelclinic.nl
GGD
🏠 Westeinde 128; ☎ 070 353 7240; 🖥 www.wkmreizigerszorg.nl/ggddenhaag.

PHARMACIES

Havinga
🏠 Prins Hendrikplein 3; ☎ 070 345 6100; 🖥 apotheek-havinga.nl

Hofstad
🏠 Korte Poten 7A; ☎ 070 346 4748; 🖥 www.apotheekhofstad.nl
Scheveningen
🏠 Badhuisstraat 163; ☎ 070 352 3223; 🖥 apotheekscheveningen.nl
Boots
☎ Westeinde 148; 🖥 070 356 1276; 🖥 denhaag.nl.boots.com
Apotheek Jan Hendrikmore
🏠 Jan Hendrikstraat 18; ☎ 070 711 2450; 🖥 artsenzorg.nl

SCHOOLS (THE HAGUE)

American School
🏠 Rijksstraatweg 200; ☎ 070 511 2400; 🖥 www.ash.nl
Deutsche Internationale Schule
🏠 Van Bleiswijkstraat 125; ☎ 070 354 9454; 🖥 www.disdh.nl
Haagsche Schoolvereniging International Primary School
☎ 070 318 4950
HSV Lighthouse Special Education
🏠 Ama lia van Solmsstraat 155; ☎ 070 335 5698; 🖥 www.lighthousese. nl
International School of The Hague
🏠 Wijndaelerduin 1; ☎ 070 328 2049; 🖥 www.ishthehague.nl
Lycee Français Vincent van Gogh
🏠 Scheveningseweg 237; ☎ 070 306 6920; 🖥 www.lyceevangogh.nl
Royal Conservatoire
🏠 Juliana van Stolberglaan 1; ☎ 070 315 1515; 🖥 www.koncon.nl
British School
☎ 070 315 4077; 🖥 www.britishschool.nl
BSN Junior School Leidschenveen
🏠 Vrouw Avenweg 640; ☎ 070 315 4040
BSN Junior School Vlaskamp
🏠 Vlaskamp 19; ☎ 070 333 8111
BSN Junior School Diamanthorst
🏠 Diamanthorst 16; ☎ 070 315 7620
BSN Senior School Voorschoten
🏠 Jan van Hooflaan 3;
☎ 070 560 2222
International Education Centre
🏠 Tarwekamp 3; ☎ 070 315 4080
Het Rijnlands Lyceum International School
🏠 Apollolaan 1; ☎ 071 519 3555; 🖥 www.isrlo.nl

TAXIS (DELFT)

A Taxi
☎ 015 261 2121; 🖥 www.ataxidelft.nl
Call Taxi
☎ 015 262 5425; 🖥 www.call-taxi.nl
Delftse Taxicentrale "Deltax"
☎ 015 219 1919; 🖥 dtdeltax.nl

TAXIS (LEIDEN)

A Taxi
☎ 071 512 3300; 🖥 www.taxidegroot.nl
Leidse Regiotaxi
☎ 071 562 2443; 🖥 www.leidseregiotaxi.nl
Taxi Sleutelstad
☎ 071 750 4978; 🖥 www.taxisleutelstad.nl
Taxi Wielkens
☎ 071 589 0503; 🖥 www.wielkens.nl

TAXIS (THE HAGUE)

De Hofstad Taxicentrale
🖥 www.htmc.nl
Taxi Centrale Haaglanden
☎ 070 390 6262; 🖥 www.tch.nl
Taxi Centrale Haaglanden
☎ 070 390 6262; 🖥 www.tch.nl

WORSHIP (THE HAGUE)

American Protestant Church
🏠 Esther de Boer-van Rijklaan 20;
☎ 070 324 4490; 🖥 www.apch.nl
Bahil'i Community
🏠 Riouwstraat 27; ☎ 070 355 4017
or 070 350 6161; 🖥 www.bahai.nl
Brahma Rishi Mission Netherlands
🏠 Loosduinseweg 717; ☎ 070 362 0961
Christian Science Church
🏠 Andries Bickerweg 1B; ☎ 070 363 6652
**Crossroads International Church
(British Junior School)**
🏠 Vlaskamp 19; ☎ 070 322 2485;
🖥 www.crossroadschurch.ni
**English and American Episcopal Church
of St. John and St. Philip**
🏠 Ary van der Spuyweg 1a; ☎ 070
355 5359; 🖥 www.stjohn-stphilip.org

Paroisse Catholique Francophone de La Haye
🏠 Bloklandenplein 15; ☎ 070 325
4671; 🖥 www.paroissetls.com
Deutsche Evangelische Gemeinde
🏠 Bleijenburg 3B; ☎ 070 346 5727;
🖥 www.evangelischekirche-denhaag.ni
Deutschsprachige Katholische Gemeinde in den Niederlanden
🏠 Badhuisweg 35; 🖥 070 355 4240
Lutheran Church
🏠 Lutherse Burgwa l 7-9; ☎ 070 396
6700; 🖥 www.luthersdenhaag.ni

Index